TRANSCENDING BOUNDARIES

Routledge Harwood Choreography and Dance Studies
A series of books edited by Muriel Topaz and Robert P. Cohan, CBE

Please see the back of this book for other titles in the Choreography and Dance Studies series

TRANSCENDING BOUNDARIES

MY DANCING LIFE

Donald McKayle

London and New York

First published 2002
by Routledge
11 New Fetter Lane, London EC4P 4EE

Simultaneously published in the USA and Canada
by Routledge
29 West 35th Street, New York, NY 10001

Reprinted 2003

Routledge is an imprint of the Taylor & Francis Group

© 2002 Taylor & Francis

Typeset in Palatino by Scientifik Graphics (Singapore) Pte Ltd
Printed and bound in Great Britain by MPG Books Ltd, Bodmin

British Library Cataloguing in Publication Data
A catalogue record for this book is available from the British Library

Library of Congress Cataloging in Publication Data
A catalog record for this book has been applied for

ISBN 0–415–27017–0

In memory of my parents
Philip and Eva McKayle

To my wife Lea

To my children
Gabrielle, Liane, and Guy

To my dance family everywhere

CONTENTS

INTRODUCTION TO THE SERIES

Choreography and Dance Studies is a book series of special interest to dancers, dance personalities, dance teachers and choreographers. Focusing on dance composition, its techniques and training, the series will also cover the relationship of choreography to other components of dance performance such as music, lighting and the training of dancers.

In addition, *Choreography and Dance Studies* will seek to publish new works and provide translations of works not previously published in English, as well as to publish reprints of currently unavailable books of outstanding value to the dance community.

Muriel Topaz
Robert P. Cohan

LIST OF PLATES

FOREWORD

Donald McKayle is a modern-day Renaissance man. He writes, he sings, he directs, he teaches, he designs, all with extraordinary talent. But he is an immortal because he choreographs. And what incredible choreography – dances like *Rainbow Round My Shoulder, Games, District Storyville, Nocturne, Saturday's Child*, etc., all part of our choreographic heritage. Donald is one of our great masters, and he has created a dance repertory that combines wit and heroism in the face of pain and loss. Imagine doing all this with warmth, charm, wit and intelligence.

Donald as a dancer was incomparable. I remember his grace, strength, power, sensitivity. His encompassing movements swallowed space with a special delicacy as he swept across the stage. His dramatic power and poignancy moved not only audiences but fellow performers.

Today one of my great pleasures is hearing Donald talk about those "good old times" which we all know were terrible. His prodigious memory comes into play with the ability to excite wonders in the listener.

I first saw Donald in 1960 when I was working for Ted Shawn at Jacob's Pillow as house manager and press agent. Donald and company danced *Rainbow Round My Shoulder* which was a recent choreography. One of those few lifetime epiphanies occurred on first seeing *Rainbow*. After that memorable performance I found myself backstage with the stage crew attempting like a bunch of bumpkins to imitate the opening of *Rainbow* when the chain gang enters from stage left moving their shoulders and legs which so powerfully and immediately expressed the hopelessness, horror and despair of their situation while emphasizing their pride and defiance.

I was trying to understand the emotion and depth of that movement by bumbling through it myself. I wanted my muscles to understand the burden and message of that movement on my soul. Imagine our embarrassment when Donald happened to walk in. It is about forty years since I first met Donald. During that time I have been his fan, manager, presenter, friend.

When the American Dance Festival (ADF) had its first Russian mini-ADF in Moscow in 1992 at the Pushkin Theater the Dayton Contemporary Dance Company performed Donald's *Rainbow*. At the curtain calls there was hardly a ripple of applause. With interpreter in tow, I quickly ran to the lobby to talk to members of the audience to determine if they hated the dance or didn't understand it or what. After asking several people, my interpreter turned to me and said, "They are all stunned to see their own recent past danced before them. They were too overwhelmed to applaud. They want to meet and talk to the choreographer."

We all want to meet the choreographer and so we shall in his book.

Charles L. Reinhart

INTRODUCTION

It is not every day that one is asked to write an introduction for one's mentor, friend, and guru. I am honored to live at the same time as Mr. McKayle – Donald McKayle – Donnie – a Renaissance man, a genius, a man ahead of his time. I haven't known Donald for as long as some of his contemporaries, but for the more than thirteen years that I have worked with him, I've been filled with rich experiences and true inspiration. I met Mr. McKayle after hearing so much about his work on Broadway and at the Inner City Cultural Center in Los Angeles, where he had his own company for many years. I felt like I already knew him; after all, I had grown up watching his work on *The Ed Sullivan Show, The Bill Cosby Show* and *Good Times* in the late 50s and early 60s. I saw *Golden Boy* on Broadway starring Sammy Davis Jr., one of my parents' idols. I also saw *Raisin* shortly after I had seen my own father, who was one of the first black actors in Denver, playing the role of Walter Lee in the local production of *Raisin in the Sun*. I had seen a road show of *Sophisticated Ladies* in Chicago and I listened as artists raved about Mr. McKayle at the cast party. What magic Donald McKayle could create! His work spoke not only to my spirit, but to the spirits of people throughout the world. I thought to myself, how could a man choreograph film, television, Broadway shows and concert work? Our mutual friend, Dr. Maya Angelou, who did a little ditty on *The Bill Cosby Show* with Donald, would probably write a poem called "the Phenomenal Man" or "the Phenomenal Hue-Man Being."

His work truly tells of the universal experience. Each work is so powerful and brilliant, so poignant and delicate; each speaks the language of the soul. He captures and communicates through movement the extra-ordinary range found in the human condition. Over the years of seeing his work on stage or on television or in film, I found myself simultaneous-ly singing, dancing, laughing, and crying. What joy this human being conjure. His genius lies not only in his extraordinary ability to create movement vital to the spirit, but also to bring us closer to ourselves and to others through his artistry, through his witnessing our passion and pain in life. He brings the life experience to the stage. He makes it accessible to all: the privileged and the disenfranchised, the elder and the child, to women and men who represent all colors of the rainbow.

I was inspired to start my own repertory modern dance company in Denver. As we were building our company, poet and co-founder Schyleen

Qualls-Brown reminded me to continue following my dream of working with Donald McKayle. After all, he was a master. *Games, District Storyville,* and *Rainbow Round My Shoulder* were all American classics and definitely masterpieces. How could I meet this man even to begin to discuss setting choreography on my company? As fate would have it, Donald would set eight works for my company, the Cleo Parker Robinson Dance Ensemble, more than for any other company in the world. He said we reminded him of his own company of the 60s. He found us feisty and very interesting. He would nurture my dancers and help develop artists like Marceline Freeman. Donald transforms dancers. He speaks of Ms. Freeman, now with my company for 28 years, as his "muse", dedicating his work to her in 1999.

He has impacted my life as a choreographer, a teacher, a woman, a wife, a mother, a daughter, a sister, and a human being. Donald McKayle lives his extraordinary life as a dancer, and as a choreographer. He totally commits himself to life's complex rhythms, discovering the textures and the shadings of each movement, of each note, of each body, of each space, of each character and of each circumstance. He always honors the past and makes a better place for the future. Blessed are the dancers that work with him as he creates in the new millennium.

Cleo Parker Robinson

1

EARLY MOMENTS

"When the ball goes round again I will dance with you." Mother smiled that wonderful way that started in her cheeks, parted her lips revealing a gleaming row of white teeth, and ended with a twinkle in her eyes. She turned briefly to acknowledge my father as he pressed the gilded wooden chair beneath her, picked up the lace fan left on the table in front of her, flicked it open, and nudged me teasingly with her elbow, "What d'you say?" I smiled back. The fan fluttered briskly as she returned my smile. "Rascal!" The mirror ball stopped turning and the lights brightened. The band on the little stage swung into a lively calypso. The lightning fast intro was punctuated with a trumpet ta-ta-ta. Daddy clapped his hands together, rocked his head to the right, placed the heel of his left hand against his ribs and threw wide his right arm. He executed a series of side steps rocking his hips. The extended right arm encircled Mrs. Samuels' waist, sweeping her away from her husband as they returned to the table, and whirling her once again out onto the dance floor. "Sit down, Samuels, he's lively tonight!" "No, Alice. Come on, let's show them a thing or two." "Go way now!" With feigned protestations, Aunt Alice followed Mr. Samuels into the calypso. Their shoulders lifted and fell in syncopation to the rhythm. Their heads turned right then left in coordination with the perky step-together-step of their feet. Aunt Alice's dangling earrings did their own intriguing dance around her graceful neck. Uncle John used Aunt Alice's absence to pour a round of whiskey for the men and a healthy double for himself. They raised their shot glasses and nodded in an unspoken toast. The sippers smacked their lips together as the liquid trickled down their throats. The gulpers let out explosive bursts of air. Their eyes opened wide and their nostrils flared. The women drank ginger ale colored with grenadine except for Mrs. Samuels who had a highball and had been talking with enthusiasm about the merits of a concoction of beer and ginger ale called a shandygaff. The women at the nearby table helped themselves liberally from the tote baskets of spirits they had carried in along with the straw hampers filled with oven fried chicken, fish cakes, scabeeched fish, coleslaw, potato salad, hard buns, and cheese. The tables were reserved in advance from the dance committee. The cover charge and entrance ticket price entitled you to a set up. Each table received glasses, ice, and mixers. Each party brought their own plates and utensils.

The West Indian community in New York City was tightly knit along class lines and highly social. The Jamaicans feigned a superiority over the "little islanders"; those from Barbados, St. Lucia, St. Kitts, Trinidad, Tobago, but none of this was taken too seriously. Mr. and Mrs. Samuels would pick up Uncle John and Aunt Alice in the Bronx, and then stop for Mother and Dad on their way down to the Renaissance Ballroom, one of several large dance palaces in the Harlem district. I had only imagined the way it would be from the grown-up's stories. Now I was really there, in this grand place with its horseshoe balcony ringing the floor below, festooned everywhere with decorations and adorned with beautifully gowned ladies. Before tonight, my brother, Philip, and I had been left at home. We were allowed to stay up just long enough to meet the company; the men in their black derbies, chesterfield overcoats, and white silk fringed scarves, the women in their Persian lamb fur coats recut into the season's mode and carrying new corday pocketbooks. Invariably the women went into the bedroom and stood before the vanity mirror making last minute adjustments, while the men waited in the living room. The men's hair was parted directly in the center and combed outwards in little pomaded waves. Each of them wore a small mustache. Philip and I would note just where each man placed his derby and wait with anticipation for the cigars to be lighted and the male stories and laughter to begin. When the men's attention was engaged, we would surreptitiously exchange the placement of the head wear. Uncle John's 7 and 3/4 would fall completely over Mr. Samuels' eyes and Daddy's size 7 would perch uncomfortably on top of Uncle John's wide forehead. "Caught us one more time, you devils!" Laughter and goodnight kisses. In the darkness of our bedroom we listened as the happy sounds faded away. Into the night we continued developing a story peopled with fictitious characters and laced with fanciful events and dialogue until sleep overtook imagination.

The calypso set was over and the lights dimmed again. A spot light hit the mirror ball and refracted light danced around the Renaissance Ballroom. Now it was my turn, wearing my first suit with long trousers, to make my maiden voyage across the dance floor. It was a waltz. The ball only went round for the stately dances: the waltz, the castillian. It was a very special moment as I led my mother onto the floor.

The first home I remembered was in East Harlem between Park and Lexington Avenues. The New York Central railway running north from Grand Central Station emerged from underground just after the posh apartment buildings of upper Park Avenue. It continued above ground through the working class neighborhoods on impressive castlelike structures of rough hewn brown stones and mortar, changing suddenly into metal gridwork at 110th Street. Beneath the railway tracks a gaggle of pushcart vendors sold their wares: produce, fish and meats maintained on ice, clothing and cloth, shoe laces, towels and linens, shoe polish and gadgets. The variety of languages and speech patterns was as manifold as the myriad odors that teased the nostrils. West Indian women sat outside the entry doorways and hawked shopping bags in a confusion of Puerto Rican, Barbadian, and other island twangs. The city fathers finally enclosed the market and built stalls for the vendors. This was a way of policing the business activities and gaining revenue, as well as providing for higher standards of hygiene. The neighborhood was mostly Puerto Rican, although black families were moving in. The Jewish and Italian families were disappearing and with them their ethnic businesses.

One day in the middle of the week, Philip and I were dressed in our Sunday clothes and taken by Mother and Daddy on an unusual trip. We walked from our home, the address of which I was required to memorize in case I should ever get lost, "I live at 57 East 111th Street." We arrived at 116th Street where the thoroughfare widened and the Park Avenue market ended. We stopped in front of a building with a bright two-tone brick facade where Mother had seen a sign advertising a two bedroom apartment. She had stopped the day before, was told it was available, and had made an appointment with the superintendent to return with the family. We were all quite excited about seeing what Mother called..."a nice new place." Mother rang the superintendent's bell. He looked through the peephole. Mother was standing in front of the door, directly in his line of vision. "Oh yes, just a minute. I'll get the key." After a few minutes the door opened and a round little man stepped out holding a key. He saw Daddy, Philip, and me standing next to mother and his face intensified into a deep shade of red. "I'm sorry but the lady that came before you came back and left a deposit... of course if you'd like, I can show it to you anyway." Mother exhaled audibly and shook her head. We left the building but Mother asked us to wait and went back inside. The walk home was strange and quiet. "Mama, why didn't we see the 'nice new place'?" Mother explained that the red faced man had thought that she was Puerto Rican and that the landlord wanted Puerto Ricans. "What are we, mama?" "We're as good as anyone else! Don't let anyone tell you different!" "Yes, mama."

The Monday after Labor Day, September 1935 finally arrived. Ever since my fifth birthday on July 6, I had impatiently waited for this day when I could enroll in the kindergarten at P.S. 101. Under the strict but loving care of Mrs. Smith, that first year of school was for the most part a joyous experience. She was a white haired woman with a smiling face. Her ample silhouette was always covered in a print dress and matching jacket. During story hour, as I sat listening to her read, my eyes were drawn to her feet which strained unsuccessfully against her shoes and puffed out in a plump arch. The sunlight streaming in from the window behind her bounced in a glowing highlight on this captured mound and led straight up her massive legs to above her knees. There, her stockings ended in a garter roll secured with a knot on the inside of her thighs, where the trapped flesh burst free. I loved the stories and Mrs. Smith's melodious voice, but wondered how she got such strange legs.

I was eager to get into what Philip teasingly called "real school." I did Philip's homework along with him so when I arrived in first grade, I was ahead of my classmates. I was always first to raise my hand with an answer to the question, always first to read out loud, always enthusiastic, causing some of my classmates to find me a little insufferable. Tensions mounted, and in second grade a trio of boys set out to get me. I had no love for fighting or believe that, if cornered, I could be victorious in a brawl; however I knew I was extremely fast on my feet. Much like the deer faced with a predator, my weapon was speedy flight. For two weeks, my adversaries unsuccessfully pursued me after school. The Monday of the third week as I dashed up the concave marble steps toward the safety of home, I remembered that mother was not there and that I was to go to my godmother's apartment on the floor below. Godmother opened the door and seeing the panic on my face, asked me what was wrong. I told her the whole tale. "You're not gonna run for the rest of your life! Now put down your books and come on and face up to them." She ushered me downstairs with a stern-no-nonsense gesture. The cigarette she was smoking dangled between her lips as she locked the door and placed the keys in her apron pocket. The heels of her backless shoes clacked noisily against the stairs as we descended. It was like the ominous tattoo of a drum accompanying an execution. Why was I being sacrificed? As we emerged outside from the dark hallway, my hopes that my foes would be gone disappeared. There they were, gathered in conversation in front of the stoop. "There he is. Get him!" "Just you hold on! One against one. Who is it going to be?" I couldn't believe what my godmother was proposing. One of the boys took his fist and menacingly ran it from one of his eyes to the other, then to his nose and to his mouth. He shook it at me and stepped forward. It was the same gesture I had mocked him with as I ran from the school yard, secure in my ability to outfox them. The three of them laughed as I turned to my godmother, wordlessly beseeching her to make it all go away. She turned me back to face the unavoidable. "Now you're gonna fight and you'd better fix him hard or I'll give you double what you let him give you." The terror of the announced alternative to any cowardice on my part unleashed my trembling fist, which landed squarely on my opponent's nose. He staggered back. "Hit him again and make him feel it!" My second blow found the same target, again true to mark. Blood trickled from my opponent's nose and dripped into his mouth. The fight was over. Godmother took me upstairs and sat me down at the kitchen table. "You won't be running home any more. Mark my words." She placed a plate of Barbadian cornmeal mush, called cuckoo, in front of me and opened a bottle of soda pop. I had always thought of godmother as an amazing woman. Her most unbelievable feat was to consume a mouthful of shad, take a sip of beer, and pull a handful of treacherous fish bones from her mouth, absolutely clean of all flesh. What she had just done for me surpassed even that.

My best friends were twin boys, whose father had a small store half way down the block from where we lived. He sold seltzer. There was nothing in the store but crates of bottles, filled and empty. We spent the after school hours playing in front of the store until closing time when he would take the twins home. I never knew where they lived. One week they were absent from school. There was a sign posted on the door of their father's store, printed in Yiddish letters on white paper bordered in black. When my friends returned to school, they told me that their grandmother had died and that the whole family had to "sit shiva." I did not quite under-stand what I had heard but figured it out to my own satisfaction and went home to explain it to my mother. "Do you know that when someone dies in a Jewish family, they all have to sit around and shiver." Mother was greatly amused by this revelation but explained that the practice was seven days of mourning and that no one could possibly shiver for such a long time.

We moved into the brand new Harlem Housing Project, where we had a two bedroom apartment filled with light, overlooking tennis courts, a river view park, and a playground. This was a landmark experiment in public housing, a first in the black community of Harlem. Everything was thoroughly modern, and all tenants had their households moved by vans that were fumigated before they were unloaded into these pristine envi-rons. Everything was wonderful in the new neighborhood, except for one major problem, the public schools. They were too few and too crowded. Mother also feared what she called "the bad element," street gangs. There was much publicity about school boys toting zip guns; home made weapons fashioned from the ends of wooden orange crates, sawed off lengths of lamp piping, cap pistol hammers, strips of bicycle inner tubes, and black electrician's tape. When finished and furnished with a 22 caliber bullet they could be lethal, to the person who fired the contraption as well as to the receiving party. The end result of this parental concern was our enrollment in the Resurrection Church School and my introduction to the dogma and ceremony of the Catholic mass. Like most children whose parents came from Jamaica, we were Episcopalians not Catholics. I was thoroughly captivated by the "costumes" of the priests and acolytes, the processionals, recessionals, the censer swinging in front of the taper boys and cross bearer. The statues, stained glass windows, tiers of devotional candles, the baptismal font, and side chapels were all mysteries to be explored. I began spending hours in the church and aspired to the priesthood. It was the theater of it all that caught me, the drilled and memorized words of the catechism becoming a performance script and, for a seven year old, one that was mostly unfathomable. "What is a sacrament?" "A sacrament is an outward sign of an inward and spiritual grace." When Mother discovered me kneeling and praying on a regular basis she removed me from the care of the good sisters. Beside, Philip had caught ringworm in his scalp and mother attributed this to the overcrowding in the classroom and the resulting jumble of headgear in the packed coat closet. The one perk of attending this school was that I was finally in the same class as Philip. Beside being able to exercise my intellectual competitiveness with my older brother, I was able to share the day's events on an equal basis with him, which drastically changed the nature of our friendship.

During our one eventful year at the Resurrection Church School, our instructor was Sister Hildegard. Unlike most of the other nuns, her face, framed by her stiff white wimple against her black habit, was quite pretty. The cincture that girded her waist had three knots symbolizing her spiritual vows and terminated in the more elaborate knot for love. This knot was sometimes put to a use obviously foreign to the spirit of its origin, as I was to witness the first day of school when my attention was drawn to a disturbance in the back of the classroom. My eyes rested on Julius who was almost twice my size. He was slow to learn schoolwork and slower yet to comprehend pranks in the making from his classmates. "I didn't want to have to show this to the new boys on their first day." Realizing I was being referred to, I turned back to see Sister Hildegard pulled a strap from her desk drawer. "Julius step forward." I watched in amazement as a scene cleverly orchestrated by an anonymous and sadistic classroom provocateur was enacted. Sister Hildegard lashed the leather strap toward Julius' trembling extended hand. With a gasp he pulled back his hand, turned, and fled, with Sister Hildegard right after him. Around the room they went. Sister Hildegard dropped the strap on the desk as she passed it, gathered up the front of her skirts and picked up speed like an Olympian. The class swiveled in rapt attention, following the pursuit. As Sister Hildegard closed the lead, she grabbed her cincture, whirled it like a lariat in a forward circle, and loosed it with force. The love knot landed with a thud against Julius' back. "Stop!" There was a swell of giggles as Julius came to a halt with a whimper. "Sit down!" Julius obeyed. Sister Hildegard angrily turned to the class. "Quiet! I will not have this! Open your books and write! I am a child of God and I will be obedient." We were instructed to number each written repetition of that command until we reached 100. That night in the darkness of our bedroom, Philip and I talked about the love knot until Mother called out, "Go to sleep now. No more talking. Morning will be here before you know it." "I am a child of God and I will be obedient."

Mother found a loophole to allow us to enter Public School 46 in Washington Heights, ending my brief sojourn as a would-be initiate. Mother's trump card in manipulating the New York school system was quite often a relative who lived within a district that would allow us to attend the school of her choice. At this moment it was her younger brother known to us as Uncle Gussy. He lived on Edgecombe Avenue, a short span of streets on a high bluff overlooking Harlem, known as Sugar Hill. I loved my visits to Uncle Gussy. It was like walking into a Hollywood movie. A long cloth canopy covered the walkway that led to the recessed front door. There, a uniformed doorman unhooked a speaking device, pressed a button, and announced our presence. He then directed us to the elevator. "We know our way. I'm Mr. Cohen's sister." The doorman smiled deferentially in reply as my Mother swept past him with a special grandeur of bearing she produced on these visits. My favorite place in Uncle Gussy's apartment was right next to the polished table where an elongated vase was always filled with tall fresh flowers. Mother called it a divan. It was a low backed velvet sofa in a beautifully curved, asymmetrical design with one continuous plump cushion filled with goose down. My only anxiety on these visits was having to meet face to face with Toussaint, Uncle Gussy's Chow, a bundle of mahogany colored fur from which dark unfriendly eyes peeked out and white teeth emerged from violet gums. I somehow believed the saliva that dripped from his purple tongue was poisonous and gave him wide berth. Bismarck, Uncle John's Alsatian, produced quite the opposite emotional reaction. He was our protector, our friend. When I was a toddler he even submitted to my mounting him like a pony; as I grew, he let me know that this particular game was no longer appropriate. Uncle Gussy was quite different from our other uncles. Beside his upscale life style, he often presented us with a new aunt. Each one was extremely beautiful and from a show business background. Aunt Edith ran the ticket kiosk at the popular Apollo Theatre on 125th Street. Some said it doubled as a drop for the numbers racket, but Mother said that talk was nothing more than unsubstantiated gossip. Aunt Edna, who followed, was originally a show girl at the famed Cotton Club where Lena Horne was the new young vocalist. Aunt Edna was flashy, always flawlessly coifed and made up to perfection. Her clothes, of the latest style, were noticeably expensive. Her fur coat was mink not Persian lamb. Uncle Gussy and Aunt Edna had a large circle of friends outside the extended family; they were not always in attendance at the ordered series of gatherings of our closely knit clan. This mysterious side of their life made them especially intriguing. Hazel Scott, the sensational piano virtuoso, and her husband Adam Clayton Powell, the flamboyant minister and politician, were their close friends. Uncle Gussy ran a nightclub on 137th Street and Seventh Avenue called Jock's Place. As Gussy Cohen's nephew I had entry even though I was underage, but I was not allowed to sit at a table where there was alcohol. I felt very special. It was exciting to be there and to see the shows. One of them introduced Eartha Kitt. At that time she was a performer with Katherine Dunham's Experimental Group and had yet to make her mark on the world of popular music and theater.

Using Uncle Gussy's Sugar Hill address, we had no trouble enrolling in P.S. 46. We climbed the endless flights of steps that snaked through the park up to Edgecombe Avenue. In case anyone saw us approaching school, we would be coming from the direction of our new address. Later when children from the Harlem Housing Project were included in the P.S. 46 school district, we took the viaduct that led from the 155th Street bridge which joined Harlem to the Bronx. On rainy days or when it had been snowing and the walk to school was not a possibility, we were given carfare and caught the trolley. Some of the boys pocketed their carfare and rode the back of the trolley, hanging on to the light fixture in a daredevil maneuver called "hitching." I would rush to the back of the trolley and stand facing them, my face pressed against the window, vicariously experiencing their thrill and the danger. One day one of my friends, even more recklessly, ran and jumped a hitch on the back of a coal truck. His fingers slipped on the dusty exterior and he fell to the pavement and was run over by a car before the horrified motorist could apply the brakes. Fortunately, I did not witness the actual event. I had boarded the trolley, while he remained behind. The school principal called a special assembly. Along with my schoolmates, that day I faced death for the first time.

Directly north of the viaduct was the Polo Grounds, home of the New York Giants. The adjacent fields were used for different local events, among which were the cricket games enjoyed by Daddy, Uncle John, and other Jamaicans and British West Indian expatriates from the Lesser Antilles. I did not understand the game of cricket nor did I have an attachment to any sport of this genre. I could not understand the passions that were spent chasing after a ball. Rather, I loved racing, swimming, diving, vaulting, which stressed body control and perfection of movement; they were beauty in motion. The cricket tournaments were yearly rituals and, in the heady Jamaican parlance, classified as "auspicious occasions". Every event that fit into this category was celebrated with food and drink. Blankets held in place by picnic baskets and thermos jugs dotted the lawn. Elegant white clothing was *de rigueur* for cricket and the West Indian community turned out in style. Daddy's crisp linen plus fours had a faint window pane plaid in a pale beige, barely perceptible but unique. He was always a classy dresser.

On warm Sunday afternoons, following church services, families would promenade up and down the avenue exchanging pleasantries, a practice known as "strolling". At ages five and four, Philip and I were dressed in identical outfits expertly crafted by Aunt Alice. Short pants of wool serge were clasped with mother-of-pearl buttons to short-sleeved crepe shirts with satin lapels. We wore berets and high-top laced shoes with turn-down socks, all in white. We sported walking sticks; mine had a curved silver handle and Philip's was topped with a carved ivory dog's head. We were the cat's meow and were ready to pose whenever someone approached holding a box camera. Daddy carried his own walking stick and wore a vested suit with a Panama hat in a soft, off-white straw. We turned the heads of passers-by, much to the approval of Mother in her georgette dress with its graceful bertha collar that fluttered as she walked.

At home, I would spend hours creating structures from our two sets of building blocks. The newer set was composed of shellacked rectangular and square pieces; the original set contained round and triangular shapes, stained red, yellow, and green. My constructions were built on the card table, giving them an elevated place of importance. My favorite groupings were turreted buildings separated by alleys and moats, connected on upper stories by bridges. If one of my fantasy installations received too much parental praise, it met with the wrecking ball of my brother's fist. Oh, it was amazing how much you could love a sibling and hate him with equal passion. Daddy would take us downtown to Barneys to shop for clothing once a year at the Labor Day Back To School Sale. Barneys dealt in good value and sensible clothes for men and boys. We both got new school clothes, but only Philip received new dress clothes; I got only his hand-me-downs. Dress clothes were for occasions and never used for casual wear or play and thus were always outgrown in almost mint condition. One year Daddy gave in to my expressions of hurt at this practice. "How'd you like a new suit too?" I grabbed him by the hand and dragged him to a rack of tweeds. I pulled out a two piece suit, jacket and knickers. Daddy laughed, placed his large hand on top of my head and tousled it lovingly. He decided to get us both the same suit, so that when I inherited Philip's next year, no one would know that it was a hand-me-down. As fate would have it, Philip stayed wiry and I got chunky. After that, I was no longer a candidate for my brother's clothing and I had my own private shopping excursions with Daddy.

In sixth grade, my last year of elementary school, the dreaded director of student traffic was my teacher. He was known as "Levine The Fiend of 414." Our classroom on the fourth floor was directly opposite the door to the stairwell. From there Mr. Levine could monitor all comings and goings. He also held sway in the boy's school yard. Twice I fell victim to his sadistic impulses. On one particular day, while I was in fourth grade,

I responded to the blast of Mr. Levine's whistle in the prescribed and practiced manner. I fell into position in my class line in front of stairway number 5. "Quiet! Eyes forward!" I heard noises in the line behind me but dared not look around. Suddenly my head was snapped forward with a jerk as Mr. Levine passed by me. He smacked the black board eraser, that he had just hit me with, on the backs of the heads of the boys in front of me. He left his mark on every boy in line. "Next time move quickly when the whistle blows!" On the second whistle we proceeded noisily up the metal staircase, dusting off the chalk as we went. I developed antennae that could sense Mr. Levine's proximity. It was unfortunately, a false sense of security. One morning late and running, I entered a deserted school yard and tripped on an untied shoe lace. I dropped my books next to a waste paper basket, hoisted up my foot, and began furiously to tie the hanging lace. As I fell forward, straddling the basket, I turned to see who had pushed me. "You're late." "Yes, sir."

Hector Gutierrez spoke a curious patois, a mixture of English and Spanish, which we called Spanglish. He was Mr. Levine's prime target for derision. "The only reason you're in school is because the sewer doesn't want any backwash!" The day following Mr. Levine's cruel insult, we were having a written quiz. Mr. Levine passed up and down the rows of desks as we worked. He stopped at Hector's desk which was directly in front of mine. Hector tipped his head and glanced up at Mr. Levine and then suddenly stood up, looking at the door. "Padre?" A man was standing at the door. Mr. Levine crossed to him and they went outside and onto the staircase landing. We all followed behind Hector, moving cautiously forward. They were speaking loudly and simultaneously in English and Spanish. There were wild gestures and then Mr. Gutierrez shoved Mr. Levine and he disappeared from our view. Mr. Gutierrez came back and said something to Hector and they left together. We scrambled back to our desks. Mr. Levine came back into the room. "Pass your papers forward." He limped as he walked. The recess bell rang and we bolted for the door, shouting and whistling without fear as we ran down the stairs. We jumped two steps at a time, and hurtled back and forth, banging against the walls. We gathered in the school yard and spontaneously roared a mighty unison hurrah.

Creating and performing the Punch and Judy puppet show was the major event in my final year at P.S. 46. It was a great success and earned a repeat performance. I loved the laughter from my classmates at the antics I created for the puppets. The snickers which had surrounded my poetry reading in fifth grade English were another matter. One residue of my close and protective family circle was a decidedly different speech pattern from the majority of students whose parents were born in the United States. I was called upon to recite "Old Ironsides". The snickers always came at the line...

> And many an eye had danced to see
> That banner in the sky.

The word, danced, was rolled off with a round and bouncy A sound. I also wanted the word itself to dance and led up to it with an accelerando and jumped off the final D quickly, leaving a little space behind it before going ahead. The sentence had a rhythmic pattern more like song than speech. That term I decided to follow my own drum, no matter how socially unpopular I might be.

I was no stranger to solitary activity but did not protest at being re-cruited into organized cultural activities. In fact, I rather enjoyed it all. I spent two winter afternoons outdoors completing a life size snow sculp-ture of a dog and sled. Mother entered it into the park department competition. It received a certificate of honorable mention which she had framed and proudly hung on the wall. I was also made the Master of Ceremonies at the May Day celebration held in the park along the riverbank. My part was small but obviously important. I was the only boy involved in the pageant. Dressed in my white suit, I had the seat of honor on the little dais built for the occasion. The ceremony opened with official greet-ings, followed by the May Pole dance. For weeks the little girls had been drilled by Miss Providence in the skipping steps. Holding on to long ribbons attached to the top of the May Pole, they converged on the pole and retreated, circling clockwise and again counter clockwise in cadence to the music. They then began an in-and-out-the-window weaving. All girls holding one color would go left. Girls holding the opposite color would go right. Over and under they went, winding the May Pole in a two-tone ribbon plait, until the ribbon lengths were too short to allow for continued dancing. It was a pretty sight and enthusiastically applauded by the spectators. Each girl was costumed as a flower. The costumes were made by the mothers from crepe paper and composed of colored petals and green leaves. The little flowers formed two files and the girl chosen as the May Queen proceeded through their ranks to the dais where I waited. She knelt on a little cushion before me and I placed a wreath of flowers upon her head. "When flowers bloom for garlands to make, I crown thee, Queen of the May!"

When my brother was five, Mother decided to take advantage of a special radio offer, announced on the Major Bow's Amateur Hour. She enrolled Philip in a tap dancing class that met Saturday mornings in a downtown dance studio. I was too young to take the class, but was allowed to stay in the back of the room and observe. Parents waited on benches outside the studio. Although I was to watch and be quiet, there was no way I could keep still. I danced along with the class, sitting down whenever I thought I was being noticed and in imminent danger of expulsion. At the end of the first class, the instructor approached Mother and pointed to me. "That's the one to watch." I had to wait until my next birthday to be eligible for enrollment, but family circumstance altered that plan and dance class was to wait for the future.

I was born at the Presbyterian Medical Center on 168th Street and Broadway, confirming my status as a native New Yorker. Regular journeys back there were mostly routine out-clinic check ups. You were kept moving along wooden slat back benches until you arrived at the entry to the examination rooms. There were, however, two major exceptions, both of which ended with my being hospitalized. The first of these was for the removal of a cyst resulting from a malfunction in my salivary glands. I awoke from the operation with a bandaged throat and with a tongue that was traumatized into an off center position of rest. The doctor assured Mother that this was only a temporary condition and nothing to worry about. He removed the bandages and the stitches. I was left with a pronounced scar. "If you ever go into the movies, you just come back and I'll remove that for you." The physician's joke, to a frightened seven year old, held a measure of prophecy. Sometime in the following year, I complained of pains, in my back, in my joints, in my neck. "Put your coat on, we're going to the Medical Center." We went through the usual process, sliding along the benches and finally reached the examination rooms; however, this time I was taken away, dressed in a funny, open back gown, and placed in a private room in a special wing. I spent two weeks in the hospital. They took two spinal taps, an excruciating procedure. I was diagnosed as having contracted polio but somehow having fought it off successfully through my own body chemistry. I left the hospital on a brisk fall day. Mother and I headed for the bus stop. I was in luck. A new double decker bus was waiting. I was anxious to get on and climb up to my seat in the front directly over the driver below so I could pretend I was driving the bus. I broke away from mother and started to run, but a few steps later I was on the ground and mother was next to me. "Don't worry, there'll be another double decker. You won't be running for a little while."

Harlem's answer to the posh Dakota Apartments on Central Park West and 72nd Street, were the Dunbar Apartments on Seventh Avenue and 150th Street, a quadrangle of attached buildings formed around an inner courtyard. The living rooms of all the apartments overlooked beautifully kept gardens. The Dunbar had been home to many a Harlem luminary, including the self made millionairess, Madame C.J. Walker. At present, the irrepressible tap dance great and neighborhood hero, Bill Robinson, was in residence. Hoping to meet him, my friends and I would hang around the arched entryway performing a well honed and practiced imitation of what we had seen him dancing in the movies. "That's it, boys." Success, at last! With a chuckle, Bill Robinson was dancing the real "Uncle Bo", just like we had seen him do with Shirley Temple. Hop, slap, hop, pat, pat. Hop, slap, hop, pat, pat. "Please, Mr. Bill, dance up the stairs." There were only three steps rising to the entrance door. He obliged with a much abbreviated version of his famous stair dance, tipped his derby, winked, and disappeared into the building.

Daddy had always held jobs which I thought were wonderful. He was the maintenance man at the Trans Lux Movie Theatre on Madison Avenue between 59th and 60th Streets, which meant I could always get in free. The Trans Lux showed newsreels, short subjects, and animated cartoons. On Saturdays, we were given eleven cents to spend on the movie features. We went to the R.K.O. Roosevelt or the Loew's Odeon on 145th Street, where we sat in the children's section. A matron in a white uniform was on duty and maintained order. One Saturday, Philip and I went to see a new Jack Benny comedy. We arrived at the beginning of the second feature, a film about a boy and his dog called, *The Biscuit Eater*. The film ended with the boy weeping over the dead body of his pet. "You crying?" "No!" "Yes, you are." "No, I'm not! You're crying!" The cross accusations escalated. Philip threw a punch. I countered. We were grabbed by the matron and escorted outside, still fussing as we wiped our wet cheeks and running noses. We never got to see *Buck Benny Rides Again...*

Daddy's next job was at the Copacabana, one of the hot nighteries fashioned around exotic locations with sultry climates. Mayor Fiorello LaGuardia had renamed 6th Avenue, the Avenue of The Americas, a nomenclature New Yorkers still refuse to adopt. President Franklin Delano Roosevelt's "Good Neighbor Policy" was in full swing and Latin American entertainment was in vogue. Central and South American entertainers were everywhere. Daddy's job at the Copacabana was again as a maintenance man. I was spending the afternoon with him during school break and he decided to entertain me while he polished the hardwood dance floor. He attached steel wool pads to his feet and glided around the floor to a samba beat. I applauded loudly as Daddy bowed at the end of this impromptu performance. My applause was echoed behind me. I turned to see Carmen Miranda and her sister laughing and calling out. "Bravo!" The Brazilian Bombshell was the headliner at the club and her famous likeness, turbaned headdress stacked high with fruits and flowers, was the logo of the Copacabana. Daddy got a new job that put the family income above the maximum allowed for residency in the Harlem Housing Project, and we moved to Stebbins Avenue in the south Bronx. The job that forced the move to the Bronx was far removed from the fringes of show business where Daddy had done service. The country was moving into a bold defense posture, and jobs were opening up in fields which had been traditionally closed to black men. Daddy was an excellent mechanic and was hired at Republic Aviation. His skill and creativity moved him steadily upward until he was repairing the planes that came back from test flights with unforeseen mechanical problems. He held this job years past mandatory retirement; they would not let him go until he had trained several men to take over from him.

Sundays at church had always been an important part of our weekly activity. At first we attended All Souls church and spent most of the morning in Sunday school while the adults attended communion service. When we moved to the Harlem Housing Project, we changed to St. Luke, a more uptown church which had a much smaller congregation. Each child was automatically a ward of every adult and was cared for constantly. Philip and I went through confirmation together under the watchful tutelage of the Reverend Denzil Carty. Exorcising devilment out of young boys, even within the hallowed confines of the church, was not always an easy task. One of our delights was to take seats in the front row of the church balcony directly over the aisle of the lower sanctuary during Candlemas, a joyous celebration of light in which candles were blessed for the year. Every church member in attendance was given a little candle to hold during the service. At marked moments in the ceremony the candles at the ends of each aisle were lit and the flame passed along until all the parishioners held lit candles and the church was aglow with light. The organist played a triumph march and the choir would lead the congregation in songs as they marched down the aisle and returned to their stalls in the nave. There was a baritone in the choir who sang with a quavering voice that undulated in a wide vibrato, constantly off pitch, especially when he reached for notes at the edge of his vocal range. His head would tremble with the effort to produce the required sound. As he marched beneath us, we would let droplets of wax fall on his bald and bobbling head. His voice coursed into notes even more foreign to the melody as he looked up wonderingly. Our expressions remained beatific as we sang out lustily and squeezed down on the hymnals until the pages creased, in an effort to keep back the laughter. Philip and I began training as acolytes under the instructions of Mr. Foote, the lay reader, and Oscar Callender, the head acolyte and cross bearer. I yearned for this position but it fell to my brother who was taller and therefore next in line. We both learned the intricacies of serving at the communion mass, apprenticing first at early morning service. At high mass we alternated as wine and water bearers. We rang the bells during the *mea culpa*, carried the missal from one side of the altar to the other, backing down the side steps, turning the corners in unison, meeting in center, genuflecting and returning to our places in rehearsed moves. We were up on our toes for the ritual of the communion service, but sometimes our attention drifted while Father Carty delivered his sermon. If our eyes closed or our heads nodded, and we seemed to be asleep we would be in for a severe tongue lashing from Mrs. Barden, a very devout parishioner with large and rheumy eyes, who wore an outlandish church bonnet with the taxidermed carcasses of exotic fowl challenging each other in a rigid battle pose above her forehead.

Pegged pants were the "in" mode of hip masculine attire. I had been saving my allowance for months to buy my first pair since Daddy refused to have any of his clothing money used for anything even remotely resembling a zoot suit. Some of the kids in the neighborhood were really hip. They wore the high waisted, pleated lounge pegs that ballooned from a twenty eight inch knee circumference down to a fourteen inch cuff. I knew such an extravagant look was an impossible dream in my family, but a conservative twenty four inch knee and an eighteen inch cuff might be acceptable. I took the subway down to Astor Place, where the subway platform opened into the lower floor of the John Wanamaker department store. I loved passing through the men's haberdashery on my way to the street level. I continued walking downtown on lower Broadway to a loft building which housed several small clothing concerns. The elevator door opened on the sixth floor directly into the factory. There were shelves of cloth, cutting tables, sewing machines, steam presses, and racks of garments in all stages of completion. I chose a gray glen plaid in a worsted wool and left a deposit. The pegs would be ready in time for me to wear them to the next Saturday Young People's Get Together at church. I was a hit with my peers but not as successful with my parents. Daddy was convinced that only hoodlums dressed that way and Mother agreed. After one season's wear, my pegs were sent to the dry cleaners and somehow got lost. I suspected Daddy, not the cleaners.

Flashing light bulbs circled around the marquee of the Grand Plaza, and the sound of driving music blared from within. Wildly flaring trumpet cadenzas and rippling percussion patterns on the timbales dissolved into a flowery piano passage as Marcelino Guerra Y Su Conjunto Afro Cubano played the "Montuno in A flat." Friday night was for dancing Latin; Dorothea Sangster was my date. The vendor at the entrance kiosk took my money and tore two stubs from the ticket roll. I never felt secure until I was past the ticket taker at the door and safely inside the ballroom. We were both underage and compensating. Dorothea wore heavy make up and an exaggerated hairdo. I camouflaged my youth, tipping my broad brim fedora at an angle that shadowed my face. The music was truly intoxicating, and the dancing was amazing. Partners competed with flashy turns, breaks, and sudden stops in provocative frozen poses. The latest craze was the coolayo, a grinding pelvic descent with legs intertwined. The older couples' answer was a sexy traditional couple dance, "Shoeing The Mare." The man straddled the woman's lifted leg and hammered at her shoe mocking the village blacksmith. He progressed forward with a chugging step. The woman hopped along backwards, vibrating her shoulders.

I attended William Niles junior high school in the Crotona Park section of the Bronx, far outside the school district for the Harlem Housing Project. This arrangement was again facilitated by the resourcefulness and ingenuity of Mother. Uncle John and Aunt Alice lived on Washington Avenue in the Bronx, where he was the superintendent of a large and well kept apartment building. Aunt Alice had fixed an extra room for Philip and me so that we could sleep over whenever necessary to establish indisputable residency credentials. Aunt Alice was an operator in the garment district and skilled at dressmaking. Mother worked with her periodically as a finisher. Mother had no love for factory work and would constantly admonish us. "Study your lessons and do your schoolwork, else you'll end up pushing the man's cart." The man she referred to was the factory boss. The job, grandiously misnamed shipping clerk, employed unskilled men to push wheeled clothes racks loaded with mass produced garments through the Seventh Avenue garment district. To reach Uncle John and Aunt Alice we took the trolley going across the 155th Street bridge and got off at Webster Avenue. The fare was a nickel and we asked for a transfer. On the Webster Avenue trolley we took back half the paper transfer and used it for a third trolley which deposited us at Tremont Avenue. We walked the two blocks to Aunt Alice, then continued to school.

My brother and I were indeed a minority at William Niles. There was one other black student. Rowena Jackson came from a family of eight sisters and two brothers, and her father was a janitor in the area. I knew janitors and superintendents did much the same work. The difference in stature was tied to the class of the building and the amenities. Uncle John and Aunt Alice had a two bedroom apartment on the ground floor of their building. A brass plaque on the door read "Superintendent". Rowena's father had a small one bedroom in the basement opposite the boiler room. A hand painted sign with a directional arrow pointed out the access to his abode, down a flight of wooden stairs. It read "Janitor". However, Rowena was able to use this address with impunity. It was, after all, her father's address even though the family lived in Harlem and both Rowena and her father were commuters. My initiation into advocacy was galvanized by the unusual events that led to Rowena Jackson's taking a stand against school policy that left her alienated and in need of a good friend. The school principal had instituted a radical shift in the vocational studies policy. For half the school year, girls were to take Shop-Woodworking, and boys were to take Home Economics-Cooking. This was an extremely advanced challenge to accepted practice in sexual role development, but stopped short of going the full distance, even within the narrow confines of available school programming. Shop also included metallurgy, which was out of bounds for young women. Home economics also included home making, which was out of the question for young men. The school kitchen was amply outfitted with stoves, ovens, sinks, shelves of pots and pans, drawers of utensils, bins of produce, and a refrigerator for perishables. We each brought with us the required kitchen attire: an apron, a cap, and potholders. Aunt Alice had made me resplendent in a full chef's apron with pockets for my potholders, and a towering white chef's hat. I was definitely the rooster in my group. The wood working class was just as popular with the girls as the cooking class was with the boys. Rowena and I met and compared notes. The second half of the school year, the classes reverted to their usual format. The boys were given the choice of woodworking or metallurgy, and the girls were to select cooking or home making. I chose woodworking and settled in to making bookends. Rowena chose home making and immediately came into conflict with the instructor and the syllabus. As in most working class households where both parents held down jobs to support a large family, the Jackson children were given early training in taking care of the home. In a family of eight girls, all knew how to cook, clean, wash the clothes, and shop for the weekly food. The school home making lab was a model apartment and the girls were assigned different chores which amounted to constantly renewing its already sterile and unlived in facade. Rowena flatly refused to dust an apartment that was not dusty, wash clothes that were clean, or make up beds that had not been slept in. "I clean my own home every week. I don't need to study this. I already taught it all to my sisters." I talked up her case with my fellow students. I managed to get a buzz going around and decided to take a stab at running for president of the Student General Organization. Taking advantage of the favored neckwear of Frank Sinatra, a young crooner enjoying a craze of popularity, I countered my major opponent Jules Podel's campaign slogan, "Mach Schnell, Vote for Podel," with a flood of construction paper bow ties marked "Don McKayle for G.O. Pres." I was victorious and spent my final year at William Niles basking in popularity. I graduated with honors in the rapid advance program and at the age of fourteen entered De Witt Clinton high school.

High school meant taking the subway and achieving the freedom to travel longer distances outside the routine of going to school and back home again. I journeyed downtown to the Broadway district and walked about looking at the posters and pictures of performers outside the theatres that lined the streets. My first introduction to this neighborhood had come as a result of my being an acolyte at St. Luke's Episcopal church. Once a year there was an all diocese ceremony to honor the acolyte. It was held at the beautiful church of St Mary The Virgin in the heart of the Broadway theatre district. It was an event we looked forward to with great anticipation. Emerging from the subway on our way to the church, we passed by a theater showing pictures of a beautiful black woman in wondrous costumes, dancing with other exotically clad black men and women. I was determined to return to that theater and investigate. My trip back downtown on Saturday afternoon led me to my first theater dance experience. The photographs were of Katherine Dunham and her troupe of dancers, singers, and musicians. I bought a ticket for four dollars fifty cents, and climbed up to the balcony to experience an event that would forever change my life. The curtain rose on a work called *Haitian Roadside*. The mood was joyous, filled with wonderful, lively dancing. Then, out walked the beautiful woman whose picture I had seen in front of the theater. She led a live donkey and sang a song, "Tix Oiseaux." I was enraptured. The number that was to leave the deepest impression on me was called *L'Agya*. It was a dramatic, narrative work and ended with Miss Dunham shedding down to a diaphanous slip as she mourned over the body of a fallen lover. From then on, I was to return to the Broadway district every possible Saturday afternoon and search the outsides of theaters, looking for pictures of dancers. At the Maxine Elliot Theatre, the moody and arresting pictures of a woman dancing were the next to catch my attention. The center placard was adorned with a large portrait. Jet black hair was swept windblown from a white face with compelling eyes and an unusually expressive mouth. Again I bought a ticket and went upstairs. What a completely different performance I was to view! The audience response was as markedly contrasting to my previous experience as was the dancing of the lone woman on the stage below. Her name was Martha Graham. None of her dance movements were at all familiar; her behavior seemed strange. In one dance, entitled *Salem Shore*, a large circle of driftwood occupied center stage. Down stage to one side, was a small railing. It appeared to be a stylized representation, a fractured section of the widow's walks that dotted the roofs of traditional coastline New England homes. Garbed in a dark and unadorned long dress, she jumped in and out of the driftwood circle, lifting and dropping her skirt with plucking, staccato gestures. From this activity she would cross down to the railing and peer forward, scanning an unseen horizon, only to return to her previous activity. I left the theater and thought a long time about what I had seen. I didn't know whether I had liked it or not, because I couldn't respond directly. I also could not forget it.

My next journey inside a Broadway theater was to see my first musical, *Finian's Rainbow*. The orchestra pit was filled with musicians; the stage was transformed by scenery. There was wonderful singing and an amazing solo dance to the mournful harmonica music of a blind musician, Sonny Terry. The dancer was Anita Alvarez, a former member of the Martha Graham Dance Company. The choreographer was the brilliant Michael

Kidd. Anita Alvarez's dance was stylistically different from the dancing in the rest of the show. It did not rely on steps but rather it used the entire body as an expressive instrument. Her character, Susan The Silent, was mute and spoke only through movement. When she took off in her solo, she exploded across the stage in arcing slides on her flanks, arms akimbo, almost spilling into the audience. It was breathtaking. Another performer took my breath away in quite a different manner. Clothed in a trailing leopard skin skirt below a bare midriff, a brown skinned beauty, with glistening hair coifed high in an extended pompadour, entered in a number called "When The Idle Poor Become The Idle Rich." I was immediately in love and commenced to hang around the stage door whenever possible, hoping to catch a glimpse of her, always with a program in hand but never brave enough to ask for an autograph. It was many years later that I was able to confess to her, "I've been in love with you ever since I was fourteen years old." The luminous Lavinia Williams seemed genuinely charmed by my guileless declaration. We met back stage at the City Center theater on the opening night of the restaging of my *Rainbow Round My Shoulder* for the Alvin Ailey American Dance Theater. The beautiful young dancer that performed the female solo in my dance was her daughter, Sara Yarborough.

At De Witt Clinton, I enrolled in a drama course taught by Mrs. Wincor of the English department. Peering at us through smoky blue lenses, speaking with a husky voice reminiscent of Tallulah Bankhead, she introduced us to Shakespeare. We read *Macbeth* and were to present selected scenes for staged presentations to the class. My classmate Andrew Siff and I were to do the murder scene. I quickly snapped up the meaty role of Lady Macbeth. De Witt Clinton was an all boys school, which severely limited the scope of the drama program.

Visits to Dr. Craig's office were never looked forward to with any emotion other than consternation. It was terror to be imprisoned in the dental chair: the towel clipped around your neck; the paper cup filled with water, "Rinse your mouth!"; the small circular sink next to the dental chair, with water swirling down its cone-like interior like a treacherous whirlpool ready to catch the jettisoned blood, "Spit out!" The waiting room had its distractions from the oncoming ordeal. There were stacks of wonderful *National Geographic* magazines, filled with fascinating stories and eye boggling photography. In a tooled leather box, there was a stereopticon with picture cards of battle scenes and memorabilia from World War I. The corner windows of the waiting room flanked a tall wing back chair. A forsaken geranium occupied the window sill. You always had to wait, no matter how early you arrived for your appointment. Sometimes the wait could be as long as an hour. One Saturday morning I was early for my appointment. I arrived at the same time as the nurse. She unlocked the door and let me in. I had purposely made the first appointment in the book, determined to get out in time for my planned trip to the theater district. I waited for the nurse to hang up her coat and hung mine right next to hers. I watched her go through the curtained French doors into the front treatment room. I dropped down in the wing back chair and picked up a *National Geographic*. I heard the nurse speaking to Dr. Craig. I looked through the lace curtains, down at the traffic. My eyes settled on the flower pot. The earth was compacted and parched until it pulled away from the sides of the ceramic container. There no longer seemed to be any vestige of life left in the geranium. I found a pencil and paper and began to jot down a title, "The Plant That They Forgot". As I wrote a rhyme scheme began to take shape. A melody played itself in my head. It was very tragic, like a French song intoned in a throaty voice by a chanteuse. The doorbell sounded and a man came in. He hung up his coat and the nurse ushered him inside. I heard Dr. Craig speaking to him. Their voices disappeared. I returned to my writing. Could he have been given the first appointment along with me? The doorbell sounded again. The nurse opened the French doors as a chubby woman entered, quite out of breath from the climb. "Oh, those stairs will be the death of me yet. They just seem to get longer every time." "Hang up your coat and come right in." I couldn't believe it. The nurse was surrendering my place without so much as an if you please. I had already been there half an hour. The room began to fill up. The nurse came out carrying a form for someone. I cornered her. "I had the first appointment." "Dr. Craig knows you're here. He'll be right with you." She disappeared behind the French doors. The hum of the dentist's drill sounded from inside. I heard Dr. Craig's laugh. I became angry. The nurse called to a man sitting on the sofa. He went in. A while later the nurse took someone else. I folded the paper on which I had been writing and put on my coat. I knocked on the French doors. A room full of people looked up at the nurse as she speechlessly listened to my words of outrage. I left, closing the front door behind me. Long before I reached home that evening, Mother and Daddy heard from a very bemused Dr. Craig just how I had given his nurse a piece of my mind.

The Plant That They Forgot

There in a secluded corner in a small red earthen pot
Stands an object withered and dying; it's the plant that they forgot.
They moved away last week and left it there alone.
The earth is parched and dry, as brittle and hard as stone.
The leaves are turning yellow and falling to the ground.
The blossoms all have vanished, the stem is bent and brown.
It breathes its last breath now; its head begins to nod.
As it leaves its earthly ruins and rises up to God.

The poem written on the back of a folded dental history sheet found its way into the January 1945 issue of the De Witt Clinton High School literary art publication, *Magpie*.

In my senior year, I was most fortunate to have Louis Allen as my English instructor. He was a wonderful teacher who loved his subject and he made you love it too. He was a poet and read us one of his poems, "Strange Fruit," a searing telling of the lynching of a black man in the South. He then played for us a recording of Billie Holiday singing his words to a haunted and pained melody. I bought the record for my own collection, but was not allowed to play it when mother was home. "Take off that woman. She just makes me feel too sad." Mother's opinion was shared by the radio networks. A distraught woman, depressed over the loss of a loved one in battle, had thrown herself from an open window. This wartime suicide was said to have occurred while she was listening to a broadcast of Billie Holiday singing "Gloomy Sunday." That song and several others by Billie Holiday were denied further airplay. "Strange Fruit" was among the casualties.

I joined the Frederick Douglass Society, an after-school group devoted to the study of black history, a subject conspicuously missing from the regular syllabus. I became a member and then president of the society. I had discovered the great black abolitionist, Frederick Douglass, some years before on my own. I hunted through the biography section of the Washington Heights Children's Library and took home every book I could find on men and women of color. I spent hours reading in the reference department. I discovered not only Frederick Douglass, but Harriet Tubman, Sojourner Truth, Nat Turner, Henri Cristophe, Toussaint L'Ouverture and a host of others. I soon exhausted the limited offerings at that branch. A friendly librarian found me wandering through the adult section perusing the shelves, and directed me to the Schomburg Collection, housed in the Harlem Branch Library on 136th Street off Lenox Avenue. It was a small room on the second floor. Locked glass vitrines held the most prized items. A bronze bust of Ira Aldridge graced a turned oak pedestal. The knowledge and information encountered there was to be a constant source of inspiration and productivity in the years to come.

I later joined a youth group called Club L'Ouverture. Named after one of my heroes, it immediately appealed to me. The club put on skits and held folk dances and folk sings. I had become deeply interested in American folk music. For several years I was a counselor at Camp Woodland, a children's summer camp in Phoenicia, New York, devoted to collecting and preserving the rich folk materials of the Catskill Mountains. The field trips searching out the singers, musicians, and story tellers, following up leads, learning the history from those who had lived it, listening to personal revelations, were extraordinary. I followed folk artists like Pete

Seeger, Odetta, and blues singers like Leadbelly and Josh White. I frequented hootenannies. The comradery was warm and genuine, and I made lifelong friends. Club L'Ouverture was a magnate for emerging young talent. C. Bernard Jackson, known then as Clarence, and Robert Nemiroff, called Bobby, were both my club mates. Clarence was a budding composer and song writer. He was later to compose dance scores for me and for Paul Taylor, and to author musicals and produce dramas and events at the Inner City Cultural Center in Los Angeles. Bobby also wrote songs and skits. He was to write and produce the musical *Raisin*, which I would direct and choreograph.

Another of my club mates, a young woman named Anna Kaufman, was taking dance lessons. She was instrumental in organizing a creative dance group with Pearl Cromone, one of the adult advisors, as instructor. The class consisted of a basic warm up and stretches which led immediately into expressive projects, improvised and performed each session. We met at the headquarters of Club Buen Vecino in Spanish Harlem, then later in a church hall further uptown. I loved the classes and decided to make a dance for presentation at one of the club's weekend meetings. It was programmed to follow a comedy skit written by Bobby, called "Buzzing The Bee", in which I played a barber. My dance was to the well known spiritual "Go Down Moses." I had no training other than my lessons with Pearl Cromone, but my efforts were met with great enthusiasm. I was the solo performer, emerging from a circle of dancers. They moved, sliding their feet along in constant contact with the floor, bodies folded forward, singing as they danced.

Anna Kaufman invited me to attend a dance concert at the Central High School of Needle Trades. She was studying at the New Dance Group and one of her teachers was giving a performance. The Central High School of Needle Trades was in the heart of the garment district and had been built in the thirties. The walls of the auditorium were covered with gigantic murals painted by artists employed under the W.P.A. (Works Project Administration). The dance series was devoted to solo artists, and that evening the curtain opened on Pearl Primus. A beautiful vision, a carving in ebony, was dancing. The opening work was *African Ceremonial*. The movements were powerful, yet sparse. It was living sculpture on view. Every curving of her spine, every thrust of her hips, every flapping of her loins, every wave of her heavily bangled wrists was a gesture from an ancestral ritual of unknown origin. A rush of pictures imprinted itself on my imagination; a sensory collage filled me. With mercurial speed and accuracy, the figure of the noble past became a sassy contemporary girl in *Rock Daniel*. Then, wonder of wonders, a voice dipped in bronze rang out in sonorous tones.

Southern trees bear a strange fruit
Blood on the leaves and blood at the root

Now she was a woman consumed with horror, recoiling from a lynching she had just witnessed. The title of the dance and the words spoken so beautifully by the actress Vinette Carrol, were from the poem "Strange Fruit," written by Louis Allen, my teacher.

Ren, ne, nay y ya bo, bi a bo bo

The clanging of a bell and the pounding sound of treading feet introduced *Shouters Of Sobo*. Within a widening iris of light the figure of a Maroon village priestess was calling worshipers to a secret gathering in the forest. In the next dance, *Hard Times Blues*, the face of hunger burst forth in desperate yet magical flight. My breath seemed suspended. Pearl Primus sprinted on a diagonal across the stage, left the ground, and walked through space. Her feet ran along the air and then she landed with the assurance of an avian creature. I turned to Anna. "I want to do that!" "O.K." "I want to dance like her!" "O.K., her class meets next week..." "No, tonight!" We went back to Anna's apartment after the performance. She taught me Pearl's *Dance Of Strength*. Slapping my shoulder, then my back, pulsing my pelvis, I whipped back and forth — first one side then the other. As my enthusiasm grew, we pulled back the furniture and stretched out, filling the small room, chanting and moving in unison. The vivid images of that evening flooded through my being and I was there again, moving with that extraordinary woman. In the exhilaration of the moment, a transformation took place. I was a dancer.

2

THE NEW DANCE GROUP

"Hello, I'm here to take the scholarship audition." "Have you ever been a student at the New Dance Group?" "No." "Where have you studied?" "I took interpretive dancing with Pearl Cromone." "Is that it?" "Yes." "I hardly think that qualifies you to be a scholarship candidate." "Anna Kaufman told me to come down." "Well I don't know, the requirements for auditioning are quite specific and..." "Please, if you don't like me, just tell me to leave and I'll go, but you can't turn me down without seeing me!" The sharp-featured woman sitting behind the desk peered at me intensely. I looked directly back into her dark judgmental eyes, almost holding my breath, silently beseeching her to say yes.

"The audition will be held down here. The men's dressing room is upstairs on the fourth floor." I breathed happily and thanked her. I took an application form from the young woman at the next desk and walked toward the stairs. Halfway down the hallway, a door was slightly ajar, and from inside came the sound of someone playing castanets. Black letters on the opaque glass door panel read,

HELENE VEOLA, DANCES OF SPAIN.

I continued upstairs, changed into my practice clothes and went back downstairs.

A few young women, each wearing a form-hugging garment that I had never seen before, were already in the studio. The room was long and empty except for a piano in the corner. There was a mirrored wall and benches along a shorter wall beside the entrance door. Folding chairs were set in front of the mirrors. As the room began to fill up, I realized that I was the only male auditioning and the only person not wearing what seemed to be the required uniform. I had on what I had always worn to my sessions with Pearl Cromone, khaki shorts and a textured beige polo shirt. I went to the front of the room and observing myself in the mirrors, began to practice the dance I intended to perform. I noticed the sharp featured woman watching me. She and several other women had come in and sat down. "I'm Judith Delman. Nona Shurman, Muriel Manings, Sophie Maslow, and I will be the judges today. William Bales will give the audition." The young woman from the office glided silently around the room with a flowing, graceful gait gathering the applications and handed them to Miss Delman. Mr. Bales entered, gave a jovial greeting to the judges and proceeded to the front of the room. He smiled and sat down. "Let's begin." Looking about, I realized that I was the only one standing. I hurriedly sat directly facing Mr. Bales. He snapped his fingers, indicating a tempo to the woman who was sitting at the piano reading a book. She closed the book and began to play. "Let's take the bounces." The class doubled over along with Mr. Bales. Peering forward awkwardly in an attempt to observe, digest, and execute simultaneously, I followed as best I could. Panic began to set in as one unfamiliar floor exercise followed another. "Let's take the exercise on six." We were asked to assume a flat back kneeling position and then execute a series of hinges and pelvic thrusts. I felt good about my ability in that area only to be challenged next to stand balanced precariously in off-center tilts with high extended legs. We were finally asked to assemble in the corner of the room. "At last," I thought, "I'm going to be allowed to do my dance for them." "I always like to see them run. I learn a lot from that." The tall blond woman was speaking. The others nodded in agreement. I was at the front of the group and sprinted across the room, only to turn back and see the women, paired off neatly in partners, running on the balls of their feet. "Please, can I do it again?" I returned and performed my version of what I had just witnessed. By the time the audition was over, I wished only that a hole would open up in the floor and I could gladly disappear. I never got to show them my dance and I certainly didn't know any of what had been asked of me. I went upstairs, changed back into my street clothes and returned to the audition room, only because good manners dictated I do so. Miss Delman's assistant was posting a list. I couldn't believe it. What had they seen? I was one of seven awarded the 1947 year's work scholarship.

My personal schedule of dance lessons included: Martha Graham technique with Sophie Maslow and Muriel Manings, Humphrey-Weidman technique with Nona Shurman, Hanya Holm technique with Mary Anthony, Ballet technique with Nina Golovina, Afro-Caribbean technique with Pearl Primus, Haitian dance technique with Jean Leon Destiné, Hindu dance technique with Hadassah, Modern Dance Fundamentals with Eva Desca, Jean Erdman, and William Bales. My class schedule was over-ambitious and so was I, eager to experience everything, a sponge for learning. My first lesson was with William Bales and I was determined to come to his class dressed like a dancer. I queried Miss Delman's assistant, Eunice Davidson, as to where I could find the proper attire. She was constantly knitting dance practice garments, and directed me to Capezio on the corner of Broadway at 49th Street, right over the Howard Johnson.

"The movement is visceral, not decorative. You've got to take the impetus from the contraction. Open your groins!" Bill, as my classmates called Mr. Bales, demonstrated the movement gripping his thighs and turning them back as his spine rounded into a powerful arc. His bare legs were a marvel of muscular definition terminating in gnarled feet, swathed in adhesive tape bandages protecting split calluses. Eva Desca also had a flair for the dramatic. She completed a salutatory sequence balanced with her arms flung open, her head held regally, with her gaze focused imperiously above the class. "Do the movement, and as you do it say, 'I am the greatest dancer in the world!'" This was my second lesson and I threw myself into the stated objective, completing the phrase with a haughty patrician glare that obviously surpassed Eva's instruction. She was smiling at me. "This time do it and say, 'Nijinsky was good also.'" Nona Shurman pounded her Gretsh Modern Dance Drum in a happy rebounding rhythm as she crossed the floor with the class in tow. Her blond page-boy bounced against her shoulders and her skirt tucked into the leg elastics of her blue leotard swished in a fluttering tail behind her. "This is from *Wind in the Willows*, one of Charles' works. Donald, Anna, lead off the diagonal." Nona's infectious good humor filled the room turning suddenly into a pointed barb at a student who dared a stylistic interpretation that she considered aesthetic heresy. "Marion, save that hunching up for the Graham classes. Open your chest, lift your sternum and dance!" Mary Anthony moved precisely, her ankle-length skirt grazing the floor, her jet black hair captured high on her head in a chignon covered by a sparkling silver net. We were walking on semi-circular paths, weaving to the right then the left of the long diagonal of the room, shifting every eight counts as we leaned into a changing center. It seemed simple enough, but one after another, the students wandered off path and failed to complete the diagonal. It was my turn, and I successfully crossed the floor. "That's it! Once again, Donald. I'll start in the opposite corner and we'll pass each other center stage."

The magic word was said, *stage*. That's what it was eventually all about. Mary emphasized the performance elements and developed the class in a cumulative massing of tasks built on thematic and motional ideas. Beginning ballet classes were exercises in character for me. I was the only boy in a class of mostly young matrons with no professional ambitions. I was Mme. Golovina's favorite, but for the life of me could not ascertain why. She liked to call me "My prince" and gave me a lot of special attention. She was an English woman with the ballerina's mandatory Russianized name. All the class terminology was spoken in French glazed with a British pronunciation that sent me hurtling to the Larousse French-English dictionary in vain efforts at deciphering. What sounded like shtay, shtay, shtay was in actuality jeté, jeté, jeté. The tights that were disallowed in modern dance classes were required for ballet. The choices at Capezio were either cotton durene jersey, which developed an unattractive bagginess at the knee halfway through class, or a coarse wool that threatened to scrape the skin from your knuckles as you pulled them up your legs and became even more lethal with repeated washings. I appealed to Eunice Davidson again for help and she graciously agreed to a lesson in the art of knitting tights. She lived a block away on 58th Street off Madison Avenue, above a cinema. A plaque alongside the entry door announced, Madame Bertha, Corsetiere – 1st Floor. You entered Eunice's domicile by proceeding through Madame Bertha's workroom to the back where a door led into a complete apartment. On the wall next to the door was a framed placard of a young Madame Bertha with upswept hair, wearing a kimono pulled back to reveal a merry widow, three quarter foundation garment which nipped in her waist and pushed her bosom high. The printed admonition below read, "No Two Snowflakes Are Alike!" Armed with a set of double ended needles for the legs, a circular needle for the body and skeins of forest green wool, I began the arduous and fascinating task of making my first pair of hand knitted tights. The sight of a six foot, muscular young man wielding knitting needles and producing what appeared to be an inordinately long and voluminous sleeve collected stares.

A series of slammed doors and heated words coming from the faculty dressing room were the precursors of the distressing announcement from Miss Delman that Pearl Primus would not be teaching any longer; her name did not appear on the 1948 Schedule of Classes. I had only studied several months with Pearl and awaited each class with eager anticipation. The classes were extremely challenging and a wonderful admixture of traditional movement and modern pedagogical discipline. Her ankle study was a particular paradox. It built the powerful legs that could produce the elevated flight for which she was famous, and at the same time required an extraordinary amount of strength. In subliminal ways, I was absorbing an understanding of what it took to make a dancer. Hard work and dedication were paramount, but without natural ability the task was impossible. I marveled at performers who held stage with great mastery and yet in class appeared flawed and out of sorts. Adding to my confusion was critical commentary often praising the "prodigious technical prowess" of these same artists. Iris Mabry, who came to class at the Graham school, and Daniel Nagrin, who attended Nanette Charisse's ballet class were two prime examples. These performers were talented creators and used technique as a means rather than an end, eschewing preconceived notions of perfection, discarding traditional goals, and developing new personal paradigms.

One of my greatest delights was my weekly class with Hadassah in Hindu dance. The centered, inner focus, the rippling arms, the deftly articulated hand gestures, the glances of the eyes, dilations of the nostrils, configurations of the lips, the intricate movements of the neck, and the voluptuous posturing of the torso; it was dessert after the wonderful meal consumed in all the other classes of the week. Hadassah was a woman of great charm who filled the classroom with a warmth that embraced each and every student.

"Dancing is a short life, Don. What are you going to do when it's over?" How could I respond to Mother's question? I just knew I wanted to dance. "You're too intelligent a boy to become a dancer." Nothing so far in my existence had summoned up such feelings. I did not want to disappoint my parents, but there was no detour from the road I saw before me. I would show them I could do it all. I arrived at the college library at eight every morning to begin my research. Through dogged persistence, I had been able to make a schedule that allowed me to fit academics, dancing, and travel into a day that started with breakfast at six and got me back to the Bronx in time for dinner and studies until ten thirty, when I was required to "get my rest."

"What made you choose this topic", queried my sociology professor as he returned my ten page annotated essay, "The Hindu Dance, An Institution Within The Hindu Religion." Although I hardly knew him, I opened up and told him of my aspirations. "Why are you here? Why don't you go and dance?" The paper was graded A. I could see I was a valued student in his eyes and yet he was advising me to leave. He sensed a passion within me that touched off something inside himself. He was wordlessly cautioning me not to give up my dreams. The next day I cornered Sophie Maslow in the break between company class and rehearsal. "I can't tell you to become a dancer, but if you want to be one, you certainly can." Sophie's answer to my probing was all the affirmation I needed. It gave me an objective evaluation and at the same time told me the choice was mine alone. Everything was happening at an unanticipated rate. The clincher that transformed me into a full time dancer was an F in statistics, a course required in the liberal arts curriculum. I had managed to get all A's and a B in Latin, which I had found deadly. I had a natural gift for languages and had received merit awards throughout all my years of study at De Witt Clinton High School, but learning a language that was taught in an uninflected routine of recitations, declensions, and conjugations seemed to be a waste of precious time. I managed to discipline myself, and aided by the strength of my knowledge in the romance languages, produced the necessary work to receive a B. I had no such helpmate in mathematics. In high school, I had great success with geometry which steered clear of arithmetic, but anything with figures was a struggle. The final exam in statistics was in two parts. The first half was theoretical and I scored one hundred percent. In the second half figures were substituted for the unknowns and arithmetic reared its ugly head. When the bell announcing the end of the exam rang, I handed in a ream of figurings:

columns of fractions that could not find common denominators, sums that were constantly changing, long division in decimals that went off the page without conclusion. I scored zero. I had never failed a class before. I left college at the end of my sophomore year and with that, I abandoned my ambition to become a biological illustrator, a desire retained from childhood. When I had turned nine and Philip was ten, Mother had decided to go back to school to acquire the knowledge for a career as a doctor's office assistant. Part of her studies included the preparation of a notebook with text and diagrams. I had drawn and colored all the muscle groups and organs for her, copying the illustrations from the encyclopedia. She confided in me that the notebook had earned a grade of Excellent and that the illustrations were singled out for highest praise. I had a real sense of pride watching Mother walk down the aisle in her white uniform. She smiled at me as she passed on her way to receive her certificate.

A flurry of excitement, faculty meetings, and a stream of observers watching classes marked the beginning of my second year at the New Dance Group. The board of directors had agreed to embark on a concert season and had reserved a two week time slot in a Broadway theater. It was a financially risky decision and the preparations severely taxed the available limited resources. The season was to take place at the Mansfield Theatre on 47th Street and was called The New Dance Group Festival. Quite to my surprise, I found myself cast in works of Sophie Maslow and Jean Erdman, and was instantly a member of a modern dance company. Sophie Maslow was remounting her successful work *Folksay*, and Jean Erdman created a new work, *Four Four Time*. I suddenly had to juggle rehearsals with two choreographers, a newly established daytime company class, scholarship work hours, and my evening schedule of dance classes, along with sixteen credits at City College.

The legendary folk artist Woody Guthrie sat downstage right with Tony Kraber playing guitar, singing, exchanging palaver, and reciting passages from Carl Sandburg's *The People Yes*. In the final large group section of *Folksay*, I circled the stage in a solo of catapulted leaps, jumping like a bucking bronco, then rejoined my radiantly smiling partner. We traveled serenely offstage gazing into endless imaginary vistas of open space. It was wonderful standing in line with a company of seasoned performers receiving the sustained applause of the audience. Sophie Maslow and William Bales held centerstage and the rest of the company flanked them: Mark Ryder, Irving Burton, Lili Mann, Nina Caiserman, Muriel Manings, Billie Kirpich, and standing next to me, my partner Andora Hodgins. Fortunately for me, there was a preview performance of Jean Erdman's *Four Four Time* at the McMillin Theatre in Colombia University, prior to its Broadway premiere. The costumes were finished at the very last moment and arrived as the stage manager called, "Half hour." There was no time for a dress rehearsal. The costumes were extremely colorful and patterned in bold, Mondrian-like blocks and stripes. I did not realize how near sighted I was until I entered the stage ready to execute a well rehearsed swirling lift; there were suddenly two women coming at me, disguised, as far as I could ascertain, in identical outfits. One was the target of my lift, but which one? They both headed for me. I was to sweep one overhead as another man entered from the wings and lifted the second woman. It was choreographed as a moment of surprise, a calculated danger. At this moment the danger was quite real. I changed the rehearsed timing and got to the meeting place of contact early, awaiting the arrival of a very surprised Billie Kirpich as Nina Caiserman breezed by with a sideward quizzical glance. I canvassed friends in the audience that came back stage to learn if my expression appeared glazed or unfocused. They assured me that eye contact was strong in my performance and that there was no hint of any problem. Yet, I wondered, what would it feel like to be onstage and see clearly?

Christmas vacation was an ideal time to put on performances for children and a wonderful way to bring new audiences and revenues into emerging theaters. José Quintero and Ted Mann had a small but highly visible theater in a converted two storey building on Sheridan Square in the heart of Greenwich Village. The basement level was made into a narrow rectangular stage space with audience seating on three sides. It was called Circle In The Square. Ted Mann invited me to produce a children's show to play at the theater during the school holiday hiatus. Two of my colleagues, Patricia Brooks and Shawneequa Baker teamed up with me to sing, dance, and draw the young audience into our performance. We rehearsed for several weeks in the cold, dark theater and spent the evenings sewing costumes late into the night in Ted Mann's one room Minetta Lane flat, as he slept soundly. A wood fire was kept burning in the fireplace and his large black German shepherd dog stretched across the hearth, periodically opening an eye to see what we were doing. The program was organized into a series of songs and dances performed by Patricia and myself with Shawneequa in charge of dropping the needle when recorded sound was used and handling the offstage madness of lightning-fast costume changes. I had fashioned a rooster dance to a recording of tablas, veena, and sitar music from India and had made an exotic whimsy of a costume with an elaborate wire framed tail of fabric feathers belted through an emerald green bodysuit. A floppy velvet cock's comb bounced on my head. I entered the stage with an exaggerated strut, moving my neck in jerky pecks and tilts, glancing about the room. Much to my surprise I could see every toddler sitting up looking at me with expressions of amazement. One little boy sucking a lollipop curled his feet up under himself on his chair and pointed a sticky finger at me. "What a funny rooster. He's got eye glasses on!" I received more laughter than ever at that performance and an enthusiastic round of screams and applause as I strutted offstage shaking my tail feathers and crowing out loud.

Shawneequa and I continued to work together and became very close friends. We lived near each other in the Bronx and spent much time traveling back and forth between our apartments. Patricia's lovely voice developed into a brilliant soprano. She became a leading artist with the New York City Opera and married Ted Mann. Later, the row of maisonettes in which the theater was housed was demolished to make way for a tall apartment building and supermarket. A new home was found in Greenwich Village for Circle In The Square. Many years later, an uptown branch was established in the Broadway district.

The New York dance world of the early 1950's existed in clusters of buildings pocketed in heterogeneous communities scattered throughout midtown and lower Manhattan. The New Dance Group was housed in an edifice that was a microcosm of the dance disciplines in vogue at the time. Above the three floors that were devoted to the varied styles and cultural forms offered by the New Dance Group, there were two other private studios. In one, Ana Ricarda, clothed in pale lavender chiffon, taught Isadora Duncan dancing to several other women draped in similar diaphanous raiment. Next door, Alexandra Fedorova Fokine taught a style of Russian ballet that was to slowly give way to the Americanized style of another Russian émigré, George Balanchine. Once a month there was a *soirée* held in Helene Veola's studio. José Greco was numbered among her many disciples performing for the invited audience of aficionados. Two blocks east, on Fifty-ninth street, La Meri's Ethnological Dance Center presented dances of the Iberian Peninsula and the Orient. One block north, on Madison Avenue, was the School of American Ballet (SAB). The principal teachers, under the directorship of George Balanchine, were the Russians, Pierre Vladimiroff, Mikhail Obukoff, and the elegant English woman, Muriel Stuart. Muriel Stuart also taught company class in ballet technique every Friday at the New Dance Group and had extended an invitation to me to observe classes at SAB whenever my schedule permitted.

Mr. Vladimiroff's classes were the epitome of romanticism. "Give me beootifool arums", he exhorted the class, as he posed at the completion of a movement phrase balanced in a curvaceous *sousou* with his wrists crossed overhead and his hands hanging like two overly ripe peaches. Maestro Obukoff indicated combinations with his hands fluttering in front of his chest as he growled in an unfathomable mixture of Russian, French, and English: "Do me like so!" As the class swung into action, Obukoff's eyes narrowed into slits and flint stone sparks seemed to flash. "You chew gum in my class. OUT!" The initial vowel of the invective rumbled from the recesses of his chest and crescendoed into a mighty roar, ending in the whip snap of the terminal consonant. The offending dancer disappeared, and the class continued with a nervous edge investing every movement. "Terrible! Same class Monday. Dismissed!" Muriel Stuart wore a long jersey skirt and soft ballet slippers with a little heel, designed especially for her by Capezio. She walked along the line of dancers at the barre giving individual corrections, adjusting the tilt of a head, rounding the carriage of an arm. As she came to a dancer at the end of the barre, she took hold of her wrist and giving it a gentle shake loosened the stored tension. "That's it now dear, lovely." As she continued across the front of the room, she passed by the bench on which I was sitting. She shook her head, rolling her eyes skyward. "Poor dear, she'll never be a dancer." The class that followed was taught by Merce Cunningham, a once a week session in modern dance. Presages of things to come.

At Camp Woodland, I had worked with a senior counselor, Carla McBride, who had a younger sister at SAB. As fortune would have it, I met her sister Patricia at the time that she and her roommate Tanaquil LeClerq were with the company affiliated with the school, a recent outgrowth of Ballet Society known as the New York City Ballet. My friendship with Patricia McBride allowed me to sit in on several rehearsals of George Balanchine's new ballet, *Orpheus*. Nicholas Magallanes danced the title role and Maria Tallchief, Balanchine's then wife and prima ballerina, danced the role of Eurydice. Tanaquil LeClerq was cast in her first important role as the Leader of the Bacchantes. Mr. Balanchine exploited her reed-like frame and sinuous strength, beginning to develop what was to become known as the Balanchine ballerina. Tanaquil LeClerq, his muse in this creation, was to become the next Mrs. Balanchine. Patricia McBride, after being appointed a demi-soloist, married, moved to England, and left behind her dance career. The New York City Ballet was to be graced years later by another dancer bearing the same name, the highly individual artist who rose within the ranks to the position of ballerina, and who was teamed so often, and so successfully with Edward Villella. Sophie Maslow's *Champion* was given its premiere at the New Dance Group Festival. It was a dramatic, narrative work based on Ring Lardner's hard-boiled story. It marked the return of Jane Dudley to the concert world after a maternity leave. She was a tall woman, trained by Martha Graham, and moved with powerful full-bodied gestures that commanded attention. She also invested her teaching of Graham technique with her own elastic and textural style. Jane played the small but important role of the mother in Sophie's *Champion*. Bill Bales played the anti-hero. Normand Maxon was his crippled younger brother; Mark Ryder was the fight manager; and Irving Burton and I were fellow boxers training in the gymnasium and competing in the ring. At the time, I was still at City College and so I prepared myself by enrolling in boxing, a class which also satisfied my physical education requirement. The class emphasized footwork, punches, deflecting blows, guarding the head and torso, and built strength and agility with rope jumping and punching bag practice. I was enjoying the class tremendously but decided to switch over to Greek wrestling after we were instructed to bring sterile cotton to be placed into our mouths between our cheeks and gums to catch the blood. The second section of the class was to emphasize man to man sparring. I had been looking at pictures of boxers for character study and had decided I didn't need a broken nose or battered face to fully and faithfully portray my role.

Jane Dudley danced her wonderful solo *Harmonica Breakdown* on the New Dance Group Festival. It was set to the same haunting music of the harmonica virtuoso Sonny Terry that had made such an impression on me accompanying the *"Pot O' Gold"* solo for Anita Alvarez in *Finian's Rainbow*. Sophie Maslow, William Bales, and Jane Dudley reconstituted their performing unit, and, in the summer of 1948, The Dudley, Maslow, Bales Trio was invited with its company, The New Dance Group, to participate as teachers and performers at the first summer session of the American Dance Festival to be held on the campus of Connecticut College. I was in residence that summer as a member of the New Dance Group Company along with members of the companies of José Limón, Valerie Bettis, and Martha Graham.

"Donald, will you take Martha up to the gymnasium. Her class has been rescheduled there." Sophie embraced Martha Graham and introduced me to her. She smiled warmly as I gazed into the face that had stared out at me from a theater placard and invited me inside some years ago. Martha opened a small yellow parasol as we stepped outside of Holmes Hall. It cast a flattering shade on her face and the woven cotton jacket she wore over her flowing black jersey dress. As we started on the path towards upper campus, a child stepped in front of us and took hold of Martha's hand. I had seen the girl peering in the window intently watching our class that morning. "Hello, you're Martha Ram, aren't you, though everyone calls you Miss Hush? I'm a dancer too and this is my dancing dress. All my friends say you're funny looking, but I think you're beautiful." The little fingers curled tightly around Martha's hand, and the little tongue kept up an endless stream of delightful chatter as we crossed the lawn to the gymnasium, where a class of gigantic size awaited the famous dancer-choreographer. She had evaded detection for weeks on a radio quiz game of guess-the-mystery-voice, and had become known to the general public, much to her dismay, as Miss Hush. Our strange journey to the gymnasium had formed an immediate bonding between Martha and myself and she personally placed me where she could watch me carefully in the large room as we sat down to begin the floorwork.

"Unite yourself with the universe. It is the spherical concept." With her left leg held in a high side extension, Martha turned on the spot and cast an accusatory glance at the class. "Now do it!" Imagery, imagination, and dynamic movement were the wizard's tools of her inspired teaching. "You must wear your skin like a beautiful garment." The entire class breathed in as one. "Word has come back to me, that someone finds this movement effeminate for men." She cast her glance to the stage full of observers, panning the group until her eyes came to rest on a male dancer. "To me, that sounds like the pot calling the kettle black. The movement is what you make of it. It is at once strenuous and tender." I was completely mesmerized by this woman and lingered on her every word, translating her directives into body sensations, recoloring, shading, and constantly renewing repeated daily sequences. "Don, you're very vulnerable." I was very pleased that she had stopped and spoken to me after class, although I wasn't quite sure what to make of her comment. In the evenings, whenever I was free, I would go up to the balcony level of the auditorium and sit in the darkness watching Martha work on a new choreography, *Wilderness Stair*, later to be known as *Diversion Of Angels*. It was fascinating to see the dance evolve and then to see it reworked and changed. Ben Belitt, the poet, had written a beautiful passage that had been included in the playbill as a program note. It ended with the line, "Joy on the wilderness stair, diversion of angels." Isamu Noguchi had done a magical backwall that placed the dance in a desert panorama. Burlap was stretched as a backcloth and punched forward with large bowls held on batons from the theater wall, with intermediary areas laced and pulled back to create a sculptural relief. When Jean Rosenthal played lights from the sides across the surface, sand dunes seemed to appear in an endless perspective. The colorful costumes against the beige cloth suggested the brief season of springtime in the desert when the cactus burst into bloom. It was a joyous work, a vibrant note created in the center of a cycle of tragedies that already included *Errand Into The Maze*, *Cave Of The Heart*, *Herodiade*, *Dark Meadow*, and would continue into *Night Journey*, *Phaedra*, and *Clytemnestra*.

Composition class with Bill Bales and Pre-Classic Forms with Louis Horst required daily choreographic work in whatever spare time was available and in any studio space that could be grabbed. Selected works from the composition classes were shown on the weekly all-school presentation in Palmer Auditorium. It was a time to share in the creative work and aesthetic responses of peers. Members of the four professional companies were encouraged to use the showings as a forum for their independent work. I found time to create and present a mini dance drama to a poem of Countee Cullen, *Saturday's Child*. It was a work that dealt with a human being discarded by society. It had no music, using only the words which I spoke as I danced, creating what was called a hybrid form by mainstream purists and highly controversial. Martha Hill, the dean of the school, called me into her office to discuss "my direction." I found this all intriguing and kept working on the piece, performing it at several informal functions. It made a mark on several important people and I was invited to join a group of artists in what was known as the New Harlem Renaissance.

The Committee For the Negro In the Arts was an elite gathering of black artists in the fields of literature, theater, music, and the plastic arts. I was the first to join in dance. Among the members were the painter Ernest Crichlow, the novelist John Killens, the playwrite Alice Childress, the actor Sydney Poitier, the singers Harry Belafonte and Paul Robeson, and Harlem's poet laureate, Langston Hughes. For a first theatrical presentation, Alice Childress adapted the Langston Hughes serial of his beloved character Simple into a musical review. The stories were originally published in the *Chicago Defender* and celebrated the mother-wit of a Harlem resident everyman, Jesse P. Semple or just Simple for short. The play was presented at the Club Baron on Lenox Avenue, a night spot famed for hosting Duke Ellington's early band. I was asked to choreograph the show and also to perform *Saturday's Child*. *Just A Little Simple* ran for several months, and I got my first good taste of working as a theater choreographer staging musical numbers and as a show performer developing a role through nightly playing before an audience. At this time the brilliant singer, actor, and political activist, Paul Robeson was under attack by the House Committee on Un-American Activities. His passport was revoked, keeping him a prisoner in his own country where his ability to earn a livelihood was severely eroded. He published a newspaper, *Freedom*, edited by Lorraine Hansbury. The newspaper sponsored a benefit concert in support of its beleaguered publisher. Harry Belafonte organized the event. I choreographed a solo dance for myself to Paul Robeson's rendition of "Bye and Bye." The concert was to take place at the Golden Gate Ballroom, a large Harlem dance palace located on Lenox Avenue, a few short blocks from the fabled Savoy. When I arrived at the hall, I found much to my dismay that there was no stage. In its stead was a band platform covered in an orange tone, raised relief patterned carpet. Lawrence Brown sat at the piano and nestled in its curve, standing in front of a microphone was Paul Robeson. I looked across at him. As that dark, resonant voice embraced the cavernous hall filling it with warmth, I found no trouble dancing up and down the carpeted risers. I moved easily within several circles at once and often became the connective link between the different groups. I was the youngster in the Committee For the Negro In the Arts, serving a wonderful apprenticeship.

The dance world was an extended family with the generations in constant close contact. I made several good friends that first summer at

Connecticut College. Four of us became rather inseparable: Irving Burton, Bertram Ross, Linda Margolies, and I. We attended classes together and met in the evenings to discuss our individual experiences during the hours when we were apart, or to revel in shared moments of high drama or comedy. We all took Dr. Lulu Sweigard's class in alternate body techniques and relaxation. We spent much of the class lying on the floor with our eyes closed listening to Dr. Sweigard's voice directing us with images. "I want you to bend your legs. Place the soles of your feet on the floor. Bring your knees and the tips of your toes together. Wrap your arms across your chest, clasping your hands around your backs. I want you to imagine the muscles of your buttocks to be the rings of a shower curtain. You will now slowly open the shower curtain." Dr. Sweigard walked among the students giving personal adjustments and encouragements. "Good, that's it. Relax. Breathe easily." She suddenly stopped. "Irving, why did you close your shower curtain?" A ripple of giggles grew into uncontrollable laughter. Class was over and the four musketeers emerged, arms laced around each other's shoulders, tromping across the green, caroling at the top of our voices. "Irving Burton, open up your shower curtain!" By the end of the summer we had persuaded Linda to put a blond streak in her hair and pierce her ears, and Irving and I had choreographed a heroic dance for Louis Horst, which he greeted with poker-faced disdain. "That's quite an opera. What do you call it, *Love In A French Canoe?*"

I was offered a scholarship to study with Martha Graham at her studio on Fifth Avenue between 11th and 12th Streets. Irving, Bertram, and I had decided to look for a loft to make into a combined living quarters and studio. We were determined to become *bona fide* artists. We found a place on West Broadway between Spring and Prince Streets. After a few weeks of standing on ladders with buckets of paint, guiding sanding machines across a floor that had previously held factory machinery, and applying coats of shellac to seal the soft wood, our artist abode began to appear. West Broadway had not yet been gentrified into Soho and was in fact an extension of the Bowery district, replete with transients huddled in doorways, and lacking retail shops or mom and pop general stores catering to the infant artist colony that called it home. My father was highly dubious about the arrangement and paid us an unexpected visit. The evening Daddy arrived he had to step over a figure asleep in the entrance and climb the long staircase of tin-treaded wooden steps. He examined the quarters meticulously, complimented our industry, and turned to me. "Where's your suitcase?" He was ready to take me back home. This was definitely not what he had envisioned for me.

With the new adult responsibilities came the necessity of finding gainful employment. I embarked on one of the many joyful aspects of a multi-faceted professional life that was to remain with me and sustain me spiritually and monetarily. I began to teach and in doing so, constantly to learn again. Judith Delman assigned me three classes of youngsters on Saturday mornings. I had to invent imaginative ways to teach technical skills to little bodies and creative projects to allow for the dance to emerge. I was very successful and was invited to teach at the Downtown Community School. They were very excited to get a male instructor to teach what they called rhythms, in an effort to confront existing prejudice toward dance as a subject for boys as well as girls. On two afternoons weekly, I met separately with each of the classes in the school. Every half hour the door to the music room, where I taught, would open and one class would exit as another entered. I was charged to combine their social studies with creative rhythmic projects. The six year olds were studying, "how water gets to our homes." The twelve year olds were studying medieval history. The little ones were eager to create mountain streams flowing into tributaries, merging into rivers, filling reservoirs, channeling into pipelines, spurting from faucets, filling bathtubs and fish bowls, or boiling over on stove tops, splashing out of forgotten pots. The older children were entering adolescence and experiencing body changes that made them uncomfortable or embarrassed. I had one twelve year old that towered over his classmates. His arms were extremely long, and his nose, ears, feet, and hands seemed to have reached their maximum growth while waiting for the rest of his body to catch up. I sensed his discomfort and was challenged. I decided to have the students devise a stained glass window in movement. There was a sturdy, built-in percussion instrument rack anchored into a wall of the music room. It had several tall vertical niches for large conga drums and square ones for gongs. It was also built in an architecturally interesting shape. The stained glass window was to be performed within the confines of the instrument rack. We visited St. Mark's church across the street and also looked at pictures of stained glass windows in books and magazines. They all decided that their gangly classmate was the perfect choice to be the angel at the top of the structure. Everything that was awkward about him was suddenly beautiful. He opened his long fingers, turned in profile, and became the archtypal archangel. His personal success transformed him, liberating his personality and energizing his performance in all of his subjects.

The Contemporary Dance Group was a cooperative dance company of skilled dancers united under the direction of Helen Tamiris, who had made her reputation as a concert artist and had also choreographed for the Broadway stage. Pearl Lang had spotted me with the New Dance Group and monitored my work at the Graham studio; she asked me to join the company. The other dancers included Daniel Nagrin, Glen Tetley, Marc Breaux, Donald Saddler, Oliver Kostock, Annabelle Lyons, and Beatrice Seckler. We were to choreograph for and perform with each other.

The idea was a noble one, but did not quite succeed. I held rehearsals on my first group dance, a work just beginning to emerge from its chrysalis, but I was not prepared to deal with the high-powered personalities, over-protective of their images, or performers in need of stardom. A concert did finally evolve in 1950, after a year's work but under a very different format. All the choreographers were indeed charter members of the Contemporary Dance Group, but the dancers were gathered outside of the company by each choreographer. The event was held at Charles Weidman's Studio Theatre on 16th Street, west of Avenue of the Americas. Among the works presented were solos by Daniel Nagrin, *Song of Deborah* by Pearl Lang, and the first draft of a work I called *Games*.

I had no idea at the time, that the definitive version of this work would emerge a year later and would become a repertory staple in dance companies throughout the country, nor did I guess that it would initiate a major national project three and a half decades later, be designated a classic, nor that it would become a prime example of American Heritage in dance. It was simply a work that came out of my observations and one that I needed to do at that time. It was a work that possessed a humanity and a genre that was both specific and universal. It was a work true to its period and yet timeless, a work that never failed to find a receptive place with audiences everywhere.

3

GAMES

Philip's in-laws, the Lewises, lived in a three story wooden structure across the street from Shawneequa's apartment building. It was the lone survivor of the original homes that once dotted Union Avenue, in the present day an architectural anachronism. You could always spot visitors to the neighborhood as they would invariably stop and stare at the little gray clapboard house sandwiched in between the dingy brick and masonry apartment buildings. Worn wooden steps led up to the entry door, which boasted carved detail and beveled glass. The Lewis family occupied the upper floor. Mrs. Lewis and her children all attended Elder Lawson's evangelical church and were members of the choir. June, the youngest daughter, had a particularly lovely voice. Elder Lawson was known as the burying preacher and was always on call for the family of a departed transgressor in need of that special push from this side of eternity. If Elder Lawson's ministrations could not intercede with the almighty in the face of a damning earthly existence, there was indeed no hope for an afterlife far removed from hell's fires. "There is so much good in the worst of us, and so much bad in the best of us, it behooves us not to speak ill of the rest of us. Do I hear an Amen?" Elder Lawson plucked the petals from a white rose and dropped them on the closed eyelids in the casket as the choir moved to the next sustained chord of the somber funeral vocalise and amens resounded around the congregation. June's pure ringing soprano sounded the opening call and response. June was not quite sure about singing with me for a dance concert; so we went to speak to Mother Lewis. Mrs. Lewis was in the kitchen where the wonderful smell of greens cooking in pot liquor on the stove top mingled with the scent of the pressing comb resting in a neighboring burner where flames from the gas jet curled about the glowing tongs. With a practiced economy of movement, Mother Lewis made neat parallel parts in the crown of her customer's head and covered the separated clump of hair with grease in preparation for and in protection from contact with the searing comb. "Donald, find yourself a chair. China, get Uncle Donald something cold to drink." "A dance about children playing. That's nice. I use to like to play Little Sally Water myself. Oh, I could play that for hours." June lasted through the first performances of *Games* at the Charles Weidman Studio Theatre but soon had her fill of show business and declined participation in further performances. "I can't be spending all my little allowance on carfare, riding the subways downtown to go to no rehearsals."

I was several weeks into work on *Games* when one of the dancers came to me. "When are we going to start working with the music?" I asked about and found that indeed dances had instrumental music for accompaniment. June and I had been singing the children's songs for rehearsals, with the dancers shouting and joining in as needed. I was quite pleased with the results. What I now sensed to be a new requirement did not faze me in the slightest. I remembered Herbert Haufrecht who had written wonderful folk cantatas at Camp Woodland. He seemed the ideal choice for this assignment. He was happy to hear from me and, after our initial meeting, set to work and had something for me in about a week's time. Although it was delightful, it just didn't seem right. With the new accompaniment, the dance assumed another texture; the quality, the very genre of the work took on a whole new complexion. It was very seductive, had all the earmarks of legitimacy, but pulled the dance into a foreign area. I explained my concerns to Herb and gave him the bad news; all his much appreciated, wonderful work would not be used. I had decided to return to my original plan of *a cappella* voices and shouts. All of this creative reassessment took time and jangled the nerves of the cast. One by one they pulled out. I canvassed the New Dance Group and gathered a group of young dancers who were eager, energetic, and actually much more in tune with the aesthetic of the work. "Donald, do you remember that work you did on children's games last year?" Daniel Nagrin was about to mount a concert of his choreography consisting of several solo dances and a new group work. He had begun to choreograph *Faces From Walt Whitman* with a cast that, beside himself, included Beatrice Seckler, Miriam Pandor, Billie Kirpich, John Smolko, and me. He did not have enough material for a full program and needed to share the rest of the evening. After a rehearsal of the Walt Whitman work, he came to me and asked if I was interested. *Games* would close the first half. I was delighted. After the concert weekend of performances at the Charles Weidman Studio Theatre, the Contemporary Dance Group ended its brief existence; however, one of the fruits of that venture was an ongoing artistic relationship among Helen Tamiris, Daniel Nagrin, and myself.

Tamiris was the choreographer for *Bless You All*, a big Broadway review, which was to star Jules Munchin, Mary McCarthy, Pearl Bailey, and Valerie Bettis, and to include a large singing chorus and a dancing chorus. I was asked to be in the chorus of dancers. It was my first Broadway show. Among my fellow choristers were Bertram Ross, Joseph Gifford, Richard Darcy, Billie Kirpich, Joseph Nash, Ilona Murai, and Gerald Arpino. Featured were also six showgirls, advertised as "a swarm of sultry sylphs," who were paid twice the salary of the dancers.

Dancer's scale in 1951, under Chorus Equity's pink contract, was seventy five dollars a week.

Helen Tamiris built two major ballets around Valerie Bettis. The first act ballet was entitled, *A Rose Is A Rose*. The setting was a fanciful modern art gallery designed by Oliver Smith. Valerie Bettis, costumed as a rose in a lovely confection fashioned by Miles White, was found center stage perched on a revolving stool in a soft rose-colored spotlight, amongst floating reproductions of paintings by Rousseau, Picasso, Lautrec, a Calder mobile, a Benin carving, and an antique urn. The works of art all came to life and reacted with the rose, culminating in a pas de deux between the rose and the mobile, as danced by Donald Saddler. At this climactic moment, a rumbling came from the orchestra, a green spotlight hit the urn and I was to emerge garbed in eight discreetly placed leaves, my bare limbs highlighted with glycerin, blossoming forth as a symbol of fruition. The creative process used by Tamiris in rehearsals was based on improvisation, a complete novelty to the show dancers who were used to being shown exactly what was expected of them. Helen called these rehearsals Exploratory Movement Sessions. I found them very close to the interpretive dance experience I had enjoyed with Pearl Cromone and threw myself into them with abandon. Tamiris would explain what she wanted. She was a master story teller and followed her compelling descriptions with the command "Make, do!" I pushed imaginary loam off my rounded back, uncurled my neck, and lifted my face. My wrists spiraled and my hands uncoiled as my torso came to rest in its final evolution. "Wonderful, Donald! That's it!" The next day when we came to my part in the ballet, I again threw myself into creating the moment. "Donald, Helen is very disturbed. The plant was so beautiful yesterday and its all gone today. She's got a lot to do and you can't let things slip away." Danny had taken me out into the hallway to deliver this amazing bit of information. It had never occurred to me that I was supposed to remember exactly what I had done the day before or that I was not free to improvise on the theme at each rehearsal. I set my part at the following session, but it was not to be long-lived. It lasted only through our first week of out of town tryouts at the Schubert Theatre in New Haven, Connecticut; then it was cut. After my appearance in the opening number, I had nothing to do in the show until my entrance in the second-act ballet. While Tamiris had gone against the traditional color line practiced on Broadway and had racially integrated the dance ensemble, that policy did not extend into any of the other areas of the show. I was left with a lot of time on my hands, a full one-hour-and-a-half break.

When the show settled into its Broadway home at the Mark Hellinger Theatre, I was able to leave at the end of the first number and walk two blocks uptown wearing full stage makeup, and rehearse for a number

Danny Nagrin, Marc Breaux, and I were creating for the Fred Waring T.V. Show. We were to be dressed in loin cloths, feather headdresses, and war paint, and dance on three gigantic drums, in celebration of American Indian Week. I was able to get back to the theater in time for the North African spoof ballet and the show finale, which came just before Pearl Bailey's second-act song, "When You Fall In Love." Pearl hated this song and was resolved not to sing it. She walked out to begin the song. The staging had her waiting impatiently for an anticipated blind date. Joe Nash walked on waving. Pearl smiled happily and started towards him. He continued on past her into the waiting arms of Elmira Jones Bey. As they exited, the orchestra played the introduction and Pearl began the verse of the song. One night Joe was out and I stepped into his part. It was just a crossover but I was determined to make the most of it. I entered with a hip street strut and took Pearl aback for the briefest of moments. Her bottom jaw hung loose, her eyes opened wide in disbelief, and she turned to the audience and said, "Don't worry darlings, he won't be here tomorrow". The crowd broke up and Pearl was given the audience's enthusiastic acceptance to say any thing she wanted. From then on, whenever Pearl was on stage, *Bless You All* was in ad-lib, double-entendre heaven. "Honey, Pearly May is just entertaining the folks. That's what they came here for!" "The next evening she spied a necklace that had fallen off one of the dancers in the *Desert Flame* ballet. "Oh my, looks like someone's lost their costume." She continued to examine the floor, then turned to the audience. "I was just looking to see if it was a two piece affair." Applause and laughter covered the lyrics which she half sung, half mumbled.

> A pigeon has to do some bill and cooing
> Before he gets to first place with the dove

"Same old bird, I'll just dance a while 'til we get to something fresh." As she started her step-touch swagger across the stage, she came to a sudden halt, her hands went to her chest and she said in breathless disbelief as she walked obsequiously with outstretched arms toward the box overhanging the stage apron: "Ladies and gentlemen, we have a celebrity with us tonight". As all eyes followed her gesture, she announced with delight, "Joe Lewis," and then with mock apology, "Oh, excuse me, Madam." The audience was like clay in her hands as she manipulated and entertained. The orchestra played softly until the last refrain which she sang out lustily as she exited, returning for show-stopping applause. Pearl's second act song became an anticipated daily event, an object lesson in showmanship. She called on all her nightclub experience. Whenever something worked it became part of her routine. A necklace placed off center right at the edge of the footlight trough was added as a permanent item on the stage manager's prop list. Whenever the on-stage boxes were occupied, Joe Lewis was in the audience. I don't know what the authors felt about this distortion of their work, but the management was clearly delighted with the boost it gave to an ailing box office. They plied Pearl with flattery, flowers, and weekly backstage visits. The other stars were treated cordially, the ensemble politely. The show girls were a different matter. "Mr. Levin, can I become a blonde?" Herman Levin's acquiescence was smothered in affectionate baby talk and embraces. The same young woman queried Helen Tamiris on the details of a simple walk in the "Presidential Campaign In Living Pictures" sketch, a visionary spoof on the future role television might play in national elections. Jules Munchin, playing a White House hopeful, announced his platform, as the show girls trooped forward forming a *tableau vivant*. "Miss Strong Constitution, Miss International Peace, Miss Natural Resources..." It was the newly peroxided platinum blonde, cast as Miss Natural Resources because of her bountifully endowed physique, who inquired, "Miss Tamiris, where are my hands?" "At the ends of your wrists, dear." Closing night the downstage wings were packed with cast members as Pearl gave her final rendition of "When You Fall In Love." As always she started the number with the original blocking, but suddenly turned to the conductor, Lehman Engel. "Honey, just keep that vamp going. Now pass me up the score." She leaned forward and took the fat accordion foldout from a surprised and smiling Lehman Engel and began to unfurl it along the apron until it reached across the entire length of the stage. "Now I'm gonna show you how this show should've been done and, honey, we wouldn't be closing tonight!" She went from number to number regaling the audience, dismissing items she found worthless and parodying others with effortless finesse. When she got to the *Desert Flame* ballet she changed pace. "Now this should've been my number. Oh, you should've seen me honey in my dancing days. I used to work the room picking up dollar bills, tens, some nights even twenties, right off the table edges, with my hands held high up above my head." She winked, laughed wickedly and started into a split, then stopped halfway down and looked offstage. "All my fellow actors, just a-crowding round in the wings. Don't worry, honeys, I'll be off soon." She recovered from her thwarted athletic move and gathered up the score, refolding it as she swung into the closing cadence of the song and handed it back to Lehman Engel on the final sustained note, trooped offstage, and returned to a standing ovation.

Putting *Games* back together was exciting. In the process, the dance found its final form. The performers were Johnny Nola as Jinx, the leader of the group of boys; John Fealy as Poor Little Johnny; George Liker as Sissy Boy; Remy Charlip as Cop; Louanna Gardner as Little Sally Water; the Beck twins, Eve and Esta as The Sisters; Shawneequa Baker and I as

The Singers. Except for Remy, Johnny Nola, and Louanna, we were all students at the New Dance Group. I had met Remy Charlip at Jean Erdman's studio where he and Lou Harrison had attended a run through of Jean's *Daughters Of The Lonesome Isle*. John Cage had composed the score for prepared piano. The session had started with John Cage and David Tudor engaged in the elaborate preparation of Jean's grand piano. A detailed chart indicated where various bolts, nuts, and rubber bands were to be placed on the piano strings virtually turning the instrument into an exotic composite gamelan. Wonderful sonorities came forth as David Tudor accompanied the hypnotic feminine trio in their mysterious choreographic incantations. Remy Charlip had a marvelous sense of humor and an offbeat imagination. He designed the costumes for *Games* and presented me with illustrations that looked like plates for a piquant, ahead-of-its-time children's book. The twins were in high waisted pinafores and Louanna in a dress fashioned from one of mother's cast off gowns. All the boys wore hats which gave them a raffish look and also provided a personal fashion therapy disguise for Remy who, despite his baby face and the fringe of black locks that encircled a beatific smile, had no hair on the top of his head. The climactic moment of the dance dictated a fragmentary streetscape for the stage environment. Louanna introduced me to Paul Bertelsen, a young designer she had met through her acting teacher, and the scenic elements began to take shape. Although the dance reflected many aspects of childhood and was set in a specific genre indigenous to various regions of the United States, it was rooted in the universal truth that play is the serious business of being a child. The chants, play parties, ring games, and shouts that were chosen to parallel the choreographic scenario were selected from my own childhood experiences, from field recordings of children's game songs collected by the Library of Congress, and from songs sung to me by my Mother. The incident that funneled all of this into its final form, and which I capsulized in the printed program note for *Games*, was an event that occurred as I was in the midst of a rough and tumble game of Steal the White Flag. It shocked my young life and was indelibly seared upon my memory.

> The streets are their playground
> Through all their play runs a thread of fear
> Chickee the cop!

"La harra, la harra, corre, run man run!" I looked up to see the figure of a cop silhouetted against the street lamp. I ran for cover, huddling with my friends, crouching on the cellar steps leading to the back alleys. We felt safe in our hiding place, knowing that if pursued we had mastered the ins and outs of retreat over the backyard fences. The exact place of every hand and foothold was memorized, including which escape alleys were open and which were false exits, ending in *cul de sac* entrapment. We could literally disappear before your eyes. But now, no one ran. Rafael was caught by the cop, trapped against the fence where he had gone to retrieve his handkerchief. It was his Sunday handkerchief, only to be worn in the breast pocket of his church suit, never to be used for everyday, definitely not for play. The policeman hit him across the legs with his billie stick and Rafael crumpled to the ground. We shouted epithets at the cop from our hiding place and suddenly panicked as a flashlight shone up at us from the base of the steps. "What you kids doing up there?" We scattered in all directions as the policeman took Rafael to his car. Somehow we all found ourselves back at the street lamp where we silently waited. Rafael came back with his mother. She did not speak English and appeared distraught and unable to comprehend what had happened. He was to appear the next day in children's court. We all agreed to go with him.

"There have been a lot of complaints from the store keepers on the street and..." "There are no store keepers on our street. We live in a purely residential neighborhood." The policeman and the judge both turned to see the source of this interruption. The judge looked at me with a quizzical smile on his face. "You're a pretty intelligent boy." This wasn't at all what I had expected. Where was his black robe, his high judicial bench, his block and pounding gavel? Where were all the things I had seen in the movies? We were in a simple room with several rows of slatback wooden chairs, a side desk for the clerk, and a larger desk behind which the judge sat. I realized that I had captured his attention and sallied forward with a prepared and memorized speech. "Are we, the children of New York City, to be brutalized by the police? Aren't they here to protect us? We were playing. Aren't we supposed to play?" The judge's smile broadened into a toothy grin and a small chuckle escaped his lips. "Why don't you play in the playground?" "We have none. The streets are our playground." "It looked like a street brawl to me." Despite the cop's feeble retort, Rafael was let go and cleared of any wrongdoing. We gathered in front of the court building and cheered our victory as Rafael came out with his mother, who smiled at me and gave me a warm embrace. When the officer was transferred from the neighborhood precinct, our triumph was complete. That summer we saw him, garbed in his dark blue uniform, patrolling Orchard Beach, looking very uncomfortable in the sweltering heat. We shouted derisive taunts at him and ran, stopping when we had reached a safe distance to once again recount the details of that fateful evening.

Danny had reserved Hunter Playhouse for the concert, a small theater within Hunter College, (now called the Sylvia and Danny Kaye Playhouse). It was one of the few venues, along with the Kaufman Auditorium of the YMHA at 92nd Street and Lexington Avenue, where concert dance could be seen. I performed *Saturday's Child* and *Songs of the Forest*, a solo work that grew out of my studies of Balinese dance with Hadassah, and the orchestral and visual depictions of the island culture by Colin McPhee and Miguel Covarrubias. I had started to work with Colin McPhee's *Tabuh-Tabuhan* but felt overwhelmed by the symphonic textures and let the idea lie fallow, awaiting another musical frame. This came in a most unexpected way. The colorful composer, Lou Harrison, whom I had met at Jean Erdman's rehearsals, had begun to drop in on the rehearsals of *Games* on several occasions. One day he approached me while holding a few sheets of manuscript paper in his hand, sat down at the piano and asked me to come and listen. He began to play from a pencil score written in an exquisite hand. What emerged thoroughly captured my attention. He had selected several melodies from the children's songs used in *Games* and developed them into little studies that shimmered with the sounds of Bali. The three chosen tunes were all inventions on a pentatonic scale and could be traced back to the Georgia Sea Islands. The natural sounds that echoed in both cultures, water and sea breezes moving through vegetation, had an amazing similarity that Lou was quick to hear, and the result was this delightful trilogy. I designed and executed the costumes after the wonderful Covarrubias drawings. I was especially proud of the headdress covered with golden flowers mounted on springs that danced in a continuous vibration as I moved.

Daniel Nagrin danced his wonderful solos *Strange Hero* and *Spanish Dance*. I stood in the wings watching and studying his magnetic performance style. He actually drew your eyes to his body in motion with a cinematic skill that was uncanny, commanding you to focus exactly where he willed. I stood next to the grand piano where Sylvia Marshall played, moving with that unmistakable kinetic rocking that seemed a trade mark of every fine dance accompanist that I had observed. She sounded a chord heavily flavored with Andalusian harmonies, pressed the sustaining pedal, then started a rolling trill with her right hand reminiscent of the flamenco guitarist's picato as she reached over with her left hand and turned the page. A sudden look of panic flooded her features and she desperately began to turn pages and then search the folder resting beside her on the piano bench, all the while continuing to play a score she knew with a memory that until this moment had never been tested. Danny, radiant with the thrill of the spontaneous ovation his performance received, bowed graciously and called Sylvia to share the applause. She walked ashen faced from the wings to his side. I don't think he sensed that anything out of the ordinary had happened but a quizzical look crossed his face as he greeted the usually ebullient Sylvia, now limp from her ordeal at the keyboard.

Games closed the first half of the program. We were overwhelmed by the audience reaction. Laughter filled the auditorium during the

"Dance of Play," audible comments of recognition continued through the "Dance of Hunger," then a sudden hush of horror as the "Dance of Terror" concluded, followed by an applause that was relentless in its fervor, a standing ovation. As I changed out of my costume there was a knock at the dressing room door and the buzz of voice outside in the hallway. I opened the door to a sea of familiar faces, friends in the audience, who could not wait to the end of the performance to come back and congratulate me.

After the final curtain fell, I took off my makeup, got into my street clothes, and went to Danny's room. "Congratulations, Danny, it was wonderful". Danny smiled and beckoned me in. Sylvia Marshall and Helen Tamiris were there. Helen curled and recurled the sausage tresses that she always wore clasped together at the nape of her neck. It was a gesture I had grown used to during *Bless You All* and knew it as a nervous outward demonstration of deep thought and concern. She seemed uncharacteristically solemn. "Your work was marvelous!" Sylvia nodded in agreement, and took me by both shoulders and shook me with pride. Danny gave me a strong slap on the back. I heard the stage manager's voice calling from the hallway. "Donald, your family's here."

 Mother threw her arms around me. "Bros, you should've seen Moms when you came out to take your bow. She turned in her seat and bowed to all the people sitting behind her." Dad chuckled as Mother threw Philip a warning look. "It was wonderful, son. And the set, it looked so good. The way I laid the painted bricks on with that sponge sure made them look real." All of my teachers, classmates, friends, parents, and families of the cast, were around me. Standing apart behind the swarm of well wishers, I noticed a familiar face from out of the past. Isabel Providence, the playground instructor from the Harlem River Housing Project who had given me such support as a youngster, was beaming proudly at me. She came forward and took my hand. "Do you remember me, Miss Providence?" I grabbed her and held her close in a huge embrace. "Thank you."

With the success of *Games*, I was thrust into aspects of the profession that were exciting and somewhat overwhelming. I was not prepared for the avalanche of performance offers, solicitations for theatrical representation, and requests for interviews. One of the people that contacted me was Bob Banner, the producer of the very prestigious CBS Television program, *Omnibus*. I was contracted to perform *Games*, the entire twenty minutes, as a major segment of the hour-long show. They rented a rehearsal space in the Steinway Building on 57th Street for us and asked for a copy of the song lyrics. On the first day of rehearsal the phone rang in the studio. It was Bob Banner. "Hello, Don. Someone from Program Practices is coming by. They've made a few changes in the lyrics. They don't amount to much, but I just wanted to let you know before they arrive."

> So what?
> So snot, down your belly red hot.
> So what?
> Chicken butt, go around the corner and lick it up
> How'd you like it, fried, stewed, or barbecued?

These lines had been expurgated and replaced with,

> Stringy hair, stringy hair
> You've got stringy, stringy hair!

"No, this just won't do. We would never say anything like this. What does it mean? Who wrote this? If you have some problem with what's there, I'll find something else, something that's authentic!" Suddenly his attention was not with me. He was watching Joe Nash and Louanna Gardner. They were practicing a section of the Dance of Terror in which Joe held Louanna tightly, both of them cowering in the shadow of the building, only to have her break free and run to help another child before returning to the hiding place and the protection of Joe's arms. "What are they doing?" "Rehearsing." A red light went on inside. I felt my teeth clench and the set of my jaw pulled against the corners of my mouth. My eyes narrowed and I looked him squarely in the face. He obviously was surprised by the racial mix of the company and clearly disquieted by what he had seen. He turned back to face my fixed and scrutinizing gaze. A professional smile camouflaged his intentions. "Okay, take a shot at the lyrics yourself." Anticipating a reply, he turned and left. The next day, three executive types dropped in before lunch. They stayed for a short while and left without speaking or introducing themselves. In the afternoon, the camera director was to come by, but in his stead, there was a message. "Don McKayle. Please call Bob Banner." "I'm sorry, Don, we have to cancel out. Of course everyone will be paid according to contract. Could you come by first thing in the morning and let's talk." "Don, is there something else you do, maybe with not all of your dancers? I remember that great number you did on the Fred Waring Show. What was it?...you know...the...the Zulu warrior...yeah, that's what it was." I watched him struggle with a dilemma that he had not created but was, by the authority of his position, mandated to solve. I rose to leave. "I've grown tired of throwing a spear."

Our weekly acting class met the next evening, and we all decided to just go on with our lives. As I walked along Sixth Avenue approaching 55th Street, I heard something unusual. Wonderful percussive sounds were coming from somewhere in the next block. The music seemed to be emanating from a darkened, recessed doorway on the other side of the street. I crossed over and discovered a strange figure covered in khaki blankets fashioned into hooded robes with a triangular leather browpiece shielding his sightless eyes. He squatted in the midst of a grouping of drums and small percussion instruments arranged in a semicircle, which he beat alternately with his fingers and soft round leather mallets. The drums were obviously hand crafted and delicately tuned to be almost melodic. The sound was hypnotic, and I was mesmerized by the dexterity of his hands as he played. "That's beautiful. What's your name?" "Thank you. Call me Moondog. What's your name?" "Donald. Where do you play?" "Here and around." I was already late for class and I had to leave. I told the dancers about Moondog and after class we all went back, but he was no longer there. Two days later, I got a call from Tony Schwartz. He had just released an album called *New York 19*. It was a collection of songs of children at play that he had recorded with his field equipment on the streets of New York City's postal district 19. He had heard about *Games* and wanted to record the rehearsals and a performance. I asked him if he knew about a street musician who played at night in the doorways of closed shops on Sixth Avenue. "Oh, you mean Moondog. Sure I've got him on tape." I went over to Tony's apartment. "Wait 'til you hear this one. It was done in a studio along with five string players recruited from the Philharmonic. It's a suite of canons in three movements. It's gorgeous." Moondog played on the city streets. These guys were to be found in Carnegie Hall. This was getting more interesting by the minute. Tony cut me wax discs. I took them home and began to immerse myself in the music. The opening movement started with the beating of drums and continued to gather individually the two cellos and three violas, until they all had joined into the melodic weavings and exited as secretly as they had entered, leaving the drums to sound the final round. The second movement was lush and rhapsodic with new delicacies of texture added in the percussion, especially a recurring rippling sound, like water playing over stones in a forest brook. The final movement was in mixed meter, a time signature that Moondog called snake time, and progressed forward with a relentless driving surge. Visual images, colors, movements, patterns, groupings, began to flood my mind. I was drawn to the verdant palette and figures of Gauguin's South Sea Islands. A mating ritual from an imagined people began to emerge. I called the dance *Nocturne*, although there was nothing dreamy or somnambulistic about it. It was, rather, a nocturnal revel.

That summer, Ted Shawn invited us to Jacob's Pillow. There were changes in the company of dancers. Ed Lum replaced George Liker and Remy Charlip was replaced by the young Arthur Mitchell. Each of the summer festival programs at Jacob's Pillow were shared by artists representing dance in modern, ballet, and ethnic forms. We were to perform *Games* and my new work *Nocturne*. The advance publicity listed us as Donald McKayle and Company. The name stuck. I built *Nocturne* around my own perform-ance ability and featured myself as soloist. Although I was to make several dances in which I performed solo roles, quite apart from the trend of most single choreographer companies of the time, this was never important to me. I was more interested in the choreographic ideas and cast the works with that as my prime motivation. The forces guiding the making of this particular dance, however, were altogether different. It began with an opening for men in which I was the motivating force. The movement, filled with large contracted jumps, dives to the floor, locomotions in supine positions, and vibratory leg and torso pulsations, all centered around me. I exited as the women entered in varied languorous and voluptuous treadings, encircling the men then standing aloof in contemplation. I returned and initiated the final groupings, climaxing in a duet for myself and my wife to be, Esta Beck. As the lights faded, entwined couples embraced slowly and descended to the floor. This dance was my proposal to Esta, an offering of love.

Esta and Eve Beck were twin sisters and fellow scholarship students at the New Dance Group. They were not identical twins and yet there was something around the eyes that tricked one at first glance into seeing double. This was a physical characteristic shared with both of their par-ents, a fold of flesh that shaded their upper eyelids and hinted perhaps at Tartar ancestry. Their dancing however was quite individual. Eve had a lovely lyric quality and was always open and vulnerable. Esta was agile and bouncy with a decided no nonsense, direct point of view. They were wonderful to watch going across the diagonal together and favorites of both Nona Shurman and Mary Anthony. I liked them from the very first and we became close friends, spending summer weekends at their family home. I caught the Long Island Railroad to the last stop on the Long Beach line and walked the few blocks to the clapboard house that was always filled with the wonderful aromas of chicken fricassee roasting in the oven. We spent hours in the waves, lolling on the beach, and returning to the house, ravenous for Mama Will's melt-in-your-mouth chicken and the wonderful talk and laughter over table games that followed. I found myself becoming closer and closer to Esta. Every evening when classes were over, I took her from the New Dance Group to Penn Station and made sure she got on the train safely. I found myself going down to the platform with her, waving good-bye as the train left, walking away an-ticipating seeing her again tomorrow, making plans, falling in love. I did not realize how deep the relationship had become until tragedy entered the idyllic world we had created and forced feelings that had been sub-merged to the surface.

Morris, Esta and Eve's father, was a traveling salesman and was always out on the road. He was a painter by avocation and brought back gouache renderings of the New England countryside that was his territory. His presence at home was always occasion for something just a little bit extra in the pot and wonderful Jewish pastries Mama Will's brother and sister-in-law, Harry and Frieda, would bring in from the city, followed by an endless spate of conversation, catching up, and sharing. Early one morning, I received a call from Esta; that in itself was unusual as we saw each other daily and saved up all our items of exchange for our meeting. "Donald, my father is dead." Tears washed the short sentence over the phone to me and the familiar voice was somehow altered in timbre and color. "I'll be right there." The train ride on the local that I caught seemed endless, but it got me in fifteen minutes before the express that followed and every minute was precious. I could not wait to get there and somehow knew she really needed me. As I came up the last block on the familiar path, I saw a small figure running toward me and I caught her in my arms and in that moment of sadness and bereavement, we shed our innocence and bonded as one.

We were married at the Ethical Culture Society headquarters on Central Park West in a simple ceremony, attended by our relatives and dance family. I spent many hours in my little apartment on Sullivan Street bent over my Japanese sewing machine making a glowing orange silk shantung wedding dress, a redingote with zillions of covered buttons running down the front closure through an equal zillion bound button holes. Esta lovingly submitted to all the extra fittings I demanded and forgave, with a smile, the dress buttoning on the wrong side. The wedding reception was hosted by Nina Caiserman in her beautiful apartment in the Hotel Des Artistes. "Here's a little check to start you off. Now don't spend it on the groceries." Nona Shurman laughed her infectious guffaw and added her envelope to the table full of gifts. There was no honeymoon hotel or ocean cruise. We spent our wedding night in the coziness of my four storey walk up. Our plans for the future included back to work the next day and the knowledge of the racial prejudice we would face in finding the place we imagined for our first home as we spoke softly of dreams, of our life together.

Ann and Paul Lovett initiated the idea of reclaiming the Brooklyn Academy of Music as a dance center. It boasted an opera house, a music hall, and various other spaces in a large well appointed building that had lost its cultural community a generation ago. The formidable feat placed before the master minds of this venture was to encourage a cultural clientele to travel to downtown Brooklyn. The opening salvo was a program of modern dance artists that would attract a large and varied audience with an opening bill that was an inspired juxtaposition of aesthetics. Merce

Cunningham was to present excepts from his *Sixteen Dances*, the work for his company of four women and himself that would launch a whole new era in dance. Jean Erdman was to perform two of her luminous solos, *Hamadryad* and *Changing Woman*. Erick Hawkins was to present sections of his solo evening, *Openings of the Eye*. I was to close the program with *Games*. We all met at Jean Erdman's studio to run through the program. When we got to Erick Hawkins' segment, he proceeded to perform his entire solo evening. He claimed that it was conceived as a single artistic thought, and though divided into subsections, had to be performed in its entirety. Both Merce and Jean who had known him from when they were all members of the Martha Graham Dance Company, exchanged blank stares then turned incredulous looks toward Erick. Before he could continue to explain all the specifics of his thought, I spoke up. "Paul and Ann, if Erick needs to do his entire program, then we will have to go on before him." Merce looked at me and smiled broadly. Ann Lovett nodded in agreement. "Erick, why don't you do the two animal sections, *Goat of the Gods* and *Disconsolate Minotaur*. They make an excellent pair." My suggestion gathered approval from everyone except Erick. The rehearsal broke up after we performed *Games*, and we left the Lovetts talking to Erick. The next day Paul called to say that Erick would do just the two sections.

The backstage of the Brooklyn Academy of Music was a very lively place. The dressing room area was a shared space that accommodated both the opera house and the music hall. On the afternoon of dress rehearsal, we played opposite a wedding; at the evening performance, there was a wrestling match next door. As I was waiting in the wings, watching Erick perform *Goat of the Gods*, I turned to see a very large and very perplexed, bathrobed wrestling contestant who had wandered onto the wrong stage. He was staring in complete disbelief as Erick, shod in high wooden hooves that covered the front of his feet leaving his heels bare, was navigating a delicately choreographed passage through the stage set of a winding path of slender wooden dowels that had the appearance of river reeds. Perhaps the sight of this gargantuan figure glaring from the wings startled Erick. He misstepped and a sharp snapping sound announced the demise of one of the reeds beneath the hoof of the god. Carlos Dyer, the designer, flinched as the dowel fell to the stage floor. The offending giant turned and retreated on slipper padded feet.

I was suddenly the bright new light on the dance horizon, the subject of newspaper articles and magazine feature stories, as the director of one dance company, and a member of four others. The New Dance Group, my parent company, was by lucky coincidence, in rehearsal recess while Sophie Maslow prepared a new choreographic work. I was the male dancer in Jean Erdman's Company and, by dint of the singularity of that position, a leading dancer. Merce Cunningham asked me to join his company for a special commission, the gala event opening of the Art Center at Brandeis University in Massachusetts. Anna Sokolow had returned from her sojourn in Mexico and extended to me an invitation to become a member of her newly constituted company. Everything threatened to crash head on in a jumble of overlapping rehearsal schedules. There were also my many teaching commitments which, along with my one-man costume construction sideline, kept me housed, clothed, and fed. Could I do all of this? The answer was yes, gladly, happily, exhaustedly, yes.

4

AT THE FEET OF THE MASTERS

Working with Charles Weidman was a new and wonderful challenge. I had always enjoyed the classes in Humphrey-Weidman technique at the New Dance Group, but the dance that Charles was remounting was quite different from the classroom studies that I had learned from Nona Shurman. Nona loved to move in large spatial patterns that coursed through the dance studio in combinations of evolving, open, lyric attitudes, or traversed the diagonal in rebounding, rhythmic phrases. Here we were dealing with Charles's early explorations into his witty dramatic gesture language which he called "kinetic pantomime."

Traditions was a dance for three men, originally performed by Charles Weidman, José Limón, and George Bachman. The trio currently in rehearsal was Daniel Nagrin, Marc Breaux, and myself. "José, do you remember George's variation coming out of the jump section?" We lined up behind José following his every move as he tried to recall another dancer's role in a work that he had performed over a decade ago. "No, that doesn't look right. José why don't you teach Donald your part. Danny, you'll learn mine, and Marc..." "Don't worry Charles, it'll all come back. It always does...or you'll just make it up and swear 'That's exactly the way it was.'" Marc's teasing caught Charles's attention. The furrowed frown of concentration on Charles's countenance melted into a smile as deep thought gave way to a tasty anecdote. "Why don't you tell them how you got that one fly away leg of yours?" Marc threw up a leg and our eyes opened wide as shin bone connected with ear lobe in a true six o'clock kick. "Now show us the other one." "Wicked!" The other leg cleared just slightly above waist level. The loose acrobatic limb was the result of a sustained injury. "Some dancers will do anything for a stretch."

We found the original costumes that had been designed for the dance by Pauline Lawrence, José's wife and a member of the early Humphrey-Weidman Company. They had been stored in a trunk in the basement. Water damage had claimed one pair of trousers but everything else, despite the unmistakable odor of mildew, was salvageable. The wide pyjama-leg pants were made from a heavy royal blue rayon crepe. They were beautifully cut and lined to give them body. The tops were from the same crepe with a diagonal swathe of unbleached muslin going from the chest into one arm in deep overlapping folds that cascaded from shoulder to wrist. The rescued costumes were sent to the dry cleaners, and I went out shopping for a matching fabric to replace the damaged trousers.

My compact two room atelier, as I was wont to call tiny cold water flat in a four story walk-up, was hidden in the backyard of a Greenwich Village row house on Sullivan Street between Prince and Spring. This area, soon to be known as Soho, was nestled in the colorful neighborhood known as Little Italy. In former days, the building in the back had served as servant quarters for a Manhattan townhouse. The front building had been converted into eight apartments, two on each floor flanking the lovely banister that still bore witness to times gone by. Although both were four-story buildings, the back edifice had the appearance of a detached playhouse. It was noticeably dwarfed in height and narrow in girth. Each floor had one green door opening into a small flat. Being on the top floor I had a great deal more light than my downstairs neighbors, a fitting tradeoff for the long hike up flights of wooden stairs. I had gotten the apartment from a student who was taking my class in Modern Fundamentals. This, along with my Saturday morning schedule of children's dance classes was the only source of income on which I could depend. Here I was, being offered my own place in the much coveted artistic community of Greenwich Village. Here I began a new way of life embracing *la vie bohème*. The monthly rent was twenty-seven dollars. Heat was furnished by a gas radiator which was quite adequate for the two doll sized rooms, except on those blustery winter days when icy winds would join the patch of sunlight coming down the chimney and snow flakes would float from the fireplace. The door to the bedroom opened inward just clearing the mattress. You literally entered the bedroom door and fell into bed. On amorous nights, with the shades drawn and the lights out, I was not ashamed to use this feature to my advantage. The furnishings which consisted of the bed, an armless upholstered settee, a small rectangular coffee table, and a bar with shelves holding an assorted mishmash of dishes, pots, flatware, a few pyrex bowls and some drinking glasses, came with the apartment for two hundred dollars. I opened up my savings, bought the decor, paid rent for the first and last months and moved in. I also bought a heavy portable Japanese sewing machine and placed it on the low table. I was ready to make my own clothes and to augment my income constructing costumes for fellow dancers. The full-sized bed would also double as a surface for cutting fabrics. Buoyed by the success of the costumes I had built for *Games* and the ones I had designed and made for my earlier solos, I was certain I could make a viable stab at a second career. I imagined this new trade of necessity dovetailing neatly with my work and class schedule and earning me some much needed discretionary income.

"That's nice Donald, but that's not the way you make a vest." Aunt Alice examined the burlap vest lined with cotton broadcloth that I had made for a solo dance choreographed to an Irish potato famine song, "The Pratties They Grow Small." "Oh, I see you've got another one cut out. Now this is a pretty print, real country. Yellow is so cheerful. You plan to wear it with these green trousers? That's lovely. You made this shirt too? That color's a beauty. How you call it now? ... Orchid!" Aunt Alice went on with her one-person conversation, asking and answering her own questions, until finally she sat down at the sewing machine and began to put the vest for *Creole Afternoon* together, executing and explaining each step as she went along. My learning at the feet of a master seamstress had commenced. She held up the beautifully finished garment. "Give Daddy and Mama my love when you see them." The yellow, green, and orchid outfit was a marvelous counterpoint to the design for my dance partner, Jacqueline Hairston. She wore a bright pumpkin-orange print ruffled skirt and a white lawn peasant blouse trimmed with an eyelet piqué, laced through with a satin ribbon. I sported a wide straw hat and fashioned a Martinique style headwrap from the orange skirt fabric for Jacqueline. I looked at the posed publicity pictures with an unabashed sense of pride and declared myself a costumer. My atelier was open for business. Matching the fabric to replace the water damaged trousers for *Traditions* proved to be an endless and unsuccessful quest. I finally found a crepe that was the correct weight and must have been the color of the garment when it was originally made. I settled for this, realizing that I had found the closest possible match. Copying the cut and constructing the lining for the trousers were giant steps beyond my sartorial expertise. Marc Breaux was most appreciative of my efforts on his behalf, but I was much more critical. The lining pulled against the outer fabric creating small unwanted puckers. I faced my personal disappointment squarely, admitted to my limited knowledge and returned to Aunt Alice for what would become an ongoing apprenticeship.

"We'll take a break now before beginning the showing. We'll start with *Sea Deep* and then do *Solstice*. Merce should be here momentarily." Saying this, Jean Erdman disappeared into her dressing room to prepare herself for her husband, Joseph Campbell's, visit and his appraisal of her new work, *Solstice*, a dance steeped in mythological references. Joe was an outstanding scholar of mythology and helped to fuel Jean's deep interest in the subject. This undoubtedly precipitated her nervous demeanor, anticipating his special scrutiny, insight, and feedback. Joe arrived as we were gathered together, testing the repair job we had just completed on the recording filament of Jean's new and modern wire recorder. The wire filament had snapped. A simple slip knot had done the trick. We turned to greet Joe as Jean emerged from her dressing room, looking radiant in an emerald green rehearsal outfit with her chestnut hair brushed neatly back from her handsome face. She kissed Joe, leaving the stain of her newly applied lipstick on his mouth and the lingering trail of her cologne. *Sea Deep*, a light hearted underwater comic fantasy, was postponed for another visit. Jean wanted Joe to see the changes my performance had brought to that work, but Joe was impatient to see the new choreography. The female ensemble was varied animal nymphs, particularized in Carlos Dyer's wonderful costume renderings by individual headdresses. Merce Cunningman was the Sun Lion and I was the Moon Bull. We did ritual battle for possession of the Earth, danced by Jean. The richly textured musical score was by Lou Harrison. The highlight of the work was a stylized male duet based on Chinese boxing with its arcane postures, advances, and retreats. Jean had brought in Chao Li Chi as a consultant and had built the vocabulary for this section on movements and attitudes he had taught us. Dancing opposite Merce was a special treat for me. We were dynamically contrasted in physique and temperament, befitting the warring forces we portrayed. As we faced off, advancing from opposite corners with high lifted leg attitudes, whipping into flexed side kicks, resolving into wide squats, regarding each other in profile glances, I was again aware of the steely tensile strength in the finely tuned musculature of Merce's dancing. I was able to play off of this with my own more sinuous movement quality to combative advantage in this bout of ritual warfare between generative and reflected light.

My initial acquaintance with Merce had been at a solo concert evening presented at Charles Weidman's Studio Theatre. He was at once an antic performer, a dance virtuoso, and a master of dramatic tension — all contrasting aesthetic venues and yet in his handling, all devoid of any borrowings from narrative devices. The works that profoundly affected me were: *Root Of An Unfocus*, a riveting dance in which increasing disorientation was dynamically heightened by a backward movement progression through space; *The Monkey Dances*, a comic romp in which he appeared as a stylized version of the organ grinder's simian companion; and *Totem Ancestor*, a dance in which Merce, with his legs folded in a kneeling position, seemed to cleave the air effortlessly. These dances left me in awe and inspired. I was treated to a new standard of excellence and filled with a desire to achieve such movement perfection. To a young dancer, he was an object lesson.

The first orchestra rehearsal for *Solstice* was a revelation. The music for the battle sequence was especially exciting. It featured the double bass in resonant arco passages, returning from savagely plucked chord clusters, and then exploding into a percussive rhythm in which the strings were beaten with a stick below the bridge of the instrument. Much of it sounded strange; it was quite different from the piano reduction to which we had become accustomed. Jean had choreographed a devilish rhythmic passage for the female ensemble in which the dance was phrased in three's while the music was in four's, providing cross accents. The dancers panicked and began to count aloud, first one, then another, until all were shouting in unison. "One-two-three, four-one-two, three-four-one, two-three-four." Suddenly there was no music, only the desperate and earnest sound of their counting. Everyone turned to face an exasperated and red-faced Lou Harrison. "How can you dance with a head full of roaring digits? Just listen to the music!" Merce and I had our own problems adjusting to the large headpieces that we wore. They completely covered our heads and extended far out in front of our faces. Merce's Sun Lion had a wide yawning mouth with the sun, a fiery painted tennis ball, held by the tips of the feline incisors. The extended bovine snout of my Moon Bull terminated in nostrils composed of a cluster of four ping pong balls, while the moon, another tennis ball, hung lazily between my curved horns. The weight of these imposing headpieces played havoc with our sense of balance. The tennis ball sun of Merce's lion and the ping pong ball nostrils of my bull were placed squarely in the center of our line of vision and caused us both to become temporarily cross-eyed. Carlos Dyer listened attentively to the litany of costume problems, made those adjustments that were in his province to solve, and left us to adapt our performances to the realities of the new theatrical environment. Jean removed herself from company problems and gave herself over completely to her own performance. Her singularity of concern was so focused that I was amazed at her observations at the end of the performance. "Why did you put all that green in your make up for *Sea Deep*? I wanted you to be cute. You looked more like a monster."

"Donald, wash your hands at the edge of the stage downleft. Remy and Ronnie, circle in place." Merce's instructions, read from a card, were the outcome of a series of coin tosses on charts containing the movement vocabulary, combinations of performing personnel, and other givens. The resulting choreographic patterns were determined by chance; preconceived notions of logic and composition were put to rest. Dance by chance was something completely unknown to me, and the fascination of discovery piqued my interest. Ronnie Aul, who had been added to Merce's company at the same time as I was, seemed to have a certain aversion to the unfamiliar. We had both been approached by Merce to augment his ensemble for a gala opening celebration of the new amphitheater at Brandeis University in Waltham, Massachusetts, just outside of Boston. The event was scheduled for early in the summer of 1952 and was to be a prestigious celebration loaded with heavyweights in the arts. The major work on the program was Igor Stravinsky's *Les Noces*, conducted by Leonard Bernstein and sung by soloists from the New York City Opera. The settings and costumes were by Ralph Alswang and the choreography by Merce Cunningham. The principal dancers were: the groom, Merce Cunningham;

the bride, Natanya Neuman; the parents of the groom, Ronnie Aul and Anneliese Widman; the mother and father of the bride, Joan Skinner and myself. The other dancers in the ensemble were Marianne Praeger, Ben Garber, and Remy Charlip. Rehearsals for *Les Noces* had a strange aura surrounding them. Merce was moody, uncomfortable with the assignment. The rehearsals for the other work, to Pierre Schaffer's *Symphonie Pour Un Homme Seul* were by contrast filled with energy and delight. Some of the vocabulary was developed in class, some of it was drawn from pedestrian movement introduced in rehearsal.

Leonard Bernstein dropped his baton on the open score in front of him and turned toward the quartet of voices singing the melancholy strains written for the parents of the bride and groom in Stravinsky's *Les Noces*. The rending moment was delivered in overlapping plaints as loss and fulfillment became entwined in an expression of pain overriding happiness. The offspring must leave their childhood sanctuaries where they have been nurtured and protected. They must now cross over the threshold of uncertainty into adulthood and face the unknowns of the traditional arranged marriage. As Phyllis Curtin sounded the final melodious tones, Bernstein lowered his chin and lifted his hooded gaze into a rapturous smile, walked over to where she stood, embraced her strongly, and planted a voluptuous kiss on the cheek of the startled diva. We sat listening as the musicians and singers brought to vivid life the wonderful music to which we had been rehearsing. "Piano, piano." Lenny squeezed his shoulders and cupped his hands around his lips pursed into a circle of hush. "Subito forte!" The maestro swung his head from side to side, tossing his hair and vibrating his arms in a dramatic replication of what he wished to hear from the musical ensemble and singers. I listened intently to information about the music and scenario that had heretofore not entered our rehearsal process. I was fascinated with the skill, command, and knowledge of this flamboyant artist. I did not realize how much this musical reading would affect my own performance. Merce sat quietly listening with a wry expression on his face as Lenny went through exaggerated entreaties, pulling depth and subtleties from the instrumentalists and singers. Despite the fact that we would eventually be on stage and the musicians in the pit, this was obviously Leonard Bernstein's show; we were simply participating artists. The next day when we arrived at the theater my suspicions were confirmed. Lenny and the singers had been assigned the star dressing rooms and we had been given the large chorus rooms. The costumes were brightly colored body suits with golden encrusted headgear and belts. The scenic flats that Ralph Alswang had designed were rendered in the style of Russian enamelware, and the whole picture was more a folkloric fantasy then the spare linear choreography that Merce had created. The amphitheater, unlike the performing shell and backstage facilities, was completely lacking in all the appoint-ments necessary for the gala opening that would take place in only a day's time. Much of the stage lights and cables arrived while we were going through our spacing rehearsal. The stage crew was respectful of our work. They proceeded with their tasks, keeping as much out of the way as possible, but conducting their operations with full voices in a boisterous cacophony. Merce, in a moment of obvious desperation, distorted a tuck leap in the choreography for the culminating nuptial night duet and soared far past the place where Natanya Neuman awaited her groom, landing smack in the midst of a trio of grips who had stopped midstage to discuss an instrument hanging problem. They moved on with nonplused backward glances at Merce, who wordlessly glided back to his waiting bride who regarded with alarm what seemed to be a slight limp in his gait, the apparent result of his impulsive move.

The next day we arrived for the final rehearsal prior to the evening's opening and were amazed at the miracle that greeted our eyes. Audience seating was fully in place. The periphery of the amphitheater was com-pletely landscaped; green turf, shrubs, flowers, and trees had somehow sprouted fully grown overnight. Merce, Joan, Anneliese, and Marianne hated the candy colored outfits they had to wear and Natanya refused to look at herself in the full length mirror, in a body suit of bridal white. Ronnie, Remy, Ben, and I wore the deeper colors of wine, emerald, rust, and royal blue. Remy clothed the Pierre Schaffer work in a wardrobe using a chance technique, paralleling the aesthetics Merce had pursued in making the choreography. He went from floor to floor and counter to counter in Filene's department store in Boston selecting items. The lighting designer refused to go along with this program and created the atmosphere and illumination based on more time honored principles.

The performance of *Les Noces* was a rousing success. Afterwards I went to look for Merce and thank him for the experience. I found a door marked with a card bearing his name. I knocked and entered. It was identical to the space we had been assigned, one of the cavernous chorus rooms. It was dark except for a lighted makeup table deep in the void and a single hanging lamp which cast a circle on the floor. Merce was in the pool of light wrapped in a robe, standing on a few sheets of newspaper, protecting his feet from the cold cement of the floor. The harsh light turned his face into a skull with his eyes receding into sockets of blackness. We spoke only briefly and I left. As I closed the door behind me, he was still standing where I had found him, privately going through what seemed to be a rite of passage, leaving an arena of dance that had become alien to him and silently dedicating himself to his personal vision.

"I've decided to create the scene with the fourteen angels in a com-pletely different way." Sophie Maslow opened a large book of illustrations to a page marked with a filing card on which she had made a few notations. We gathered around to view the visionary drawings of arch-angels by William Blake. I was engaged as a member of the opera ballet with the New York City Opera. The choreographers were Sophie Maslow, Charles Weidman, and Robert Pageant. This was Sophie's first year with the New York City Opera and she was to choreograph revivals of *Hansel and Gretel, Aida,* and a new opera, *The Dybbuk.* Charles was returning as resident choreographer to remount his production of *A Love For Three Oranges* and a new production of *The Tales of Hoffmann.* Robert Pageant was in charge of the choreography for *La Traviata.* Raymond Sachse was the resident stage director. He utilized the ballet to augment the opera chorus in crowd sequences and give movement to static passages in which the choristers would invariably gather in arranged groups, dig their heels in firmly, watch the conductor, and lustily sing and gesticulate. We had no formal rehearsals for these assignments, but were told what to do, and sent to the wardrobe room where we would scrounge for costumes from racks and trunks marked for the opera in question. Then, we would pick up our props from the property table, usually lanterns for the ubiquitous "Let's make merry," villagers-romping-on-the-green sequence, wait to be counted down by the onstage prompter, and enter in weaving, skipping patterns, breathing life into the *mise en scène.*

The rehearsals for *Hansel and Gretel* were, in contrast, full and detailed. Even the major singers, Peggy Boninni, who sang Gretel and Frances Bible, who sang Hansel, rehearsed with us for several days. The *corps de ballet* was augmented to fulfill the requisite number of fourteen. Sophie engaged Ethel Winter from the Martha Graham company as soloist. Ethel's lovely, lyric quality was put to advantage in floating lifts, in soaring suspensions held high by the four male dancers. I was one of the arch-angels; the other three were Al Shulman, Marvin Gordon, and Harvey Lichtenstein. Harvey was later to become the much honored executive director of the Brooklyn Academy of Music. On the day of the dress rehearsal for *Hansel and Gretel,* I arrived early but found Marvin, Al, and Harvey already there. I heard raucous laughter coming from the dressing room and opened the door to find Marvin in a long white dress with tiny golden wings sprouting from his shoulder blades. As I stood in the doorway joining in the mirth, four wig blocks were carried in, bearing identical long blond sausage-curl wigs. As they were placed on our dressing tables, we absolutely dissolved into uncontrollable guffaws, until tears filled our eyes and our sides ached from the inability to stop laughing. None of us could finish a complete sentence, but managed to ask if these were really what we were supposed to wear. "These are the costumes for *Hansel and Gretel.* We usually have fourteen little girls from the ballet school." The wardrobe lady shrugged and closed the door as she left. We quickly got into our gowns, wings, and wigs and faced each other. A vagrant blond curl fell across Marvin's cheek and rested there beguilingly pointing toward his broken nose bridge, a prizefighter in drag; Harvey's shaggy, John L. Lewis eyebrows and hooked nose jutted out in alarm, a peek-a-boo family of wrens nested in a blond shrub; Al's unshaven pug and pursed lips were caught up in a gesture of shock, undeniably an escaped hood from the musical comedy *Kiss Me Kate*, somehow lost in opera heaven; blond ringlets trembled around my sepia complexion, a peroxide cherub in a quartet of questionable seraphs. We took our places backstage and mounted the escape steps for our heavenly descent. We were the last four angels to float down to earth through the parting curtains of clouds, where we hovered over the sleeping Hansel and Gretel. My first task was to assist Harvey in lifting and rocking the somnolent Hansel; a role that was traditionally assigned to a mezzo soprano. As my curls brushed across Frances Bible's face, and she cracked open her closed eyelids and caught a glimpse of me, she began to shake with laughter. The harder she tried to hold back her mirth, the more impossible control became. This infectious state of affairs quickly spread across the entire stage, and the ballet ended in a shambles of hilarity.

"Where are my ladies for the 'Barcarole'?" Raymond Sachse faced Charles Weidman who was just entering rather unsteadily after a two cocktail lunch. I was warming up as a matter of discipline, although my role in the first act was only to whirl silhouetted behind a screen with another dancer for twenty seconds. "Charles, what do we do in these orange costumes?" Wearing a midriff-two-piece outfit with chiffon veils flowing from a jeweled-cap headdress, Lila Lewis accomplished an inquisitive spin in front of Charles and Raymond Sachse. "Ba ... Ba ... Bacarole?" Charles stuttered helplessly and looked aghast at Raymond. The ladies of the ballet crowded into the elevator bedecked in their vibrantly colored diaphanous raiment, and accompanied Charles up to the fifth floor rehearsal room where he proceeded to make instant choreography for the Barcarole sequence in the upcoming act of *The Tales of Hoffman*. I joined them after my twirling vignette and watched Charles' clever groupings, supine floor loungings, and pseudo-oriental arm gestures take form. He finished just as the assistant stage manager arrived to lead the courtesans to their places on the scenic barge. The choreography that had been created in twelve minutes was to remain unchanged throughout the season.

Michael Oshansky, an émigré from the Russian theater, was the brilliant makeup artist employed by the New York City Opera. He was to have a chance to indulge his specialty in the bizarre and macabre, creating the makeup for *The Dybbuk*. The new opera was steeped in the supernatural and in Jewish mysticism. The dancers were beggars at a wedding feast and each of us emerged from Oshansky's ministrations more ghoulish than the other. He used heavy grease paint and crepe hair to completely obliterate our natural features and transform us into his fantasy. I was a cripple and ambulated with the aid of a crude crutch. The grease paint, putty, crepe hair, and spirit gum finally in place, I turned and found an unrecognizable harpy with a sallow yellow face, one eye lower than the other, a wispy mustache, and an unkempt gray beard staring back at me in the mirror. Oshansky had enlarged the mole on Anneliese Widman's cheek from an attractive beauty mark into a disfiguring wart. We were all transformed, not just superficially but deeply. Our new theatrical personas took over our performances. We surrounded the sideboard, customarily set apart to feed the unfortunate, and grabbed at the real foods that edged the table encircling the inner mound of fruits and meats made from wax. Anneliese, now a toothless crone, scurried over to me and stuffed a cookie in my mouth catching my unruly facial hair and causing me to pull the captured strands from my teeth and disengage the crumb and crepe hair mixture from my tongue.

There were no full rehearsals for repertory items such as *La Traviata* or even the grand opera, *Aida*. There also seemed to be little coordination between the choreographers and stage directors. I was instructed to take the crystal ball from the count in *La Traviata*. Never having met any of the performers except for my fellow dancers, I supposed that the person holding the crystal ball must, by deduction, be the count and went for it. This was not the staging rehearsed by the singing ensemble and a small tug of war ensued. In *Aida*, we entered one whole passage too early in the temple scene, only to arrive at our places and hear once again the melodic cue repeated as the startled chorus sang and moved about us into their next tableau. This happened to be a felicitous mistake and was kept as part of the staging. I had never rehearsed in costume the triumphal celebration with my partner, Beatrice Seckler, and try as I might, I was not able to keep the accordion pleated nylon of her garment from floating beneath her feet as I lifted her and tried to lodge her securely standing on my thighs. With arms raised aloft, she was the figurehead of a choreographic formation in the shape of the prow at the helm of the royal barge. She momentarily abandoned her majestic demeanor and picked up the hem of her dress in order to execute the movement. The short pleated skirts that Harvey Lichtenstein and I wore in our gladiator fight sequence were also a problem. The drawstring inside of Harvey's waistband was full of dry rot. It broke midway through our stage battle and the skirt landed about his ankles. Without missing a beat, he stepped out of the circle of fabric and finished the dance in his trunks.

On tour, we often had big-name guest stars jobbed in by the local impresarios to sing the leading roles and to guarantee full houses. They arrived with their own wardrobe and staging. Quite often the resulting stage picture was garish and the stage action clashing. In the scene set in the café of Lillas Pastia in *Carmen*, our diva always remained standing on the table as we danced. Blanche Thebom, who guested with us in Detroit, wore a bright red costume dripping with ballfringe and, unbeknownst to us, began to dance in the same locale in which our choreography had been staged. We smashed into her, sending the diva reeling and knocking askew the black wig that covered her ankle length amber tresses. She quickly retreated and was helped back onto the table by a kindly supernumerary.

My life as a professional dancer in New York City was beginning to find its eclectic shape. I moved with liquidity from one modern dance company to another. I performed in increasingly varied arenas; dance, opera ballet, television, musical theater. I studied with wonderful dance teachers in modern, classical, and cultural forms. My career as a choreographer was also spreading from my own concert works created for Donald McKayle and Company to accepting assignments in theater and on television. My teaching jobs were expanding and bringing me into new circles.

Martha Graham taught at the Neighborhood Playhouse, the outstanding theater school under the direction of Sandford Meisner. The students, all actors, brought a completely different physicality to her classes. She asked me to demonstrate for her and I found my weekly hours there fascinating. While she was always extremely articulate and eloquent, her images and associations were especially heightened with the actors. One young man, who was preparing a role in which his character had a maimed hand, had covered his closed fist with red candle wax, turning it into a loathsome bloody stump. The Graham floor work executed with this handicap was quite bizarre and his rhythmic sense, which under normal circumstances was a bit shaky, ceased to exist. Although he placed himself in the back of the class, he was definitely not out of harm's way. Martha's eyes focused on him and narrowed in annoyance at his self indulgence. He was saved from impending chastisement by the entrance of a young woman, late for class, clothed in cotton durene tights that were ill fitting and bagged at the knees. She made her way to the back of the room and whispered to the young man, pointing to his red waxed fist. Martha's target suddenly shifted and that unmistakable voice sounded forth. "On my way over here, I passed the Algonquin Hotel and saw Peggy Ashcroft there, leaning against the front door, looking like the wrath of God. She's earned the right. You ... get out!" A pointing finger at the end of a flung gesture sailed across the room and caught the young woman before she could sit down to join the class. She cowered for a moment, looked unbelievingly at the accusing finger, and left the room.

The second New Dance Group Festival was scheduled to take place in Billy Rose's Ziegfeld Theatre. The downstairs lounge boasted Salvador

Dali's paintings of watches hanging limply from the edges of tables within phantasmagoric landscapes. I was scheduled to perform *Games*, and was listed with the other choreographers, including Sophie Maslow, who was to present *The Village I Knew*, in which I would also appear as a performer, and Anna Sokolow who was presenting the New York première of *Lyric Suite* and had cast me in the opening solo. Anna had returned from a self-imposed exile in Mexico and was mounting the work she had choreographed to Alban Berg's music. The *Lyric Suite* dancers were threatening to become what she had sworn, prior to her departure, never to have again: another New York dance company. Controversy, challenge, confrontation, and fierce loyalty were constant companions wherever Anna Sokolow plied her art. In Mexico, her followers were known as the Sokolovas and were in ongoing competition with the followers of Waldeen, a dance artist who followed in the proletarian tradition of the great muralists, Rivera, Siqueiros, and Orozco. Working with Anna was as inspiring as it was demanding. "Turn, stop, turn, stop, again, stop, again, stop, turn, stop, head and arms up, relevé, stop!" I carried my lifted focus over an imaginary horizon and down through space like some mythic avian colossus, hands fluttering into a blur, tilting in a forced arch knee bend then flipping backwards into an upturned crawl with legs unfolding in long, liquid strides. "That's it. It's like tasting. Devour the space! Cut through it! Longer, lower, hold it there!" I felt like an exquisite all powerful feline, in constant readiness and physical command.

"Donald, I've never seen you dance like that before." This sincere, heartfelt compliment coming from Pearl Lang after the première performance of *Lyric Suite* caught me utterly by surprise. Pearl had extremely high standards and was not overly generous with praise. The review by P. W. Manchester in *Dance News*, noting my "physical magnificence," clearly described what I had accomplished in response to the challenge of working with Anna, a remarkable and demanding artist. There was an aura of toughness about her and an observation of the human condition at its most vulnerable that filled her work. The following year Anna's company was securely in place and she began the making of a fifty-minute work examining the faceless people in the windows and behind the doors within the thousands of apartments in the impersonal and sometimes cold New York City. Kenyon Hopkins wrote a wonderful jazz score which was performed live by a fabulous group of top-notch musicians including the amazing bassist, Charles Mingus. Anna entered the private realities and fantasies of her cast of characters in a series of dance groupings choreographed on and around wooden chairs representing the rooms where each lived alone. My section was called "Panic" and dealt with fear, cries for help that go unheeded resulting in obsessive behavior, and a final catharsis. I awake from a deep and troubled sleep and sense danger. I run to my neighbors. They ignore me or turn away. I return to my room and to my paranoia, crouch fearfully in a ball, beat my head repeatedly against the floor, a move accomplished an inch short of damaging physical contact, roll on the top of my head in disorientation, and finally stagger back to my chair where I collapsed. Anna would rehearse this section for an hour without letup. I left those sessions exhausted; I had to sit quietly to slowly come back to reality. I designed and constructed the costumes for *Rooms* under Anna's watchful eye. Costume was almost a dirty word; clothing was what she wanted. I wished to satisfy her aesthetic directive and yet heighten the desired reality with a palette that captured and furthered the individual moments. I was determined also to enhance the body line that we worked so hard to achieve with properly cut garments. The men's outfits were all shopped and consisted of cotton pants, T-shirts or tank tops, and a raglan sleeved club jacket for Jack Moore's jazzbo solo, "Going." The women's garments were all constructed and in the trio for the three young girls dreaming at their windows, I was able to bring some sunlight into a very dark piece with pastel hues and the use of voile and lawn fabrics. Beatrice Seckler's role was very much like the Blanche DuBois character in Tennessee Williams's *Streetcar Named Desire*. She existed in her own magical world and shunned reality. I found a chiffon print in claret, sienna, and forest green and dressed her for her fantasy. The dance was built on a series of runs with arms outreaching, traveling in, around, and through, avenues of chairs. The gown was designed ankle length with bared shoulders and circular sleevelets, held with elastic, at the same line as the bodice which cut across the bosom and swept backward, fluttering in graceful trails behind her as she ran toward arms that never appeared to receive her.

"Anna, it was like spending an evening with Kafka." "So what's wrong with that?" "Nothing, it was wonderful but very depressing." "Good!" Muriel Stuart embraced Anna and backed away as the growing swell of friends and colleagues pushed forward to greet the little powerhouse who had just premiered a troubling, sensitive, and uncompromising work. As I stood watching, Charlie Mingus approached me. "Hey, man, you were something else. I got a piece you got to do with me. I'm working on it now." I was surprised and excited about this. We exchanged phone numbers. "I'll get in touch with you when things are ready." Jane Dudley and Sophie Maslow were next to me. "You were just great." "Powerful!" The event was a triumph and at the same time not everybody's cup of tea. Anna was animated, excited, argumentative, and all in all, in her glory. Comments were flying back and forth. The crowd was boisterous and opinionated.

Why I had been recruited to perform in John Cage's *Imaginary Landscape Number 4*, I will never know, but I found the idea intriguing and imme-

diately accepted. I did not know what was expected of me. I was not a
musician, and though there were many at the initial rehearsal in the same
professional limbo-land, there were also some very *bona fide* musicians
present presumably to participate in an equal capacity with the fledglings.
The work was a sojourn in the area of captured sound. The composition
was scored and conducted by John Cage in a manner befitting its completely unorthodox instrumentation. *Imaginary Landscape Number 4* was
written for twelve radios and twenty-four players. The radios were set up
on individual tables along with two chairs for the players and a music
stand to hold the notation. My task was to manipulate the amplitude and
volume knobs, which were marked with numbers from zero to nine. My
partner, David Tudor, operated the station dial. We both were challenged
to watch the score and the conductor. We were constantly surprised by
the emissions that ensued, from silences to cacophonies. It was very
entertaining to us as participants and had all the fun of a wonderful parlor
game. The performance was at the McMillin Theatre in Columbia University and was presented by the American Music Alliance, a gathering of
composers of widely differing aesthetics, joined by their commitment to
the making of new music. I had never attended anything like this before
and was not acquainted with most of the composers on the program. The
audience was filled with members of the Alliance, other artists, and students. It began with a duet for tuba and thunder stick and progressed
through works using traditional acoustic instruments and voice in unusual combinations. Applause came from different pockets of the highly
partisan audience and conversation between selections was heavy.

Peggy Glanville Hicks had taken newspaper reviews written by Virgil
Thompson and set them to music in the style of the composer being
critiqued. It was a clever *pièce d'occasion*, a pithy satire. The singers were
excellent and manipulated the sometimes murderous vocal writing with
aplomb. Rumblings of indignation began to erupt in the audience as she
began the section on Stravinsky with layered rhythmic and harmonic
quotations that evolved into the baritone solo. "Stravinsky's neo-classic
music..." Laughter became mixed with an undercurrent of vocalized discontent, and jockeyed back and forth across the auditorium. As the work
segued into the section on Arnold Schoenberg and the twelve tone scale,
Stephan Volpe could not contain himself and stood up red faced and
shaking. "Boo! Boo! Booo!" The evening was well on its way, a cultural
happening. We were yet to follow with *Imaginary Landscape Number 4*. An
interval preceded us so that the stage could be set with our tables, radios,
music stands, and the warren of electrical spaghetti that we required. We
went to our places and a smiling John Cage entered to the conductor's
stand and faced us. At the two rehearsals of the work we were well aware
that the snatches of programs entering and leaving, the occasional crackles

and squeals would be unpredictable. We were not however prepared for a seemingly endless spate of almost perfect quiet tainted only by the sound of the page turn and a single naked popping sound interference. Suddenly a snatch of a Mozart chamber work broke the near silence. "Leave it on!" The voice came from the balcony. Other voices began to speak to the stage. The din grew louder and louder. We continued at our tasks following John who was now beaming with a grin that went from ear to ear. What a success, a true Parisian scandal.

"Donald, can you join the cast of *House of Flowers*?" "What ... when?" "Right away. Alvin is out. I need you to dance with Carmen." Herbert Ross was on the phone. Alvin Ailey had failed to wear his knee pads for the "Slide-Boy-Slide" number and had torn open the flesh covering his knee-cap executing a knee slide that traveled across a scenery track in the deck. He needed to be hospitalized. Carmen De Lavallade and Alvin had been brought into *House of Flowers* by Herbert Ross when he took over the choreographic directorship of the musical from George Balanchine. Balanchine had been replaced along with his equally illustrious colleague, Peter Brook, the show's director. The stellar cast of the musical included the ever popular Pearl Bailey and the dynamic Juanita Hall. Their offstage rivalry was the spice of their onstage characters, two warring madames of neighboring *maisons de joie*, Madam Fleur played by Pearl Bailey and Madam Tango played by Juanita Hall. The show marked the debut of the eighteen-year-old Diahann Carroll and introduced the Watusi-like Trinidadian, and Renaissance man, Geoffrey Holder. The dancing ensemble was a Who's Who of the future. Herb Ross had reunited the two former Lester Horton dancers, Alvin Ailey and Carmen DeLavallade, in the film *Carmen Jones* and brought them to New York for *House of Flowers*. Along with Carmen and Alvin, Herb had also brought the young Cristyne Lawson. The three Californians joined a company that included Arthur Mitchell, Walter Nicks, Louis Johnson, Albert Popwell, Pearl Reynolds, Leu Comacho, and Glory Van Scott. Dancing with Carmen was a magical experience and when Alvin returned, I stayed on as a cover learning the rest of the show from the stage manager, Lucia Victor and the dance captain, Walter Nicks. My first time in the full show was quite a roller-coaster ride. The understudy rehearsals did not include the company, only me, Lucia, and Walter. "Well, you do one chorus of *yanvalou jennou* entering and one chorus circling the duchess and when they say *Agué*, you get possessed." Aside from my careful watching of the dancers from the wings, Walter's slow and meticulous delivery was the sum total of my rehearsal for the voodoo scene. Fortunately for me, I had paid close attention to Albert Popwell since I was scheduled to go on for him at a Wednesday matinee. Lucia managed to call the dancers and Miriam Burton, who played the Duchess of the Sea, onstage at half hour for a quick go-through. "Well, now you enter with two choruses of *yanvalou*..." "Oh, hurry up, Olsa, just spit it out. We ain't got but fifteen minutes and we've got to get dressed and made-up." Louis Johnson's sharp interruption of Walter Nicks' tedious recital was greeted with laughter. Walter had earned the nickname, Olsa, from his constant practice of the Swedish language in preparation for a second teaching stint in Stockholm and Göteborg. Walter already spoke several languages and all were delivered in the same precise rounded tones that marked his English speech. "Just stick with me. You're my partner in every number." Cristyne's words brought relief to what was becoming an anxiety ridden experience. I sailed through the "Two Ladies in the Shade of the Banana Tree" number and was really feeling my oats in "The Bamboo Cage" parade into the cockfight. This was a lively stage-cross in front of Oliver Messel's beautiful bamboo curtain. It was fashioned from horsehair tubing that glistened in the stage light. The number was a free and improvisatory song and dance and my West Indian heritage came out in full bloom, much to the delight of my fellow performers and especially to Enid Mosier. She was what we Jamaicans called a "little island Turk," someone who hailed from the Lesser Antilles. In the big "Mardi Gras" number I was in trouble. I could not figure out how to put on the costume, which was a feathered headdress in the shape of a horse's head and feathered trunks with a fluffy feather boa for the horse's tail. Albert Popwell's head was two sizes smaller than mine and the horse's head sat precariously on the top of my skull. The proper entry into the trunks was a puzzle to me. I finally got into them and discovered only as I was standing in the wings ready to go on that I had the left thigh opening around my waist, which probably accounted for the scratching of the displaced quill ends against my flesh. I danced my way over to Cristyne only to find Alphonse standing in what I thought was my spot, looking at me quizzically. "What are you doing here?" I saw Pearl Reynolds winking at me with that captivating smile of hers, nodding her head and beckoning me to join her. I started toward my new place just as Alvin was coming down the aisle of dancers in a swift arm flinging run. One of his hands hit my jaw, knocking the horse's head over my eyes and sending me reeling blindly, luckily toward the wings, into Lucia's stage manager desk. There I remained until the number ended.

After the close of the show, Alvin Ailey and Cristyne Lawson joined my company and danced in *Games* and *Nocturne*, as had Walter Nicks and Arthur Mitchell before them. Our relationship as colleagues and friends was very close and included my costuming of Alvin and Cristyne for a private audition for the musical, *Jamaica*, choreographed by Jack Cole. I recreated my epic dance-theatre work, *Her Name Was Harriet*, renaming it *They Called Her Moses*. It was a sprawling canvas of dance and drama with many details drawn from scenes in the life of Harriet Tubman, ex-slave and conductor on the Underground Railroad. Two of the sections from this work were inspirational to Alvin in his later masterwork, *Revelations*, although treated quite differently in dramatic texture and vocabulary: the solo I choreographed for him, "Run, Brother, Run" and "Wade in the Water", a dramatic fording of a stream in the flight to freedom of a band of fugitive runaways or *passengers*, as they were called in the ante-bellum parlance of the abolitionists.

The noise of the film threading through the sprockets was the only sound coming from the eight millimeter projector. I sat on the floor of the front studio at the Martha Graham School of Contemporary Dance on East 63rd Street viewing the silent film recording of *Dark Meadow*. It was one of the works that Martha had told me to learn when I accepted her offer to join the company for a tour of Asia under the aegis of the United States State Department. It was an overture in government sponsored cultural exchange, orchestrated by politically enlightened officials who suddenly realized that our heretofore under-exported performance arts, when brought to the peoples of the world, would inform them that we were more than the ubiquitous Coca Cola or the sum of our other corporate faces in their nations. Music and dance were the forerunners in this inspired program as they were immediately accessible, requiring no translation.

Robert Cohan was in charge of the men's rehearsals for *Dark Meadow*. I was learning Mark Ryder's role, Bertram Ross was learning Dale Sehnert's part. We were studying the entrance with the fetishes prior to the revealing of the leading male generative figure behind the phallic totem which dominated the center upstage area in Isamu Noguchi's massive sculptural setting. "We'll have to look at Louis' piano score in order to fit the movement to the music. There are all kinds of pencil notations written in. Gene should be here soon and we can sort it all out then." Eugene Lester entered as Bob was speaking, opened his briefcase, took out the score, and flipped through the pages until he came to the part we were watching. He went to the piano and began to play, accompanying the silent film. It all seemed to fit except for a repeat in the music he had overlooked. "Sorry, I should have returned to the *dal segno*." We turned off the film projector and began to dance the stylized ritual entrance.

The ensemble sections of *Dark Meadow* were prime examples of the finest of Martha Graham's choreography. Even devoid of all theatrical connotations, they stood on their own movement values as exquisite pieces of dance art. There was an early section for the female ensemble entitled "Tale of Ancestral Footsteps" that was particularly beautiful. I always managed to get to those rehearsals to study the craft and marvel at the absolute simplicity, the rhythmic richness, the architectural texturing, and the joy of performance that happened for the dancers. Unfortunately, I would never perform the work. Various circumstances caused it to be dropped from the repertoire, mostly economics, which tends to be art's arch-enemy. The scenery was just too bulky, too heavy, too expensive to be transported around the world. Also, Martha had not involved herself in any of the rehearsals. Stuart Hodes, who was to partner her in the role created for Erick Hawkins, became increasingly agitated with sessions that were scheduled for him and Martha, in which he constantly ended up working alone.

The other repertory piece that I was to learn was *Diversion of Angels*. Paul Taylor and I were the new men added to the company, and we had our initial rehearsals together. The other men, Robert Cohan, Stuart Hodes, Bertram Ross, and David Wood had been with Martha for varying amounts of time and shared the responsibility of teaching us. The female ensemble had four new members: Ellen Siegle, Ellen Van der Hoeven, Donya Feuer, and Cristyne Lawson. In *Diversion of Angels*, the Yellow Duet was danced by Helen McGehee and Stuart Hodes with a quality of playful abandon and dare-deviltry that was delightful, and a sense of partnering that was unique. Bertram Ross danced the White Duet with Linda Hodes, the former Linda Margolies now married to Stuart Hodes. Robert Cohan again brought his elastic phrasing to the Red Duet, now danced with Ethel Winter.

Ethel, who was learning the role from Pearl Lang who had originated the part, came out of those rehearsals with steam rising from her ears. "What's wrong, Ethel?" "That bitch refuses to teach me the dance." "Why ... what do you mean?" "She keeps saying, 'Martha never choreographed this section.'" "Why don't you just ask her to teach you whatever the hell she's been doing for the last seven years?" The next day the part was learned but there were wonderful idiosyncratic movement transitions that were to remain with Pearl Lang and enter her own growing repertoire. It was indeed a strange dichotomy that those very movements when presented in the Pearl Lang body of work brought accusations that they were derivative. Once you had relinquished an idea to Martha, it was artistically appropriated and became the unquestioned property of the regent. If you worked in an analogous aesthetic, the accusation of plagiarism became almost inevitable. The Graham movement vocabulary and performance quality was so unique that, wherever it popped up, it was immediately commented on and traced back to its source. Martha's training was so all-encompassing that she was able to allow company members to choreographically fill a large gap in an unfinished dance work.

Ardent Song had premiered in London in 1954, the year before the beginning of the Asian tour. One of the three movements of Alan Hovhaness' lush score had an extended section that had not been choreographed. Opening night at the Saville Theatre, the dancers designed a rotation scheme in which each would enter and dance as long as inspiration carried and then execute a raptor-like swooping turn as a signal to the next in line. One would enter as the other exited. Linda demonstrated the process to me. Some pretty exciting things could have happened within this game-plan. Martha was now to finish and revise *Ardent Song*, and had offered to build it around me as an enticement for my joining the company and as an artistic challenge. That it was indeed. The dance sections were designed on inspirations and myths attendant to the mysteries surrounding the phases of the moon. It was, as were many of her works, ritualistic and celebratory. It was never clearly explained to me whether the central figure that I performed was celebrant or sacrifice. I chose, in turn, to play both aspects and thus in a dance painted on a pagan canvas I added colors from the Judeo-Christian mythology. The dance opened with the metaphor of a journey. On a boat, like construction of fabric, I was discovered in a sculpted cross-legged kneel with my arms lifted above my head and my upturned palms shading my heavenward gaze. From behind the small sail the figure of my adoration was revealed, holding a pearly conch shell next to her ear in which the sound of the ocean reverberated. Linda Hodes danced this opening duet with me, which was succeeded by two other duets, first with Helen McGehee, and then with Ethel Winter. Each was bridged by ensemble sections. The silvery sail of the barge dissolved into a gentle ocean on which the full moon painted a lustral path and commanded the tides to deposit me on dry land. Abandoned there, I was placed in sacrifice to a nocturnal priestess of a lunar cult. Here my role was passive and reactive. The priestess was danced by Helen McGehee in a costume she had designed and executed, with appliquéed serpents that wound about her limbs and ended with their heads held rigidly in her hands, their sequin eyes glistening and their red satin viper tongues protruding. Helen's wiry hair was back-combed and let loose in an electric frizz that encircled her tiny face in a charged halo of shock. She always gave an absolutely possessed performance and as I lay on my back, limbs spread-eagle before her, and she jumped repeatedly in the groin triangle between my legs with her feet flexed and her eyes glaring maniacally, I was flooded with fear of grave physical danger. I was then deposited into a crater made from yards of pebbly-surfaced fabric, the color of volcanic ash, which rose into three peaks wound around Matt Turney, Ellen Siegle, and Ellen Van der Hoeven. The eruption of this no longer dormant volcano symbolically spewed me into the heavens where I was united with the lunar goddess, and we rode together on astral beams.

Martha began rehearsing the opening duet. Linda Hodes had started dancing in the children's classes at the Graham Studio at 66 Fifth Avenue. Martha had a genuine feeling for Linda, and it showed in the way she worked at those rehearsals. She also seemed very excited by what I brought to the role. She would give ideas, suggestions; I would create; she would mold and change. The process bogged down in the ensemble sections where there always seemed to be an undercurrent of bickering and some unhappy partnering combinations. Martha had taken my wife, Esta, into the company, a rather unorthodox decision on her part, since Esta had not come out of her studio. She had been originally trained by Gluck Sandor and then had futhered her studies at the New Dance Group, where she had received a heterogeneous dance training, including Graham technique with Sophie Maslow and Jane Dudley, both charter members of Martha's company and featured dancers in her early works. Esta had a real feeling for the Humphrey-Weidman technique and personally most enjoyed her work with Mary Anthony in the Hanya Holm technique. She had no real kinetic bonding with the theories of contraction and release and never finished a Graham class with the same elation that followed a workout with Mary Anthony. She was thrilled and excited about working with the Graham Company and going on this remarkable global tour, but also very apprehensive about the work and her lack of preparation at the Graham studio. She felt very insecure at just not being part of the in-group.

All of the company had to take a series of inoculations against a host of tropical maladies. The shots were delivered by needles of varying lengths into the arms and buttocks and were subsequently recorded on our visa applications. Our travel documents were handled by the company management and the completed passports were returned to us filled with colorful stamps and flowing foreign alphabets. We were vaccinated against typhoid, typhus, diphtheria, smallpox, cholera, and yellow fever. Some of the inoculations were single shots, some were in a series of two or three shots. Many in the company reacted badly to this onslaught. Some had to go to bed; others could not lift their arms. Rehearsals became a nightmare; there was much to be learned. One day, Esta was the only ensemble woman left, valiantly trying to rehearse in a passage she hardly knew, and that was the day Martha attended rehearsal. "Don, I know this is going to be difficult for you, but I have to let Esta go. It's just not working out." By the end of that fateful rehearsal, I had been primed for some disaster, but this was more then I had expected. I was torn and did not know what to do. Esta was devastated, but insisted that I stay with the company and go on the tour. I would write from everywhere and we would share the experience through my copious letters. We would meet in Israel, which was the last stop on the tour, and come back together through Europe. A set amount was to be deposited from my salary in our joint account and would accumulate to take care of Esta's air passage and our household while I was away.

Martha began to withdraw herself more and more from the company, to concentrate on her own performance needs and to prepare herself for the ex-officio ambassadorial role she was to assume. She made a brief appearance at a rehearsal in which Ethel and I wished to show her our work on the final duet in *Ardent Song*. She had left us with a sketch the week before; we had fleshed it out and needed her feedback. She watched us very closely. We finished and turned to her. "You're very beautiful together. It is quite magical but it needs something. It...it..." She rose and walked about us. We followed her turning to where she now stood facing toward the studio door. She reeled around, looked at us, and cast her hands into the air. "It needs more ...sá–da, sá–da." Saying this, she wheeled about and left the room. We looked open mouthed at each other. "Sáda ...sáda...?" We both released our incredulity in a spontaneous chuckling that swelled into solid open throated laughter. We were to continue to sá–da, sá–da for the rest of the tour.

Charles Green was our impresario and called the company to his Rockefeller Center office to impress us with his savvy and to give us a pep talk on the breadth and magnitude of everything he was accomplishing for us. Stuart's eye caught something in the literature lying about that disturbed him and called a meeting of all the dancers, back at the studio. Charles Green had an inactive dummy corporation that served to buffer him from any personal liability that might arise in the transaction of business on our behalf and had decided to use it as the entity that employed us as dancers, staff, and technicians. It was a corporation he had registered when he was presenting José Greco and was called Iberian Attractions. Stuart wanted no part of Iberian Attractions and insisted we be hired under the heading of the Martha Graham Dance Company. We all concurred; there was no dissent. Martha attended the meeting and was in a heavy state of agitation about the use of her name by a business administration outside of her circle of control. She took Stuart, as the spokesman, to be an adversary. She was used to getting her way and advanced threateningly toward Stuart who was leaning against the small fireplace wall. She walked with a lifted open palm brandished at him. Stuart grew rigid and faced her defiantly, his arms opened from his sides. Martha caught his attitude in mid-stride but would not stop or change her course. She brought her hand down with a loud slap on the mantel-piece next to Stuart's shoulder and spat out an invective through clenched teeth. "Okay, so now you've made my name Lux Soap!" She left the room slamming the door behind her. The meeting was over.

Charlotte Trowbridge called me into the front studio which had been transformed into a costume workroom to begin the draping of my costume for *Ardent Song*. She had pulled all the existing costumes for the dance and had hung them on hangers about the room. She fingered a bolt of moss green wool jersey. As I stood before her, a bare pallet clothed only in my dance belt, she began by passing the moss green jersey over one shoulder and clasping it with a safety pin at my waist. The door to the back room opened and Martha passed through on her way to the front door dressed in an overcoat and hat, and pulling on leather gloves. "How about this shade, Martha?" Martha stopped momentarily and looked me up and down. "Ursula refuses to make me a new dress for *Night Journey* unless I get a new brassiere." Ursula lifted her gaze from the sewing machine in front of her and looked at Martha, peering over the glasses which rested on the tip of her nose. Martha did not return her gaze but continued on her path out the front door without acknowledging Charlotte's query. Charlotte sighed and went back to her task. Ursula Reed and Nellie Hatfield exchanged knowing glances and continued stitching. Two hours later I was getting out of Charlotte's creation, a task requiring the help of both Charlotte and Ursula as I was a minefield of straight pins. Suddenly the door opened and Martha entered bearing a large brown paper bundle, tied twice around with twine and clasped by a wood and brass department store package handle. She tossed it on the cutting table, grabbed a scissors, snipped open the string, clutched the exposed edge of the wrapping paper, and with a flourish let loose a dozen or more brassieres. "Now can I have a dress?" Ursula answered Martha's bellow, purring in soft, round, perfect speech. "It's all cut out, you can have a fitting tomorrow." There was a twinkle in her eye which was mirrored in Martha's return glance as she went into her room. Nellie gave a short little chuckle as she put on her hat and picked up her pocket book. "See you tomorrow."

Both Ethel Winter's husband, Charles Hyman, and Helen McGehee's husband, Umaña were going on the tour as members of the crew. Martha could find no organizational use for Pearl Lang's husband, Johann Mitchell, and rumor was that this was the reason Pearl had refused to go on the tour. The veracity of the gossip not withstanding, Pearl was around regularly during the last week of rehearsals, helping with the wardrobe. I came into the front studio midweek to speak to Linda, and could hear Martha's voice in the adjoining room. The door opened and Martha came out. "Look what Pearl gave me." She opened a wooden box and displayed a razor sharp double edged dagger. "She says it's very useful for sharpening eyebrow pencils. Isn't she sweet." She closed the box and went back into the room where Pearl sat, shutting the door behind her. Both Linda and I put our hands across our mouths until we were in the outside hallway where we exploded in laughter.

At last the awaited day before departure arrived. Last minute shopping completed, we delivered our luggage and trunks to the studio for shipment to the cargo plane. A final dress parade of *Ardent Song* was scheduled and Martha kept me after the others had left. She took a scissors to all of Charlotte Trowbridge's work, opening seams, redraping, pinning, tucking. "There, now that's more like it. Don, you looked absolutely hermaph-roditic before. Nellie, finish this and pack it with the others." "Yes, Martha." Martha left to walk to her apartment, one block east of the studio. Nellie got up from the sewing machine, took the costume with the pins and open seams in tack, and packed it as it was and closed the case. "No, I'm too old for this. She'll never look at this again." Nellie put on her hat, picked up her pocket book, and went home to fix her supper.

The next day, I entered the four-propeller airplane that was to take me on my first flight and found my seat next to the little window. I searched the observation deck and found Mother, Dad, and Esta leaning against the rail, wrapped in their overcoats against the brisk fall weather. We waved good-bye. Armed with Dramamine pills against airsickness and brimming over with anticipation, I settled back into my seat and started my journey around the world.

In Mother's arms.
Collection of Donald McKayle.

Mother and Aunt Alice in
summer finery.
Collection of Donald McKayle.

With Philip in Central Park.
Collection of Donald McKayle.

Philip, Dad and I in the
Harlem River Housing Park.
Collection of Donald McKayle.

From *Creole Afternoon*.
Photos by Carmen Schiavone.
Photos © Bennett and Pleasant.

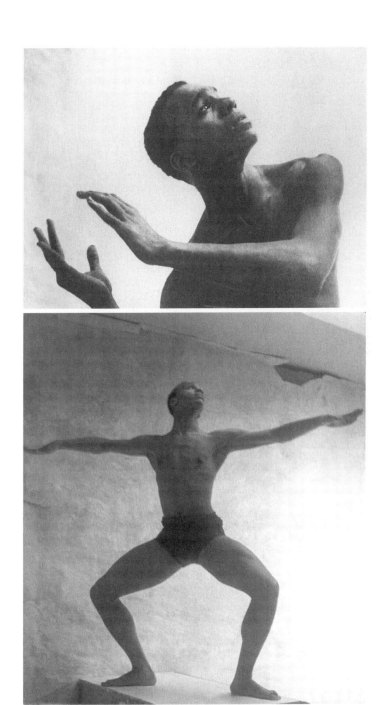

Photographic studies by Carmen Schiavone.
Photos © Bennett and Pleasant.

Photographic study from Jane Dudley's
Appassionata,
Carmen Schiavone.

Aerial moment at Jacob's Pillow,
John Lindquist.

5
AROUND THE WORLD

The trip from New York's Idlewild Airport to Tokyo took thirty-six hours, and though it seemed endless, every long leg of the journey held revelations. We spent about an hour in the San Francisco Airport, then boarded a Japan Airlines flight on the way to Honolulu. The change in demeanor, care, courtesy, and service aboard the new aircraft was a good introduction to the completely different culture toward which we were heading. In Honolulu, we were taken to a hotel near the airport for a pre-arranged meal. We returned to the airplane to find the stewardesses garbed in kimonos and our succeeding meals were served on lacquered trays with Japanese dinnerware, including *hashi* (chopsticks) instead of knives and forks. You could get western utensils but everyone took the opportunity to get one-on-one instructions on how to handle these simple and effective eating tools. Finally, a day and a half from our initial New York departure, we arrived in Tokyo. A welcoming committee stood on the tarmac to greet us. Photographers arranged us on the stairs of the aircraft and snapped away as we smiled and waved. We went through passport control and were finally loaded into vehicles with the steering columns built on the right and were whisked away on the opposite side of the road to the famous lodging designed by Frank Lloyd Wright, Tokyo's Imperial Hotel. I lay down for a short nap and fell into a deep sleep.

A strange musical sound awakened me. I went to the window and looked out on the last vestige of dusk as darkness fell upon the city which was immediately emblazoned with neon. The displaced reveille that had awakened me was sounded by the *soba* (noodle) man announcing his presence with a traditional short melody played on a wooden flute, as he pushed his cart through the street below. I got dressed, found Matt Turney, and we went out to spend our first night in Tokyo on the Ginza. We passed another *soba* man and suddenly heard a more familiar sound clashing with the noodle vendor's ancient melody. We followed the strains of a small jazz combo and arrived at an amazing-looking building. It was painted a vibrant shade of orchid and trimmed with white gingerbread. A white stallion reared across its facade. Japanese characters with Roman script below announced *Shiro Bashi* (The White Horse). The eye-catching exterior was matched by the inside of the establishment, where a cascading fountain was the focal point of three widening tiers of white wrought-iron balustrade balconies, the first of which housed the small and very good jazz combo. Young people filled the cocktail tables, crowding the tiers around and above the band. The walls were covered in satin in the same intense shade of orchid, tufted with white, satin-covered buttons. The young people sitting, talking, listening to the music, and sipping beverages were referred to as *avecs*; the borrowing of the French word was Japanese slang for couples on a date. The female singer who joined the all-male band sang "Love Is A Many Splendored Thing" in a rich jazz vocal style with only the slightest flaw in her English pronunciation. It was staggering to realize, upon meeting her, that she spoke no English and had learned the lyrics by listening and phonetic copying.

"Did you see the schedule Charlie posted? We have a lecture-dem tomorrow." "What exactly will we do...a class...repertoire...what?" I was quite concerned about the undesigned and unrehearsed lecture demonstration. Linda Hodes was calming and seemed to take it all in stride saying that it would be all sorted out at the afternoon rehearsal. We met on the stage at the Sankei Kaikan, the building of the newspaper that was sponsoring our performances in Tokyo. The beautiful, intermediate size concert hall that was part of their operation would be our main performance space. Martha arranged us in places for the floorwork sequence that would open the demonstration. Things went along well enough until we started progressions in space. We took partners and proceeded from upstage to downstage doing a tilted off-balance lean with the lifted leg reaching into a low side step, resolving into a pulsing torso shift from contraction to release which thrust us back into the initial lean. Paul Taylor and I went through the sequence together. "Paul, watch your hands." Martha looked disturbed as she focused on Paul's decorative and highly individual approach to the movement. "What do you want me to watch about them?" Paul answered tartly and continued his stylistically renegade performance. Martha was agitated and would not for a second countenance insubordination or loss of control. "That's it! Only the senior members of the company will perform tomorrow." Paul picked up his rehearsal bag and left immediately. I gathered that I was canceled as well. The new women, Cristyne, Donya, Ellen Siegle, and Ellen Van der Hoeven appeared somewhat taken aback by this arbitrary chastisement. They knew what they were doing. Why didn't Martha have the directness to put the scissors to the cloth where it was damaged rather then throw out the whole bolt. Following the dismissal of half the company, the rehearsal petered out on its own accord. The senior members caucused to strategize on what to do under any and all probabilities. The rest of us went to get dressed. Ellen Van der Hoeven brooded and hung around. "Martha, when will I become a senior member of the company?" "When you become a dancer." Instead of leaving Martha's lack of grace alone, Ellen chose to answer back. Martha would have none of it and slapped her across the face. "You should be glad you're an old woman or I'd slap you right back. The trouble is, you don't know what it is to love anyone. I don't have to stay here, you know. I'll call my Richard and he'll bring me right back home." The tour had started off with a bang, and we had yet to do our first performance.

Martha's art and Japan were a perfect match. Not only were we a tremendous hit with the public, but journalistic critiques were filled with thought, honest discourse, and erudition. I was completely unaccustomed to such artistic scholarship in our own newspapers or periodicals. It was particularly thought provoking to read the translations of commentary on Isamu Noguchi's set for *Cave of the Heart*, discussed in relation to the ancient and modern principles of Japanese landscape architecture.

The first week in Tokyo, I was performing only in *Diversion of Angels* and was able to stand in the wings and watch the other dancers. Martha's performance in *Cave of the Heart* was as dramatically powerful, if not physically as terrifying and dangerous as it had been seven years ago at the American Dance Festival. At that time, I was doing service on the stage crew in Palmer Auditorium and, therefore, had a parallel viewing opportunity and could now render a true comparison. I remembered those pitched over revolutions balanced on one leg with the other leg flung high and the head cast low. These turns, which were to become a staple of the Graham vocabulary, had been named cave turns because they had been developed for the serpent heart solo in *Cave of the Heart*. In the early performances Martha had thrown herself at an angle that caused the tail of hair dangling from an upswept, off centered point on the crown of her head to touch the floor and inscribe a perfect circle around her standing leg while the lifted leg pointed skyward. At the climax of the solo she left the stage with such rage and power that Mark Ryder was posted to stand in the wings and catch her for her own safety. Now though the drama was all still there, the physical abandon had been altered and she needed no security net waiting in the wings.

"Ow!" The scream was a loud and real expression of pain. "You stuck that pin right into my flesh." "It shouldn't be there anyway." Donya and Martha glared at each other with equal venom. "How can you wear this dress with all that extra poundage. Take it off and leave it with Bethsabee." The Baroness de Rothschild had come on the tour with us but insisted on a real job, outside of her role as benefactress, and had been put in charge of wardrobe. Martha dismissed Donya with a wave of her hand and turned to me. I was the next to be fitted and was a little apprehensive after what had just occurred. Dressed in only my dance belt, I stood in front of Martha. She unwound a length from a bolt of jersey and threw it over my shoulder. She clamped it to my waist with a cinch of wide elastic held together with a safety pin and continued to wind the jersey through my legs and upward. She held me tightly between her knees with the viselike grip of her inner thighs as she draped and pinned. A startlingly handsome costume emerged. I was also instructed to take it to Bethsabee. My costume was so twisted in places, it would need to be sewn on a power machine. I was afraid of pins hidden under layers of drapery that would remain undiscovered, only to emerge in performance and stab me. I would also have to work with this garment and readjust the choreography. There was a slashed pocket like drape around one leg leaving a full loop of fabric that could be a booby trap in executing all the floorwork. I thought of Nellie Hatfield's prediction and how right she had been. The costume that Charlotte Trowbridge had so carefully designed and built for me was nowhere in sight.

"It is a terror and a challenge to be here, for this is a dancing nation and we place our hearts at your feet." Our first official reception took place in a ballroom and Martha gave a glowing speech that we were to hear at every stop on our itinerary. Each time it would be delivered with only minor variations or interpolations of bits of local information that had come her way; it always sounded fresh, spontaneous, and heartfelt.

The first row of the balcony overlooking the ramp at the Kabuki Theater was a choice location and securing it was quite a prize. I had a local dancer, Nobuo Iwamura, to thank for this maneuver. We had met at the function following the opening night performance at the Sankei Kaikan. He was a soloist with the classical ballet which had just finished its performance season prior to our arrival. He had essayed the leading male role in *Jardin Aux Lilas* under Antony Tudor's tutelage and had made a personal triumph. He also spoke English very well. He accompanied me to the Kabuki and explained the action, the intricacies of the onstage performance, and the audience participation. It was wonderful to experience a traditional and time honored art form that had not suffered the petrification of elitism that encased the opera and symphony in the United States. Of course these were both importations of European origin and unfortunately carried all the baggage imposed on them by the American upper crust, who looked upon our indigenous forms as crass modernism or vernacular, lowly pursuits. As I was to discover on this tour, one would have first to be a prophet abroad before receiving tribute at home.

"What's going on?" "Those are the fans expressing their approval of the actor. He has played a double role, the faithful wife in the first half and the courtesan in the second half. This is the final scene, the ritual death." A great clamor of voices and rhythmic shouting from the audience accompanied the mutual tying of the obis by the tragic couple and the piercing of the daggers as the revolving hydraulic took them down midramp clasped together in a death embrace as the lights faded. The excitement in the theater was palpable. No one hushed the natural vocal response, the visceral participation, the act of partnership between audience and players. It had all the warmth and celebration of the antiphonal call and response heard in the gospel church and none of the shushing heard at symphony concerts, delivered with glares of chastisement directed at the untutored who had the temerity to applaud between symphonic movements.

The Noh drama, antecedent of the Kabuki, was sparsely attended at the performance I viewed and seemed to live within a time warp of unchanged tradition. An entrance ramp led to the main stage where the musicians sat without scenic embellishment. Torches were used for illumination. The actors wore masks and proceeded down the ramp with measured step at a pace that allowed for the perception that the masks were changing expression. The angle at which the actors approached the torches caused shadows to fall and linger on the surface of the masks. A tilt of the head produced a smile, a lowering of the head dredged forth deep sorrow. Comic or evil characters moved more swiftly and their personas, which were veiled in trickery and lacked vulnerability, did not reveal change on their countenance. I sat hypnotized, not realizing that three hours had passed.

We had a special performance scheduled at the large Ernie Pyle Theatre which was situated across from the side of the Imperial Hotel. It was the home of the Takarasuka, the largest popular theater in Tokyo and we were therefore able to investigate at close hand some of the technical wizardry of the modern Japanese theater. I had marveled at the production values in the competing Kokusai where I had seen *Autumn Dances*. Both theaters had schools that trained young women who were chosen through arduous auditions and then became attached to the theater first as apprentices, then as ensemble members, some rising to the rank of featured performers, and one or two eventually to stardom. Just as the Kabuki and Noh were all male, these theaters were all female. The star was invariably the lead male impersonator, excellent in vocal work and in several styles of dance: including traditional Japanese forms; western forms such as flamenco, jazz, tap, and classic ballet. The scenic effects were amazing: a waterfall of recirculated grains of rice transformed with magical lighting into a plunging cataract; a planetary journey in space with comets flashing over the heads of the audience and the milky way receding onstage into infinity; the leading lady descending from the fly gallery seated within a giant chrysanthemum singing "The Unchained Melody" in Japanese; a line of girls in the tradition of the Rockettes, known by some strange cultural aberration as the Atomic Girls, performing a lively unison routine in which their costumes, at the pull of a drawstring, turned, in perfect synchronization, from white to red. Despite their proliferation of copies and one-better versions of our popular entertainment and vernacular arts, there was no experimental or individual modern dance art apparent.

Judging from the capacity to absorb and assimilate, it seemed only a matter of time until the onslaught of our visit would spawn new ventures. My own appetite for knowledge of the indigenous arts was ravenous; my perceptions and conclusions constantly seemed to reinforce one another.

The theater in which the Kagaku was presented was obviously constructed without the comfort of a six-foot-tall, long legged American in mind. Fortunately for me attendance was sparse, and I could easily extend my legs over the seat in front of me since the stalls were raked in the manner of an amphitheater. This ancient court orchestra appeared to be similar in age to the Noh as they shared some of the same musical resources: a wind instrument whose double reed was constantly moistened in a container of water and whose prolonged wail, always on the verge of resolving, never arrived at a settled pitch; a flat circular drum held on the shoulder and struck with a sharp rap at the end of a phrase. The entire musical experience was unobtrusive, almost as if it had been specifically designed over generations to be the most excellent background.

The Bunruku puppets were exquisite in every detail, with beautifully painted faces, wigs of natural hair, and costumes in fabrics, patterns, and tailoring in perfect scale for their miniature proportions. The expert puppeteers were clothed in black from head to toe and were symbolically invisible. Sitting in the small theater within a major department store, I felt as if I had somehow wandered into a Lilliputian version of the Kabuki.

Each night as we left the theater, there was a crowd of people holding programs to be autographed. Always among the group was a young girl with the most exquisite face filled with huge dark eyes and a radiant smile. I smiled back. "I am Donald McKayle." She nodded knowledgeably and pointed to my picture in the souvenir booklet. "And you?" "Takako." She giggled and thanked me again. Whatever would she do with all those autographed programs?

The ceremonies at the Chinsanzo Gardens began with a reception beneath an open-sided canvas tent. The afternoon was arranged on behalf of several dance artists deemed national treasures and was in honor of Martha Graham and her art. Michiko Ito, who had worked with Martha in New York during the early stages of Martha's career in the Greenwich Village Follies, was there. The speaker at the podium was reuniting them and venerating their age and longevity. Martha bristled at the inference of senior citizenship but rose graciously to accept the honor and once again spoke of "... a terror and a challenge ... and we lay our hearts at your feet." We went next into a beautiful building within the serene gardens. It was amazing to find so peaceful a place in the heart of a bustling modern metropolis. We sat on cushions in a shoji-screened room. In a niche to the side were two musicians; one played the koto, and the other was blind and played the samisen. As the music began, the screen at the back of the room parted and a dancer emerged in a sea blue kimono, her face whitened with rice paste, her eyes outlined in black, and her painted mouth a slash of red. Her wig was stiffly lacquered in place, except for a curved caracole on her temple that parted as she raised her head and opened her eyes. She was the master artist of the Suzuki school and performed a classic tale of a pearl diver who is chosen to go into the depths of the sea and recover a magical pearl needed for the survival of the community. It is guarded by a dragon and the only way to obtain it is by placing it within a slit cut just over the diver's heart, causing her death. But the pearl is safe since the dragon will not touch a dead body, which then floats to the surface where the pearl is retrieved. The continuity of the village is thus insured, and the diver's memory is eternally honored. She moved forward with her feet sliding along the surface of the tatami mats approaching the waters' edge. As she entered the surf, she kicked lightly at the opening of her kimono causing it to flip over, revealing the white lining, which became foam and wave caps as she descended into the sea. She withdrew a fan from her obi and opened it across her face so that its silver surface glistened against her cheek, framing her face as she sang a high pitched plaint. She shut the fan against the palm of her opposite hand and with a swift lateral gesture, it became a dagger slicing her heart. Her voice rose then fell in a sad cry. The fan was reopened and tossed into the air turning as it fell from silver to gold to silver. She retreated from the spot marked by the fan and danced a slow exit, turning back before she left so that the loose curl of her wig covered her eyes. She was gone. We were all mesmerized. The musicians left, and our hosts waited until Martha, who was in a deep state of absorption, looked up. They came over to her, bowed, and helped her to rise from where she sat.

We were escorted in twos and threes to the tea ceremony. A time set aside for the appreciation of beauty – what a wonderful idea. The vessels were presented so that the bamboo pattern design faced us as the young woman in her elegant silken kimono poured the pale green liquid and offered us the porcelain cups. As we accepted, we were instructed to turn the cup so that the design faced the pourer as we drank. Time slowed and we became contemplative, open, and receptive. The taste of the green tea was strange and unfamiliar, but pleasant. Pale green confections in lovely shapes were set in front of us. The slightly sweetened bean paste was absolutely unpalatable. Linda nibbled politely on the tiny bite she had wisely taken, artistically returning the remainder to the plate in front of her. I rolled the whole little pastry I had chosen around in my mouth, softening it for the inevitable final chew and swallow that ended with a wry, eyebrow lifted, eye blinking, I-did-it smile of bravery. Bob surreptitiously disgorged himself with a deep and gracious formal bow, plopping his mouthful into a waiting handkerchief that he deftly tucked into his jacket pocket. As the light filtering through the shoji screens changed to dusk, the wisdom of *In Praise of Shadows*, Junichiro Tanizaki's essay on beauty as perceived in traditional Japanese aesthetics was clear. The woman who had conducted the tea ceremony was bending to remove the trays and the glow of late sunlight that highlighted the back of her neck revealed in chiaroscuro a beautiful arabesque set off by the stiff collar of her kimono.

Bob Cohan and I planned a visit following the evening performance to the Yashiwara, Tokyo's red-light district. On the street outside the stage door, we hailed a small taxi and scrunched together in the back seat. A slender necked vase attached to the narrow column between the doors contained a thoughtfully arranged floral grouping of a single Fuji mum and delicate reeds. We left the center city and were soon in a warren of small streets and then suddenly on a wider artery where women sat in open doorways waiting for, or conversing with, prospective customers. The cab dropped us in front of a theater. We purchased tickets at the kiosk and went inside to view Japanese burlesque. Many of the comic routines that opened the entertainment were incomprehensible to us, but an energetic semi-nude adagio team followed, not unlike the ones on view in Las Vegas. The dancers wore G-strings and executed acrobatic lifts and passionate embraces. They were covered head to toe in metallic paint; he was silver and she was gold. The dance was performed to Bobby Capo's popular Latin recording of *"Baballú."* We left without seeing the rest of the show as we were to join the company for a late supper at a restaurant known both for its atmosphere and its excellent tempura. We arrived later than the appointed hour and were met by two kimono clad hostesses waiting for us at the entry. They bowed profusely and led us through a lovely garden whose small size was brilliantly camouflaged by the plantings and the meandering of the path. We went over a little drum bridge hearing the sound of water from the stream beneath and after an abrupt turn came upon a lighted doorway. We were escorted into a room where our colleagues were already gathered at a low table, sipping tea. We shared the details of our visit to the Yashiwara and were guided through a hallway into another room, centered around a semi-circular lacquered table backed by a lacquered screen. We sat on floor cushions with our legs extended downward into a pit beneath the table. At the echoing sound of a large gong struck with a padded mallet, the lacquered screen rotated and two chefs seated before glowing braziers revolved into view. They executed a deep bow as the turntable on which they were seated came to a halt. They knelt on cushions facing woks which were surrounded by trays of beautifully sliced vegetables and meats fanned out into attractive designs. The hostesses passed among us pouring sake into our porcelain cups. The chefs were busy dipping items into bowls of batter and crisping them in hot oil, transferring them from draining racks onto lovely square table trays that were brought to each of us with bowls of sauces for dipping. The meal was magnificent, and we all overate and drank a constant flow of sake until we realized that we must turn down our cups or they would be continually filled with the sneaky liquid. The chefs bowed, the gong sounded, and they revolved out of view. After a final serving in the antechamber of sliced fruit and a scented tea, contented and drowsy, we were taken to taxis. Our hostesses stood at the gate as the cabs drove off.

Nobuo Iwamura and his sister were at the airport to say good-bye. I left them and joined the others gathered on the steps of the plane for our final picture in Japan, waving farewell to new friends and a wonderful fortnight. We landed in Manila and I could see men in shirtsleeves wheeling the debarkation steps up to the airplane. The aircraft door swung open like the hatchway to a furnace and a blast of fiery air rushed in. I stepped out into the withering heat. We were taken to a hotel surrounded by tropical foliage. Porters in light cotton formal overshirts with white on white embroidery bustled about, carrying our luggage, and showing us to our rooms. English was spoken everywhere. That evening we had our first USIA (United States Information Agency) reception and I found myself in the midst of colonial society, American style. We had been instructed not to sit clumped together in a group, but to spread ourselves among the tables and mingle with our hosts and their guests, and to be pleasant and informative. I found myself at a table with someone from the staff of the United States cultural attaché and a couple from the American colony. The husband was with an American firm and had been brought along to the reception by his wife who clamored for inclusion in every vestige of home. She feigned great cultural savvy and exhibited a wagon load of misinformation on Martha Graham and the modern dance. The gentleman from the cultural attaché's office was letter perfect on all the information contained in the advance material furnished by Charles Green's office. He owned a well digested copy of Bethsabee de Rothschild's book, *La Danse Artistique aux Etats Unis*. Martha instinctively sensed the climate of this group and saved her "terror and a challenge" speech for the reception hosted by the Philippine government and attended by the president and first lady. At that reception, we were greeted by music played on indigenous instruments and entertained by dancers performing the Tinikling, a national dance in which twin lengths of giant bamboo were held horizontally and pounded rhythmically against the floor as dancers skipped dangerously in and out of the clashing poles. Martha was greeted personally by the first lady and presented with a beautiful Maria Pañuela gown of embroidered silk organdy and matching backless open toe mules. The first lady wore an exquisite example of this national dress with its gossamer butterfly sleeves standing in stiffened puffs from her shoulders. Martha was genuinely charmed by the intimacy of this lovely gift which fit her to perfection, but she gave the mules to Ethel Winter. Martha's wide feet with their high arches and toes that curved backwards would never grace such delicate footwear.

The trip through the countryside, climbing upwards toward the magnificent vista point at Tagaytay was an eye-opener. Anywhere a seed dropped it seemed to germinate into lush growth. How could a country so verdant with riches bear such poverty? "They're basically lazy. It's just passed on from generation to generation. It must be in the genes." I found myself silent to any further conversation with the Americans who had brought me up to view the awesome panorama that spread out before my eyes. I had promised to be pleasant, not polite. I could not wait to be rid of them. I was intolerant of intolerance, the colonial mind, the condescension, and all that "white man's burden" rubbish. I was eager to get to Indonesia and away from the lingering oppression that was a stagnant suffocation hanging densely in the Philippine air.

We came down in Jakarta on the island of Java where, instead of hotel accommodations, we were placed in private residences. I was in a lovely district called Kabayoran. It was easy to remember the lilting sound of my telephone number, ampat, ampat, lima, lima. As in most island cultures, there was the music of water in the sound of the language. Ellen Van der Hoeven was home and very happy. I was suddenly aware of how tall she was in comparison to her compatriots. Her Dutch ancestry was as clear in her physique as her Indonesian heritage was etched in her features.

Our performances were sellouts, and filled both with people from the city and people who traveled in from distant parts of the island. It was wonderful to be dancing for the people of the country and to be showered by them with specially arranged performances of dance, theater, gamelan concerts, and marvelous parties. Indonesian cooking was glorious and the consumption of a full rice-table with its myriad dishes of varied and succulent flavors almost demanded a following day of rest. While fruit is offered after such a magnificent meal to help cleanse the palate, the durian that we were served had an altogether different effect. Durian is a cousin to the jackfruit which I had heard so much about from my father's tales of growing up in Jamaica. In Indonesia, durian was considered an aphrodisiac and highly prized by virile young men; raging hormones often spawned raids on durian orchards. The large pod was sliced open by our host and the pungent aroma that came forth was something akin to a strong cheap brandy. I popped a fleshy seed into my mouth and the shock of the taste was enormous. It was like biting into an overly ripe creamy cheese that owed its flavor to fermentation. Such a sensation might definitely have deep repercussions.

A length of beautiful batik swathed the loins of the dancer as he entered slowly. It curled between his legs, and trailed behind him. He stopped, slid his fingers along the edges of the cloth that was clasped in the jeweled girdle about his waist, opening it to reveal a ceremonial dagger. He kicked the train of batik to one side with a sharp flick of his leg and turned his head, crowned with a curvilinear coronet, into profile. He became the living embodiment of the wayang shadow puppet that I had purchased as a souvenir. The graceful artist performing this elegant Slendang was a colonel in the army. You were considered uneducated if you did not dance. Here was a culture in which art was a part of, rather then apart from, life. I wondered to myself, "What would it be like to see General Eisenhower dancing for visiting dignitaries?"

Singapore was a crowded, busy, bustling port city. We stayed at the Raffles Hotel, made legendary by Hollywood movies and the seductively sinister Sydney Greenstreet. Mosquito netting was draped from canopies about our beds, and a ceiling fan, though not really necessary at this time of year, hummed pleasantly overhead. There were goods from all over the world on sale here at marvelous prices. Not far from the teaming city were beaches of clean, white sand which were amazingly devoid of crowding humanity.

Paul Taylor dove through the wave and was gone. I watched the churning foam and suddenly realized that Paul had not yet resurfaced. I rose from the sand and walked into the water. I don't know how long I scanned the stretch of sea. Fear erased logic and each second became an eternity. Suddenly there was a ricocheting of two, three, four porpoises in and out of the water, and then I saw Paul. How close he was to these wonderful creatures was impossible to tell but he seemed to be following them. Some twenty minutes later, Paul was walking toward me from a point far down the beach. As he approached he looked exhilarated and was smiling. He was holding a beautiful bivalve which he wrapped in his towel before diving back into the water. That evening in the room we shared, he placed a file of ocean bottom creatures on the window seat. They were exotically beautiful but by the next day, removed from their saline environment, they had begun to lose their luster and to expire, exuding a vile odor. While we were out, they were confiscated and disposed of by housekeeping.

The raw silk suit that Bob had had made to measure by a Chinese tailor was ready the next day as promised, in time to be packed for departure. Unfortunately, it would soon give evidence that a few more days were needed for proper inner construction to guarantee its ability to hold its original shape. It was just one item in the frenzy of shopping that infected the entire company and that resulted in lingering problems for the rest of the tour.

The cargo and baggage situation had been resolved in terms congruous with economic necessity. Some of the overload was being returned by sea, including the burdensome set for *Dark Meadow*. We each had to take care of our personal bags; the company was responsible only for our make-up cases and performance items. We had to respect established airline weight restrictions or be prepared to pay personally for excess baggage. It was wonderful watching David Wood trying to walk normally, carrying a flight bag in which he had sequestered a solid stone Buddha head. Paul had purchased a collection of stuffed birds that were to be placed on pedestals of varying heights, along with a yet-to-be found ostrich or other exotic egg, and were to form the scenic elements of a yet-to-be choreographed work. While other members of the company were buying jewelry, silks, and antiquities, Paul bought a Chinese farmer's straw raincoat and hat. He packed it in the wardrobe trunk scheduled for shipping. There was some doubt about whether it would be allowed through U.S. agricultural inspection on return.

Some words can conjure up romantic notions. For me, one of them was the name, Kuala Lumpur. I knew nothing about this city in Malaysia but the sound of its name was music. I liked to roll it off my tongue, connecting it to mystery and pleasure. As often is the case with romantic musings, reality looms in sharp contrast to fantasy. The brown river that ran through the city was the source of its name; it meant muddy banks. The surrounding countryside was ravaged with the scars of strip mining of tin ore. British colonial power was in full force here in a most repugnant manner. In many ways, we had a lot of adjusting to do. We were told to be thankful for the little lizards that climbed the walls of our hotel room or scurried away across the floor. They were wonderful exterminators and with them as roommates, you needn't fear the dreaded scorpion. A much larger reptilian relative silhouetted against the screen covering the window did not elicit any such gratitude, and I closed the shutters as double protection.

The theater where we were to perform was built early in the century and lacked the electrical capacity needed to power our lighting and sound equipment. A generator was brought in. Opening night, after the first dance, I returned to the dressing room to find my open container of Albolene cleansing cream covered with captured insects. A rip in the window screening and the lure of the lights had turned the room into a bug sanctuary. Small flying and crawling creatures were everywhere.

"Who's Martha Graham?" "She couldn't be anyone much, or why would she come to Kuala Lumpur?" This exchange, saturated with disdain, came from two taffeta-frocked matrons with drawn faces capped with tightly permanented coiffures. They spoke between sips of gin gimlets, sputtering their snobbish blather as if their mouths were filled with mashed potatoes. Without a word spoken among us, we had collectively abandoned the policy of mixing and stood together shunning the bored free-loaders. "Isn't it wonderful that you came to entertain us." "We're not entertainers, and we didn't come here to dance for you. We're here for the people of this country and were expecting to meet them." The affronted woman drew herself up in a huff of indignation. The USIA official took me by the arm and introduced me to several local couples who had attended the concert and were deep into a discussion about *Seraphic Dialogue*. Their commentary was a rapturous detailing of the linear set of glowing brass tubing and the lush vivid costumes that recreated so imaginatively stained glass windows.

The backstage dialogue surrounding this work was not always seraphic nor of heavenly or divine inspiration. Martha had distilled and developed her solo, *The Triumph of Saint Joan*, into *Seraphic Dialogue*. I had seen the original at the Juilliard School with the orchestra placed on stage behind a scrim. Ellen Van der Hoeven was to dance the role of Joan the Warrior. She had an amazingly pliant body, long beautiful lines, and an open, expressive face. Alas, she also had rhythmic problems which worked against her, especially in the battle sequences. Martha had taken the role away from her, given it to Helen McGehee and cast Ellen in the supporting role of one of the attendant saints opposite Ellen Siegle. At a matinee performance, highly temperamental and smarting from this obvious demotion, she got into an argument over a series of inaccuracies in the darting jumps relayed back and forth between her and Ellen Siegle. The dispute continued into the dressing room and escalated into a struggle. Martha heard the commotion, entered the room with paper cups filled with water, and dashed them into their faces. Instead of calming or defusing the situation, it inflamed it. Ellen Van der Hoeven was infuriated. "I'll kill you!" Ellen Siegle was pressed up against the dressing table in terror. Charlie Hyman rushed in to separate the two, slipped on the puddle of water and landed flat on his back. Bertram followed in quick succession and met with the same fate. Matt Turney finally took command, ushered everyone out of the dressing room, and told the two Ellens to sit down and get ready for the next dance. Her voice was calm and precise. It cut through all the shouting and soothed the growing physicality like a cool breeze.

The magnificent city of Bangkok floated on canals that transported, irrigated, washed, and gave life to its teeming population. I was very happy there, for despite hardships that were everywhere, I sensed a joy in the voices of the people and in the play and laughter of the children. I spent hours in the shops examining the beautiful handicrafts, going through bolts of stridently colored, full-bodied silks. I found a lovely pair of black star sapphire earrings and added them to my collection of presents for Esta. A party was held at the palace in our honor, hosted by the uncle of the king. His majesty was known to be a great jazz aficionado and a reputable hot clarinetist. The party was an out door fête in the magnificent palace gardens. Everyone decked themselves out in their finery and flashed their newly acquired jewels. Our host turned out to be a wonderful conversationalist and began to regale us with a story of a dangerous jungle hunt and capture. On cue lights came up on the small island across the lagoon and revealed a small elephant. "This young fellow is the prize of a fateful journey into the interior. We were on the trail of a rogue tiger that was terrorizing the villagers and suddenly came upon this stray. He was very young and finding him alone was most unusual. We approached him with caution. His cry of fear as we came near was answered by a fierce trumpeting. We turned and faced the charge of his protecting mother who, having found her lost calf, thundered to its defense. We had no time to escape, I fired my rifle and the great beast fell just yards from where I stood my ground. The baby screamed aloud. I turned to see a huge bull approaching at full speed. I fired again..." At that moment the young pachyderm punctuated the story by relieving himself in a great pile.

The plane that we took on the flight to Burma (now Myanmar) came down for refueling in French Indochina (now Vietnam). The airfield seemed to be a temporary landing strip left over from World War II. Perforated strips of metal were laid into the clay and took the place of the tarmac. A ladder was released from the airplane door. We clambered down in the rain and were taken, by men carrying waxed rice paper umbrellas and wearing straw raincoats and coolie hats, to a shabby, cramped structure. The skirts, stockings, and heels that had been dutifully worn by the women were clearly most inappropriate.

Because there was no theater in Rangoon (now Yangôn) suitable for the company, we were scheduled to dance on the grounds of the Shwe Dagon Pagoda, one of the most important of Buddhist holy places. It was swarming with worshippers, visitors, and monks in saffron colored robes. Vendors of religious articles sold small papers of gold leaf that were placed on the forehead of the Buddha in adoration. The glittering statue literally dripped with these precious metal offerings of the faithful. In a large open space adjacent to the pagoda, an outdoor stage was built according to specifications sent ahead by our technical department. The floor was teak wood, beautiful to look at and a joy to dance on. Because our performances took place on hallowed ground, they were overflowing with monks grouped together in patches of saffron yellow amongst the capacity audiences. Children and young men climbed the trees outside the surrounding fence and watched from on high. Unaccustomed to western theater traditions but realizing that applause was a part of the foreign ritual, the audience would clap loudly as the curtain opened and the dancers assembled for bows. The applause would then dutifully cut off immediately as the curtain closed. For each successive curtain call, this automatic response would be repeated.

"No, that's not what happened." We all turned to the nine-year-old boy who had just interrupted his mother's garbled recounting of Martha's performance in *Cave of the Heart*. She had mixed together thumbnail sketches of several Greek myths, a dash of saltiness remembered from newspaper reports of Judith Anderson's backstage life in gossip columns sent from home, with a soupçon of the monody by the vengeful heroine of Robinson Jeffers's *Medea*, "... because I loathe you more than I love them!" Now seeing all eyes upon him, the lad grabbed center stage and adopted the retreating contracted body stance that Martha used as she danced her venomous solo. "She was a wicked witch, but very beautiful. She was also very jealous of the young princess, because the prince loved her more then he did the beautiful witch." He threw his hand forward in an exact replication of Martha's gesture. "When she did that, you could tell just how she felt. So she killed the princess and the prince found her dead. Then the wicked witch got into her golden chariot and rode away, far up into the sky. She was so evil then, that nobody could touch her." He finished and went back to sipping his Pepsi Cola, as we all applauded his absolute comprehension of the dance action that had so baffled his elders.

"Merry Christmas. Coffee, Sir?" How to make Christmas in the tropics? Except for the cheerful greetings of the hotel staff, there were no traces of the holiday anywhere in the city. We had a company party planned for noon, and I set out, determined to somehow summon up Christmas in Rangoon. That afternoon we all piled into cars that took us to a Chinese restaurant for a special holiday meal. It was reputed to be one of several excellent restaurants in the city. The restaurant lived up to its reputation; the meal was magnificent and we all sat happily around in its afterglow and exchanged holiday favors. Luck had somehow directed me to a shop where I was able to find individual cards for everyone. I had carefully chosen each one and circulated around the table handing them out. Lee Letherman passed out little packets from Martha and Bethsabee. Inside carefully folded white papers, I found a pair of cabochon moonstones, a rectangular garnet, and a large emerald cut pink topaz. We all had received unmounted stones encased in jeweler's paper. Amidst a chorus of oohs and aahs, we examined each other's loot. Linda called for a toast. "Here's to *Bijoux* Christmas, 1955!"

"Fly CAT, huh?" Matt Turney gestured to the smiling pilot pictured on the wall poster standing proudly in front of a streamline airplane. Then she gazed out of the air terminal window at the aircraft that awaited us. In her succinct and precise way she encapsulated our dismay at the journey we were about to take to Dacca, the capital city of the eastern section of the divided Pakistan. The airplane was reminiscent of ones I remembered from World War II films, with a grim faced row of paratroopers sitting in a file against the rounded exposed ribs of the unadorned cabin next to the open bay, ready to plunge into space. As the plane took off, we bundled into our overcoats, pulled on our gloves, and wrapped scarves around our throats. A sliver of light from the great outdoors passed through a tiny fissure in the otherwise sealed seams of the fuselage, and with it a chilling draft. Sneezing and coughing, miserable and in bad temper, we arrived. I drew a hot bath immediately and immersed myself, allowing the water to drive the cold from my body. I found extra blankets in the closet, piled them on top of the light cotton throw on the bed, and nestled deep within their warmth, determined not to get sick. My therapy was successful, but luck was not with everyone. A half a dozen of the company remained in their rooms suffering with terrible colds, unable to come down for meals let alone perform. The large company works, *Diversion of Angels* and *Ardent Song* could not be presented. Fortunately all of the female soloists had graduated from roles in the corps, so a cast could be assembled to dance the followers of the revivalist in *Appalachian Spring*. This would open the rearranged program followed by *Errand Into the Maze* and *Cave of the Heart*. Stuart was hale and hearty, Bertram and Bob wan but willing, Martha stoic and stern. She had to dance in every work and finished the evening drawn, exhausted, and sheet white. Her partners had sensed the physical drain and wordlessly rose to her support. Stuart's minotaur-creature of fear was more horrific then ever, and Bob's, husbandman in *Appalachian Spring* glowed with warmth. It was an altogether amazing performance and one never to be repeated or even approached. It also marked a turning point in Martha's performing career and in the approach to the roles she would choreograph for herself. The stage for her future works would become dotted with scenic resting places where her heroines would languish in dramatic postures or engage in striking manipulations of costume elements.

An elegant and handsome Pakistani left the bar and crossed over to us as we entered the reception. He congratulated us and asked us to join him for a drink. "I'm having lemonade but I'm sure I can scrounge up something more exciting." He looked squarely into Ellen Siegle's eyes, "If you'd like, I'll ask?" His penetrating stare was characteristic of the male population in Dacca when they encountered the uncovered faces of the women in the company. The veiled women in this Moslem city were draped with layers of clothing and filled the streets carrying bundles and clutching the hands of children until the sun set and the muezzins sounded. Then, as if some unseen and selective giant vacuum magically whisked them away, the women would miraculously disappear, leaving the city a nocturnal male garrison.

Ellen's handsome swain, a manufacturer of saris, was arduous in the pursuit of her beauty. Ellen thrived on his solicitous attention and in all the commotion this caused in the tight familial gossip of the company and with Martha who doted on intrigue and the possibility of scandal. He invited Ellen, and she invited a few of us, to his factory. He cautioned us of a certain delicacy in this journey and swore us not to reveal the whereabouts of his studio to anyone. All of this lent an extra measure of fascination to the outing. Of course he needn't have worried. Separated from the hotel or the theater, none of us had the foggiest notion of where we were at any time. We left the city and entered the environs, passed through several villages until we arrived at a small whitewashed clay building surrounded by a high wall. He honked the horn, someone opened a gate, and we drove inside an inner courtyard, scattering chickens pecking in the dust. He led us through a low doorway. Inside several looms were laid out horizontally on the earthen floor. Women sat in front of them, their legs descending into shallow pits below. Muslin cloths covered the already woven fabric while nimble fingers tossed shuttles wrapped with silk and gold threads back and forth, and bare feet worked pedals that changed the shutters between each crossing. A chicken wandered in through the open doorway. Our host lifted one of the covers to reveal an exquisite length of shot-silk, bordered with a pattern of gold. The opalescent surface changed from green to crimson as it was touched. He lifted one cover after another, revealing cloths of equally dazzling beauty. He led us out of the building and into another hut where two women working with ancient Singer sewing machines, stitched the tight *cholis* bodices. These machines were identical to the foot pedaled model Aunt Alice used to have. I had grown up watching Auntie sew on the old machine. I often wondered what happened to those wonderful old machines. Now I knew.

Just before New Year's Eve we arrived in Calcutta, our first stop on the vast subcontinent of India. Nowhere before that day had I so questioned the meaning or value of human existence. Families slept on the streets in such numbers that the sidewalks resembled packed hospital wards after a disaster but without beds, blankets, sanitation, or comforts of any kind. A man strained to pull a wagon loaded with kindling because it was cheaper to hire him than it was to feed a bullock. Rickshaw wallahs ran through the streets, pulling wire-spoke-wheel rickshaws, their hard, bare, flattened feet slapping the earthen roads. I turned a corner and came, with a gasp, face to face with a fierce-eyed holy man carrying a trident, his forehead painted with white symbols. Everywhere, the sacred Brahman cows roamed freely. "Why don't you take pictures of our monuments? Take pictures of the filth in your own country."

"Come mister, I'll be your guide, very cheap. Come mister." The young boy grabbed Bertram Ross's right hand and led him away from the gathering of staring men standing between Bertram, his camera, and the young woman with a toddler clinging to her as she nursed an infant hidden in the folds of her wrappings. It was the same young boy we had seen standing in front of the hotel when we arrived, and whose offer then to serve as our guide we had waved off. His proposition seemed now not only prudent but appropriate and wise. Rows of numbered lockers lined the side streets and held the meager possessions of these people, giving them legal addresses and legitimizing their right to endure this existence of misery. The division of India and Pakistan had left thousands disinherited and the government with no apparent solution for the homeless masses. At the same time the Maharani of Jaipur matched with the American, Althea Gibson, in an international tennis competition, was to be married, and preparations for the occasion were a fairy tale of riches come true. Pictures of the painted, jeweled, and ornamented royal elephants and their tenders were enough to boggle the imagination in this land of stark contrasts. A peacock flew from a tree with bare branches thick with sleeping bats. The regal bird opened its opulent tail as it landed and dragged up a cloud of dust as it strutted about, emitting a harsh screech from its elegant throat. The flying nocturnal rodents in the tree above hung upside down like dried fruit, their bodies hidden beneath folded leathery wings. Women in long dark wrappings ran after bullocks, snatched up their warm droppings, and placed the dung to dry in the sun to be used later as fuel for heating and cooking. A man, with his painfully thin frame bare but for a loincloth and turban of homespun cotton, pushed a rotary treadmill which operated a primitive irrigation system, while the government labored to introduce the windmill.

We celebrated New Year's Eve at the home of a friend of Craig Barton. His large and well-appointed flat boasted an enormous patio covering the roof of the downstairs sitting room. It was bedecked with lanterns for the festivities and overlooked stretches of Calcutta transformed into a nighttime loveliness, wrapped in a cloak of darkness, dotted with buttons of light. Ellen Siegle's suitor arrived in Calcutta at the same time that Ellen's mother arrived from the States and swept into the hotel lobby, a ravishingly beautiful woman swathed in fur. The coincidence of timing had all the markings of Martha's heavy-handed interference. Bob Cohan was still making plans to somehow get to Angkor Wat, although the forbidden temples of Cambodia were getting farther and farther away, and the possibility of crossing into Tibet and glimpsing the Dalai Lama was becoming more feasible and equally adventuresome. Donya Feuer had gone to the American Embassy to try and contact her father who was a stage manager touring with the *Porgy and Bess* company in Russia. She had succeeded in lighting Martha's short fuse that exploded without warning at any action that brought attention to Donya's strong individuality. "You've caused an international incident. Just look at you, hanging out in the sun without proper covering, red like a slab of beef. What are we going to do with those shoulder marks in *Diversion of Angels*?"

We had been invited to several concerts of classical Indian dancing, but one was very special. Shanta Rao was giving a performance in our honor. She had championed the revival of Mohini Attam, the female school of Kathakali, and was also an exponent of Bharata Natyam but with a personal approach flavored by her work in the more aggressive and highly controversial Mohini Attam. Her wonderful open face with its square jaw and her broad shoulders separated her immediately from the oval-faced voluptuaries carved in the stone of the temples. I went backstage with the rest of the company to meet this artist, who, like Martha, was a giant on the stage but in reality diminutive. Martha and Shanta Rao greeted each other with a silent moment of genuine mutual respect.

A side trip to Agra took us through the countryside and opened views of everyday life in the interior that we would never have seen in the major cities that dot the coastline. The legendary symmetrical beauty of the Taj Mahal was encased in scaffolding for cleaning and the reflecting pools were a jumble of images disowning the serenity for which they were famous. Our guide on the tour to the nearby Red Fort extolled the masculine prowess of its builder, Shah Jahan. We were taken into his chambers and through those of his wives and his concubines, with their stone screens, carved in lattices of intricate caracoles and arabesques through which peering female eyes could see and not be seen. The inner courtyard was marked off with a huge Parcheesi board and raised thrones where the Shah and his favorite wife would sit beneath a canopy and play, moving chosen concubines from square to square with the throw of the dice. A sly smile crossed Matt Turney's face. "How about that, living doll Parcheesi!"

We were back in the bus on the way to our next stop, a renowned silk merchant whose establishment bore the royal coat of arms, declaring it a purveyor to Her Majesty Victoria, Queen of England and Regent of the British Empire. We were escorted inside where the air was delightfully cooled, purely by the magnificently crafted tropical architecture, and where the walls were covered with shelves glistening with silken saris and gossamer mousselines. We passed through a vestibule where a glass-topped shadow-box table in the center held a royal blue silk carpet, encrusted with jewels bezeled with solid gold cording. A wall-hung shadow box held the triangular insert of a train for a silk peau-de-soie gown, marked with diamantes patterned in a glistening sunburst, designed for Queen Mary. We were brought cups of jasmine tea and sat on soft tooled leather hassocks as one more luxurious sari after another was flung open in front of us. We had no money to purchase anything but functioned as an appreciative Amen chorus for Bethsabee and Martha who pondered, selected, and bought. Our stay in Madras was tantamount to a wonderful tropical holiday. Once again we were hosted by individual families. I was fortunate and stayed with a lovely young couple. They had an airy, comfortable villa in a fine section of the city. He was a tea merchant. I went with their housekeeper to visit one of the markets where foods were sold. There were flies everywhere. They crawled over the faces of little children who had given up the useless effort of brushing them away. A donkey twitched his flank muscles and switched his tail when they landed on an open sore. I suddenly realized that one of the virtues of the pungent curries that seasoned the meats was its counteraction to the attack of flies. They literally covered the butchered slabs, rising in swarms as a portion was lifted for inspection, only to return as it was replaced, causing the chop to resemble a steak encrusted with black peppercorns. Two pullets ran out of a doorway and I began to laugh. Except for a sparse ringlet of feathers around their necks and a few downy tufts hanging askew from their tails, they appeared to have been plucked bare and to have somehow escaped the stewpot, clucking a noisy and naked retreat into the streets. I found a nearby cloth merchant and inquired about bleeding madras. "I beg your pardon sir, but all of our fabrics are of the highest quality. These plaids are dye fast. They do not run, nor do they bleed" I realized that bleeding madras was as foreign here as a New York steak was to a Manhattan restauranteur.

On our day off we were invited to a vegetarian meal prior to an evening performance by Balasaraswati, the recognized leading living exponent of Bharata Natyam and a revered artist. The meal was served on a long, low table. We sat on cushions with our legs folded. A bowl and pitcher were brought around and we washed our hands in streams of warm, lemon-scented water and dried them with soft towels. There was a plantain leaf placed in front of each of us, and aromatic rice, bean pastes, chopped salads, yogurts, and vegetables were served onto these glistening mats. We watched our hosts and imitated them as they gathered the food between cup-shaped fingers, carried it up to the mouth, and with a gentle snap of the thumb, popped it onto the tongue. The aromas and flavors were magnificent and the absence of fats was a welcome cleansing of the palatte.

Balasaraswati stood on stage with her weight resting against one hip, her head and shoulders counterbalanced in the classic peaceful position of repose, an icon of feminine grace, at once delicate and at the same time coiled, ready to lash into motion. She was surrounded by five musicians, who were all masters of their instruments. The tabla player was especially captivating as he drummed his complicated rhythms while singing counter-rhythmic syllables in that wonderful South Indian way so reminiscent of jazz scat singing. The opening pure dance was arduous and blended seamlessly into a padam of expressive narrative dance where the lips, eyes, nostrils, and the entire musculature of her face was featured against the yearnings of her responsive torso. I was in the presence of a great artist, and I wished it never to end.

We left India for a week's stay on the island nation of Ceylon (now Sri Lanka.) The capital city of Colombo was our home base. The days were hot, but the island was verdant, with trees everywhere, bringing shade and purifying the air. At night, the sea breezes brought a lovely cooling. A small bus took us on mountain roads up to Kandy. Along the climb, we passed working elephants moving timber and walking with amazing grace and sureness of foot. Our destination was a performance given by a male troop of Kandian dancers and drummers. Their performance style was virile and exciting and markedly different from anything we had seen in India. In their vibrant red and white costumes, they were a magnificent sight. We stopped for a late supper, and I sampled a fish curry that was the fieriest meal I had ever eaten. I had no idea what kind of fish I had consumed but after several beers to quench the flames racing about my mouth, I was so mellow I ceased to care.

Our performances were beginning to find their own place in the changing and yet routine schedule we followed. The constant repetition of the small repertoire had its benefits. It allowed ensemble passages to become enriched and solo roles to be honed. It also permitted idiosyncrasies to spore and sometimes obscure the original choreographic intent. Peals of raucous laughter drew my attention outside the dressing room door, where the female ensemble gathered in their handsome *Night Journey* costumes. The Daughters of the Night looked strangely bizarre holding each other and laughing with such abandon that their driftwood-pierced hair extensions threatened to become dislodged. "You said what?" Matt and Ellen Van der Hoeven were in the center of the group and tears streamed from their eyes, sending trails of mascara down their cheeks. She said, "What's the count?" I said, "What's the count, hell! What's Helen doing?" Helen McGehee was the Leader of the Chorus, the central figure among the Daughters of the Night. The choreography for the chorus was filled with percussive body contractions executed exactly on the musical pulse, with each pelvic thrust piercing the heart of the beat. Helen had taken to anticipating the beat. Just when all of her followers had become expert in that approach, she suddenly switched to an after-beat echo. Matt had simply given up and decided to follow her, come what may.

Our hotel in Bombay sat on an embankment overlooking the port. The harbor had been aptly nicknamed the Queen's Necklace for its nocturnal resemblance to a royal gorget with its perfect circle of glittering lights. On our arrival, we were invited to a special party in honor of Dag Hammarskjöld, secretary general of the United Nations General Assembly. It was held in a huge tent with a ceiling of gloriously configured, brightly colored cotton pieces, stitched in bold patterns, swirling from mirrored centers. Two ferociously snarling stuffed Bengal tigers benignly guarded the entryway and a red carpet directed us through the festive tables to the magnificent spread of foods and the bar. I was extremely careful of everything I chose to eat. I bypassed the tempting display of crudités, because of the use of human fertilizer and the possibility of internal disease. I drank only bottled water. That night I awoke with a violent gripping in my stomach and rushed to the bathroom, where I stayed ...sick ...very sick. What could have caused this? I finally returned to my bed and after hours of tossing there, alternately crawling back and forth to the bathroom, I narrowed the possibilities of my misery to the only likely culprit. I had drunk a vodka gimlet with ice. I was sure that the ice cubes contained the agent of my malaise. The next day, the doctor visited me and diagnosed a mild case of dysentery. I was put on medication and not being able to hold down food, spent the next two days in my room. By the end of this awful siege, I had lost almost ten pounds. Being a dancer, I looked proudly at my streamlined body, but had little strength to move it about. My first effort to dance was, of all insane things, standing on my head and throwing my legs up against the wall. I had a fear of being upside down and was determined to conquer it so that the cartwheel-into-balance section in *Diversion of Angels* would cease to be a personal nightmare.

By the time we reached New Delhi I was hale and robust again. We were there at the time of the Independence Day celebrations and were allowed to attend the rehearsals in the stadium. Dance from every part of India was on view. What a varied and heterogeneous nation! The dancers were representative of the finest from every province and tribal group. The costuming and musical accompaniment were as diverse as the movement vocabularies. One group, with towering headdresses, seemed strangely akin to the Hopi dancers of the American Southwest. There were men skillfully costumed to appear as if they were on horseback; their dance was a ritual mock battle. The Naga Hill Tribesmen performed an ancient warrior's dance. A group of small boys, from a village bordering Burma, performed with pairs of rounded bell-cups attached to one another with string. As they danced, one of the bell-cups was held and one thrown upwards, landing inside the other with a lovely ringing. We wandered about the open field in the midst of this extraordinary cacophony. Tomorrow they would be presented in an arranged rotation, but now they practiced all at once, somehow hearing only their own music and never violating each other's space or formations.

The newspaper photograph of the company, posed on the steps of the plane when we landed in Karachi, was in marked contrast to its twin on our arrival in Tokyo. No one was waving and there was an aura of fatigue permeating our practiced diplomatic expressions. Karachi, the capital of West Pakistan and a more modern city then Dacca, was the seat of the government. Our stay there was uneventful and we headed for the port city of Abadan, a refinery and shipping center of oil-rich Iran. The air in Abadan was saturated with the heavy scent of oil. I felt as if I had acquired a mineral film on my skin: my tongue seemed coated. I spent the days in my hotel room with the air conditioner on full blast against the oppressive heat and the cloying penetration of petroleum. I could not wait to leave. We loaded into the two-engine DC 3, buckled up and started our trip to Teheran.

The flight took us through mountain passes, and from the 105° Fahrenheit temperature of Abadan we moved toward the cool 60° temperature of Teheran. The overhead rack on the DC 3 was a continuous shelf with a fat elasticized rope holding the articles stowed there. The plane suddenly began to pitch and seemed to be falling through space. Jackets and hats tumbled from the shelves; miraculously, the travel cases remained overhead, either lodged against the elastic rope or sliding noisily back and forth. I gripped the arm rest of my seat. Several of the dancers had pulled out air-sickness bags and some already had their faces buried in them. Martha's face was drawn, white as a sheet. Her eyes stared forward and then, with the next pitch of the plane, shut tightly. The stewardess tried to help but had to return to her seat and strap herself down. "We are not falling. The plane is rising." The collision of frontal systems created an atmosphere that was impossible to navigate and we had to return to Abadan. We disembarked and headed for the waiting area, where the company besieged the restrooms in an all-out, mass invasion. An hour later, we were aboard the DC 4 which carried the scenery and costume. The four-engine plane could rise above the weather and though we were not entirely spared from turbulence, we made it safely to Teheran. Strangely in years to come, Martha would credit this terrifying flight as the inspiration for *Errand Into the Maze* which had its premiere in 1947, some nine years prior to this journey. In fact, this tour would mark Martha's final performance of *Errand,* and precipitate a new era in the Graham company in which Martha would begin to pass on her roles to other dancers.

I stayed in a small hotel in Teheran. My room was compact and tidy with beige walls that gave it a dingy appearance. The hotel was run by a devout Parsi family. Above my bed they had hung a painting of a man either asleep or laid out on a funerary bier. Above his head a raptor loomed, wings and talons spread wide. It was rather gruesome, but I would not risk offending the concierge by asking him to remove it. I could not help but shudder as I remembered riding by the Tower of Silence where the dead were placed and where the kites and vultures constantly circled overhead.

We did not meet the Shah but were invited to the palace as guests of the Queen. The opulence of the public rooms was overwhelming. The elegance of the Queen in her beautifully tailored western clothes was the complete antithesis of the women that filled the streets of Teheran in their shapeless black wrappings. Western culture had made strong incursions here but the grasp of Islamic fundamentalism was tenacious. The State Department had decided, for what I am sure were non-artistic reasons, that our appearance in Baghdad was of extreme importance. Bethsabee was adamant in her desire to have the company appear in Israel. For reasons never properly explained, the performances in Baghdad were canceled. While we could not have traveled to Israel from Baghdad, we were able to do so from Iran, but this was not something the State Department wished officially to sponsor. Bethsabee underwrote the passage and we flew from Teheran directly to Tel Aviv.

Israel was different from any country that we had visited. There was a sense of pioneering and group purpose that seemed to be a part of the very fiber of existence, as essential as any vital fluid. The arts were a necessity, a part of this vitality, and our visit was front-page news. Although French was the diplomatic language, Israel had long been under a British mandate and English was the second tongue. European and American performing arts were greatly in evidence. There was an excellent symphony orchestra, a fledgling opera, several small modern dance companies, and the ubiquitous recordings of American popular music. We visited Gertrude Kraus, an exponent of German modern dance, in her home in the artist village of Ein Hod. Mia Arbatova taught classic ballet in her studio in Tel Aviv, but there was no professional classical company waiting for her aspiring students. We performed in Tel Aviv at the Habimah, the national theater founded by Russian immigrant disciples of Stanislavsky. Our performances in this charged atmosphere were filled with excitement and a new energy. Our engagements in Tel Aviv, Jerusalem, and Haifa were filled to capacity and we presented the entire repertoire. Martha and Bethsabee were housed in the Dan, Tel Aviv's five star hotel, and the rest of the company were put up next-door at the Kate Dan. We gave a lecture demonstration as our initial performance event and the ecstatic response of the audience, crowded with dancers and other artists, was overwhelming.

That night as I lay on my bed ready for sleep but still wide awake with excitement, I heard the rap of a pebble against the window glass, and then another. I went to the window and looked down at the street below. The figure of a young man was caught in the light of the street lamp. "Dani, come, we go!" It was Abshalom Sela, one of the dancers from the Inbal Dance Company. I dressed quickly and went down. He took me to his family home where his mother had prepared a magnificent spread of Yemenite foods; I sat down to a meal with his parents and seven brothers. They were all part of the Magic Carpet enterprise, in which the Israeli government had transported the Jewish populations of Yemen and Aden to Israel, the Promised Land, *Ha'aretz*. "Tomorrow we go to Masada for a *cumsitz*." The next day, we arrived at the base of the desert fortress where, in Biblical times, a group of zealots had held out until their death against a Roman legion, rather than submit to conquerors and slavery. It was dusk by the time we completed the arduous climb to the summit. Around a blazing campfire, a group huddled, swaying and singing to the accompaniment of ceramic drums and wooden flutes. Abshalom leaped over the flames and began an amazing performance circling the fire, dancing in a crouch, a dagger clamped between his teeth. The voices dropped out and the drumming and the sound of the flute grew wilder. We sang, danced, laughed, and drank spiced coffee until daybreak. "*Boker or*, morning light, now we sleep!" Back at the hotel, I closed my eyes to slumber, happy and content.

Martha was scheduled to perform *Errand Into the Maze* on our return to the Habimah. It had been out of the repertoire since that fateful performance in Dacca. She was agitated and fitful and shunned rehearsals, spending her time designing and having a new costume made for herself. The day of the performance, we were told that we could not watch from the wings and were advised by Stuart to stay clear of Martha. Linda and I went up to the projection booth. Instead of the usual white costume, boldly slashed with black rick-rack that stood out so clearly against the wishbone shaped sculpture of Isamu Noguchi's set and the black and bone costume of the Creature of Fear, a strangely garbed figure stood on stage as the curtain rose. Martha was clothed in a red, white, and black dress with a flying back panel and a large green fig leaf appliquéed on the white front panel just beneath her navel. Her hair was coifed with an elongated horizontal chignon at the nape of her neck and dangling side-locks falling against her cheek bones, reminiscent of the *peot* curls worn by devout Hassidic men. The ornate costume undermined the simplicity of the concept and diluted the intensity of the movement, causing a confusion of intent. It was never to be seen again, and this was to be Martha's final performance in that role.

At last Esta arrived and we spent a glorious time together. As the tour began to wind down, we were left with free days to do with as we wished. I had so much to share with her and we had so much to discover together. We roamed through the souks and savored the scents rising from the open sacks of pungent spices, rifled through the hand-embroidered Bedouin dresses, bargained with the merchants seated over a cup of tea, visited the ancient and modern sites, climbed the hillsides and picked bunches of wild poppies which we brought back to decorate our hotel room in Jerusalem. When we returned to our room after dinner, the bed was turned down and the poppies were gone. The next morning after breakfast, they were back in place. "*Calaniot lo tov ba lylah*. No to sleep with *adoni*." The little Moroccan woman who cleaned our room was emphatic. We were not to go to sleep with the poppies in the room. With an involved pantomime and spurts of English and Hebrew mixed into a charming cocktail, she told us that we would be drugged. *"Lo geveret! Lo adoni!* Madam, Mister, no!"

"Bye... Catch you in Paris... Call me when you get back... Good luck getting through customs..." The tour was over and everyone went his or her own way. After a last day in Israel, Esta and I started out for Europe and the honeymoon we had never had. It was winter and cold, but we were excited and happy. It rained our entire three days in Athens, clearing up the day we left. We visited the Acropolis and wandered through the drizzle into a little restaurant. The waiter and I had no language of communication and the menu was totally incomprehensible. He gestured that I follow him and took me back to the kitchen. He opened pots and I sniffed and pointed ending up with a wonderful meal. This little place became our sanctuary and we were greeted with affection by our new friend whenever we arrived. He'd bring out things he thought we'd like and we ended up sampling most of the menu along with some special treats prepared just for us.

Rome was clear and crisp. I had the phone number of an old friend, Ted Barnett, and called him when we arrived. I hadn't seen him in years. He had settled in Rome, was enamored of the city and loved to show off *"Mia Roma."* He took us to his favorite vista points, pointing out architectural wonders with sweeping gestures. *"Como se dice in Inglese...edificio?"* "Building, Ted, building." I couldn't hold back the laughter. In the years that Ted had settled in Rome, he had gone Italian, stumbling over his native tongue.

Paris was windy, gray, and leafless, and London was either covered in rain or wrapped in fog. We spent our days in the museums and our evenings at the ballet or the theater.

"How're you doing, world travelers?" Mother laughed and embraced us and welcomed us back home. We settled into our apartment on 57th Street and had fun finding the right places for all the momentos of the journey. At the Salvation Army, I found a lovely, round, cherry wood Queen Anne dining table, cut the legs down to coffee table height and polished it to a warm glow. We got a wok and threw a sukiyaki dinner party, greeting our friends at the door swathed in silken kimonos.

In the final days of December, 1956, I stood at the nursery window at the Klingenstein Pavilion with my nose pressed against the glass, making silly faces at the little girl who had just been born into our lives. The nurse brought another baby out and I turned to see Stuart Hodes going through an identical new-papa routine. Both of our daughters had been conceived in the Holy Land; they were born a day apart. On the cusp of the new year, I stood outside Mount Sinai hospital hailing a taxi. It was a frigid morning and I turned up my overcoat collar and wrapped a muffler around my mouth and nose. An empty cab spotted my gloved hand and approached. As I stepped forward to grasp the door handle, the taxi pulled off. The cabby rolled forward to where Stuart, who had just come out of the entrance door, was waving. Stuart opened the cab door and asked the driver to wait while he got his wife. He gestured to me and we went inside together and brought Esta and Linda out with our Gabrielle and their Catherine wrapped in swaddling. As we piled into the taxi, the cabby looked in the rear-view mirror and compounded the affront with a shrug. "Thought you were going to Harlem." We chose to shun him silently. Cuddled together against the blustering winter wind, we started our journey home and our new lives as parents.

Photographic study from *Nocturne*. Photo: John Lindquist.

Donald McKayle. Photographic study by Marcus Blechman.

6

RAINBOW ROUND MY SHOULDER

Gaby sat directly in front of me, with her legs folded, her elbows resting on her thighs, and her knuckles supporting her chin as she gazed intently at me. I raised my body up from the elongated lunge that had brought my palms to the floor with a slap, and flung my arms open wide and my head upward. Gaby's little body echoed the rhythmic rise and fall of the movement, and the expression on her face grew serious as her eyes filled with concern.

> Takes rocks and gravel to make-a
> To make a solid road oh well-a
> But it never gets done lordy mama
> Lessen captain's got a gun oh well-a

Three summers before, when Gabrielle was just six months old, I started the seed and gestation process that would eventually give birth to *Rainbow Round My Shoulder*.

It was a long drive from Manhattan up to Crystal Lake, a summer resort nestled on the shores of one of the many lovely lakes that dot the some-times rugged, sometimes rolling countryside of endless greenery in upstate New York. The Catskill Mountains brought back fond memories of Camp Woodland. I enjoyed passing through the charming one street towns. Discovering a previously unknown niche was a happy home coming. I had been hired for the weekend as the "dance talent." I wasn't quite sure what I was going to do, but I knew I was responsible for dancing in three shows. Except for *Saturday's Child*, I had no solo works. Les Pine and Joe Sargent were the directors of the entertainment staff. They had assured me that it was a piece of cake and not to worry. They had worked with me on a sketch they called *Ash Can* for an Actors Equity Broadway benefit and I had composed the movement for it on the spot. This, they said, was just more of the same and required no special preparation. I was not so sure.

"Hello, I'm Leon Bibb." "Hi, I'm Donald McKayle." " Joe and Les told me that you'd be here this weekend. Maybe there's something we can do together." "Oh, I'd love that. I've got your record. It's great. How about 'Tol' My Captain'?" Leon and I bound ourselves together with a length of chain we found behind the kitchen. Leon held pieces of rock in his hands. The rehearsal was a wonderful happening. We fed off of each other's creativity, inventing the moments as we progressed. The only sound accompanying Leon's rich baritone was the crashing of the rocks together and the sound of my breathing. The busy preparatory activity in the dining hall came to an abrupt halt. The din of clattering dishes and silverware ceased as all eyes turned to the stage. If the power of that moment could be accurately gauged by the expressions on the faces of the staff watching us or in their spontaneous applause when we finished, we were creating something very special.

"Ladies and gentlemen, the stirring voice of Leon Bibb and the powerful dancing of Donald McKayle performing 'Tol' My Captain,' a chain-gang song from the prisons of the American South, a song of men who must do forced labor, breaking rock in the hot sun under the watchful eye of an overseer leaning on his rifle." Applause followed the MC's announcement as we waited in the wings. Leon, holding the rocks, looked back at me curled on the ground beside him. We nodded to each other. "Here goes." The rocks crashed together and Leon entered the stage with a labored gait, dragging the chain behind him. As he lurched forward heavily, I emerged crawling sidewards, traveling behind him. The clanking of the chain and the crashing of the rocks accompanied our mean journey. I finally found myself free of the chain and soaring defiantly as Leon's voice grew darker and more defiant. A culminating leap brought me back to the chain, which I wound about my wrists with a snap, pulling it tensely against Leon's ankles. Leon opened his arms wide as his voice glided upward to the next octave. I fell to the floor as the rocks crashed together and the lights went black.

"Bob, it was really magical, powerful stuff. There's a whole dance here." "Oh yes, the prison songs are amazing. Have you heard any of the Hall-Johnson arrangements?" I sat with Robert DeCormier in his Greenwich Village apartment leafing through song collections, manuscripts, and onion skin copies of arrangements that Bob and his partner Milton Okun had done for vocal groups that specialized in folk music. The songs from the southern chain gangs were unique. They were an accompaniment to heavy physical work and their uneven musical structure paralleled the rise and fall of the pickaxes swung by the men as they sang, ending in an explosion of breath that added a beat to the measure between song lines. The lyrics were in turn biting, sardonic, angry, plaintive, filled with bitterness and despair, or wistful with an ever present glint of hope. What to choose from this rich source? I knew I would use "Rocks and Gravel" from Leon Bibb's album and that he would be the lead singer calling out to the response of a male chorus. I had already had one exploratory session with several dancers and the movement ideas had flowed easily and potently. The energy in the room had been unmistakable, and an eagerness and desire to be part of the evolving work was everywhere. I had carried that excitement to a solo rehearsal with Mary Hinkson. The dreamlike images that emerged to Leon's rendition of "Dink's Blues" formulated the female role as a symbol of freedom for the imprisoned men. "What about this one?" Bob strummed heavy, strident chords on his guitar and began to sing.

> I've got a rainbow, huh
> Tied all around my shoulder, huh
> I'm goin' home, huh
> My Lord, I'm goin' home

The melody was short, spare, driving. The coded lyrics were filled with despair, but always held an ever present glimmer of hope. Rainbow was the prison slang for the tool used to break rock for road beds. The pickaxes glistened as they were swung, sometimes creating their own fleeting rainbows, arcing spectrums of color reaching into space and quickly vanishing. We had found the thematic anchor for the work and the title *Rainbow Round My Shoulder*. I gathered a group of men together: Harold Pierson, Jaime Rogers, Jay Fletcher, Gus Trikonis, Charles Moore, and Alfred DeSio. We began to work on the opening dance to "Rocks and Gravel."

The curtain opened; the lights came up on the cyclorama. One after another, the seven of us slowly emerged, silhouetted against a hot amber sky, chained to each other with clasped hands, our faces flung back as if slapped, our backs rounded over with an imposed weight, rising up only to be slapped again. The movement was relentless and purposefully repetitive. Our bodies were being used as tools, and yet an ever-present defiance colored the movement with a sardonic and seething rage and a dangerous humanity. The men collapsed on the ground for the midmorning break and their minds immediately filled with visions of freedom. Their varied musings were personified in the dream figure of a woman, a composite of all their longings, all their fantasies, alluring, tender, nurturing, and always just out of reach.

Working with Mary Hinkson was an unbelievable joy. Movement just seemed to pour out. The images were clear and exquisitely revealed in her inspired dancing. She entered as if lifting a slip over her head, dropping it, and stepping into the pleasure of a gentle shower, delighting in the feel of the water running down her body, anointing her limbs with scented lotion, and reveling in her own loveliness. She was at once free, a flighted bird, and then a rooted reed bending supply in a violent storm; the sensual caress of intimacy, and then the prison visit window clanging shut; the face in a snapshot that would never be seen again, and then the tiny disappearing figure waving farewell on the train platform. The respite over, the men must return to their labor. One young man clinging to his reverie, recalls the hot and heavy pursuit of a girl called Nancy. Mary returns transformed into a teenager, delighted with her blossoming woman's body and the power she suddenly has over the boys. She flounces on, high stepping, a cabbage rose bouncing teasingly atop her head, knowing she is being carefully watched and pretending not to notice her admirer. She leads him on a merry chase and then, with playful triumph, slips out of his embrace. Alfred DeSio, finding his arms empty is briefly thrust back into the reality of the prison work, but suddenly imagines the touch of female hands on his shoulders. He races back in time to realize that these are the hands of the only woman he has ever really known. Mary, now a young mother looking for her missing son, finds him forgetful of his chores and lost in play. These are his mother's hands. "Yes ma'am, yes ma'am, yes ma'am!" Al was suddenly calling out loud, deep in his thoughts, tears rolling down his cheeks. He had a beautiful voice and picked up the lyrics, blending in with the tenors.

> I can't read her letter for crying
> My time's so long
> Lord my time's so long

It was my turn to move out as Al whirled back into the pattern of the men's dance. I picked up his lead and joined into the song. The singers were arranged on steps leading from the orchestra floor up to the stage level where Leon stood. The guitarist and Milt Okun, the conductor, were at the base of the pyramid. There was a wonderful rhythmic swaying and a charged performance electricity rocking the chorus as they sang.

> That old letter read about dying
> My tears run down
> Lord my tears run down

Mary, now my wife, entered again as if emerging from a dream, coming to take away the rage that consumes me and to reclaim the man she married. It is difficult but we find each other in the dance and she tries to heal the scars of injustice, drain off the bitterness and fill me with her love. She is gone and desperation echoes in the emptiness that remains. Something explodes inside of me and I goad the men into a break for freedom. Shots ring out. Al and I are hit. He dies in the arms of his companions. I make it a few steps further reaching for the arms of freedom. As I fall dead, Mary's dream figure waves a last good-bye and fades.

> Another man done gone
> They killed another man
> He had a long chain on
> Another man done gone.

The audience would not stop applauding. The next day the phone rang incessantly with well-wishers, congratulations, people who had crowded back stage at the Kaufman Auditorium but who just had to talk to me again. "Hello, Donald, this is Jack McGiffert. I'm Aida Lioy's husband. She told me all about your triumph yesterday and convinced me that it is a must for *Camera Three*. Do you know our program? We're on CBS every Sunday morning."

Sunday was the day devoted to culture by the television industry. The morning hours were filled with programs featuring the arts. Drama, dance, music, literature, and the visual arts would find their way into presentations of biblical or inspirational texts sponsored by the religious community. You could find a costume drama on *Look Up And Live* or a dramatic ballet on *Lamp Unto Thy Feet*. *Camera Three* was different in that it had no doctrinaire sponsor. It was a secular network presentation with a broad cultural focus. I remembered all too well my last encounter with *Omnibus* and the narrow, racially biased outlook of the Sunday afternoon sponsors.

"Donald, should I shave?" Still holding the telephone receiver in my hand, I rubbed the sleep from my eyes and squinted at the clock on the bedside table. The illuminated radial dial read 4:05. The darkness in the room told me it was still nighttime, and that I should still be asleep. "Who is this?" "It's me, Jay. I wasn't sure how I should look for camera." "Just come as you are and bring your razor with you. We can decide when we look at the monitor, or we could just use it to slit your throat." There was no use trying to get the remaining hour of scheduled sleep. I was now wide awake. We had had a lengthy dry rehearsal the day before at the CBS studios on 57th Street between 10th and 11th Avenues; today we were on camera. The shoot was at the movie house converted into a television stage on 9th Avenue and 54th Street. We had decided on an opening cameo. I entered against a dawn cyclorama. A dog barked in the distance and the sounds of early morning filled in around me. I bent down and rose effortlessly, as if lifting a heavy object to my shoulder. As my body settled into an arrested pose, Leon entered singing. He crossed down to a rustic table and sat on the edge. I began to dance in pounding, scooping movements. As Leon sang the last line, the picture faded to black and the camera picked up the host, James McAndrew, to introduce the show. This segment was to be repeated at the end of the show using all of the men. Leon and Joe Crawford, one of the singers with the most lilting light tenor voice, had decided on the song and made an instant vocal arrangement. I had choreographed the passages on the spot, and it proved to be an excellent frame for the dance in this particular setting.

"Liane, just you wait and you'll see I'm right. Won't she, Daddy?" I picked up Liane, who was not yet a year old, and rested her on my knee.

Gabrielle kept talking to her and, though Liane had no words yet to answer back, she seemed to comprehend her sister's explanation. She shook her head with disbelief that today she would see her father dancing on the television.

Our call at the television theater was at 7:00 in the morning. We had an hour to get warmed up, find our way around the studio, and prepare ourselves. We had met the camera crew and the technical staff when we had our dry run with the director, John Desmond. Now we were surrounded by all the other personnel that worked behind the scenes to make the shows happen. The ones that seemed to be catching the dancers, attention were the concessionaires who spread out a table of pastries, fruit juice, and coffee. I wandered around the cameras which were mounted on pedestals with thick rubber wheels for quiet maneuvering. I did a few small jumps and realized there was absolutely no spring to the surface on which we were to perform, that underneath the gray battleship linoleum was only a poured concrete slab. Soon it was time for camera blocking. A stage manager with earphones called "Places!" We started the process, listening to the director's voice over the loudspeaker and re-orienting ourselves to an offstage that was next to the camera, alongside the operator and the cable manipulator. The singers were gathered in a semicircle around an overhead boom microphone. They were next to the table where Leon sat for his on-camera opening solo, singing into his own overhead microphone. The rehearsal went smoothly and except for a few changes in the new prologue and epilogue, it was exactly as planned. We met the host, James McAndrew, and listened to his introductory and closing remarks. The writer had equated the thrust and breadth of my creation to the works of Berlioz, Dostoyevsky, and Goya in which beauty had been wrung from misery. We were given a break and time for us to get into makeup and for the director to give notes to the crew. The makeup room was an entirely new experience. We sat in large cushioned revolving chairs, like the ones in barber shops, while two makeup technicians applied what we would need for camera. A hairdresser stood by. These technicians followed us onto stage and stood around watching the monitor with boxes of tissues to blot excessive perspiration and combs and brushes for off-camera touch-ups. On the way to the stage I passed a room where a sixteen-millimeter film camera was set up in front of a monitor to record the direct shoot that was to be beamed out live to all CBS hookups across the country. This kinescope would be the remaining record of that performance.

Liane giggled with delight and ran noisily into my arms when I returned home. Gaby stood by with a happy glow about her face and an expression that told me she had a hundred things to say as soon as I was ready to give her my undivided attention. "Oh, Donald, you should have seen Liane. She kept going to the back of the TV trying to see how you got in there." Liane giggled, tore herself away from Esta and ran over to the television set. "Daddy, it was just like before, but different." "How so, Gaby?" "Well, you were dancing but the space was moving around you, and sometimes you were very close, and then you'd be far off again like before." Yes, it was different dancing before a camera. I missed that dark space out front in the theater, hearing the little coughs, the rustling of playbills, whispered conversations, and other small sounds of life. In its stead was a silent roving Cyclops with its large staring glass eye and an entourage of earnest gentlemen-in-waiting following after their inquisitive master.

"Donald, do you get *The New Yorker* magazine?" "Hi, Mary, everyone's been calling and talking about how beautiful you danced, people I bump into on the street, the students at Juilliard and at the studio. What's in *The New Yorker*?" "You've got to pick up a copy. There's a story, a little piece of magazine fiction, that describes our duet in *Rainbow* as a sort of moment in the life of one of the characters who's at home Sunday morning having breakfast and watching TV. It's just a bit and gives no credits but it's us to a tee." "Oh, Mary, great news! Papa Shawn called. We've been invited to perform *Rainbow* at Jacob's Pillow." Ted Shawn had been deeply moved by the telecast and had filled my ear with compliments and grateful thanks at what he termed "my falling heir to his credo, celebrating the power and beauty of men in dance." We would appear on the program with Barton Mumaw, the former leading dancer of his men's group, performing *The Banner Bearer*, thus creating a bridge across the generations and thrusting the continuity of his aesthetic strongly into the public eye. The summer he had invited us to Jacob's Pillow to present *Games* and *Nocturne*, he had declared himself a fan. The programs at the Pillow were a mixture of dance genres, with modern, classical, and world dance forms always represented. Marina Svetlova was to dance the *Dying Swan* just before *Rainbow Round My Shoulder*. She arrived, carrying a shaker intended for the dispensing of grated parmesan cheese. It was filled with powdered rosin which she proceeded to sprinkle over the entire stage. The crew swept the stage for us but the residue of the powder clung in the crevices between the floor boards and was a disaster for us, tearing at the soles of our bare feet and catching our thighs as we lunged into slides. After a treacherous dress rehearsal, we returned to the theater to find Mme. Svetlova's lethal weapon and hide it from her. As we entered the hall we heard the music for "Rocks and Gravel" playing and there was the stage crew, dancing their hearts out in a replication of what they had remembered from our performance. Front and center was the young Charles Reinhart (later to become director of the American Dance Festival and one of the leading figures in the international growth of Modern Dance.) Charlie was giving instructions to his fellows as they joyously danced, oblivious to our presence, sweat running down their faces, screaming in unison as they jumped forward.

Jack McGiffert's promise that there would be another Donald McKayle opus on *Camera Three* became fact the following year. *Rainbow Round My Shoulder* had been so successful that he plumbed my repertoire for other works that would have the same pungent ingredients: vibrant group dancing, vital pivotal characters, choral singing surrounding rich solo voices, and an American story that reached the heart. I listened to all his specifications and replied without a moment's hesitation, "I've got the work you're looking for."

Remounting *They Called Her Moses* was exciting for me. I asked Robert DeCormier to restructure the music with the idea of tightening the sprawling fifty-minute work into the requisite television half-hour format. I also pared down the cast by combining characters. The work was set in the final moments in the life of Harriet Tubman. Realizing that her health was failing, she gathered her friends around her and led her own funeral service, singing the songs that had been so important to her as a conductor on the underground railroad. With this theatrical stroke, I was able to travel freely in time and place, and the work achieved a focus that had been missing. Jacqueline Walcott, who had played the child in the original version, *Her Name Was Harriet*, took on the role of the young Harriet, with Miriam Burton as her vocal counterpart, the dying Harriet. Arthur Mitchell and Kathleen Stanford were the couple with a newborn infant carried in a basket, determined that their child would never live as a slave. Robert Powell was the Quaker boy who befriended the frightened and lonely slave child, played by Sylvia Waters. Carmen DeLavallade and I were the young lovers who chose dangerous and uncertain flight rather than suffer possible separation on the auction block. The work was powerful as a television dance drama and the music was published by Lawson-Gould as a cantata for chorus, solo voice, and narrator and enjoyed regular performances by choral groups around the country.

"Mr. McKayle, this is Gian Carlo Menotti speaking. I would like you to come to Spoleto this summer and bring your wonderful ballets, *Games*, and *Rainbow Round My Shoulder*. It is very important. You will come, yes?" "Yes," I replied, without hesitation. An invitation to participate in the Festival Of Two Worlds in Spoleto, Italy! It was, a real measure of recognition and artistic arrival. "Good, we have a meeting at the office on 57th Street, upstairs in the Steinway building. Arthur Mitchell, you know him, yes? He will call you about when."

Arthur had become a real star with the New York City Ballet, which for a black male dancer was quite a feat. George Balanchine's description of ballet in answer to John Martin's query at a symposium on dance held in the auditorium of the Museum of Modern Art some years prior had never left me. "Ballet, she is an exquisite woman, with skin the color of a peeled apple." This, from the master of the new American ballet, could not possibly give Arthur a foothold. By description, he was either patently unfit and unwelcome, or more charitably, a tolerated interloper. The male presence in Balanchine's world was of secondary importance, primarily a foil for the presentation of the female figure in motion, and Arthur's chiseled, handsome features and glowing brown skin would be ideal for the task of showing off Balanchine's idealized ballerina. In fact, Balanchine never used Arthur as an exotic, but cast him in roles which were perfect for his technical and performance abilities. The only other black face in the New York City Ballet at that time was another male dancer, a former co-cast member of *House Of Flowers*, Louis Johnson. Louis appeared in Frederick Ashton's *Illuminations* as one of the four cavaliers that partnered Tanaquil LeClerq in the role of Sacred Love. Louis had been trained in Washington, DC, at the Jones-Heywood School of Ballet, which had also produced Chita Rivera and Sylvester Campbell.

Arthur's administrative role in the formulation of what Gian Carlo Menotti called New American Ballets had evolved from his *de facto* assignment as assistant to Joe Layton, one of the three choreographers. Paul Taylor and I were the others. We both had dancers from our own companies and fellow colleagues that we could pool to do our works. Joe worked mainly in commercial theater and chose his casts by the time-honored Broadway audition procedure. His singular contribution to the personnel that would compose the company was Ralph Lynn. Ralph was the brother of Bambi Lynn, the lovely, lyric dancer that Agnes DeMille had used so effectively in *Oklahoma*, the show that had forever changed the role of dance in musical theater. Ralph had let his dance career lie fallow for a while and had been working as a stage manager. Putting together a company which would please the three choreographers had been left to Arthur, who was also participating as a dancer. Arthur was excellent at this task, exhibiting a facility and political finesse that would serve him well as spearhead of his emerging company, Dance Theatre of Harlem.

Paul was to do one work on the major program, a dance called *Meridian* which was designed as a trio for himself and two other dancers. He would bring his company members, Dan Wagoner and Akiko Kanda, to perform their original roles and would flesh out the choreography with other dancers in group passages that were to be added. He had chosen one dancer as his contribution to the team, a young student from Germany whom I had taught at Juilliard. She was an unusual artist: Pina Bausch. My contribution to the program was the largest, as two of my works were to be presented, *Games* and *Rainbow Round My Shoulder*. I chose Dudley Williams, William Louther, and Robert Powell, who together with myself, Arthur, Dan, and Ralph, would comprise the male ensemble for *Rainbow*

Round My Shoulder. Mary Hinkson would repeat her role as female soloist. Kathleen Stanford, Mabel Robinson, and Akiko would be the three girls in *Games*. Mary would make her debut as a vocalist, singing the songs with me. The rehearsals would start in a rented studio in Manhattan with me, and with Joe Layton, who was doing a new choreography to a score by Carlos Chavez. Paul would work in his own studio on the trio, setting his times around our needs and completing the new group passages in Spoleto. There was to be a program of small works, mostly premieres, to be presented later in the festival; it was to be rehearsed in Spoleto. Arthur was in charge of all the scheduling. He also would demonstrate for Joe Layton, who was skilled as an idea-man and a fine director but was not a mover.

Finally we were in Spoleto, a tiny Italian village nestled in the Umbrian hillside. It was a town of historic importance with its own Roman amphitheatre and aqueduct. Its fourteenth-century chapel, situated perfectly on a rising knoll, was a jewel of design and acoustics. Spoleto had two fine theaters: the large house, Il Teatro Nuovo, and the Caio Melisso, a miniature opera house of exquisite proportions. Menotti had rediscovered this sleeping city and brought it back to its former glory. He was now enthroned in the hearts of the townspeople as the new Duke of Spoleto. I was taken to my residence in the home of a local family, a room with my own adjacent bathroom. I also had use of the kitchen and parlor. My room had a small bed, a chair, an armoire to hang my clothes, and a dresser with a mirror, a porcelain washbasin and pitcher. The tall narrow window in the corner looked out on the winding cobblestone street that curved around to the front door. The bathroom was filled with sunlight pouring in from a high horizontal window that was hinged at the base and opened and shut with pull chains. I stood on the edges of the ball and claw-footed bathtub to see what was outside: a magnificent view of rolling hills, farmhouses, orchards, stone fences, and a small stream. I unpacked my suitcase, gathered together my rehearsal clothes and audio tapes, and went out to explore the town.

This was the third year of the festival which had started in Spoleto in 1958. The city was very proud of its role as the new cultural Mecca and had proceeded happily with the arduous and painstaking work of restoring the Roman amphitheatre, as well as mounting a stage for outdoor performances in the market place in the center of town. The year before, Jerome Robbins' Ballets USA had performed to enthusiastic response, and the first year John Butler's modern ballets had opened the festival. We had run into an unfortunate setback during our rehearsal period in New York and Gian Carlo was anxious to get everything back on course. Joe Layton had not been successful with his ballet making. Movement invention had dried up, and no amount of craft, professionalism, or showmanship could fill that void. He seemed to lack direction or view-point. Arthur had literally given up on supplying movement ideas, so Joe eventually withdrew from the project. Gian Carlo had brought in Herbert Ross to create the new ballet and Herbert had brought along his wife Nora Kaye, the former ballerina with American Ballet Theatre and the New York City Ballet. She was the brilliant interpreter of the dramatic works of Antony Tudor and the center of Jerome Robbins' sensational explorations into the procreative cycle of spiders, *The Cage*.

The rehearsal hall was the same size as the stage and was even con-structed with the same gentle rake that sloped upward from the orchestra pit, giving an excellent view to the audience but creating hazards for our dancers. Pirouettes in place were not a great problem but a chain of turns going downstage threatened to spill the dancers off the stage edge. Leaps upstage were a constant surprise as the landing foot hit the floor sooner than expected.

Gian Carlo seemed genuinely beguiled by the performances of *Games*, *Rainbow Round My Shoulder*, and the trio version of *Meridian*. He was surrounded by a staff of designers and technicians, and they all began to speak at once in Italian with occasional short forays into English for our benefit. Nora and Herbert were in a small caucus with Arthur and kept turning from their huddle to point to an individual dancer while making notes. Paul stood on the side smiling enigmatically. The dancers clumped together, exchanging stories about their accommodations. The stage manager was bilingual and our link with the staff and crew. To be ready in two weeks for the *prova generale*, the final dress rehearsal that was traditionally attended by the press and critics, was an enormous task. The local chorus had to learn the music for *Rainbow Round My Shoulder*. The set for *Games* had to be built. Paul had to set the group passages in *Meridian*. Herbert had to choreograph an entire ballet. Gian Carlo was filled with optimism about the successful completion of this gargantuan schedule. He gave a sense of security to all of us. *"Bravi tutti*. Now we must talk soon about the second program for the Caio Melisso. We meet Friday for a risotto at my villa. Until then, *Ciao."*

Rainbow rehearsals were in the morning and *Games* rehearsals were after lunch. The dancers spent the rest of the time divided between sessions with Paul and rehearsals with Herbert and Nora. I was free to visit the scene shop and watch the set for *Games* come together or sit in on the choral rehearsals for *Rainbow Round My Shoulder*. The stage manager had assigned a sturdy Wollensak reel-to-reel tapedeck to me for the *Rainbow* rehearsals, but I was participating as a dancer and needed someone to work the playback. "The *bobina*? No problem, it is all arranged." "Who will be in charge?" "Lui." He pointed out one of the men, and I went over and gave him the rehearsal tape. "From the beginning please, Louie. *Da capo per favore,* Louie." It wasn't until the end of that week that it suddenly became apparent to me that there was something behind the pleasant smile that he gave me every time I called his name. After rehearsal, I went over to him and ventured a question. "Louie...?" Immediately the secret smile again as he turned to face me. "*Como si chiamo?* What is your name?" "Giuseppe." This time the smile became laughter that broke spontaneously between us. I had misinterpreted the stage manager's *lui* as he pointed him out to me. I had been calling Giuseppe, *Him.* Bob Powell, with a chuckle, recounted how his housekeeper bowed to him the first evening he arrived and said, "Sera," to which he had replied, "Robert," thinking an exchange of names was being requested. "Well, it soon dawned on me that there were too many people, both men and women, with the name Sarah. They were all just being friendly, saying 'Evening' to me."

The sound coming from the room where the singers were rehearsing was glorious and though the melodies were undeniably familiar, I could not fathom the language they were singing. I opened the door quietly and went inside. Howard Roberts was conducting the Italian singers. He stopped the rehearsal with a tapping of his baton on his music rack. "*Buon giorno, maestro.* Gentlemen, our choreographer, Donald McKayle." The chorus applauded briefly before returning to their scores. I saw Julian Jackson, Mary Hinkson's husband, sitting in the back row and went over to him. Julian had volunteered to sing and had been seated with the baritones. I looked over his shoulder at the score in amazement. There were two lines of lyrics. The top line was in English and the line below was a phonetic transliteration for the Italian choir.

> Heard that my woman gonna leave me
> Herd dat mai uoman gona liv mi

Not only were the words unintelligible, but the vocal sound was also out of character. The singers were all trained in *bel canto* and the velvety, rounded, and covered tones that they produced had nothing to do with the wide open, raw vocal sound required for the work songs. This was especially true on the grunts and intoned calls that gave these songs their special character.

"Well, what do you propose we do? We cannot bring an American choir over." "Gian Carlo, I asked them to sing along with the audio tape and listen to the sound of the American voices. It worked wonderfully. Also you have the main vocal line sung on the tape by Leon Bibb and none of the singers can duplicate his authenticity. The sound engineer seems to think he can blend the live and recorded music and produce a completely acceptable mixture." "Well, Donald, you are most adamant. Perhaps you are right. We'll see." I left Gian Carlo and headed for the *mercato* to find something to eat before the afternoon rehearsal. I took the path through the narrow street lined with antique, art, and specialty shops. I was moving from the room I had been assigned by the festival housing into the flat that Charles Saint Amant and his partner had rented for the summer. Charles had been a dancer with John Butler's company the first year of the festival and had returned this summer to run a shop. They had two extra bedrooms, one already spoken for by the Israeli mime, Juki Arkin. The other was for me. I would have complete run of the place without the awkwardness of being a boarder in someone's home. I think it was the scorpion that had dropped from the ceiling of my spartan bath into the tub just as I was to step in that had prompted my search for a new domicile, and had felicitously led me to these new accommodations. I was to pass by their shop and pick up the extra key. "Hello, you are Donald? Charles told me to expect you." I looked into a lovely face. "Yes, hello to you. I'm Donald McKayle." "Rita Nardi, I manage the antique shop over there. Charles wants us to join him for lunch. Everything here is closing for the afternoon. We open again at four. Plenty of time for a leisurely meal and a rest before the evening." "Your English is wonderful." "No, but *grazie*. Come, let's go."

"Herbie, that's awful." Nora Kaye sat on a wooden chair at the edge of the stage, framed in a semicircle of coffee, sandwich halves, pastry, and bottled water. She took another sip of coffee, hefted herself from the chair, and walked over to where Herbert Ross stood with a hand on his hip and a "well, come and show me what you mean" expression plastered across his craggy face. Nora proceeded to execute the movement in question with her head turned in sharp profile and her hands clasped behind her back. "Something like that. Give it some punch." Herbert's dubious gaze softened as the dancers repeated Nora's version. He turned to her and nodded. Nora returned to her nest, picked up the pastry, took a bite, and followed it with a gulp of coffee. There were only two more days before the *prova general*, and a host of last minute preparations were taking place. The afternoon run-through was to begin in half an hour and the stage manager told Herbert he would have to give up the stage to the crew. The weary and nervous dancers welcomed this intrusion and quickly picked up their rehearsal bags and went up to their dressing rooms to rest or outside to smoke. The stage crew brought in the set for *Games* and began to put it in place. It was the original Paul Bertelsen design, but the execution was entirely different. The fragmented tenement walls were constructed of plywood instead of upson board and the scattered bricks were inlaid and textured rather than painted on. My father had been very proud of the way he had laid on the bricks, dipping a rectangular kitchen sponge in the paint tray to give them realistic dimension. He would have loved the craftsmanship displayed by the Italian scene shop. The broken window in the doorway was sugar glass and the street lamp was com-

pletely three dimensional and electrified to light up on cue at the beginning of the "Dance of Terror."

The cast for *Games* was very ready for the opening. The new members,
Robert Powell, Ralph Lynn, Akiko Kanda, Mary Hinkson and the veter-
ans, Dudley Williams, William Louther, Mabel Robinson, Kathleen Stanford,
and I had become the tightly knit community that was necessary for the
successful rendering of this dance. Akiko was having the time of her life
in this work. She was from a well-to-do Japanese family and participating
in the rough and tumble of this very American work seemed pure ecstasy.
Half of it was sharing in universal truths she understood completely. The
other half was a wonderful learning process of cultural and class differ-
ences. "Momma dress me up and I go out to play." "No, you dress yourself
and play until Momma comes home from taking care of somebody else's
child to take care of you."

> I do love short'ning bread
> Momma love short'ning bread
> Poppa love short'ning bread
> Everybody love...

"Green light!" Akiko stopped dead in her tracks. This was her moment
to tag me in the window and call out the next game. It was also an abrupt
choreographic transition in which the dancers went from the series of
crouched movements that made up the "Dance of Hunger" to a gleeful
run. Akiko's shock was echoed by the entire cast. None of them moved.
It was a complete halt of all action. Saying green light had been an
impossibility for Akiko. The R and L consonant sounds were an anathema
to her and invariably the word came out as "Gleen right." Akiko labored
over this nightmare moment and had almost resigned herself to defeat
when suddenly, success! I clapped my hands to shock her into moving
and as she led the company in the leaping circle, everyone standing in
the wings applauded and she beamed back proudly, a smirk of trium-
phant confidence. Julian gave Mary a big hug as we came offstage after
our bows and laughed at their new summer careers as vocalists. I stood
in the wings to watch *Meridian*. Paul and Dan carved out the space in
shifting shapes of weighted volume only to be bisected by Akiko's exquisite brush stroke movements. The new corps waited in the wings to
execute a scurrying cross from stage left to right. There was something
transpiring among them as they prepared themselves, grasping their knees
and folding over. They looked at each other with wicked smiles curling
the edges of their lips and a glint of delight flashing from their eyes. As
they started across at a double time clip, the mischief afoot revealed itself.
The only one apparently not in on the scheme was Pina Bausch who, at
the start, was positioned in the middle of the group, and who soon found

herself left in the dust of her fleet companions. Pina realized the sudden
change and tried in vain to keep up with the others who, arriving in the
wings turned back and waved her onward with delight. As she entered
the wings they all cheered and embraced her; she half-heartedly smiled,
accepting the slightly cruel joke. Pina had been losing weight steadily and
her dietary habits showed evidence of a serious eating disorder. Mabel,
who was close to her, noticed that she carried around a calorie measure-
ment booklet and constantly consulted it. She never finished the meager
and strangely assembled meals she ordered and took stolen glances at the
little pamphlet that she held hidden in her lap under the table. She carried
a chocolate bar and nibbled on it for strength. She began to show a loss
of energy and her muscle tone began to decrease with her dwindling
muscle mass. Kathleen, who was a disciple of the Joe Pilates "Return To
Health" method, had engineered the little plan to shock Pina, as well as
for just pure devilment. Paul, dancing down-stage of them, was somehow
oblivious to these goings-on or he would most likely have retained it as
a permanent part of the choreography. It was perfect for his madcap brand
of antic humor.

Rainbow Round My Shoulder came after *Meridian*. The plan for the live
singers mixed with audio tape worked like a charm. Even the critics who
attended the *prova* did not realize the slight deception. It was quite an
education for me to see music critics sitting with scores in their hands
watching the performance and turning pages. I had been brought up on
journalists who had been assigned to write on dance, some switched over
from the sports page, and whose only qualification seemed to be strong
opinions rather than professional knowledge or scholarly criteria. *Rainbow*, as always, was a difficult dance for the male ensemble. It proved to
be a real problem for Ralph Lynn who was out of shape and found this
comeback a baptism of fire. Dan Wagoner also had some difficulty performing the series of wild body-folded air turns that led into "Take This
Hammer." He invariably landed with a loud crash before executing the
torso tremble that finished the phrase. Arthur had been with my company
and had danced in *Games, Nocturne,* and *They Called Her Moses*, but was
new to *Rainbow*. He was dancing the young man and little boy duets with
Mary, and was excellent in the role, but insisted on convoluting the climactic end of the dance in order to produce a perfect back attitude before
collapsing dead at the feet of his companions. I had a summer-long battle
ridding him of this classical dance affectation. The Herbert Ross ballet was
the commissioned world premiere and closed the program. It was a
professional and well crafted piece, but lacked an artistic point of view
or compelling *raison d'être* and paled in comparison to the other works.

The second program of dance, scheduled in the tiny Caio Melisso, was
a group of chamber works featuring new dances by Paul Taylor and

myself, Paul's humorous and macabre *Four Epitaphs*, and mime pieces by Juki Arkin. It was part of an on-going variety format established the first year of the festival. Jack Venza, then a young scenic artist-in-residence, had designed a curtain emblazoned with the show title, *Album Leaves*. Gian Carlo had incorporated the curtain as a permanent fixture of the popular afternoon program. The curtain functioned as a roll drop. It was revealed at the beginning of the performance when the opera drape was swagged opened. It was raised at the opening and lowered at the interval and at the finale. An early dance on the program was Paul's *Tablet* with Dan Wagoner and Pina Bausch. Paul took advantage of Pina's wafer-thin physique, clothing her in a white body suit and painting her face white except for a circle of orange encasing her eyes, nose, and lips. Dan was extremely solid in comparison and was in an orange body suit with an orange face except for a circle of white surrounding his facial features. When the lights came up on a motionless Pina Bausch, there was a gasp from the audience and a woman's voice spoke aloud, *"Guarda la morte!"* (Look at death!) A sliver of light widened from Pina's heels, past slender calves and thighs, to a blunted triangle at the joining of her legs, where it terminated in a squared off crotch. With her head tilted slightly to the side, the bones at the back of her neck glistened in pristine white, and a ghostly apparition took shape as she became *la morte*, the personification of death.

In New York, Gian Carlo had introduced me to the young artist that was this year's recipient of the festival's scenic design commission. He had designed a back cloth which was a canvas drop painted on both sides; when it was back lit, a new design would emerge. I had conceived a fantasy work set in a legendary primordial forest. I was not cognizant of the dimensions of the Caio Melisso when composing the dance and now found the work cluttered on the tiny stage with its precarious 6% rake. I had become disenchanted with my contribution to the program and wanted out. My desire to pull out was greeted coldly by Gian Carlo. "Donald, the young man arrives tomorrow to look at his curtain. I cannot send him home because you are suddenly disenchanted. I know you can work out your problems. He comes from the airport straight to the rehearsal. You will have something to show him." I returned to the stage and sent home all the dancers except for Mabel and Bob. I did have an alternate plan secretly brewing for "just in case"; "just in case" had abruptly arrived. I put on a tape of Debussy's solo flute composition, *Syrinx*, and began to quickly put together a lustful encounter of a woodland satyr and a maiden. Robert and Mabel were marvelous to-gether and the short composition fell into place that afternoon. The young designer had fancied this event as his *entré* into the limelight and was displeased not to find the major work that we had initially discussed. I explained the limitations of the stage environment and left him to pout and lick his wounds.

The first technical dress rehearsal of the entire program was followed by a production meeting at Gian Carlo's villa. He was entertaining an assortment of people who, at his initiative, had attended the run-through and had been invited to sit in on our gathering. Plates of risotto and glasses of wine mixed with laughter and idle conversation. "It's a nice program. *Bravi!* We all enjoyed ourselves, but there are things that can be better. *Vero?*" He turned from speaking to us and segued back into Italian, continuing a conversation with his guests that our entrance must have interrupted. Paul, Juki, and I exchanged glances and tried to contain our annoyance. "Donald, I think your ballet should be dressed different. Blue jeans would look marvelous against the backcloth. Don't you think so?" He left me without waiting for a response and turned to his house guests for verification. "*Vero?*" They nodded and continued with him in Italian. I could contain my displeasure no longer. "Gian Carlo, I am tired and it's very late. You and your friends continue your party. We'll talk about this when you're ready to have a professional meeting." I got up and left the gathering and a suddenly speechless Menotti.

Both of the dance programs were well received and the houses were filled. Our three leading ladies, Mary, Akiko, and Pina were suddenly stars. They were profiled in all the newspapers. *La dolce vita* was still enjoying its heyday and paparazzi and gossip columnists were everywhere. The Festival Club on the Corso Mazzini, brainchild of an American-born contessa-by-marriage who was dedicated to life in the fast lane, was the after-theater hang-out for the beautiful people. The social scene surrounding the *Festival dei Dui Mondi* vied warily for prominence with its cultural and artistic mission. Rita Nardi, whom I had met earlier, and I were constant companions and had become an item of idle chatter with the denizens of Spoleto's night life. Rita had introduced me to all the principal players of this summer madness in which she was a brilliant, if somewhat reticent, star. Her face filled the four-column corner of prominence on the front page of the social section in the evening paper under the headline "*La Volta Misteriosa*" (The Face of Mystery.) I was not her only admirer.

New American Ballets was now playing in repertoire and other programs were entering the festival roster at a dizzying pace. The opera from Hamburg brought in a mammoth production, *The Prince of Homburg,* that could not be physically accommodated in its entirety on the stage of the Teatro Nuovo. Two short plays by Tennessee Williams were being mounted at the Caio Melisso with an excellent American cast which included Jo Van Fleet, who was married to my former teacher, William Bales, and the new young Cuban actor, Tomás Milian. I went to the Festival Club hoping to find Jo Van Fleet.

I saw Rita across the room and went over to her table. She introduced me to a striking and exquisitely groomed woman seated at the next table, surrounded by three men. "Donald, this is my mother." "*Buona sera*, how do you do." "The performance tonight, it was magnificent. My congratulations." I thanked her and shook hands with her companions who echoed her praise. "Donald, let's dance." We squeezed our way onto the tiny dance floor, filled with couples swaying to "*Arrivederci Roma*". "What's the matter, Rita. You seem tense." "It's Tomás. He's been pursuing me. It's too much, and tonight he made a pass at my mother. She is very angry. Can we get out of here?" The air on the Corso Mazzini was pleasant after the smoke-filled room. A breeze was blowing as we walked along the deserted street, past the closed coffee shops, holding hands. Rita turned her face to me and a little smile twinkled in her eyes. "*Donato, grazie*." I stopped and as I turned to her, I noticed a form moving toward us. I suddenly felt a foot in my back, and I was thrust lurching forward against the sidewalk barrier decorated with flower pots. The geraniums crashed to the ground, and I turned to see a woozy and angry-faced Tomás Milian, unable to hold his own equilibrium, toppling backward from the force of his own blow. I fell on top of him. We grappled, rolling over each other and succeeded in demolishing several other floral decorations before we were separated. Tomás's friends were laughing at him. Rita grabbed hold of me and shouted angrily at my subdued attacker. She insisted on going straight to Gian Carlo and lodging a complaint. "Oh Tomás, he's such a naughty boy, such a naughty boy..." Rita and I left Gian Carlo and his ubiquitous guests in a buzz of excitement over this new bit of tasty gossip. I took Rita to her flat. It was an amazing warren of rooms on the second floor of a venerable building with a large coat of arms hanging over a huge baronial carved entry that remained permanently shut. Inside of it was a smaller door through which you entered and exited. Arched colonnades graced a balcony that opened from the living room, which was richly appointed with antique furnishings. We stood on the balcony looking out over the hillside below, touched by a wash of moonlight. "Donald, I think it is time we go to bed." She took me by the hand and I followed blissfully after her through a vestibule where she opened a door and suddenly I found myself in the hallway facing the stairwell. "Goodnight, Donato. *A domani*." I turned back to her as she finished speaking and found myself facing a closed door and listening to the ancient lock as it clicked shut. As I stepped through the downstairs doorway and onto the cobblestone street, I laughed out loud. What an end to an evening of surprises.

"Mr. McKayle, this is Stanley Chase. I am producing a new musical, *Blues Opera*. It's an updated version of *Saint Louis Woman*. Robert Breen has been working on it for a few years now and will be the director. It's his concept, his baby. He asked me to call you about doing the choreography. We rehearse here for three weeks, and then at the fairgrounds in Brussels, before the opening in Amsterdam. Opening night is a royal command performance for Queen Juliana of the Netherlands. Quincy Jones and his orchestra are part of the cast. Billy Beyers will be sharing the orchestrations with Quincy. Howard Roberts is doing the choral arrangements. He says that Donny's the best. What shall I call you? What do you say? Interested?" "It sounds wonderful. Donny will do fine. What shall I call you? When do we start?"

Was *Blues Opera* (subtitled *Free and Easy*) a musical, or was it a folk opera? Robert Breen definitely leaned toward the latter definition. He had successfully remounted the Gershwin opera *Porgy and Bess*, which had toured Europe to great acclaim and which had made stars of Leontyne Price, William Warfield, and Avon Long. He was riding the comet's tail of this meteoric hit and the conceptual milieu of the new production was surrounded by ghostly apparitions of its predecessor. For many of the singing cast it was old home week, and they picked up with each other where they had left off a few years prior. The presence of a renown jazz orchestra as part of the onstage environment was a bold and original stroke. Among the players were some of the best instrumentalists in the field including: Clark Terry on trumpet, Melba Liston on trombone, Patti Bown on piano, Jimmy Cleveland on guitar, and Jerome Richardson and Phil Woods on reeds. I was allowed to cast a couple, or at the most a trio of two females and one male, as the dancers in the show. The major part of my work would be staging the singers and instrumentalists. There was very little dialogue; most of the original Arna Bontemps book, *Saint Louis Woman*, had been excised in the plan to mirror *Porgy and Bess*. I had engaged two members of my company as the dancing couple, Charles Moore and Jacqueline Walcott. Now I was maneuvering for a third dancer.

"Frances, this is Donald McKayle, how are you? I'm doing *Blues Opera*, the big Harold Arlen show. We play Europe with Harold Nicholas as the lead and then come back to the States where Sammy Davis will take over. I've got a part for you. There are only three dancers in the show and a large cast of singing divas." Frances Davis seemed eager and excited about my call but I sensed a dab of tension in her voice when she broached the question of salary. I told her it was Equity union scale and what I understood that to be for Europe. "Shit, I give her more than that just to stay home." The gravely voice on the other end of the phone was unmistakably Miles Davis, the trumpet jazz-man whose icy and slightly evil demeanor in person was light years away from the searing heat of his music. He had been on another extension, eavesdropping on our conversation. Frances was a creature of joy and I wondered how she had ever come to marry Miles Davis. She had been cast in *West Side Story* and opened the show under her birth name, Elizabeth Taylor. The Equity rule which assured each of its members undefilable uniqueness, insisted that only one actor could hold title to a name and it was on a first come basis. Frances had legal claim to her name but was being pressured to change it in deference to the international film star who was being wooed to the stage and could certainly not be expected to change her name. When I joined *West Side Story* on Broadway as dance captain, at Jerome Robbins's invitation, Elizabeth Taylor had already dropped Elizabeth for her middle name, Frances; her last name was yet to be changed by marriage. I had been invited to a post-wedding celebration at Frances and Miles's duplex apartment. A beaming Frances opened the door and asked for my coat as she ushered me in. I took off the stylish gray Persian lamb chesterfield that I was sporting and handed it to Frances". Ooh...nice!" Frances stroked the coat and cooed as I laughed, enjoying her warm flirtatious spirit. "Yeah." Miles grabbed the coat from her, opened the closet and tossed it inside on the floor. I looked after him as he turned and walked away and saw Jackie Walcott on the stairs talking to someone. "Jackie, look who's here."

Jackie's descent down the stairs was like fizz rising in a glass of champagne. Jackie and Frances were both effervescent spirits and great friends. It would be wonderful to have both Frances and Jackie in the show, but that was not to be. Miles and Frances came to a final rehearsal in New York and sat next to Quincy watching Jackie and Charles dance a sultry duet to "One For My Baby and One More For The Road." A wistful expression crossed Frances's face as they danced. Miles looked on with a countenance of impassive immobility.

We were finally on our way, off to Europe, with only a fortnight left prior to our royal command performance. Only the first act was blocked, and we had yet to see the set which was being built in Europe. The orchestrations were incomplete, and Robert Breen did not see eye to eye with Quincy Jones and Billy Beyers on the musical style of the show. Esta, Gabrielle, and Liane were all going with me, and we had secured our little family niche on the plane. Gerry Gray, my third dancer sat behind me waving to Frank Rehak, who had come to see her off. At last we were up in the air. Liane and Gabrielle had dozed off and Esta took the opportunity to also get some sleep. I heard sniffles coming from behind me and turned to see Gerry taking a small cellophane packet from her pocketbook and showing it to Norma Donaldson who was sitting next to her. "These are my Daddy's curls, oh honey: I miss him already." "Don't look like you cut those from his head." "Oh no, darling. Got these from the best part." Gerry kissed the little packet and fell laughing through her tears into Norma's arms. I closed my eyes and drifted off. When I opened them again the cabin was quiet except for a group of musicians playing poker. Norma was stretched across the two seats behind me fast asleep and Gerry had found solace curled up in the arms of Oki, our Swedish musician, who, like Frank Rehak, also played slide trombone.

Transplanting the family to Europe in transient dwellings was a huge challenge, to which Esta and I did not always measure up. In Belgium we were housed in a compound near the rehearsal site of the abandoned fairgrounds on the outskirts of Brussels. Gabrielle adjusted wonderfully and made friends easily with the neighborhood children. Language, which was an insurmountable barrier for Esta, seemed not to bother Gabrielle in the slightest. She led her new playmates, teaching them ring games, which they took to with great relish. Their singing in the courtyard was a source of delight. The words floating back to us were all gibberish until the refrain, which was shouted out lustily.

Ashes, ashes, all fall down

Screams of laughter would follow as they tumbled about and then bounced up to begin again, circling and mumbling nonsense lyrics to the familiar melody, anticipating the coming moment of joy. In Amsterdam, we were lodged in a hotel where English was spoken, and the routines of securing the necessities of food, laundry, and diversion became simpler. I was so involved with the show that I was of little domestic help. The children were always glad to see me at the end of the day, but whined when I left in the morning, and absolutely could not understand why I would come back for dinner and then leave again.

The show was a sleeping monster that refused to move out of its state of hibernation. Robert Breen seemed mired in the repetition of directorial strokes from his production of *Porgy and Bess* and had characters moving about the stage without purpose. The set had been constructed in two different scene shops. In the process of assembly it was discovered that the upper level did not match the lower floor. The entire support structure had to be completely revamped. Without access to the set, further scene blocking was arrested, and we remained in a gnawing state of limbo. Robert Breen spent countless hours on favorite details, and I had to steal people away to rehearse dances. He was particularly enamored of a section he called "The Lumping." In this scene the villain was surrounded by the female ensemble, who sighed and moaned as they rubbed their undulating torsos, goading him on as he manhandled the hapless and little-loved madam of the gaming establishment. It was a particularly unattractive sequence that played into prurient fantasies. Robert Breen never tired of it and watched wide eyed, sipping from a glass of Tang that his dutiful wife always had ready for him. Days slipped away and we seemed never to get to the end of the show. The day before opening night arrived, and we were still incomplete. The seldom used Equity rule that allowed for an uninterrupted twenty four hour rehearsal prior to opening night was put into force. At the twentieth hour, the cast was lying around the set, some of them fast asleep, and Robert Breen was exhorting an exhausted leading lady to "curve a little more when you leave the staircase." Irene Williams had no voice left and was in tears. I had a costume and was cast as the conjure man. I roamed around the stage whispering directions to the musicians who were at a complete loss. Mercifully the stage manager at last called time, and we were sent to our dressing rooms to make up and to take sustenance in the croissants, sandwiches, and coffee.

"Places." I suddenly realized as I picked up my tray of voodoo *gris-gris* from the prop table and took my place between the house curtain and the theater drape, that my voice would be the first heard by the audience. The royal command performance had been canceled, but a hostile crowd noticed the empty royal box and awaited the culprits as the house darkened and the drape opened. We managed to survive Amsterdam and Utrecht and proceeded to Paris where, word having already spread of our calamities, ticket sales were extremely slow. Stanley Chase relieved Robert Breen of his directorial duties in an angry scene, and I was asked to take over the helm. We had no real second act. There was no author to craft the missing pieces. We had only the Harold Arlen score with its wonderful songs, and the remnants of a story outline. I met with James Baldwin in a small café on the left bank and he agreed to take a stab at what he called, "a horrible, sophomoric mess." The next morning I arrived at the Alhambra Theatre on the Place de la Republique and found that we were not going to continue. The show was bankrupt and had been shut down. Stanley Chase spoke to the cast of a possible regrouping in the States with Sammy Davis, Jr. That evening we played our last performance, and though I gave a preshow talk to the cast, exhorting them to make this last performance a memorable one, I was not prepared for the interpretation they would give this directive. That evening, I witnessed the time honored theatrical practice of "burying the show" at the final performance. Clark Terry rolled his pants legs up and stuffed his feet into Stradella Lawrence's high heels as he took front and center, playing his trumpet. Cast members roamed the *pasarella*, a curved walkway that circled out from the stage in front of the orchestra pit, playing with the audience. This arcane piece of theater architecture was a fixture of the girlie shows, staples of French music hall tradition, that allowed high-rolling, lecherous men to ogle the show girls and chorines at close range. This final performance was indeed memorable.

A flight back to New York had been arranged for the next evening. We sat around the darkened theater waiting for our company manager to arrive with per diem money to pay our hotel bills. Mitch Brauer came in through the stage door carrying a large brown paper bag filled with crumpled franc notes. "This will get you to the airport. Don't worry about the hotel. I've taken care of that. Go home and pack." My heady entry into big-time show business had ended in a disappointing fizzle. Was this symptomatic of the genre? Did I want ever again to put my trust in someone else's hands and lose all control over my work? I longed to be back in the studio with my dancers.

"I'll ring for the *ascenseur*, Daddy." I laughed with Gaby. A lot had been happening in addition to the demise of the show. I promised myself; "Remember to enjoy each moment, it will never happen again." I loaded the suitcases onto the waiting elevator and went back to our room for a final check. Esta placed Liane in the stroller and pushed her down the narrow hallway runner for the last time. I took Gabrielle by the hand and followed, closing the hotel room door behind me. Liane twisted around in the stroller to make sure we were all in tow.

The plane cabin was quiet and except for a single reading light shining up ahead of me, darkness blanketed the forms curled uncomfortably in sleep. I gazed into the blackness outside the window and wondered what lay ahead for me. I was coming home months earlier then scheduled and had no opportunity to warn anyone of the change of plans. I had substitutes teaching my classes, subletees in our apartment, dancers on hiatus who had perhaps made other allegiances. I had reached Mother and Dad by phone and we had commiserated together. "Don't worry yourself son, something else will come up. We'll let everyone know. We've got the list of numbers right here by the phone." Picturing them at the airport waiting for us, I finally surrendered to the weariness I had been battling and drifted off to sleep.

7

DISTRICT STORYVILLE

"Donald, Riverside Records has picked up *Come and See the Peppermint Tree*, and they're talking about another recording." "What happened to Washington Records? I thought we were a big hit? Didn't they give us a second release?" "Alas, we are not the problem. They went belly up. We're one of the lucky ones, Riverside bought out our contract." Making *Come and See the Peppermint Tree* with Evelyn Lohoefer had been, for me, a delicious gambol in another part of the creative forest. The prospect of a second chance was immediately appealing. Evelyn and I had met at Connecticut College where the Summer School of the Dance had become the official home of the American Dance Festival. I had returned to the six-week school as a member of the faculty and the American Dance Festival had presented my company in concert at the Palmer Auditorium. Evelyn accompanied my morning technique class, sometimes abandoning the keyboard and going under the lid of the baby grand, beating the strings with mallets or strumming and plucking them with her fingers as she sang a vocalise or wielded a rattle. We immediately befriended each other and spent hours outside of the class talking, singing, and making music together. Evelyn lived in Washington DC and was a dance accompanist and composer. The offer from Washington Records to make an album of children's songs resulted from Evelyn's work with the Erica Thimey "Children's Dance Theatre." I traveled to DC to work with Evelyn on the twenty-three songs and narration that became *Come and See the Peppermint Tree*. When the record was completed, Evelyn came to New York and together we played the demonstration tape for Lucas Hoving, Louis Horst, and Martha Graham. They were all enchanted by it and wrote blurbs for the back of the record jacket. Martha was genuinely intrigued with the imagination of the material. She sat with her arms folded across her lap, bent forward in rapt attention as she listened. "Don, you're becoming quite the talked about young man these days...and now this. What else are you up to?" I smiled broadly at Martha's flirtatious questioning. "I'm working on a new dance. It's a big work about the birth of jazz in New Orleans. It's something that started on the tour."

Everywhere I went on my world journey, from the very first night in Tokyo, I heard jazz. It had started me thinking. I realized that jazz music was America's real ambassador. The State Department had sent us out as cultural attachés to the world, but jazz without the benefit of any ex-officio title, had beat us to the punch. It was already there. What was there about this music that made it so communicative to people everywhere, no matter how alien it seemed at first? Its joy was infectious and natural, with the pulse, rhythm, and sounds of human laughter. Its sorrow plumbed the depths of genuine pathos, its song the sound of weeping, moans, and deep sighs. It demanded continuous creativity. Improvisation was marrow to the bone of its being, and, like great storytelling everywhere, it was immediately accessible. It had roots that were deep and tenacious, reaching across continents and oceans and, nourished with blood and with tears, had flowered into this ubiquitous and beautiful weed.

> New Orleans, 19 and 03... District Storyville...cradle of jazz...out to the graveyard the brass bands mourned death...coming back they screamed life... Horn was king and the followers did mighty battle for the crown...music from every corner of this demimonde... 19 and 17... District Storyville closed forever...but the music goes on... everywhere

This short dedication followed the title and listing of creators on the playbill that was distributed at the Kaufman Auditorium on April 22, 1962. It was not an easy distillation of all the thought, research, conception, choreography, and rehearsing that resulted in the premiere that afternoon of *District Storyville*. It was rather the concerted effort of Louise Roberts who functioned as manager, public relations coordinator, creative advisor, and general chief cook and bottle washer, along with Charles Blackwell who among other things was stage manager and technical wizard. They had compressed my overabundant notes into this salutation. This was my most ambitious work in size and I welcomed the partnership of several creative allies.

Dorothea Freitag was a brilliant pianist who had composed and played for Katherine Dunham and had worked in theater. I approached her with the idea of working on a dance built around the birth of jazz in New Orleans and she was immediately interested. "Bring all your records and books over. I've got tons of stuff here. We can spend an afternoon around the piano." Dorothea folded back the index of *Mister Jelly Lord*, snapped the binding of the paperback edition open, and placed the reduced notation on the music rack of the baby grand. I sat on the bench of the adjacent upright and peered over her shoulder as she finished cleaning her rose tinted eyeglasses with a small embroidered handkerchief, burying the rhinestone studded frames within her blond curls. She tapped her right foot on the pedal in a bright tempo, and then released her fingers upon the piano keys in a riot of notes as Tony Jackson's *Naked Dance* came stridently to life in a display of breathtaking virtuosity. "Oh, that's a good one and so is this." Jelly Roll Morton's *The Crave* received the same fullblown reading. We spent the entire afternoon and early evening playing tunes, looking through manuscripts, digging out remembered sources from hidden suitcases, accordion files, and boxes. "What do you think of this one? I think it's kind of pretty." "It's beautiful, so melancholic. Who wrote it?" "It's mine. I've got lots of tunes. I think some of them will work just fine."

"Normand, Dorothea is something else, I've got a tape from our session. Yeah, I'll be right over." Normand Maxon lived on 54th Street between 2nd and 1st Avenues. I had met Normand at the New Dance Group where we took classes together and had been members of the Dudley-Maslow-Bales Trio's dance company. Having graduated from the Parson School of Design, Normand had dabbled in fashion, but was presently working as a coordinator of sets and properties for a fashion photographer. His coexistent dance career had also included a few brief sallies into choreography and the formation of his own dance company. I had been a dancer in his first and only group work, a psychological dance drama to a symphonic score of Carlos Chavez. Linda Margolies, Marian Shapiro, Normand, and I were the soloists. We had auditioned the work for inclusion on the YM-YWHA Audition Winners' Series and it had been selected to be presented on a shared bill. The final rehearsal had been foolproof and then, true to the old superstition, at the performance disaster struck.

We took our beginning positions, the curtain opened, and we waited for the music to begin. Marian Shapiro was downstage right with her leg lifted and her head up in a position of precipitous balance, for which she was famous. Linda was in a crosslegged seated position upstage center, and I hovered over her in a tilted balance with one leg pointing skyward and one arm pointing to the ground. Normand was hidden behind Linda and me, waiting to emerge, and the ensemble was off stage ready to enter. We waited – no music. Mercifully after what seemed an interminable pause, the curtain closed. "What's going on? What's happening?" "Sorry, Mr. Maxon. A temporary technical snafu, we're ready now. Places, everyone, the curtain's opening." We returned to our positions. The curtain opened and once again...nothing. Normand was beside himself. "What's going on? Why is this happening?" He suddenly grabbed hold of my lifted leg, as he continued his babble. In a fierce stage whisper and without flinching a single muscle, I commanded, "Let go of me!" Normand released his hold and continued his distraught monody. The needle whooped as the record suddenly found its voice, and Marian dovetailed her opening section to the place where the music had started. We were finally off to a bumpy start. "Never again!"

Normand's words were not idle threat. After that performance, he put away all personal desire for choreography, but became an indefatigable resource for my creations and for Alvin Ailey. He started these alliances as a photographer and graphic artist, creating posters for our annual concerts. They were unusual pieces and the way the black and white photography blended into the print was pacesetting. He created a masterful poster for me to announce the premiere of *Legendary Landscape*. I was photographed in a bulky black sweater, hands clasped overhead, single source side lighting sculpting my features, and the black of the sweater filling the rest of the poster with the white print bouncing forward boldly. This poster won a Pepsi Cola Graphic Award and was exhibited with the other advertising prize winners.

"Look what I found today," Normand exclaimed enthusiastically. "It's just the look that I'm after." "Normand, this painting is the same as the one on the record album." I placed the double album, *Jazz Begins*, spread wide alongside the open pages of the issue of *Life Magazine*. Normand and I had simultaneously found the same pictorial sources. We excitedly launched into the design elements of the work. There were two sets of costumes to delineate the two very different parts of the work. The first set, for the opening, "Funeral Function", consisted of uniforms for the marching band, country cottons for the "second liners", and the raggle-tag outfit that would follow the young protagonist, Little Lou, throughout the dance. The second set would be the satin and gauze finery for the Countess and the *filles de joie* of the brothel, and the brocade vested suits of the Sports and Tailgate Ramblers, the clientele in the "Sporting House Saga." "How many women are you using?" Normand queried. "Well there's Pearl Reynolds, she'll play the madam. I call her the Countess, after the Countess Willie Piazza, who ran one of the finest houses in the Tenderloin and was famous for her octoroon ladies of the night. She ruled over them with a fierce hand, carrying off her adopted European royal lineage with affectations like a monocle and a foot long diamond studded cigarette holder, used to puff on black Russian cigarettes." "Oh, Miss Pearl, she's divine." Normand paused thoughtfully. "I want her in virginal white. Let's drape those wonderful hips tightly and drop a heavy swag of fabric from her crotch to play between her legs when she walks her walk, and a rhinestone coronet, and lots of pearls and rhinestone jewelry, and a stand-up pouf of crinoline and netting to frame that wonderful face." I continued Normand's thought process without interruption. "Give me a trail of chiffon hanging from the back of her neckline, something that she can fidget with when she gets annoyed at the girls and something to toy with when she's acting coy with the customers." "Who are the three girls for the lesson?" he asked me. "I call it 'A Matter of Instruction' when the madam shows the girls the basics of how to peddle their wares. There's Jackie Walcott, she's the newest recruit and doesn't get things right. I think of her as a well-endowed country girl trying to make her way in the big city, naive but clever, and terribly funny. She's also never worn high heels before and falls all over herself. I call her Sugar Lover and she'll dance the comic bedroom scene with Herman Howell to *The Crave*. He's known as Willie the Pleaser. Then there's Shelly Frankel. She's Titanic, the sultry sophisticate. She'll dance the trio with the Countess and the King in the first section of the Carving Contest, 'Calling the Children Home'. The third girl is Thelma Oliver. She's Stingaree. As far as she's concerned, she's the main attraction of the establishment, has nothing but contempt for her sisters in sin, and is furious at being called to this tiresome brush up rehearsal. She challenges the Countess's authority by breaking into a brief snatch of her shimmy dance which she'll perform in full later, to Tony Jackson's *Naked Dance* – a little something I call 'An Entertainment.'" The twinkle in Normand's eyes and the sly wicked smile that creased his face led to a rush of tantalizing description. "Well, I want them all to look like they've just gotten out of bed and are half dressed, in underwear, step-ins, and wrappers." "Great, Normand! How about putting them in Spanish shawls with lots of knotted fringe? It'll look wonderful in movement." "Good, I can combine the shawls and the underwear. I've got a lot of ideas for the gowns. I want Jackie in bright orange with diamond shaped geometries on her hips, outlined in rhinestones. We can also play with the crepe inside of the fabric there for a little texture. And I'm gonna put her in a crisscross halter neckline. She's got a magnificent pair of knockers. Might as well show them off. You don't see a bust like that very often with dancers. Here are some color swatches of the crepe-backed satin. The dark mossy green will look wonderful on Louanna with her blond hair. The fuchsia's for Mabel Robinson. Against her chocolate brown skin, it'll be a knockout. I've made this funny little thumbnail croquis sketch of her dress. There's a big cabbage rose covering one breast, attached to invisible netting." "They're great, what about the men?" "I haven't done much on them yet. I want the band jackets to look like the ones in the magazine. I have to get to the suits." "Normand, how will we be able to afford all of this?" "Don't worry about that. I've got my sources. I can promote a lot of this and charge it off against the propping. A lot of firms will donate for credit in print ads. I just have to find ways to use what we need for the dance in the ad set-ups. Look what I've got here." Normand opened a carton filled with spools of shiny red thread. "What's this for?" "I'm gonna string these together for the beaded curtain entrance into the sporting house parlor. And I've got boxes more in gold to make a drop for the bedroom scene with these heavy silk drapery tassels hanging every now and then. They'll be ours tomorrow when I'm finished with the shoot. I promoted them from Coats and Clark. I use them behind a lingerie model. She's stepping out of a porcelain bathtub filled with pearls. Maybe I can incorporate some pearls too. I've got a tub-full. I just have to con the transport for the use of the truck to get the spools to the dance studio.

We can string them there and keep them in the storage closet until the concert. Oh God, we'll need the truck twice more. They're pretty damn heavy, but they'll look great."

The stage went dark at the end of the "Funeral Function," as Little Lou, William Louther, raced after the disappearing parade of musicianeers and second liners. The audience went wild with applause which continued until the lights came up on the back of a solitary female figure in glistening white satin, her head hidden in an erect pouf of stiffened net studded with diamantes, from which chiffon kerchiefs trailed down her spine to the floor. With a jeweled hand placed on her hip, Pearl Reynolds turned to reveal the Countess in a state of regal agitation. She flounced forward, walking her walk, as Dorothea, in black satin, proceeded nonchalantly down the aisle of the theater and was helped slowly down into the orchestra pit by the trumpeter, Clark Terry. She placed a huge ring on the piano rack, waving off the glaring Countess, and began the sultry raunch of "A Matter of Instruction." The music Dorothea had arranged and orchestrated from the authentic sources and her own compositions was a seamless triumph. In fact the atmosphere in the Kaufman Auditorium was giddy with excitement. From the opening drum roll as the funeral cortege entered the stage and the distraught widow threw herself across the coffin, little murmurs and chuckles of recognition bounced around the audience and peals of laughter and applause greeted section after section. In the coda, the *filles de joie*, led by the eternally haughty Countess, made their final exit behind the downstage scrim. Little Lou, in front of the scrim, danced a rapturous solo carrying the gleaming cornet as he left the stage traveling in the opposite direction, symbolically taking the music out to the world. The curtain fell. The audience was on its feet. Bill Louther could not believe the ovation he received as he came forward to bow. He stopped in his tracks midstage, genuinely overwhelmed. His jaw went slack for a brief moment as his eyes widened in disbelief and then a huge smile captured his features and he bowed and bowed and bowed.

The day before events at the theater had not been so happy. Pearl Reynolds could not be found anywhere. Finally, she arrived an hour late from an appointment with a lady who had meticulously applied individual false eyelashes to beautify the just-don't-talk-to-me-about-it eyes she flashed as I approached her. Normand and the lighting designer, Nicola Cernovitch, were battling over the few available pipes needed to mount both electric equipment and scenery. Nick gave in, alloting pipes for the gold spool drop for *The Crave*, the mirror drop for *The Naked Dance*, and the downstage black scrim for the "Funeral Function". It was up to Normand to solve the upstage opera drape and red spool drop as well as the midstage chiffon trip drop on the one remaining available line. Charlie Blackwell came to the rescue by utilizing the auditorium's upstage black velour traveler for both the opera drape and the red spool drop, rigging the operation with pulleys, large safety pins, and a covenant of secrecy obtained from the house crew with a little payola. The free line went to the chiffon trip drop which was encased in a little wooden box operated by a device Charlie had fashioned from a frozen orange juice can and clothes line. It all worked like a dream. On cue, the center of the upstage black velours swagged open to reveal the four sports standing behind the shiny redspool curtain. As Stingaree laughed lasciviously and tossed her silver lamé dress overhead the pink chiffon cascaded down in front of where she stood, posed wantonly on a moveable mirrored stage, with her voluptuous torso reflected in the oval mirror that hung behind her. The sports lifted her and she grabbed hold of the chiffon drape which tumbled over the grouping as they left stage with Thelma held high, kicking with wild abandon. The audience screamed its approval.

The company had undergone some changes in personnel, which was always to be expected in the quicksilver world of concert dance. Carmen De Lavallade took over the female solo in *Rainbow Round My Shoulder* and the Countess in *District Storyville*. She was superb in both roles and brought several unique gestural interpretations to "Fare Thee Well" that became permanent additions to *Rainbow Round My Shoulder*. When her natural, patrician bearing was allowed to dissolve into a wicked shimmy it was irresistible and idiosyncratic. The only absence that caused me anxiety was Eliot Feld. He had been so wonderful as the Pensacola Kid, challenging, with his pulsing, vibratory intensity, the sultry long-legged blues of Gus Solomons Jr's King in the "Carving Contest." A crippling cramp had suddenly developed in his leg in the climactic moments of *Rainbow Round My Shoulder*. He danced beside me in "Take This Hammer" and after the diagonal leaping section, as we fell to the floor and began the slashing crawl back to the corner, I noticed his calf muscle stretching against his trousers in a stiff rectangle. As I rose to start the leaps again, he continued off into the wings. "Eliot, what's wrong?" "I don't know." Eliot managed to come back on for the curtain call and did a wonderful performance of *District Storyville*. I received a worried but determined "everything-would-work-itself-out-and-be-all-right" telephone call from his mother. Eliot was suddenly shooting up from the diminutive lad I had taught when he was twelve years old and who seemed then to be destined to stay miniature in size. His all-at-once growth pattern had precipitated the problem and time was the only remedy. I missed him sorely although Louis Falco gave the role a no-holds-barred sizzling rendition.

We were part of the gala inauguration of the Summer Dance Festival, held at the Delacorte Theater in Central Park. Walter Terry, the critic from the *Herald Tribune*, gave the opening remarks and introduced the mistress of ceremonies. He tiptoed up to the microphone which was set for a person much taller than him. "I'll just have to stand on full *demi-pointe* to present to you *prima ballerina assoluta*, Alexandra Danilova." The weather in the park that evening was perfect; a crescent moon hung overhead and was reflected in the little lake that backed the stage. Ruth Saint Denis opened the program with her mystical dance, *The Incense*. She was an ancient lady by then and walked with great difficulty, stepping out with one foot and dragging the other up to meet it. She could execute this limited meander in any direction and with her impeccable sense of rhythm and unfailing theatricality, she made this handicap appear to be a chosen dance maneuver. In pale chiffon drapery, with cottonsoft white locks, framing her delicate face, she sprinkled grains of incense on the glowing coals in the brazier beside her and, as the smoke rose, her arms rippled bonelessly. Even the loose and hanging flesh seemed a magical part of the incantation. It was amazing to watch her finish this glorious performance and then be helped painfully off the stage in the darkness. We followed with *Nocturne*, danced to live music, with Moondog and his wife playing the percussion. Al Brown had assembled the quintet of cellos and violas, utilizing several of the instrumentalists from the New York Philharmonic who had made the original recording. After a classical pas de deux and an intermission, we closed the program with *District Storyville*, and once again brought the house to its feet. *District Storyville* was the highlight of the Summer Dance Festival. *Life* magazine featured a two-page photo layout of all the participants grouped on the outdoor stage surrounding Joseph Papp, the executive producer of "Shakespeare In the Park."

"Hello, Hilly Elkins here, I'm doing a show that I want to talk to you about. Do you know the Clifford Odets' play *Golden Boy*?" "Oh yes, I saw the movie with John Garfield. He's from a poor Italian family and plays the violin. His father wants him to be a concert artist and he decides to become a boxer, which breaks his father's heart." "Exactly, our version is like that but with a big difference. First, it's a musical. Charlie Strouse and Lee Adams have done the songs and I've got Sammy Davis Jr. to play the Golden Boy. The family is black, and his father wants him to be a concert pianist. He goes into the fight business and falls for his white manager's girl. It's an inter-racial love story. Pretty hot, eh?" "You've got Sammy Davis? Wow!" "There's lots of dance, including a prize fight scene between the Golden Boy and a challenger. It's the scene where he breaks his hand and ends any possible career as a pianist. Everyone's talking about your jazz ballet. This is a serious show with big entertainment values and with the black/white love story, very controversial. We think your're the man for the job. Interested?" "Sounds wonderful. Yes!" "Great. Who's your agent?" "I don't have an agent." "Well, get one. You'll need someone to represent you, to make your deal. You and I, we just talk about the show. Maybe you've got a lawyer?" "No. I'll get an agent. When is this all beginning?" "In the fall; we've got some time. Clifford Odets passed away, you know, so we've had to do some shifting of plans. I'll arrange a get-together with Charlie and Lee. You'll get to meet Peter Coe, our British director, when he arrives from London. The choreographer was our missing link. Now with you on board, we're right on target."

Becoming part of a creative team in the Broadway theater was light years away from anything I had yet encountered. The session with Charles Strouse and Lee Adams was stimulating, but nerve wracking. I must have passed the test because a face-to-face audience with Hilly Elkins was already in place by the end of our meeting. Hilly and I met in the dining area/conference room of his flat. It was decorated with all the trappings of a theatrical set, a miniature throne room. Hillard Elkins sat in a magnificent armchair at the end of an antique empire table, polished until its rich patina exuded a dull glow. He rose to greet me with a warm smile, set within a small face with intense shining eyes. He was elegantly tailored in an exquisitely cut European suit, and nattily barbered, a manicured hand grasping mine in a hearty handshake. Pictures of Napoleon Bonaparte covered the walls of the alcove. As Hilly handed me a glass of wine, despite his prematurely graying hair, he seemed a dead-ringer for the little emperor, whose portrait peered at me over his shoulder. A hollow round container stood in the corner with an assortment of walking sticks that were all harbingers of death. Shielded within their elegant facades were concealed rapiers and razorsharp daggers. Hilly smiled with pleasure at my fascination with his little collection.

With the sure offer of a major Broadway show which had a guaranteed super star leading man, getting appointments with prospective agents was a lark. I met with a handful of private agents who were an admixture of hard sell, false sincerity, fascinating perversity, and yeah-who-are-you-and-how'd-you-land-this-big-one. I made strong mental notes and followed my chemical reactions. The next step was the large agencies. "You're a newcomer, you could get lost." I put the admonition in the back of my mind and took the elevator up to the penthouse in the MONY building on Seventh Avenue and 55th Street, where I had an appointment at the William Morris Agency. The elevator opened and Marcello Mastroanni stepped aside to let me out. He was an idol of mine, and I took this as an omen of good fortune. "Mr. Youdelman will be right with you. Have a seat." Before I could select a magazine from the end table, the double door to the inner offices opened. A smiling man pushed the eyeglasses back on his nosebridge and called to me with an outstretched hand. "Don, come on in. I'm Bob Youdelman." I hit it off with Robert Youdelman immediately. He had done his homework. He knew who I was and what I did. He was reasonably acquainted with concert dance and didn't need a basic course in aesthetics. He was warm and down to earth. He answered my questions directly and posed ones that I hadn't asked about the William Morris Agency and what it could do for me in the entertainment industry. He didn't seem overly happy when I told him I didn't want William Morris to participate in my concert career, but said he would convey my wishes to Nat Lefkowitz, the head of the agency. He was sure that everything could be arranged.

The waiting period leading up to the commencement of rehearsals for *Golden Boy* was not an idle thumb-twirling time. I immersed myself in a long rehearsal period ending in my second large concert at Hunter Playhouse. The stage there was only slightly larger then the Kaufman Auditorium which had cramped the full company sections of *District Storyville*. However, its configuration and orchestra pit gave the illusion of spaciousness. I also had managed to develop a wonderful relationship with Joe London, the rather problematic theater manager and was able to have access to equipment and technical assistance that was off-limits to other renters. Joe's daughter was a student in one of my children's classes and had broken the ice for me with her father. His reputed cantankerous nature never surfaced with me, and I was in fact, the beneficiary of unheard of largess. Ten years previously, in 1952, I had premiered *Her Name Was Harriet* at Hunter Playhouse, and Joe had donated the use of choral platforms for a full upstage riser and even had his student crew move the bulky items in and out without charge, completely on his own initiative. When I called to request this concert date and rehearsal days he greeted me as if it were only yesterday that we had last spoken. This time the technical demands of Normand Maxon's design were much more sophisticated. When we finally met at the theater, a large dollop of Joe's legendary irritability greeted me. Normand had conceived a setting for my new work, *Legendary Landscape*, from research on secret society huts of Papua New Guinea. Robert Blackburn had designed and executed the grouping of totem figures surrounding a low opening at the center back of the stage. They were made from *papier-mâché* over chicken wire framing and required assembling and detail finishing at the theater. Joe was not pleased with Normand, Bob Blackburn, or with their assumptions about the use of the theater that they considered part of the contractual privileges. I was able to smooth Joe's ruffled feathers, but I had a slight mutiny on my hands with Pearl Reynolds and the four other women over the large headdresses that Normand had designed. They were built on buckram frames and covered with yarn to look like rows of finely plaited hair on skulls that had been reshaped from birth by applied bindings. This along with the raised tattoo trapunto welting on the abdomens of the skin colored leotards, a clever design duplication of ritual sacrification, were derived from an African tribal civilization a halfworld distant from New Guinea. The cultural anachronism was not the problem, it was rather the discomfort and the sudden disorientation of balance that the headdresses posed. The look of the scenery and costumes was startling, especially the design for Gus Solomons Jr., whose body and face appeared to be painted with swirls of ash, like the ceremonial figures in the wrestling bouts of the Kau tribal rites – again a distinct and different cultural source. I convinced Pearl that it was just a matter of adjustment and that I would take the time needed to deal with all of her concerns. I gathered a mumbling and slightly truculent cast together on the stage. I told them how wonderful they all looked, how striking Normand's designs were, and that in the theater there were basically only two kinds of people: problem makers, and problem solvers. I assured them that I was one of the latter, had no use for any of the former, and that I expected their full and total collaboration in making everything work. Normand was grateful for my support and for my genuine belief in his work, but continued to nibble away at his fingernails. I left him to secure the silver loops for ear ornaments to the headdresses. He had backed off from any further ornamentation but was now emboldened to complete his designs with this final touch.

Leon Bibb was not able to appear in *Rainbow Round My Shoulder* and I had replaced him with a young singer who had been a general understudy for the men in the European tour of *Free and Easy*. Howard Roberts was conducting and agreed that Robert Guillaume would be an excellent choice. We were not able to arrange the male chorus in the formation that had proved so felicitous at the Kaufman Auditorium. Bob Guillaume stood at the proscenium and Howard and the choir were in the pit and were only visible to people sitting in the balcony. Bob had not committed the lyrics strongly to memory and panicked midway, although all he had to do was to listen to the choral antiphony and the vocal answers would have led him back. As stress compounded alarm, he left the portal and began to wander toward stage center in front of the dancers. Jaime Rogers shouted the correct lyrics at him and directed a sharp kick in the choreography at his rear which sent him quickly back to his spot. It was a strange and distorted performance with everyone trying to make up for the mishaps, but the adrenaline level was so high that it transferred to the audience who greeted us at the end with wild hosannas. Shelly Frankel took over the female solo and brought an alluring sensuality that was never duplicated by any of the many excellent soloists who later essayed the coveted role.

"Donald, I know something that you don't, and it's marvelous, and I really can't say, but congratulations and you'll soon find out." "Jack, what's all the mystery, tell me." "I really can't." Jack Mitchell smiled wickedly. He was a master at gossip and intrigue. Jack was a superb dance photographer. He had invited me to view the contact sheets and several prints of his own personal favorites from his last session with the company in the dress rehearsal at Hunter Playhouse. There were some excellent capturings of the duet from *Rainbow Round My Shoulder* with Shelly and myself, and phenomenal aerial moments with Gus Solomons Jr., suspended in space above the female ensemble in *Legendary Landscape*. Normand's wonderful costume and makeup transformed Gus's torso and face into the images that were later to be celebrated in Leni Riefenstahl's photographic essays on the peoples of Nuba.

A letter from the Awards Committee and a congratulatory phone call from Ben Sommers finally revealed the essence of Jack Mitchell's pronouncement. I was the recipient of the 1963 Capezio Award. The honor which had been bestowed in former years on such notables as Martha Graham, Ruth Saint Denis, Louis Horst, Lincoln Kirstein, Sol Hurok, Doris Humphrey, and Barbara Karinska, was awarded to me at a luncheon in the St. Regis Hotel. The letter was signed by the selection committee: Martha Hill, Anatole Chujoy, Walter Terry, and Emily Coleman. From my seat on the dais, I smiled at Esta seated at the table amidst this high-powered quartet and at the adjacent table where Mother and Dad, Aunt Alice and Uncle John sat beaming. Sydney Poitier presented the award in a delightful speech detailing our friendship and his appreciation for my art. He read the citation:

> The Capezio Award, 1963, to Donald McKayle
> For his translation of deeply rooted American folk materials — street games, cries, chants, modern blues, and brash but poignant jazz expressions — into theatre dances of interacial cast which faithfully reflect life in our land.

I posed for pictures with Sydney, Dame Alicia Markova, and Carl Van Vechten, the photographer, who requested a session to add my image to his collection. The framed citation with its illuminated letters went home with me. The accompanying prize, a check for one thousand dollars, went with Normand for a new brochure using the copy from Capezio Award booklet. Normand had become intrigued with the high-powered language of public relations specialists. He came up with a program credit listed in all playbills and on all promotional materials for Donald McKayle and Company that caused me no end of embarrassment.

> Donald McKayle is a Normand Maxon Attraction

It not only reeked of a commercialism that was alien to my work but was misleading, as Normand had no management organization nor any stable of artists to present. Charles Reinhart was in charge of bookings for the American Dance Festival and was the first to inquire into the propriety of the claim or its desirability. I recounted my conversation with Charlie to Normand and he agreed to remove the offending line, but I could sense that he was disturbed by the implied criticism and questioning of his ambitions or motives.

That summer I choreographed two large works and presented them at the Palmer Auditorium as part of the American Dance Festival, *Blood of the Lamb* and *Arena*. They were very different in content but were both dramatic dances. *Blood of the Lamb* was a distillation of impressions from James Baldwin's novel *Go Tell It On The Mountain* and drew its characters and setting from the black church. C. Bernard Jackson wrote an original piano and vocal score for the work. *Arena* was taken from another literary source, Mary Renault's novel of ancient Cretan ritual, *The King Must Die*. Normand costumed the two works and in *Arena*, he used gold fabrics and large fake gemstones to recreate the opulent descriptions of Mary Renault's prose. I was the royal bull and Louis Falco was the daring bull dancer who had to execute the *salto mortale* between the bull's horns, which were my constantly raised arms, shielded in stiffened golden vinyl edged with gold cording. Sylvia Waters was the Cretan Goddess standing on an altar of bull's horns carved from styrofoam and sandblasted to look amazingly like stone. Her bosom was bared above rows of pleated skirts and she clutched venomous vipers in her hands. The ample breasts were rubber and the serpents were fabric and sequins over wire. The end result of Normand's detailed work was not the royal riches he hoped to portray but a garish palette that evoked Las Vegas rather then ancient Crete. For all my efforts and the exhaustion of my central role, carrying Louis Falco around on my back, being ensnared by Dudley Williams and Raymond Sawyer in a dense net, the choreography fared no better, and I was forced to write it off as a failure.

Blood of the Lamb was chosen to be presented at the State Theater in Lincoln Center at a major presentation emanating from the American Dance Festival, and I was pressed into having the music orchestrated so that it could be played by the State Theater Orchestra. I fought this plan with great conviction as I could not fathom how the conventional instrumentation of the symphonic orchestra would be able to fulfill the gospel character of the vocal portion of the score. I also did not "hear" a string section in the music. Simon Sadoff was to conduct the program. He was most adamant about the necessity for the orchestrations and the use of the orchestra. I knew Simon very well from his work as music director for José Limón, whose work was also to be presented on the program. I respected his integrity and musical knowledge, but was convinced that his wishes had more to do with his appearance as the conductor than with what was proper for my work. C. Bernard Jackson, who was known as Jack to everyone, welcomed the challenge to orchestrate his music and was the one who finally got my acquiescence. Never was I more sorry that I had not stuck to my guns and ignored the host of forces working against me. Much of the music was unrecognizable in its new incarnation and certainly did not support the emotional or dramatic fabric of the dance. I returned to my dressing room and sat in abject silence, slowly removing my makeup and angrily kicking myself for lack of fortitude. A knock at the door disturbed my inner conversation. "Come in." I turned to greet the pair of faces I saw reflected in the dressing table mirror. "Charlie, Lee, how nice of you to come." I studied the concern in their faces and launched into a lengthy monologue on the events that had led up to the abortion they had just witnessed. They seemed to understand, shook their heads and offered words of condolence. It was rather like being at a wake; after they left, I felt worse then ever. Would this unfortunate failure damage my prospects with *Golden Boy?* They seemed genuine in their statements of reassurance, and anyway I had a signed contract executed by William Morris. Normand came in with a grave expression, chewing at a hangnail on his left index finger with nervous concentration. "Normand, you look worse then I feel." He reached inside his jacket front and pulled out an envelope. "Wait 'til you read this." I opened the folded page inside the envelope and gazed at an exorbitant bill for the copying of the score. This was the last straw. I told Normand to take it back to Simon and tell him I didn't want the score, had not ordered the copying, and that he could keep it all. Simon was furious as he had signed the order sheet and was liable for the bill. Normand received the bulk of the abuse and condemnation as byproduct of the fallout from his overambitious production claims. His spirit was crushed. He wanted to sever all connection with my work and took responsibility for all the recent run of bad fortune. Sensing his distress, I was able to separate myself from my own wound licking and come to the emotional rescue of a good friend and colleague.

AGMA was the performing artist's union that had jurisdiction over the events at Lincoln Center. It had intercepted the company paychecks and had them delivered to us minus dues and other union assessments. Dudley Williams stormed into my room with fire leaping out of his eyes and demanded to know where his money had gone. I took a pen from my rehearsal bag, turned over my paycheck, endorsed it, "Pay to the order of Dudley Williams," handed the net amount of twenty-seven dollars and change over to him, picked up my belongings and walked out into the bustling Broadway traffic.

Waiting for me at home was a message to call Craig Barton at the Martha Graham School. "Donald, how good of you to call back so promptly. Bethsabee has settled in Israel and is planning to start a dance company in Tel Aviv. It's to be called the Batsheva Dance Company. That's her Hebrew name, Batsheva; she's now Batsheva de Rothschild. She wants to know whether you're able to go to Israel as the first teacher for the new company and maybe you could do a work for them? Some of the dancers are here studying at the studio and at Juilliard, but the ones in Israel need a teacher. They've been studying with Rena Gluck but she's a member of the company and they all need to work together as a group."

I marveled at the vagary of fortune and how so much good and bad could be served up, consumed, and digested at the same time. I got out my passport and set about preparing myself for the Holy Land. I took out the audio reel of the Ernest Bloch score to which I had choreographed *Out of the Chrysalis* for the Juilliard Dance Theater, Doris Humphrey's conservatory company. The theme for that work was one I had wanted to revisit and this might be just the opportunity. Anyway, I was extremely fond of the music and wanted another crack at it. Perhaps another inspiration would replace the original. The starting date for *Golden Boy* had been pushed back and the excursion to Israel dovetailed neatly. I would arrive there at the conclusion of the high holy days and begin work in Rena Gluck's studio while the floors for the new studio were being completed.

The flight to Tel Aviv's Ben Gurion airport was interminable, but finally the airplane wheels were on the ground and all around me people burst into applause as a joyous chorus of "*Heveinu Shalom Aleichem*" filled the cabin of the El Al super jet. Rena Gluck's smiling face was among my greeting party, and I was taken to my temporary lodging in Batsheva de Rothschild's flat on Dubnov Street where I could get some rest. That evening Gary Bertini, the musical director for the new company, was conducting a concert of chamber music, and I was invited.

A repeated rapping awoke me from a deep sleep. Where was I? I was completely disoriented. Crack ... there was the sound again! I arose in a strange room and followed the rap to a window. I looked out and saw Rena in a garden courtyard below. She had been unable to awaken me with the downstairs door buzzer, and was throwing pebbles at the bedroom window. A smile broke across my face as I waved down to her and realized I was once again in Israel. I unpacked my suitcase, stepped into a hot bath, and as I soaked the jet lag from my body I wondered what adventures would hail me on this first night in Tel Aviv.

Lea Vivante in *Spanish Dance*. Costume design by Donald McKayle.
Photo: Martha Swope.

8

LEA

There was a buzz going through the intimate audience sitting in the museum auditorium waiting for the concert of chamber music to begin. Pleasant smiles and *Shalom...* greeted me as people passed by on the way to their seats or stopped to chat with Rena Gluck and were introduced to me. The musicians filed into their places and a round of applause marked Gary Bertini's entrance to the stage. He acknowledged the audience with a short bow, turned, picked up his baton, and began the concert. My attention wandered from the maestro's conducting as the pleasant sounds of the introductory selection filled the auditorium. Amidst the sprinkling of khaki uniforms on the male and female soldiers and the blending of muted and traditional jacket colors, a shapely back in brilliant purple caught my attention. Rising from a collarless neckline was a standing ruff of vibrant green organza, crested by a sleek coiffure of jet black hair. As I stared at the exquisite sight a few rows ahead of me, a flickering highlight bounced from a golden earring; a pair of startling green eyes returned my gaze. As I continued to look, an elbow from the young woman sitting next to the illusory vision jabbed into the purple fabric. A small quiver gently tossed the crescent of black hair. She turned back to face the platform where the conductor, acknowledging the applause, smiled warmly and bowed. I looked down at my program for the title of the next piece.

In the intermission, I headed for the queue at the water fountain, and was surrounded by people. "When did you arrive?... How long will your visit be?... What are your plans?... Do you know Rina Schenfeld?"

"Welcome...."

"She's at Juilliard."

...A single word of greeting in a lovely accented English and once again the green eyes look directly at me...

"She'll be returning to join the new company."

...A profile of pursed red lips touched the spurting water at the fountain....

"Do you know Moshe Efrati?...Ahuva Ambari?...Oshra Elkayam? They study at the Martha Graham School in New York."

...She was gone.

Rena did not have to wake me by pelting pebbles against the glass. I was up bright and early the next morning, awakened by a different and even stranger sound. A hollow and incessant thudding jarred me from a lovely dream. I opened my eyes in the still unfamiliar surroundings and lifted my head from the pillow to get an unmuffled reading of what I was hearing. The repeated thudding seemed to have found an echo...but no...the rhythm and timbre were slightly different. Suddenly voices interrupted the cacophony. I went to the courtyard window and saw the source of my wake-up call. Two women were leaning out from their balconies and gesticulating at each other with curled reed carpet beaters. Clouds of dust sprung from rugs thrown across the balcony rails as the women once again struck up their rhythmic antiphony. The puffs of gray rose, blended into the morning light that bounced along the surfaces of the tree leaves and vanished into the garden below. I heard the click of a door closing and wandered into the kitchen where I found a plate of orange slices, coffee, and a spread of breakfast breads waiting for me. I sat down to this lovely and unexpected sustenance and prepared myself for my first meeting with the Batsheva Dance Company.

Rena Gluck's studio was on the street level of a small building in central Tel Aviv. What was unique about it was the wooden floor, the generosity of a special bequest from Batsheva de Rothschild, and a rare commodity anywhere in Israel. As I listened to Rena talk about the tender care given to the immaculate maintenance of this prized possession, I remembered with great clarity some seven years earlier being taken to a lookout vista point in a kibbutz near Jerusalem when, as part of the Martha Graham Dance Company, we were given a tour of the environs. To reach this vantage point we had to pass a rather foul-smelling garbage dump. There, highlighted against a barren and rocky terrain that stretched as far as the eye could see and set apart like a precious jewel displayed on velvet, was a solitary hillside covered with trees. "Come back in ten years, it will all be this green and beautiful," said the proud voice of our prophetic young guide. He was suddenly sharply remembered, as Rena took off her shoes before entering. I went off to get into my practice clothes and re-emerged to find the studio filled with dancers stretching and warming up on the glowing hardwood floor.

"Welcome." The same lovely green eyes looked up at me. "Did you meet Lea last night? She was at the concert." "*Shalom*," Lea smiled at me as she acknowledged Rena's introduction. "This is Galia, Ruti, Ehud, Shimon, Rahamim..." I listened closely to the unfamiliar names as Rena introduced the dancers. They rose and came directly up to me and greeted me warmly. I repeated what I heard after each name. A gentle giggle bounced around the room. "Ra-cha-mim." Try as I might, I could not properly produce the throat vowel of the second syllable of Rahamim's name. "Rami ... ?" Rahamim shrugged indulgently and acquiesced.

Vigorous sustained applause and happy faces, shining with perspiration, followed the final slow warm-down. "*Yofi!* ... *Toda!* ... *Fantastic!* ..."

The dancers crowded around me. "Would you like a coffee?" "*Cafe afoock
... Pamaim.... Nes bishvili.... Cafe turqui.... rak kos mayim....*" I sipped the sweet
rich concoction and answered a stream of eager questions. Lea looked at
her wristwatch and rose to excuse herself. "*Lhitraot mahar....* See you
tomorrow."

The first rehearsal on the restructuring of my choreographic ideas for
Ernest Bloch's *Four Episodes for Chamber Orchestra* progressed with great
energy and excitement. The dancers were all responsive and eager to
grasp every nuance of movement. I was experimenting but a theme and
shape was quickly emerging. "That's enough for today. We'll continue
after class tomorrow. Thank you." That evening Rena made a little party
at her house in my honor. She was responsible for the training of Israeli
dancers in Graham technique. This occasion was perhaps as much a
celebration of the beginnings of the reality of Bethsabee de Rothschild's
dream as it was a private gathering to honor me. It was, I could perceive,
also quite unorthodox for Rena and her students to socialize. "Donald, do
you remember Moshe from Juilliard?" I looked at the man who had just
entered but did not remember him. He was Rena's husband and they had
met when he was in New York as a violin student. He was now a member
of the Israel Philharmonic and had just played a concert at the Mann
Auditorium. Rena went into the kitchen to prepare a plate for Moshe.
Galia and Lea came over to me. "We want to take you to Jaffa, to a
wonderful club where we can dance. They have great music and Shoshana
Damari is there. Do you know of her in America? She's a wonderful singer
and Jaffa is very special." I thanked Rena for the party and bid her
goodnight. She seemed a little upset that I was leaving. I made the excuse
that I was tired and that Galia and her husband Arik had offered to take
me home.

The old port city of Jaffa was a fascinating scramble of little streets and
Arab houses. We had to park the car and go on foot through the maze
of alleys down to a lighted doorway in one of the domed and arched
buildings marked with a sign... Omar Khayam. We arrived in time to hear
the end of Shoshana's set and the band began to play dance music starting
with a hot rumba. Galia grabbed me and led me to the dance floor, and
we soon cleared the space with an inspired *rumba caliente*. The music was
sizzling and Galia was a wonderful dancer. She had emigrated from
Argentina and had a sultry Latin personality. She was also full of fun and
given to impulse. She wouldn't let me off the floor as one rumba led to
another. The band's Latin set segued into a tango, I led her back to the
table and asked Lea for the dance. "You looked so wonderful dancing all
those fiery fast numbers with Galia." She rose to follow me back to the
dance floor. A small smile crossed her face and she looked boldly at me.
"Tango is a passion of mine, but you couldn't possibly know that." I

placed my arm around her waist and she rested hers across my shoulder. Our hands joined and we swept with the music. I looked into her sparkling green eyes. "Tango is for lovers."

Rehearsals and classes progressed wonderfully that week in Rena's small studio. The next week we were scheduled to move to new and larger quarters. Rena opened her purse and pulled out an envelope. "What are you doing tonight? I have two tickets to Habimah. They're doing *My Fair Lady*. It's a marvelous production with an excellent Hebrew translation by Dan Almagor." "I think you'll enjoy it even without the language." I went to the dressing room door and knocked. "Lea, would you like to see, *My Fair Lady*? I have two tickets." Lea looked directly at me for a few silent moments as if her mind was racing. "Yes. I'll meet you in front of the theater. I have to make arrangements. I'll see you there." The door to the dressing room closed behind her and a flurry of conversation followed the click of the latch.

The crowd was beginning to disappear inside the theater when Lea alit from the taxi. A shapely leg, shod in an attractive but precariously high spike heel, emerged from a slit in a fitted claret velvet Chinese dress. White satin stitched embroidery and caracoled frog closures adorned a diagonal path above her bosom to the mandarin collar that graced her lovely neck. Her raven tresses were piled high and clasped with a tall ivory hair ornament that ended in a playful dangling of carved flower bells. "I'm sorry I'm a little late. I had to get a teacher to cover my class. I teach at Imbal twice a week." "You look beautiful." "Thank you," she demurred with a tilt of her head. "You look beautiful too .... or should I say, very handsome? ... Excuse my English." "Thank you. Your English is perfect."

We turned heads on the way to our seats. We were in an excellent location, center mezzanine. The wonderful score and familiar settings were marvelously captured by a first rate cast and production. The Hanya Holm choreography had been remounted by Crandall Diehl. Without understanding a word of the dialogue, I marveled at the sound of Hebrew alliteration that so astutely echoed the original English lesson captured in the Alan J. Lerner lyric, "The rain in Spain falls mainly in the plain." The tortured cockney flower girl's attempts to properly pronounce the repeated diphthong, found a fascinating counterpart in the Moroccan immigrant's nightmare with the sound of the rolling R of the Hebrew letter *Resh*. "What are the words that they're singing?" "*Barad yorad bderom safarad haerev*. It means, the hail is falling in the south of Spain this evening."

I paid the cab driver and walked Lea to the door of her apartment building. A wild screeching stopped me dead in my tracks, and I turned toward the direction of the frightening sound. "It's only the parrots calling out to each other. I live behind the zoo. The night creatures love to serenade us. We get used to it." I turned and looked at her smiling at me with amusement. "Goodnight. I had a wonderful evening. Thank you." I bent down and kissed her lightly on her forehead and walked away. When I turned to look back, she lifted her fingertips from her forehead and waved. "*Laila tov.*" I wandered off into the night not quite knowing where I was heading and not very much caring, full of strange and wonderful feelings.

"Donald... Donald... Where are you going? The studio is in the other direction." "Oh, thank you. I am constantly lost in this city, but I do meet lovely people who help me find my way." Lea's smile broke into a little laugh. "This way, just a few streets." Rena brought me a steaming cup of *cafe botz* and sat down on the floor next to me. "Have you decided on your cast?" "Yes. I want you and Galia and Lea. I will use just you three women and one man, Ehud. I call the dance *Daughters of Eden*. You three live in paradise. One day a stranger comes into your idyll and nothing is ever the same again." I sipped the sweet thick coffee called, most appropriately, mud, as Rena went off to the dressing rooms to spread the news.

"Batsheva says I should alter the title because there is no way to say it in Hebrew. She says I would have to say Daughters of the Garden of Eden ... *Benot Gan HaEden*." "She's right." Everyone chimed in with an unsolicited opinion, an Israeli custom that could charm or annoy. "Why not call it just Daughters of the Garden ... *Benot Hagan*?" I thanked Lea for her suggestion. It was a perfect solution. I let Ehud go and asked him to return in two hours. I would start on the first movement with the women and then would work with him on the adagio third movement, which was to be a duet with Galia. By the time Ehud returned I had completed the opening section and was well into the scherzo-like second movement. I was on a roll and didn't want to stop. Galia, Rena, and Lea's torsos were drenched with perspiration and their faces flushed and exhilarated. I noticed a bright red spot on Lea's high instep. "You're bleeding." "Yes, it's a floor burn from the fall you gave in class. I must have lost the band-aid in the rehearsal. It's nothing." I noticed similar marks on Rena and Galia and a shiny translucency on Ehud's arch as he came from the changing room. I turned back to Lea. "So these are the feet that speak such beautiful poetry?" Lea looked up at me, a quizzical expression crossing her face, as a little buzz of exchange passed between Galia and Rena. Ehud smiled and winked at me.

"How did the duet go this afternoon?" "Wonderfully; I think I'm more than halfway through the music, and I really like what I have done. They're both beautiful dancers and marvelous together." "Yes, Galia is very special and so is Ehud. We were partners in Bimat Mahol with Rena Shaham. Would you like a Campari?" Lea placed a tray with glasses, ice, and a bottle of sweet vermouth on the little table in her combined parlor bedroom. The rattan furniture was covered in a green brocade and piles of colorful pillows tumbled about the double bed snuggled in the corner of the room. A small kitchen, a bath with a separate water closet, and a bedroom with an armoire, a toy chest, and a crib completed the small flat. "Where's the occupant of this sweet little room?" "Oh, he's visiting with my parents. You'll meet Guy, maybe on the weekend. Do you like children?" "Very much. I have two daughters, Gabrielle and Liane." Lea handed me a glass of vermouth and lifted hers to me. "To a wonderful stay. I hope you will be happy here."

Happiness was a meager word to describe the state of euphoria that filled every precious day; however, I ruefully realized that my sojourn here must come to an end. *Daughters of the Garden* poured out of me effortlessly. I was beginning the final movement that followed the duet. "Donald, why do you have me jumping and turning, and you give Galia all the soft lyric movements?" "You are a brilliant flame, burning, leaving sparks behind you." "Oh?" "Rena is solid and experienced. Galia is open and vulnerable. Your role is elusive and unpredictable. You three together make a classic trio. Combined you have unity, a wholeness that approaches the divine." "And Ehud, what about him?" "He fulfills the promise of the beginning, you know, those hateful slow rises from a low crouch with the leg extending and the head lifting." "Oh, they are impossible. At the very start of a dance to have to balance on one leg with your head up, looking into the lights." "The very last moment of the dance, Ehud will return again, skipping across the ground, bounding from one arm and one shin, like a flat rock skimmed across a lake. You all swirl around him and wrap together into a final spiral. Your combined bodies shape a pattern of infinity."

"*Yma, Donald, kelev yam, kelev yam!*" "He loves the seals. In English, you call them sea lions. In Hebrew, we say sea dogs." Guy ran to the enclosure where the seals were honking loudly and pushing each other out of the way in a hungry rough and tumble over the fish that were being tossed to them. He was a delightful child filled with vigor, always on the move. We had met at the new studio on Ibn Gvirol Boulevard, the former Ron Academy, where the company had moved once the new wooden floor had been laid. Guy was entranced with the shiny wooden panels. He ran across the length of the studio and slid on his knees under the grand piano. He was a three-year-old bundle of energy with beautiful large blue eyes in a wide open face. In a voice with a surprising low timbre, he kept talking to me until I would understand what it was that he was trying to convey. It was a wonderful learning session of instant Hebrew with a marvelously patient little teacher. I gathered from the impish smiled that covered his face when I spoke back to him in the new found language, that he was amused and delighted with the progress of his big and willing pupil.

Erev shabat and *shabat*, Friday evening and Saturday, comprised the weekend when all work ceased. While shorter than our weekend of two full days, it was a true time of rest, faithfully observed by both the religious and secular population. This *shabat* I was to meet Lea for a stroll on the Dizengoff and then we were going to her parents for lunch. It was to be a relaxing afternoon, but I sensed the seriousness of making a good impression. I dressed myself in a jacket, tailored from a rich paisley of warm earth colors and went to Hakalir Street to pick up Lea. She came to the door of her apartment dressed in a striking sheath of glowing Damascus silk, in tiny stripes of myriad hues like a *haute couture* Joseph's coat of many colors. We strolled down Dizengoff stopping in coffee shops, meeting friends, window shopping, looking at shoes displayed in Sasson, Lea's cobbler who hand-crafted exquisite Italian-style footwear, and finally turned off on Arlozerof and walked down the *shdera*, the tree-lined center of the boulevard, and turned on Ibn Gvirol towards her parents' home in a *shikun* built on the banks of the Hayarkon River. "There she is, peeking out from behind the blinds of the balcony. News travels fast in this little city and I'm sure she already knows where we've been this morning." "Well, we're quite a colorful pair, definitely something to talk about." I was fed a beautifully prepared meal. The centerpiece was a cold loaf composed of various ground meats wrapped in alternating layers around hard-boiled eggs and carrots. The attractive appearance of the marbled shaded slices was as rewarding as the delicate taste. I weathered a friendly but intense grilling on my profession, family, and schooling, and managed to convey my joy of life, ambition, and my happiness in their country. I apparently passed the charm test, but the happiest news to them seemed to be my plans to return to the States and the big Broadway show that awaited me. "When do you leave?" "In a week." "So soon? Will you come back for the *premiera*?" "I don't know. It would be wonderful."

A telegram was waiting for me in the Batsheva office. "Need you back. Please call collect. Hillard Elkins." "Hilly, it's Donald. What's up?" "We've discovered someone for the show, a terrific singer/dancer, a truly sensational talent and a knockout beauty, a real looker. We want her. You've got to come and see her." "I only have a week left on my contract here." "I know but we need to make a decision right away. Peter Coe is here and he wants to meet you, and he won't make the decision without you. We're sending a round trip ticket, TWA first class. There's a big party the day after you arrive, upstairs at Sardi's. See you there." François Shapira, Bethsabee's company manager, personally took me to the TWA office to pick up my ticket and deliver me to the airport. "You must be quite an important man. They're spending a fortune on you for these few days. It all seems in order." I thanked him for his help and took the small bag from him that I had packed for my three-day intercontinental twirl. "I'll be fine from here. See you in three days." He insisted on going with me as far as customs. I acquiesced. I knew he was being responsible and was genuinely concerned that everything go smoothly for me, but there was something about him that I just did not like. There always seemed to be a hidden agenda when he was around, and I felt discomfort and distrust.

The crowded party upstairs at Sardi's was a virtual who's who of show business. Sammy Davis was the center of attraction; he was accompanied by his wife, the lovely actress, Mai Britt. Billy Daniels who was to co-star in the play made a debonair appearance surrounded by a bevy of young women. Kenneth Tobey had been cast as the fight manager and was in a small group speaking to Peter Coe. His craggy face and shock of red hair were well known to any Hollywood film buff. Hilly took me over and introduced us to one another. "Donald, do you remember me?" I looked at the striking blond woman standing between Peter Coe and Ken Tobey, and although something was very familiar about her, I could not remember where we had met. "Paula ... Camp Woodland ... opera work-shop ... Rose Bampton ... Wilfred Peletier ... am I striking a familiar chord?" Was this vibrant, sophisticated young woman speaking to me with a smoky voice the Paula I remembered? Was she really the light lyric so-prano, graced with a clear open sound, always clothed in sundresses and modestly coifed in home-permanented mousy colored brown hair? "I see you already know Paula Wayne. She will be playing Lorna." Hilly guided me across the room to a small circle of people engaged in lively conver-sation marked with sharp bursts of laughter. In the center of the group was a bubbly and beautiful young woman who certainly lived up to every superlative of Hilly's telephone description. "Lola, I want you to meet our choreographer. You two will soon be seeing a lot of each other. Donald McKayle ... Lola Falana." A brief meeting with Peter Coe completed my transcontinental fête and the next day I was back on the jumbo jet, luxu-riating in first class service and arrived in Tel Aviv a day later, completely disoriented and exhausted.

My last week in Israel was filled with events, engagements, night life and a succession of farewell parties by all the friends I had made in my short sojourn. *Daughters of the Garden* was completed and a small, elite, and enthusiastic invited audience of friends and aficionados attended a studio performance. Lea and I went back to Omar Khayam to listen to Shoshana Damari and dance. The last night came and we banished sleep completely, loving each other and promising each other that we would somehow be together again. As the first light of dawn crept in through the cracks in the blinds, a pair of turtle doves fluttered their wings noisily on the window sill and began to sing the saddest song as they coupled. We held each other tightly.

Galia and Arik were downstairs with their car at the appointed time to take us to the airport. I piled my suitcases into the trunk and crawled into the back seat next to Lea. We pulled away from the curb and started the short drive to Lod airport. "Ay, we're almost out of petrol." "Arik, *koos emak! Mah atah omer!*" "It's Shabat, nothing's open." Arik and Galia railed at each other. I smiled inwardly, hoping that I'd somehow miss my flight. Arik stopped on a little side street and backed the car up to a parked vehicle. He opened the trunk and pulled out a section of rubber hose. He unscrewed the cap to the gas tank on both cars, plunged one end of the hose into the tank of the parked car, sucked heavily on the other and plunged it rapidly into the tank of his car. He then bent over and placed his ear on the hose. A smile broke across his face. "*Shigaon*, bull's eye, we'll soon be on our way." "Ay Arik, if someone catches us, we'll soon be all in jail." "Don't talk *shtuiot*. We're out of here." Arik closed the trunk of the car and pulled off just as someone emerged from a doorway and started to move down the street towards us. We all broke into laughter, and Arik led us in a rousing chorus of a favorite song of the Trio Hayarkon, "*Ezeh Yom Yafe*" (What a Beautiful Day). "My ticket I don't have it. It must be back at the apartment." "Donald, it's not meant that you should leave me." Arik whipped the car around in an illegal maneuver and headed back to Hakalir Street without dropping a beat. "*Tov, tov, tov, tovli a lalev!* (Good, good, good, in my heart, I feel good!)"

I looked out of the little airplane window to where Lea stood, her fingers laced through the chain link fence, her gaze searching for me. I waved bravely as the plane door closed. She waved back, but did she really see me? I crossed my wrists and executed a gesture from *Daughters of the Garden*. Success, she smiled and echoed the movement back to me. We kept waving as the plane moved off and turned onto the runway and she was gone. "Buckle up your seatbelt, sir." I sat back in my seat and fastened my seatbelt as tears rolled unheeded down my checks. I closed my eyes, swallowed deeply, and felt a strong pang in my chest. Was my heart breaking? Could such a thing really happen? I had never experienced such desperate feelings in my life, such pain, such heaviness. Mercifully sleep that I had pushed away at last embraced me and the next thing I remembered was the attendant bringing up my seatback for landing in Paris.

I looked at the gargoyle that stared back at me from the washroom mirror and shuddered. I splashed cold water on my swollen eyes, lathered my hands and covered my face with suds, rinsed and toweled, brushed my teeth, combed my hair, and decided a change of shirt was in order. I wandered through the elegant shops in the terminal and spotted a knitted silky shirt in Rodier of Paris. As the salesgirl wrapped it for me, my eyes fell on a lovely knit suit. It was a deep blue and next to it was a knitted shell in a warm apple green. I added this to my purchase. I would bring this home for Esta, but as I left the shop, I knew she would never see it. My mind was filled with the memory of those green eyes staring at me over an arc of organza on that first night weeks ago in Tel Aviv. There were other things for Gabrielle, Liane, Esta, Mother, and Dad in my suitcase. A new pain gripped me and opened a window on something that had vanished in a slow erosion over the past five years. Was what I now felt real? Was I now ready for such a commitment? I obviously had not been a decade earlier when I swept a bereaved friend into my arms and promised to take care of her forever. I twirled the heavy silver band around the fourth finger of my left hand. "*Goofenu ve nishmatenu, yahad l'olam.* That's a big order, Donald." "Yes, I know.... Our bodies and souls eternally together." The remembered conversation backstage after a concert as Natanya Neuman read the inscription on my wedding ring, brought other memories crowding into my consciousness. I would soon be back home and I must face my dilemma with honesty and responsibility, and decide what was really best for my two beautiful daughters. A mixture of joy and sadness blended with courage and cleared my mind. I hurried back to the gate to reboard my flight.

Gabrielle and Liane stood at the bay window and watched me as I walked down the street. I looked back at them and smiled. Their eyes remained fixed as they pressed their hands against the glass. I would be back on the weekend. We had made plans but they did not seem to understand what was happening. A change in fortune and a sharp rise in rent in our high-rise apartment at Park West Village had left us crowded into a studio flat in a west side brownstone that belonged to Esta's mother. She had moved in with her brother and his wife so that we could have her little apartment to tide us over. The cramped living conditions had only magnified the problems our little family was experiencing. The landlord wanted us out but was especially happy when I left to move in with Louise Roberts, a good friend that I had met while teaching at the Downtown Community School. The immediate future was unsettled and stressful but the decision to separate was one we both agreed was best for all. It was not, however, the best way to enter into rehearsals for my first Broadway assignment, but the dance auditions were in a few weeks and I buried myself in preparations for *Golden Boy*.

A trumpet blared and a rapid roll-off on bongo drums was answered by a wicked dance rhythm sounded on the conga drum. The crowd roared and began to sway and to clap on the off beat as a fiery tune rose from the trio of musicians sitting ringside in Madison Square Garden. The boxer who had just concluded a winning round stood in his corner holding the ropes and smiling. Handlers crowded around him and eased him onto a little stool. A woman jumped into the aisle and began to dance. The crowd was filled with Latinos and this was their hero. I had witnessed this total adulation when one night I went to a midtown Cuban restaurant and midway through one of my favorite meals, a delectable plate of *picadillo*, José Torres and his entourage had entered. Everything in the restaurant suddenly centered around his pleasure and everyone seemed to understand that service would not be the same as usual in his presence. The bell rang for the round to begin and the music came to a halt as José Torres sprang up from his stool and went forward to face his opponent. I watched his stance, the way he crossed his powerful arms over his chest and face so that he resembled an armored tank with his vital middle section fully protected with impenetrable sheets of steel. Seconds later his opponent was on the canvas, the referee was standing over him counting. José Torres was dancing just outside the stretched arm of the referee and the crowd was on its feet. The music blared again and it seemed as if everybody was screaming, jumping, or dancing. The aisles were packed with vibrant bodies and the entire scene was wildness. I knew immediately what the fight sequence in the second act of *Golden Boy* would be. Jaime Rogers would play Lopez, the bantam weight favorite that Joe Wellington, the Sammy Davis character, was to challenge. It would be the scene I had just witnessed, except the challenger would eventually emerge victorious. I had met Jaime and his sister Polygena doing their act, "The Kids from Puerto Rico", and had invited him to join my company. He was a dynamic little ball of unflagging energy and a great asset in the growing company repertoire. I had asked him to be my assistant on the show and play the role of Lopez which would involve him as a performer in this vital and terrifying scene that was the high point of the second act. We got together at the New Dance Group and planned the combinations that would be given at the dance auditions. I explained to him my ideas for the fight scene and a broad smile broke across his face as he assumed the José Torres crouch and shook back the shank of well-greased hair that he constantly held in check with a handkerchief wrapped around his forehead. Yes ... I knew I had made the right choice.

Every day I sat and wrote an aerogram to Lea, went to the post office and mailed it express. Every morning the postman would ring the bell with an express letter from Israel. On Monday the weekend bonanza would mean two. If nothing arrived before I left the apartment, I knew it would be waiting for me when I returned in the evening. When the weather turned to spring, I would sit in the park at lunchtime and write about what was happening, what I was feeling, what I was doing or seeing at the moment. The letters were long-distance conversations. I got books on introductory and conversational Hebrew and began to add a few sentences in Hebrew each day. I practiced the curved script written from right to left arduously on scrap paper, before I transferred it to the letter.

The preliminary chorus auditions for *Golden Boy* were jammed. The bare stage of the Majestic Theatre was a sea of dancers. Among the faces of people stepping up to the little table and showing the Equity lady their union card, I noticed Mabel Robinson and Lester Wilson, both members of my dance company and former students. I knew I wanted them for the cast. This show, unlike so many that I had auditioned for as a dancer, was to have a completely racially integrated cast. The whole theme of the show was built around an interracial love. Clifford Odet's original drama had been set in an Italian family and focused on the dissolution of a father's dream for his son to become a concert violinist. The boy decides to fight his way out of the grips of Lower East Side urban poverty and take a shot at the Golden Gloves and the tangible lure of the prizefight game with its perceived promise of fame and fortune. The musical had transferred the family into the black ghetto of Harlem in New York City, and the father's vision was that his son would be a concert pianist. There was no way to bypass open casting with such a story and this was a landmark moment in the history of the Broadway stage.

I remembered having gone to audition for *Subways Are For Sleeping*, a musical set in New York City, and having been stopped by the stage manager and told, "Sorry, but we're not using Negroes in this show." "Well, I'm here to dance for you. Maybe after you see me, you'll change your mind." That day, I had danced my heart out. I had been determined to be the best I could. I was fired up by the injustice of the situation and could not fathom the city of New York without a black presence, certainly not in its ubiquitous subway system. The Equity lady had informed me of the policy at the door in an effort to ward off trouble and embarrassment. I had flashed her my Equity card. "Is this card valid and up to date." "Why, yes." "Am I on your delinquent dues list." "Why, no." I had swept past her as she feebly tried to justify an untenable position. I had finished the audition combination and was startled when the dancers waiting to go on broke into spontaneous applause. The rehearsal pianist had stopped playing and the choreographer had come over to me. "You're terrific; I'm sorry I can't use you." I had thanked her, gathered up my things, acknowledged, with all the grace I could muster, the compliments coming at me as I made my way through the dancers waiting to go on, changed back into my street clothes, walked past the Equity lady who averted her eyes. I had welcomed the blast of wintry air that slapped me across the face. It wouldn't be the last time that I stood up for my rights.

The shiny cover of the new script was stamped in shimmering gold letters, GOLDEN BOY. I turned to the act opener, "The Manly Arts." I listened as Lee Adams and Charlie Strouse presented the number and I began to think of ways to stage it. It was a bright and snappy tune with happy colloquial lyrics in the best tradition of Broadway musical comedy.

The problem, as I saw it, was that this was not a traditional musical comedy. It was not a comedy at all, in spite of some of its fun filled moments. This was a hard hitting drama and the opening had to deliver the show's content with a wallop. It would be very difficult for Sammy to make his brooding entrance after the cheery lyric and bouncy melodic line. It was also misleading to the audience to set them up for a show that would not be forthcoming. My feelings became abundantly clear to all after I staged the number, which came off quite successfully on its own terms, but which stood out like a sore thumb in the context of the rest of the show. I met with Peter Coe, Charlie Strouse, and Lee Adams and described to them my impressions from the gritty atmosphere of Stillman's Gym on Eighth Avenue where hope burned eternally in the novice trainees as well as in the punch-drunk faces of the has-beens. This, I thought, was the atmosphere we needed for the musical opening of the play. Charlie and Lee began to work immediately on the new idea and the number that emerged, "Workout," grabbed the audience viscerally. They responded with strong sustained applause that carried over to welcome Sammy as he made his entrance. The rollicking satirical, "Don't Forget 127th Street," was the absolute other side of the coin, filled with all the fun and spice, steeped in an age-old tradition of black humor, "laughing to keep from crying." Sammy was the center of this big company song and dance number and had the wonderful special assistance of Lola Falana and Theresa Merritt.

I had worked with Theresa Merritt the year before on a gospel/spiritual songfest built around James Weldon Johnson's *God's Trombones*, a small book of sermons in the venerable tradition of the itinerant black country preacher. *God's Trombones* had been made into a musical play, *Trumpet's of the Lord*, by the actress turned director, Vinette Carrol. Recognizing one of the earliest manifestations of American theatrical forms in the black church, she had begun to develop a body of theater works with the commanding presence of the preacher as the main actor, the support of the choir as the chorus, and the vital participation of the audience as the congregation, with call and response as the completing element of the total theater. Something had gone awry with Vinette and the producer, Theodore Mann, and I had received a phone call in upstate New York. We were completing an arduous bus tour with my little company in which we had to share travel accommodations, with the set for *Games* lashed to the seats in the back of the bus to keep it from traveling down the aisle. "Donald, this is Ted Mann. You're a hard man to track down." "Ted, what's up? How'd you find me?" "Patricia called Louise Roberts. They both send their love. Look, fellow, I need you in New York now. I've got this show scheduled to open in two weeks and we're in trouble!" As fortune would have it, we were scheduled to drive back the next day. I met Ted in the

tiny Astor Place theater on Lafayette Street as soon as I could get downtown. He had called in Howard Roberts as I had suggested and we put
our heads together to remedy what seemed like an impossible problem.
The three principal actors were all first-rate, Lex Munson, Al Freeman Jr.,
and Cicely Tyson. Theresa Merritt was the leading singer but proved to
be a gold mine as an actress and all-round stage presence. Howard augmented the small choir with a few needed voices and I went about the
tasks of directing, choreographing, and refocusing the drama. The theatrical premise was a platform service bringing three famous preachers from
around the country together in a once-in-a-lifetime meeting of spiritual
greatness. Each would tell the biblical stories from creation to crucifixion
with parallels to the black journey in the new world, culminating in the
age-old question, "Where you gonna be on that great gettin' up morning?"
Ten days later we gave our first preview to an ecstatic audience response.
On opening night we sat around the radio at Ted Mann and Patricia
Brooks' apartment in a post-performance gathering slated for a celebration that could not begin in earnest until the reviews came in. "*Trumpets
of the Lord* opened tonight and it is a smash..." Cicely burst into tears and
Ted and Pat went around pouring champagne. Theresa burst into a song.

> Have you been through the fire
> Have you been through the flood
> Have you been through great trials
> Have you felt His precious blood

By the time *Golden Boy* arrived in Philadelphia for the final rehearsal
week prior to our out of town opening at the Shubert theater, we had
already begun to experience great trials. The fire, the flood ... and the blood
... were waiting in the wings.

Sammy was surrounded by the accoutrements and special perks that
befitted his stature as a superstar but were decidedly alien to the atmosphere and practice of legitimate theater rehearsals. His personal man,
Murphy, was always at his beck and call to supply him with another pack
of cigarettes or to freshen his drink, a bourbon and coca cola served in
an icy silver goblet. He seemed to have an amazing tolerance for this lethal
concoction and he also smoked incessantly. By the end of a full rehearsal
day, the stage floor was a carpet of cigarette butts. We had additional
rehearsal spaces set up in the John Bartram Hotel for Joyce Brown to
conduct vocals and for me to work with Dorothea Freitag on the dance
music. Dorothea was a master at lifting music-fills from the song score
and developing them into exciting compositions for dances or as underscoring for scenes. She was credited: "Dance Arrangements and Incidental
Music by Dorothea Freitag;" her contributions were sizeable. The music
for the prizefight was pure Freitag gold although she never was

recognized as its true composer. Sammy arrived for fight rehearsals with Murphy in tow carrying all the usual paraphernalia and, additionally a silk bathrobe emblazoned with an initialed crest which he threw over Sammy's shoulders at every break. The rehearsals with Sammy and Jaime were magical. All the planning, with me dancing Sammy's part against the movements I had designed for Lopez, paid off in the smooth and exciting execution of a dynamic sequence. The third day, the repetition, the bourbon, and the nicotine got to Sammy and he balked angrily. "All this work for a lousy ten thousand a week!" Despite my efforts, I could not control myself. Jaime and I looked at each other and burst into laughter. Sammy grudgingly joined us in mirth, but the rehearsal was over. The next one would have to wait for the stage.

It became increasingly clear that Sammy was beginning to feel a sense of panic. I had gone through a similar period midway through rehearsals in New York and felt a great empathy for this amazing talent burdened with the stress of this new testing of his stardom and weighed down with all the attendant baggage of his lofty position. My personal alarm had gone off when I realized how different a medium musical theater was from concert dance and the sense of my lack of apprenticeship began to gnaw at my confidence. It was good having my company members around me in the cast. They were able to restore my level of self-belief whenever it began to waver. I choreographed a trio for Jaime Rogers, Mabel Robinson, and Lester Wilson that really sizzled. It was greeted with accolades from the production hierarchy, and suddenly other areas of the show that were trials became easier to resolve.

Preview week in Philadelphia was chock full of incidents. On the weekday matinee, a vision in yellow chiffon splashed with white polka dots, wearing a beribboned yellow broad-brimmed straw hat, with a Yorkshire Terrier tucked underneath her arm, glided through the backstage door and was directed to Sammy's dressing room. The door opened on the completely redecorated star dressing room with the walls covered with pictures of family and friends. Sammy screamed with delight and embraced Elizabeth Taylor as the little Yorkie yapped loudly and struggled to be put down. Elizabeth Taylor's eyes actually were the sparkling violet prisms of Hollywood myth and she was every inch the realization of her legend. The following day a giant yellow Western Union Telegram mounted on a four- by eight-foot board arrived for Sammy from his Hollywood cronies, known as the Rat Pack. Saturday matinee rolled around and Sammy did not arrive for the half-hour call. He was nowhere to be found. Murphy was at his wit's end and Hilly was climbing the walls. He had called Mai Britt, who knew nothing of Sammy's whereabouts and was distraught with the news. Peter Coe called everyone together and announced that Sammy's understudy would be ready to go on and that he needed everyone's full support. As the house lights dimmed a spot hit the curtain and Peter Coe stepped out and explained to a very disgruntled audience that an amazing young man, Lamont Washington, would be playing the role of Joe Wellington and that they were in for a special treat, the discovery of a new star. As the orchestra began the overture, the din of feet against the marble steps leading down from the balcony, and the crush of people crowding the aisles and rushing the box office windows in the outer lobby demanding their money back was frightening. Sammy Davis was billed over the title of the show, and if he was not playing they had every right to a refund or, as the management would prefer, an exchange of ticket for another performance. The small audience that remained experienced a performance played to the hilt and gave Lamont a standing ovation. Sammy returned looking like the wrath of God and explanations for his disappearance were never given, but his voice was shot and his emotional level was very fragile. Other areas of discontent, grumblings, and straightforward malice surfaced and began to spread contagiously through the cast. Buried passion, unfulfilled ambitions, and outright cutthroat competition appeared in unlikely places. The first casualty of this cancer was Peter Coe. It is almost axiomatic with shows in trouble that the producers, the stewards of the ship, throw the director to the sharks without a second thought. The inevitable consequence of this miscalculation is that all allegiances, partnerships, and visions end up in legal battles, arbitrations, and lawyers' fees. Peter Coe refused to take his dismissal lying down and arrived at the stage door for the performance. He was told that he had been barred from the stage area. He went around to the front of the house and found the doors to the inner lobby locked. This hasty maneuver was against every fire regulation and, in disbelief and outrage, he banged furiously on the glass doors. A panicked house manager called for Hilly Elkins. Peter turned as Hilly entered from the manager's office and the two of them went at it loudly in the outer lobby.

Peter left the show without my having a chance to talk to him and Arthur Penn was brought in from Hollywood. A meeting with Charlie Strouse, Lee Adams, and Tony Walton, the designer, was convened. Hilly's back went into spasm and he attended propped up against a slant board. I came to the meeting but was told that I was needed to keep the cast in active rehearsal during this troubled transition. Arthur Penn began to redirect the dialogue scenes and the ballads and principal numbers. All of this was done on the stage with him walking around amongst the actors like a cinematographer. In a break, I asked him if he'd like to come out front and see the full stage picture and listen to the vocal projection of the actors. He gave me a quizzical look and thanked me. Hilly called me at the hotel and told me that he was bringing in Herbert Ross to help

Arthur with the staging of the principal actor's solo numbers. He then explained that dramatic scenes were Arthur's strength, but he had requested help with the musical part of his assignment. "Herbert Ross's help is needed to make the show the success it should be." I smelled a rat but told Hilly that I respected Herbie's work, and believed "we could both work together with the new director to make the show the success it should be." Hilly perceptively caught the emphasis of my words and agreed. "Yes, we'll all work together."

Herbie restaged the party sequence at the top of the second act as a decadent penthouse in the sky gathering with Billy Daniels singing "While the City Sleeps," as he slowly peeled a nylon stocking from Sally Neal's raised leg. The new staging helped set up the emotional bankruptcy of the hero, Joe Wellington. Herbie, with Nora Kaye constantly at his side, went on to set a light-hearted song written to showcase the charisma of Sammy's famous night club persona. As he strolled through a hastily assembled park setting, he suddenly burst into a song and danced a soft-shoe routine. While the conventions of musical comedy might allow for this textural inaccuracy, this was a musical drama. I found the choice of this purely showbiz formula completely in contradiction to the rest of the play. When Herbie's hand suddenly extended to the opening, "Workout," and threatened the integrity of my work, I put my foot down and protested loudly to Arthur Penn. "Is this what you want to do to the show? Did you sanction or request this?" Arthur expressed complete ignorance and denied culpability. I restored the number to its original form. As I stood in the back of the theater that evening watching, Herbie came over to me. "Oh, I see you've changed it back." "Yes, I most certainly have!" He shrugged nonchalantly and walked away.

At the final note session before opening night, I sat in the orchestra seats with the creative staff, Sammy, and the rest of the cast, listening to Hilly giving his final pep talk. Elliot Lawrence, the music director, passed me a gift box tied with a gold cord. I looked down the row and saw small packets in everyone's hands. My eyes found Sammy at the end of the row. "Open it. It's for you." I gulped a whispered thank you against the litany of Hilly's fervent go-out-there-and-give-'em-hell routine and opened the box to find a gold Bulova Accutron watch. That evening I went to Sammy's dressing room and expressed a proper appreciation for his generosity and handed him a present I had picked up for the occasion in Philadelphia, a pair of antique gold cufflinks shaped in the form of two golden orbs connected by a curved gold bar. They reminded me of barbells and struck me as just the right momento of the prizefight atmosphere. I wrote a little card in Hebrew letters, which I had been practicing in my daily correspondence with Lea. The Hebrew letters were followed by Roman letters and an English translation — *Mazel Tov* — Good Luck. Sammy looked at me with a raised eyebrow as if to ask, "Are you trying to steal my act?" I revealed to him the source of my Hebraic fascination. He smiled warmly and wished me, "Good luck tonight and back in the Holy Land." The show was a huge success. My work was singled out for praise, and I was proud that I had fought so hard for its integrity.

"Lea, *Golden Boy* is a sensation and promises to be on Broadway for a long time. You will see it when we arrive in New York. Say you will come and share my life with me. 'Ani ohav ohtacq.'" I love you. I signed the short and fervent wish with a salutation in Hebrew, "Lecallah shelli," followed by an ardent closing, "Miaroos shelach, Donald."... To my bride, from your fiancee, Donald.

The rest of the week was a much needed wind-down period from the stress of the show and filled with a bursting anticipation of Lea's reply to my cross-Atlantic proposal. At last the little blue envelope arrived:

> "Donald, ahoovi, yes I can't wait to come to New York, see *Golden Boy* and yes ... share our lives. I have read your proposal over and over and it fills me with joy and your lovely words in Hebrew bring such laughter to my soul. My aroos, in Hebrew you must not leave out the letter Vav or aroos becomes ars and you are no longer my fiancee but become my pimp.
>
> Ani ohevet othah ... I love you,
>
> Lea."

With Carmen DeLavallade in
Rainbow Round My Shoulder.
Photo: Normand Maxon.

With Esta Beck in *Nocturne*.
Photo: John Lindquist.

Alvin Ailey, Ernest Parham,
Cristyne Lawson, and
Kathleen Stanford in a
performance of *Nocturne*.
Photo: W. H. Stephan.

With Shelley Frankel in
Rainbow Round My Shoulder.
Photo: Jack Mitchell.

With Gus Solomons Jr. and Lester Wilson (back to camera) in a performance of *Rainbow Round My Shoulder*. Photo: L. Picariello.

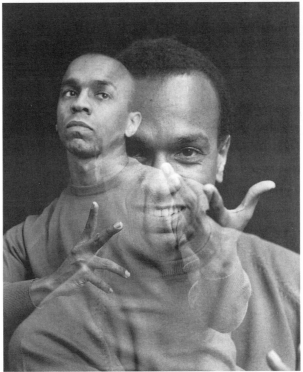

Donald McKayle. Photographic study by Michael Avedon.

Gus Solomons Jr., Sylvia Waters, and Lester Wilson in *Nocturne*.
Photo: Fannie Helen Melcer.

Eliot Feld and Shelley Frankel in a rehearsal for *District Storyville*.
Collection of Donald McKayle.

Cleo Parker Robinson and dancers in a scene from *The Emperor Jones*. Collection of Donald McKayle.

With Anna Sokolow and José Limón
at the State Theatre, Lincoln Center,
New York City.
Photo: Jack Mitchell.

With Paul Taylor, Ethel Winter,
and Matt Turney in Tokyo, Japan.
Photo: Y. Hayata.

With Louanna Gardner, Esta McKayle, and Eve Beck in *Games*.
Collection of Donald McKayle.

Alfred DeSio, Eve Beck, and Louanna Gardner in *Games*.
Collection of Donald McKayle.

Jacqueline Walcott, Shelley Frankel, and Gloria Jones in a stage rehearsal for *District Storyville*. Collection of Donald McKayle.

Jacqueline Walcott and Herman Howell in *District Storyville*. Photo: Oleaga.

9

STARTING OVER

The row of taxicabs at the El Paso airport ready to transport passengers to hotels for the lucrative quick-one-day-divorce in the Mexican border town of Juarez, was there waiting exactly as Eliot Lefkowitz had said. Normand Maxon had recommended Eliot Lefkowitz. He was in the firm of Weissberger and Frosch, a high profile theatrical law partnership which listed Elizabeth Taylor on their roster of famous clients. Normand had reasoned quite sensibly with me, "If they can take care of Liz Taylor's domestic affairs, they certainly can handle yours." I declined the cigarette offered by the cab driver as he lit one for himself and proceeded to strike up a conversation with me. He knew the lawyer I was going to see. "His office is right across the street from your hotel. Juarez is a fun town. You see the *abogado* in the morning. You leave tomorrow in the afternoon. Tonight you have some fun. My sister..." "No thank you. Tonight, I need to sleep."

Flying back to New York, I retrieved the packet of divorce papers from my attaché case and leafed through them. The Mexican lawyer's signature at the bottom of the last page was an indecipherable convolution of bold swirls. I was relieved that this was accomplished and yet at the same time filled with a great sadness. The document in my hands was as much an urn containing the ashes of the last ten years of my life as a passport to the future. The future of my imagination was all aglow, the prospects of converting imagination to reality were wrapped in haze. How would I get back across the world to Lea? How would I be able to bring her back with me? What would she think of this strange country and would our love withstand the forces marshaled against it? The immediate future was much clearer and I looked forward with anticipation to my role as choreographer for the major CBS network television special conceived and produced by Harry Belafonte, scheduled to be aired early in 1965.

The Strollin' Twenties was set in Harlem at the height of its cultural renaissance and the cast and creative staff were from the cream of black entertainment, arts, and letters. Langston Hughes, the acknowledged poet laureate of Harlem, had written the book of..."that dusky sash across Manhattan," as well as the lyrics for its title song, "Strollin'." In my early childhood I had been a participant in that Sunday afternoon Harlem practice during its waning days and had much to add to the concept, feeding ideas to Langston and Harry Belafonte, and working to visualize these ideas with musical director, Howard Roberts, designer, Tom John, and director, Charles Dubin. Handling the schedules and temperaments of the stellar cast that included Sammy Davis Jr., Diahann Carroll, Nipsy Russell, George Kirby, Gloria Lynn, Joe Williams, Duke Ellington and his orchestra, was awesome. Paula Kelly, who had started dancing in my classes at the New Dance Group and was now a performer of amazing power and personal charisma, was my assistant and lead dancer. Together we planned the audition for the sixteen member dance ensemble. It took place in a rented rehearsal room in the basement level of a West Side building. Many of the dancers in attendance were directors and members of leading concert dance groups and the atmosphere in the room was buoyant with camaraderie, rather than heavy with competition. The outfits that the women had chosen for this occasion were a riot of color and allure. I had invited my good friend Alvin Ailey to watch the audition. Alvin was always on the look-out for dancers for his growing company and this was an opportunity for him to see the best in one fell swoop. Among the women following Paula as she demonstrated the audition combination was a tall majestic willow of a dancer garbed in black and wearing woolen leg warmers over her ballet tights. She was a complete contrast to everyone else in the room and immediately caught my eye. She was a newcomer and did not join in the friendly banter that filled the space as the dancers vied to attract attention with a little extra personal something added onto the movement as given. The tall ballerina with the closely cropped head was all business, eager to execute what she saw, and very concerned with stylistic accuracy. Paula was indeed a hard act to follow. Wanting an uncluttered viewing of the striking newcomer, I called out, "Would you take those funny looking things off of your legs before you do the combination." The tall serious lady in black looked a little taken aback at my suggestion but went off to the side to comply. At the end of the audition I had narrowed down the field of excellent dancers to a group that included William Louther, Dudley Williams, John Parks, Vanoye Aikens, Louis Johnson, Raymond Sawyer, Bernard Johnson, Claude Thompson, Mary Barnett, Barbara Alston, Carmen Hilton, Cleo Quitman, Sandra McPherson, and Diana Ramos. Alvin sat on the steps leading up to the street exit. He moved to the side as the tall woman passed by him on her way out. His gesture called me over. "Who is that girl ... the one who just left?" "Yes, she's wonderful, isn't she. I just don't see her blending into an ensemble, but what an exciting talent." I filed through the cards that the dancers had filled out for me and pulled out the one written by Judith Jamison and handed it over to Alvin.

The dancers were the backbone of the show, augmented by a large off-camera singing chorus. The scheduling and stroking of the principals kept Harry busy around the clock. Sammy arrived an hour late for his big tap number, "Doing the New Low Down," and everyone else was put on hold to accommodate him. As we watched him execute his charm in song and dance from the control room, Mai Britt glowed with excitement. Sammy came into the booth to view the take and Mai embraced him warmly. "Oh Sammy, you're so cute!" Sammy bounded back into the studio for another take. He felt he could do some things differently. The door burst open and an excited production assistant entered, speaking at the top of her voice. "Diahann Carroll and her whole entourage are walking down the hallway headed for the elevator. She's been ready in costume and makeup, waiting to go on for two hours and when she saw Sammy back again on the monitor, she just blew it. She's got a hundred little pink bows in her hair for the "Honeysuckle Rose" number and they're shaking mad!" Harry flew out to intercept Diahann as another assistant came in through the door. "The mothers of the children for the Joe Williams/Gloria Lynn duet are asking when they can take the children home. We've brought cots and blankets to their dressing rooms so that they can sleep. It's way after their bedtime already. We're also heavy into overtime with the dancers." Somehow it all got done. Diahann Carroll was beguiling, falling backwards in an ecstatic swoon into a cape lined with roses , supported by an adoring ensemble of men as she sang, "Honeysuckle Rose." The children were awakened and their drowsy condition was perfect for the tenement family number. The last day, the big production finale with Duke Ellington at the piano leading his famous orchestra with the full dance ensemble led by Paula Kelly was a thrilling closing. Harry was able to relax, cutting up with the comics. He seemed to enjoy most of all an esoteric period piece done by George Kirby, imitating a vintage grand opera tenor emoting, "I want to know where Tosti went when he said 'Good-bye Forever'."

"Donald, I've got a project to present to you that I hope you will find interesting." That unique Belafonte voice was filled with excitement as well as its characteristic gravel. "Habib Bourguiba Jr. has invited me to assemble a group of artists to travel to Tunisia to view the indigenous performing arts of his country and give an educated opinion as to their viability as cultural exports to the United States. I've already received enthusiastic acceptances from Norman Dupaur and Ralph Alswang. Will you round out our group?" My acquiescence was immediate. The prospect was exciting. Not only would I have first hand experience with the people and dances of cultures of which I knew virtually nothing, I would also be just a hop, skip, and a jump away from Lea. I would be able to bring along an associate. Louise Roberts was thrilled with the offer to go along and help me with the written report that I would have to submit at the end of the tour. A final document, a summation of the four individual visits, would then be presented to Habib Bourguiba Jr.

Louise and I were greeted at the international airport in Tunis by an envoy who brought us to our hotel in the capital city, gave us our schedule for the following day, and wished us a pleasant rest after our long journey. The next morning, Habib Bourguiba Jr. was eager to meet with us and speak about the cultural riches of the peoples that inhabited his country. The recorded history of Tunisia dated back before the ancient Phoenician civilization of Carthage. Rising up from the deserts of the Sahara and sticking out like a beckoning finger into the Mediterranean Sea, it had been a constant target of conquest throughout antiquity. The son of the Tunisian president was a frequent visitor to the United States and a great fan of the world folk music that Harry Belafonte had made so popular. He was eager to bring the music and dance of his country to global prominence. Among the monarchs and sheiks that ruled most of the oil rich Middle East espousing narrow world perspectives, his father, Habib Bourguiba, was a leader of enlightenment. We were introduced to a pleasant young man who would be our guide. Abdul spoke no English but fortunately he was conversant in Spanish and French and we communicated in an unorthodox patois that moved seamlessly in and out of both languages.

Our first afternoon, spent in a rehearsal room with a local troupe of women devoted to Tunisian national dance forms, was an altogether inauspicious beginning into our inquiry. Abdul sensed our disappointment and explained that tomorrow we would get into the interior of the country and experience the real thing. The following day we arrived at Sousse, the beautiful coastal resort city on the Gulf of Hammamet, in time for a wonderful luncheon with the director of the theatrical facility housed in the ancient Roman amphitheater overlooking the Mediterranean. He explained that there was a great interest in theater, and people traveled long distances to attend. Last year's production of Shakespeare's *Othello*, translated into Arabic, had been an inordinate success with vocal inter-action between the stage and audience members as they voiced their opinions on the dramatic action. We left for Sfax where we were greeted by an engaging troop of musicians who performed in dance-like rhythmic cadences while executing acrobatic feats. The center of attraction was a stalwart fellow wielding mallets, beating a large bass drum suspended in front of him from a parade harness, all the while balancing on his shoul-ders a slender young man who was playing a piercing melody on a tsouka. As the double-reed player bobbed with the stride of the drummer, he flipped the braided tassels hanging from the pointed cuffs of his upper sleeves in circular paths around his arms in a playful filigree dance. Other events of the week included a visit to the ruins of Carthage and a shopping trip to the market in Suq al Arba'a. The days were constant sunshine and our journeys took us from the verdant vineyards that pro-duced excellent wines into the desolation of the desert that stretched

endlessly about us. There was mystery as well as majesty in the commanding barrenness. A ferry brought us to the Island of Jerba and to a wonderful
meal in a hotel filled with German and Scandinavian tourists. When our
repast was over, Abdul took us to view the highlight of our sojourn, an
extraordinary gathering of Berber musicians and dancers. The dancers
performed a virile leaping dance. On heavy staves, they vaulted high into
the air over the heads of the drummers who played vibrant crashing
rhythms on skins stretched across large bowl-like drums hollowed from
trees. A chorus of song was included in this amazing performance. Abdul
asked us shyly if we would spend the last night of our stay in Tunisia as
the guests of his family. "It would be a great honor. Our home is humble
and my mother has never entertained foreigners."

"Tell your mother it would be our honor; thank you."

Abdul's mother placed steaming bowls of couscous in front of us and
disappeared back into the kitchen. The granules of fluffy wheat were
mixed with fish, vegetables, garbanzos, plumped dried apricots, fresh
grapes and sprinkled all over with a fiery sauce called *harissa*. A sweet
soft drink cooled our palettes and a cupful of pomegranate seeds gave a
tart finish to this glorious meal. We retired to a couch of tooled leather
pillows where we reclined, sipping sweet tea, and listening to Abdul's
pleasant voice as he sang songs accompanying himself on the oud. The
home was above the family business and the main room opened out on
the flat rooftop of the store below which doubled as a patio. We were given
a small comfortable room for the night and awakened the next morning
with the sound of birds on the patio and the busy patter of Abdul's mother
in the kitchen. We washed our hands and face in a basin, and she poured
rinse water for us. The kitchen was a tiny room and the cooking element
for the magnificent meal prepared the night before was a single portable
Primus stove, a sort of primitive Bunsen burner with a pump to activate
the vaporized oil fuel supply. A tank above the water closet held water
for the toilet. The two footprints imbedded in the floor of the room marked
the proper positioning over the hole which caught the flush of water that
was released with the pull of a chain. A deft jumping maneuver took you
away from the gushing flow and out the door, safe and undrenched. This
hospitality was all the more meaningful when we realized that we had
been given Abdul's brother's room and that the whole family had moved
into the large communal chamber to insure our comfort. We thanked them
profusely and bid them good-bye. Abdul took us to the airport and asked
us not to forget him and to please tell our countrymen about his country's
dance and music and that Arabs are not like those in the story of "Ali Baba
y Los Cuarenta Ladrones."

"Oh Donald, Donald, You're really here. I got your letter with the news
and then a telegram from Rome." "We had to go to Rome to pick up a

flight to Tel Aviv. There are no connections between Tunisia and Israel. This is Louise Roberts. She'll be staying a week ..." "I hope it's all right, Lea. Donald's told me so much about you, I had to meet you ... and being so close ... and I wanted to take the opportunity to visit Israel ..." "You are welcome to my home." We took a taxi from the airport to Hakalir Street and Lea left us to settle in and hurried off. There was a showing of *Daughters of the Garden* that evening in the studio and she had classes to teach at Imbal. She had rearranged the apartment to accommodate another guest and had left a little meal for us. A lovely bouquet of flowers for Louise once again said "Welcome."

Several rows of chairs had been set up on risers at the end of the studio. I found places in the front for myself and Louise. Bethsabee de Rothschild arrived with Martha Graham. I stood up and waved to them as they moved into chairs a few rows behind. "Hello, Don. What a wonderful surprise." Martha smiled warmly at me as she spoke and Bethsabee waved and echoed the greeting. Rena, Galia, and Lea entered and took their places for the beginning of the dance. The audience quieted and the music began. As Rena's slow rise from the crouched opening position was followed by Galia and Lea, I heard Martha's voice muttering and then a quite audible, "Damn them!" I was too concentrated on the dance to turn and see what was going on behind me. The three women and Ehud danced with great passion and I was excited and pleased to see my work and to hear the warm response of the audience. I rushed onto the studio floor and they all swarmed around me in a gigantic embrace. "Lea just told us you are here....We didn't believe it....You look wonderful.... How'd you like your dance? We love it!" " It's beautiful and so is the way you dance it. Thank you." Others crowded around and I managed to pull Lea off to the side. Bethsabee was smiling and talking to Rena but Martha remained where she had been sitting and looked agitated. "Donald, I got here at the last minute from my classes and told the others that you were here. We didn't have any time to talk. We had to come right to the studio and dance. Martha has been here for a week and she's been changing your dance. Without a word exchanged between us, we all went back to the original version you choreographed. She's furious."

Martha's hands-on-and-meddle interpretation of the role of an artistic director was obviously not mine and in complete contradiction to everything I understood about artistic integrity. Bethsabee wandered over to where we stood and took me off to the side excusing herself to Lea. "I received your letter and am happy to see that the possibility of your being here for the premiere is indeed a reality. We have been able to put together a very respectable opening repertoire and not only to have Martha here for *Herodiade* and the excerpts from *Clytemnestra*, but now to also have you here for *Daughters of the Garden* ... it's quite a gala beginning." "Yes, it all worked out. Providence was with me." "In your letter you wrote every-thing the costumes for your work should not be. You didn't write what they should be." "Well, I'm here now and I will take care of that with Galia." My letter to Bethsabee was calculated to keep Martha's hands away from placing her stamp on the wardrobe for my work, "... no weltings, no divided skirts, no rick-rack, no capes, no head ornaments, no elastic strappings." I had never contemplated the necessity to add a caveat against choreographic tampering as well. Fortunately, my physical presence re-moved Martha from any further unsolicited dalliance with my work.

Sitting on the jumbo jet and looking out the window at Lea's father standing at the same fence where one year ago Lea had stood waving good-bye to me, I was filled with a sense of deliverance. I squeezed Lea's hand as I leaned over and waved with her. Arieh looked disconsolate and alone in the line of well-wishers crowded together at that last good-bye point. He had met with me in an effort to dissuade me from taking Lea to the United States. "She is a Sabra born of five generations that have always returned to this land. Such a flower cannot grow elsewhere." Guy, the sixth generation, was boarded with a family that took care of children. There was a great curing to be done to heal the wounds resulting from our audacious move.

Our journey back to New York took us through three cities where I had arranged for us to stay with friends, fellow Americans expatriated in Europe. Our first stop was Rome and we stayed in the studio apartment of Norman, my sculptor friend from Boston who had settled with his son in the artist colony in Trastevere. The first morning there, the little fellow knocked at our door and entered with a pot of coffee and a plate of rolls from the cafe downstairs. He placed them on the table and crawled into bed with us snuggling up to Lea with a stream of conversation in a mixture of English and Italian street talk. Lea hugged him tightly and thanked him for breakfast. She missed Guy just as much as her little visitor missed his mother. In Paris we bunked down on the couch in Jackie Walcott's living room. Paris was still in the grips of winter, and not the same romantic place of strolls along the banks of the Seine that I had remembered. At London Airport, Cristyne Lawson was to pick us up. I left Lea waiting for the luggage while I went to answer a page. On my return, I found Lea smiling benignly at a porter who was regaling her with a steady stream of conversation as he placed our bags on a trolley. "Donald, I haven't understood one word he's said to me. Is this English that he's speaking?" The man's thick North Country accent was as unfathomable as his con-geniality was contagious. I thanked him with a generous tip as he loaded our bags into a taxi and told the driver, "Marlabon Lane," which turned out to be spelt, "Marylebone Lane." Cristyne and her husband Graham's mews house was charming and their little toddler daughter, Lisa, was a joy. She delighted us by playing an endless game of tumble, down a stack of canvas covered foam rubber cubes, all the time articulating the arches of her tiny feet with the exquisite finesse of a ballerina. We started on the last lap of our journey to New York with wonderful memories of our European holiday and with the addition to our luggage of some prize items that Lea's wonderful eye had spotted on our tours through the shops; an exquisite pair of green Italian leather boots from Rome, elegant kid gloves and hose decorated with clocks from Paris and, from a London arcade, a beautiful Russian enamelware box on which was pictured a fairytale fantasy.

The foreign visitors' line at the New York International Airport moved at a snail's pace, but at last Lea was through and we queued up for customs inspection. I searched the glass barrier enclosing the overhead balcony and found Gabrielle and Liane standing with Mother and Dad and Louise. At last we were together embracing and all talking at once. I introduced Lea to the family while Louise went to get taxis. She arranged that I take a cab with her, Liane, and Gabrielle, while Lea went in another cab with Mother and Dad. I suddenly realized that Lea and I were separated for the first time since leaving Israel and wondered how she was faring. It was comforting to know that she was with my parents as I hugged the girls to me and began to answer their myriad questions.

Al DeSio opened his ten room Riverside Drive apartment to us and we settled in and began the adjustment phase of our new life. Lea knew nothing of winter clothing and considered being muffled up in heavy outerwear and overshoes ugly and unattractive. She proceeded to brave the snow storm that greeted us mid-March in a high fashion asymmetrical suede suit and succeeded not only in ruining the beautiful matching green suede and purple calf leather pumps but also in suffering a mild case of frost bite. We went shopping and she found an empire-waisted woolen overcoat in a wonderful rich shade of red, snow boots edged in fur, gloves, and a fur and wool hat that covered the ears. From her very first excursion into the New York department stores, she emerged looking smashing as well as being warm and protected. Harry Belafonte was having a private showing of *The Strollin' Twenties* that evening and I took Lea, garbed in her new finery, to meet Harry. So we began her introduction to my colleagues and to aspects of my work that she had never seen.

Mike Thoma, the production stage manager, was standing at the back rail of the audience as we walked into the Majestic Theater to see *Golden Boy*. He had heard that I was back in the country, was happy to see me there, and wondered if I would be coming backstage with notes. I assured him that I would see him afterward and, following warm introductions, we found our seats. *Golden Boy* had been nominated for the Tony in the Best Musical category and I spotted several voting members scattered around the orchestra and in the mezzanine. I had also been honored with a Tony nomination for Best Choreography. It was a wonderful perform-ance and my critical observations were in areas in which some of the personal additions of the excellent cast had stretched dramatic moments or made for distortions in the timing and balance. Some of their discov-eries were pure gold, though, and exactly the sort of enrichment you dream of in a show.

"What d'you want?" I looked at the menacing man who answered my knock at Billie Daniel's dressing room door and could not help but notice a bulge under his jacket. "I'd like to speak to Billie..." "He's occupied. He can't see no one." "Tell him that Donald McKayle, the choreographer, is here to see him and that I..." "I said, he's busy and can't see nobody!" With that the door slammed closed. Was I in some sort of bad movie or did I really experience these last few minutes? I turned to Lea standing next to me and noticed Mike Thoma at the end of the corridor. "What's the scene with Billie?" "Oh, I should have warned you about that. It's a long story. Jaime will fill you in. He's waiting for you upstairs with the kids. They all know you're here." "Tell him I'll be right up after I see Sammy." Sammy was in high spirits; Murphy, and George Rhodes, Sammy's musical director, and Rhode's wife, Shirley, were all happy to see me. Lea made quite a hit with Sammy who gushed unabashedly. "You're a lucky man. What a knockout! Pleased to meet you." "Shalom, pleased to meet you. You were wonderful tonight, everything Donald promised me and more." "Thank you." "No, thank you. It's a marvelous show." We managed to meet most of the dancers and singers and many of the actors and, after giving some notes, went out to the watering hole next to the stage door with Jaime. "Oh, Billie? Man, that's a gas! Didn't you hear about his old lady?" "No, Jaime, fill me in. Why does he have that hood back stage?" "Protection, man. His old lady caught him in the sack with someone else and took some pot shots at him. Man, he was running down the hotel hallway in just his shirttails." "You mean his new wife...that sweet young thing? I can't believe it." "That's the way it went down. Believe it or not. Anyway, now he's got a bodyguard."

Finding our own apartment, getting back into my teaching schedule at the New Dance Group, spending the weekends with Gabrielle and Liane, were just some of the activities that were sprinkled with the endless social functions that accompany such a major change in life. Lea had left all of her friends behind. Except for Hadassah Bedoch, a dancer with the Imbal Dance Company who had married an American and moved to New York, she knew no one. All of my relatives were eager to meet the mysterious Israeli beauty that I had brought back with me, and a large family get-together was arranged for that purpose. The aunts turned out a magnifi-cent Jamaican spread that was truly a feast for visiting royalty. There were distant relatives present that I hardly knew. Two cousins, who had only recently arrived, came with bottles of dark Jamaican rum, and the festivities quickly accelerated into high gear. A rolling island twang began to saturate the speech and idiomatic patois replaced the king's English. I noticed Lea across the room with an expression of perplexity crossing her face.

I introduced Lea to my friends. She made an immediate linkage with Aida Lioy, a dancer schooled in Spanish dance. The art of flamenco had been a passion for Lea. When Aida agreed to give her classes, it became the focus of her day. Aida rented a studio on 67th Street off Central Park West on a rotating schedule with Pearl Lang. The studio was run by two ancient ladies known as the Peters sisters. Lea's concentration and ambition were as amazing as was her progress in those intense private sessions. She began amassing a library of Spanish music, recordings, and literature, sought out Spanish dance performances and classes wherever she could and was soon enrolled in Mariquita Flores's flamenco dance class at the Ballet Arts studio in the Carnegie Hall Annex.

Robert Arthur called me from the Bob Precht offices to invite me to choreograph a summer replacement television series. Bob Precht was Ed Sullivan's son-in-law. I had worked for him when he was the line producer for the *Ed Sullivan Show*, staging numbers for The Supremes prior to Diana Ross' emergence from the trio as the ultimate star of the Motown singing group that also included Mary Wilson and Frances Ballard. The weekly show, *Fanfare*, was scheduled for thirteen episodes and featured the affable New Orleans trumpet player, Al Hirt. Bob Precht promised me five female dancers that would be regulars on the show. I chose an excellent dance ensemble with Paula Kelly again as my assistant and lead dancer. The other women included Barbara Alston, Vicki Di Chiaza, Beth Howland, and Donna McKechnie. They formed what would become a trademark television identity for me, "The Donald McKayle Dancers." I was responsible for the weekly choreographed show opener and for at least one additional dance number that would sometimes feature a guest star such as Liza Minelli. A televison dance number was approximately two minutes and thirty seconds in length and the rehearsal period for the entire show, prior to camera blocking, was three days. The sets and costumes for the featured weekly numbers were also designed and executed within the same time frame. Fortunately the show opener and home set were locked in place which allowed us to concentrate on the new material. If anything didn't work out by the day of camera blocking, the creative staff and cast were thrown into a high pressure situation. We would have to come up with a replacement item in a day and a half. I was being increasingly petitioned by Bob Arthur to utilize items from Al Hirt's song book for dance numbers, besides the weekly opening to his well known tune

"Java." I listened to Al's many recordings and decided on his version of "Tin Roof Blues." I conceived the number as a highly sophisticated dance on revolving piano stools with the dancers caught in supple body moldings or grouped in spirals with the crane camera rotating overhead three hundred sixty degrees. The dancers wore long bias-cut white alix jersey gowns and opera length gloves. The dance emerged as a sultry and sizzling winner. Everyone was excited about the beautiful, high aesthetic that was achieved. "That's a real class act, Don." I thanked Bob Precht for his praise and turned to Al Hirt who hadn't commented. "Yeah, Don, it's real pretty. I just love it ... but that's not the way we do "Tin Roof Blues." Ya see, I stand in the middle, Buba's on my right, Pee Wee's on my left, and we sway." Al's description of the staging of "Tin Roof Blues" is exactly the way it appeared on the show and the choreography, set, and costumes were dropped as of that moment. I settled in immediately to choreograph a replacement number to Dave Brubeck's "Blue Rondo a la Turk." The music was in mixed meter, a delightful challenge to me but a hellish rhythmic nightmare for the dancers. I was smarting from the summary dismissal of my work and relentlessly pushed to outdo myself on this assignment. We finished the day with a fully blocked and extremely complicated number. The dancers were in a state of exhaustion and mental fatigue. Beth's eyes welled with tears of insecurity, and Barbara just sat on the rehearsal studio floor shaking her head. Paula kept practicing a particularly tricky sequence. Pepe arrived with the baby in the stroller and took a very weary Vicki home. As luck would have it, the wardrobe could not be completed for the shooting deadline, and we got a reprieve. The number would be shot out of sequence the following week and would be edited into the show prior to airing.

Edward Villella and Patricia McBride were scheduled as guests on the show, and I was given the opportunity to create a special dance for these two illustrious stars from the New York City Ballet. I was able to engage the brilliant jazz reed player and composer Jerome Richardson to create a special score for a dance fantasy. The choreography was designed especially for the camera and these extremely exciting artists who worked on it with a great appetite. Alas, once more, my work would fall victim to Al Hirt's ax. "No, I want them to dance that Tchaikovsky dance, just like I saw them do it at the ballet." Al was adamant. He was very exercised about this, breathing heavily as his face flushed with color. The disappointment for Eddie and Patricia was only second to Jerome's, who pleaded with Bob Precht to at least let him hear the band play his music at the rehearsal scheduled later in the afternoon. I was angry at what was definitely a cavalier attitude toward my own creative investment.

At this moment a remembered incident, that occured during my tenure as choreographer for the *Ed Sullivan Show* when Bob Precht and his entire production team had been held hostage by the demands of a celebrity dancer, helped to give some measure of balance to my wounded spirit. Rudolph Nureyev and Margot Fonteyn had been booked in as a star attraction to perform a classical *pas de deux*. They arrived and Rudi came out to examine the television stage while Fonteyn went to the dressing room to change for rehearsal. Rudi did a few movements on the tiled surface and frowned. "No good. I can no dance on this!" The stage manager and the director rushed over to see what was the matter. Rudi scowled at them. "This floor too hard, no jump. I no dance on this!" Turning on his heels he walked off toward the dressing room, leaving a flurry of excitement in his wake. Bob Precht was summoned and went off to the star dressing room in a flash to assure Mr. Nureyev that whatever he needed for his performance with Miss Fonteyn would be arranged to his satisfaction. This was marvelous. I had never seen such action for a dancer before. We had all killed our legs and backs dancing on the poured concrete television studio floors laid over with just a thin sheeting of linoleum tile. Resilient floors, so necessary for dance, were a no-no for television and the steady tracking of the cameras. Nevertheless, they constructed a dance floor from raised risers overlaid with a masonite subfloor and then covered with tiles to match the look of the rest of the television studio. The cameras practiced moving around the outskirts of the resilient island and then Bob Precht called Nureyev in for an inspection. Rudi did a few small jumps, a run, and a pirouette. "Good." Bob Precht and the director sighed with relief. "Okay let's begin the camera blocking." "Camera blocking?" "We need to set the camera moves as you and Miss Fonteyn are dancing." "No, now is time for my rest." Leaving an open mouthed assemblage, Nureyev repeated his haughty turn on his heel and returned to his dressing room.

Reorganizing my own company and getting back to the full charge and responsibility for my own work was a welcome change. I also took on the challenge of performing again in a very demanding repertoire. I staged *Daughters of the Garden* for its United States premiere in which Lea and I performed the central duet, and in *Rainbow Round My Shoulder* I danced my original role with Paula Kelly as the multi-faceted figure of the Dream, Sweetheart, Mother, Wife. Charles Reinhart was our company manager and booked us on an East Coast tour.

Lea and I found an apartment on 110th Street between Broadway and Amsterdam Avenue and started housekeeping with just a bed, a card table, and four folding chairs, all gifts from my parents. Slowly furnishing our home together and finding things that we enjoyed was a wonderful process. A year rolled by from the day we had arrived together at John F. Kennedy airport, and we decided on the date of our marriage. Eliot Lefkowitz advised me that until the legal kinks with New York State's rulings on Mexican divorces were finalized, it would be best to get married out of state. We chose the neighboring town of Riverside, a lovely suburb of Greenwich, Connecticut. Once before, I had been present at a wedding in Greenwich. It had taken place in the private home of a justice of the peace. I was best man for Domingo Rodriguez when he married Esta's sister, Eve. As the vows were being exchanged and the justice intoned, "Do you take this woman to be your lawfully wedded wife?", all of the quaint little clock collection that hung on the walls began to chant, "Cuckoo, cuckoo." Try as we might to continue with the required solemnity of the occasion, the entire wedding party dissolved into contagious guffaws.

Lea and I were married on the first Sunday in May 1965, and Mother was elated. She surmised that since we had chosen Mother's Day for our wedding, it was our gift to her, and she beamed with delight. We planned a simple ceremony with just a few guests. Mother and Dad gave a reception at their home for our friends and the relatives. Dad embraced Lea and said with joy and relief in his voice, "Now I can call you daughter." The ceremony was witnessed by my parents and a few good friends, including Normand Maxon, Hadassah Bedoch, Jaime Rogers, and Louise Roberts. Jaime snapped away with his camera, but the negatives were somehow misplaced. Mother's little brownie camera captured the only existing photographs of our wedding. They were good pictures but carried the trademark of all of mother's photos of me: the top of my head was cropped off. Lea found a lab that studied other pictures of me and was able to fill in the missing slice of cranium and add additional background to one of the snapshots that we particularly liked. It was an unstudied moment with none of the stiff posed formality of standard wedding photography, just two young people in love looking into each other's eyes. As tradition would have it, Lea's beautiful dress of lavender lace was kept secret from me until our wedding day. Gabrielle and Liane did not attend the ceremony but they were at the final fitting of the wedding dress and were the only ones to share this special moment with Lea. Ursula Reed, who made all of Martha Graham's costumes and had constructed Normand Maxon's wonderful designs for *District Storyville*, made Lea's outfit with its triple tiers of graduated flounces falling from an empire waist and a mantilla for her head. She skillfully matched the floral patterned filigree to create the triangular shawl with a flawless scalloped edge. She covered a satin purse and edged satin gloves with the lace in a complete realization of Lea's designs. Holding a small bouquet of lavender orchids, Lea was truly a breathtaking bride.

"Hello, this is Martha." "Martha who?" "I'm sorry to disturb you on your nuptial night, but I'm sure it's not the first." After a bizarre one-sided conversation, I hung up the phone. "Lea, that was Martha Graham." "What did she want?" "She said she couldn't make it to the wedding because it was in Connecticut." "We didn't invite her to the wedding. She must have heard about it from Ursula." "What a strange call. It's three AM." "When you arrived so unexpectedly in Israel for our *premiera*, Martha asked me to a meeting and tried to persuade me to stop seeing you. She told me about not taking Esta on the Asian tour. She somehow felt responsible for the breakup of your marriage." "She said what?" "I told her, 'Martha, from ten until four I'm here in the studio to work for you. After that, what I do is none of your business.' I don't think she was used to dancers speaking that way to her. She left the room very angry." "But she seems to like you so much." "After that, she treated me with respect. When she was casting *Clytemnestra* she asked the three of us who had learned Cassandra to dance the solo together. Ahuva Ambari and Hadassah Bedoch both grabbed hold of the one prophecy stick that had been made for a rehearsal prop. I let the two of them fight over it and went to the janitor's closet and got out the broom. She gave the role to me."

Donald McKayle and Company were scheduled to be presented on the 1965 Brooklyn Academy of Music's Modern Dance Series, and I gathered the dancers together and began preparations for a program that would include a new work, *Wilderness*, and two other dances from my repertory, *Nocturne* and *Daughters of the Garden*. The premiere dates of these three items roughly spanned my choreographic history, 1952, 1964, and 1965. Beside the brand new *Wilderness, Daughters of the Garden* was also unknown to New York audiences. Later, I was asked to stage *Daughters of the Garden* for the Harkness Ballet which had yet to make its all-important New York debut.

Lea and I arrived at the Watch Hill, Rhode Island, estate of Rebecca Harkness in a chauffeured station wagon filled with our luggage for a month's choreographic residency, our new basset hound puppy, Yofi, and five cages of exotic birds, including finches, thrushes, honey creepers, and a black headed red South American siskin. The attendant took us up to the far wing of the mansion and ensconced us in Mrs. Harkness's mother's suite. The spacious quarters were decorated entirely in white with blue accents. The housekeeper looked at our menagerie with dismay as he set the cages down on the luxurious white carpet. Light streamed in through the windows on both sides of the bedroom which overlooked the bay and the Harkness's private golf course. A trio of nuns with their black habits fluttering in the breeze were running gleefully at the waters' edge. Bright blue tennis shoes padded the wet sand as they frolicked. Lea put the leash on Yofi and took her out for a walk. I had spotted the puppy in a pet shop window and immediately fell in love with her doleful sad eyes and brought her home. Alas, she had lived in that cramped pet shop environment for too long and resisted all our attempts at house breaking. We had enrolled her in a training course in preparation for the summer residency but had little faith that our efforts would prove successful. We lined the tops of the bureaus and chests with brown wrapping paper and placed the aviary in its new and magnificent setting, then we covered the bathroom carpet with newspaper and left Yofi there for the night. In the morning we found the papers filled with evidence of Yofi's presence but she was nowhere in sight. The attendant appeared and with a smile informed us that our little hound was happily lodged in a kennel with a long run and excellent food, where she would be well cared for and that we would be free of worry as to her wellbeing during our busy rehearsal period. For the first week we had the entire wing, with its spacious and fully equipped kitchen and small screened porch, to ourselves. The second week John Butler arrived to begin working with the dancers, and the following week Alvin Ailey joined the roster of choreographers. The three of us shared the wing but, except for Mrs. Harkness's private quarters, we were free to roam about the rest of the estate with its forty-two rooms and fourteen kitchens. On our first night there, Lea and I were invited to a dinner in the main dining room where Rebecca Harkness sat at the head of an enormous formal dining table set with beautiful linens, silver, and glowing candles. She sat me at her side and after looking Lea over with a swift and appreciative eye decided to seat her at the other end of the table where the two of them could not possibly be perused in the same glance.

Rehearsals were held in a light and airy studio on the second floor of the former fire house. John Butler had cast Lawrence Rhodes as the lead in his *Sebastian*, and Alvin wanted Dennis Wayne for a major role in his work. Aside from those two dancers, I was free to cast anyone. I chose a lovely Belgian artist, Panchita De Peri, to dance the duet with Salvatore Aiello and cast Bonnie Matthis and a promising young dancer from the corps in the other female roles. In the remounting of *Daughters of the Garden* on my own company at the Brooklyn Academy of Music, Jerry Grimes had danced the duet with Yuriko Kimura; Lea had danced her original role. Ruti Lerman and Rahamim Ron had come from Israel to New York for a year's stay and I cast Ruti in the role originated by Rena Gluck. The scenario for the new work was based on the biblical wanderings of the Hebrew tribes in the wilderness, the loss of faith, and the building of a golden idol to worship. I cast Lea against William Louther in a passionate duet which was the center of this complex piece. In rehearsals they looked wonderful together but little by little Bill began to reshape and change his role in subtle and devious ways... an extra holding of a balance... arriving a fraction late for a support... a change of focus. It became obvious to me that I was experiencing a power play and something that had to be nipped at the bud. With the Brooklyn Academy of

Music engagement close at hand, I sat and listened to Bill as he reeled off complaint after complaint in an effort to justify his obnoxious rehearsal behavior. It all sounded so alien to the work I was doing. I decided to sidestep the past and deal with the present. I insisted on his adherence to the choreography. Bill began to arrive late for every rehearsal, coming in with a container of coffee and a Danish pastry which he proceeded to consume, further delaying the process. While he nibbled at his breakfast, I began to shift things around, taking music that had been used for choreography for him, and giving it to someone else. He was suddenly on the floor and ready for rehearsal. It was a tiresome exercise, but with performance only a week away, it became necessary.

Nocturne was the opening work on the program, and Bill was dancing my role. He was striking in the men's dance and Rahamim brought a vibrant assertive openness that was characteristic of the way the Batsheva Company had danced the work. As the women entered in the second movement, I sat back and waited for the duet that I had choreographed so many years ago for Esta and myself. Connie made her passage downstage but Bill was not there. She circled around a nonexistent partner and as she came to rest in her final pose, Bill suddenly emerged from the wings and joined her. I raced backstage to see what had happened. Connie was silently steaming, and Bill looked me squarely in the face and puffed on a cigarette. "I was so thrown when I saw the program, I just didn't know what to do." "What are you talking about Bill? What about the program?" "Look at my name. It's on the same line with Lea and Jerry." "So what! I made no arrangement with you to become a diva. This is a dance company not a Broadway show." "You even put Lea's name in the center which automatically makes it more important than my name." "There is no excuse for not fulfilling your artistic role. I'm sorry if I tarnished the tinsel on the imaginary star on your dressing room door, but we've got a premiere coming up and you'd better concentrate on that!" I was furious as I went back to my seat and fearful of what might happen in *Wilderness*. Bill danced with all the brilliance his pliant physicality could muster, but he was icy cold and up to all his devious tactics, calculated to undermine Lea's performance. It saddened me as I remembered the ingenuous youngster who had stopped in his tracks as he heard the ovation that greeted his performance in *District Storyville* not so many years ago. *Wilderness* was not successful, but the rehearsal process had been so distasteful that I never went back to it.

Lea and I stood at the gate waiting for the passengers to come off the jumbo El Al jet that had just landed. The first passenger out was a smiling five year old clinging to the hand of a stewardess with a big tag clipped to his jacket, exhibiting his name in phonetic misspelling from the Hebrew, Gai Eylon. Lea ran to Guy and hugged him closely. I followed and bent down so that we were face to face. *"Shalom Guy, mashlomha?"* *"Tov."* He pulled Lea close to him and whispered. "He wants to know if he really has a bicycle, and where is it?" We hailed a taxi, and took Guy home to our apartment on 110th Street where his little room had been decorated with loving care in anticipation of his arrival. Toys were everywhere, and in front of the window was a shiny new bicycle. After a promise that he could take his bike for a long ride in the morning, he agreed to look at his other toys and following a late and little-touched supper, he went to bed piling all his new toys into the bed with him and insisting that the bicycle be placed close to the bed where he could reach out and touch it. Living for a year in a home with children where everything was shared had left its mark on him. A new six-week-old Saint Bernard puppy, who had inherited the name of Yofi from the basset hound we had never been able to housebreak, was brought into Guy's life and the two became fast friends. An elderly lady had admired Yofi Number One while she was out being taken for a walk, and Lea had handed her over to the woman, leash and all.

On the weekends Gabrielle and Liane would stay with us. I now had three children and suddenly needed three arms, one for each child to hold onto possessively when we went out to the playground. Guy's English improved at a remarkable rate with the two girls as playmates and siblings. His other tutor was the television tuned into cartoons with the volume up to an excruciating decibel. "Gigantor, the great beeg robot!" Guy sang at the top of his lungs. With the advent of school, he came into contact with classmates who chided him on his faulty language skills, a problem that he often settled with aggressive behavior. Gradually he adopted his new language and tried to forget his mother tongue. The dusky timbre that had colored his speech in Hebrew was replaced by the imitation of what he heard in the schoolyard and he began to speak New Yorkese with a high-pitched vocal swagger. He demonstrated his acceptance into the pack with the chanting of a playground taunt.

Baby, baby, stick your head in gravy.

The second line was mostly in an imagined language.

Lasha hala bubble gum, send it to the navy.

With a little research, I was able to give him the proper line and ward off any further embarrassment.

Wash your face with bubble gum and send it to the navy.

10

HOLLYWOOD

"Hi, Donnie, it's Nick Vanoff. Want to come out to Hollywood?" Nick Vanoff's voice on the phone swung me back a decade or so to Charles Weidman's studio theater on West 16th Street in Manhattan. Nick was, like all of us, a dyed-in-the-wool modern dance fanatic. He took care of the studio for Charles in exchange for classes and a bunk near the light booth to hunker down in at night. He was also courting Charles's lead dancer, Felicia Conde. "Felicia and I live in L.A. now. I'm producing the Hollywood Palace. We're on ABC. I need you out here. Miriam Makeba, the wonderful South African singer, will be starring with us next month. We'd like to introduce her with a dance production number. I think this one's right up your alley. What d'you say?" "Of course, congratulations!"

Nick had in mind "The Zulu Chief," the same song that I had been asked to choreograph and perform in 1950, on the Fred Waring Television Hour. Ray Sax had been the show's line producer and his wife, Nadine Gay was the show's weekly choreographer. Nadine with her partner, Peter Hamilton, were featured guest artists with the Charles Weidman Company. I had danced the number with Nadine's assistant, Marc Breaux, also a Charles Weidman alumnus, now a Los Angeleno. In the early fifties the familiar harmonies of Fred Waring's Pennsylvanians had delivered the vocals. Now, in 1968, it was to be the thrilling and authentic sound of Miriam Makeba. No matter how deeply felt, my interpretation of the material was ignorant of authenticity. The dancers chosen from the audition were men who spent their childhood in Watts or Compton or who had recently migrated west, answering the seductive call of Hollywood. They were trained in studios featuring tap, swing, and acrobatic dance or they were émigrés from Club Harlem in Atlantic City or some such sister club. One dancer, Carlton Johnson, stood out. He had the respect of all the others. I immediately made him my assistant and began the rehearsal process. The dancers were not used to dance directors with my drive or technical demands. Many were laid back. They came to rehearsals straight from poolside or from the beach with sand in their hair and sunshine lazing their muscles. Miriam was not pleased with the results of our work. "Who is this Zulu Chief.... He is our king. In this song we pay homage to our ruler. He is wise as well as strong and cunning." She threw herself into a pattern of movement. But when the dancers imitated her, they had little of the desired texture. It just was not in their bodies. Only Carlton rose to the occasion, and I was able to develop a brief interlude for him with the other men forming a stately processional which led the camera to Miriam Makeba as she sang.

Other television specials led to increasing journeys to the West Coast, and in 1969 a part-time residence in the Hollywood Hills. Finally an offer came to choreograph a prime time musical series to feature Leslie Uggams, the delightful young singer/actress/dancer who had made such a hit on the *Mitch Miller Show*. We were guaranteed thirteen episodes with the possibility of being picked up for the rest of the season of twenty-six. This meant moving Lea and Guy to Los Angeles. Gabrielle and Liane had moved with Esta to Boston; so while I could not see them on a weekly basis, it had been still possible to spend some time together. Now it would be very difficult. I found a house in Beverly Hills, walking distance to Wilshire Boulevard, where I could catch a bus to the CBS studios on Fairfax and Third. Guy was enrolled in a wonderful public school, and Lea and I started driving lessons. I chose Carolyn Dyer to be my assistant and she began to drive me to rehearsals.

Carolyn was a New York dancer that I had cast in the 1968 Broadway show *A Time For Singing*, based on the Richard Lewellyn novel *How Green Was My Valley*. This moving story of life in the coal mining villages of Wales had previously been made into a classic film. The musical, starring Tessie O'Shea, Ivor Emmanuel, Shani Wallis, and Laurence Naismith, was authored by Gerald Freedman and composed by John Morris. I had worked with Gerry and John, in the 1963–64 season, on several plays for Joe Papp's "Shakespeare in the Park." The last was the highly successful production of *The Tempest* with Paul Stephens as Prospero, Kathleen Widdoes as Miranda, James Earl Jones as a green tongued Caliban, Charles Durning in a wonderful comic role, and Karen Black as one of the goddesses. The dance ensemble included Pearl Reynolds, Thelma Oliver, Harriet Clifford, Don Martin, Charles Moore, Ella Thompson, and Takako Asakawa. Esta was then my assistant and midway through the rehearsal period was called into full staff authority. In the second week of rehearsals, a slit had opened between my toes. The podiatrist who examined my swollen foot sent me to a general practitioner, who took one look at the foot and the blue vein that was traveling up the inside of my thigh toward my groin, and sent me directly over to the Medical Arts Center. The swelling was lanced, and I was hospitalized for several days with a drain and saline solution treatments. "Caught it just in time. You're a lucky man. If the infection had gotten to the lymph glands we would have been in serious trouble." I had to send my choreography in diagrams and explanations via Esta, who visited me twice a day. When I returned, I was quite pleased with how it had all turned out. Carolyn was not the only New York dancer who had followed me out to Los Angeles. The gypsy hotline was in full operation and my growing reputation as the new hot choreographer in the business brought a huge turn-out of aspirants answering the audition notice. The packed rehearsal hall was peppered with familiar New York faces. Midway into the second week of rehearsals I received my first call on the set. It was from Lea. "Hello Donald, I've got my driver's license. Bring me home a car."

Relocating to Los Angeles also meant establishing myself in the Beverly Hills branch of William Morris. I had no contact there, no personal agent, no Bob Youdelman to oversee and guide my career. In Los Angeles the bright new item on the agency horizon was packaging for the rapidly mutating television industry. Musical variety shows were in the forefront of home screen entertainment. It was a natural for the few mega-talent agencies that handled the top name entertainers, directors, song writers, and choreographers to offer their services and guarantee the best to the industry. Agencies that could deliver the sexiest talent packages became the new super-stars and fabulously rich. The benefits that accrued to the talent from this new practice was that the agency no longer withdrew commissions from fees. It was taking its cut off the top, and conflict of interest stipulations prohibited double taxation. As a result, I was shuffled around from agent to agent according to who was handling the packaging for the show that desired my services. I began to know the lot of them in the television pool. Suddenly, early in 1970, there was a new voice on the phone to me from William Morris. I was being asked to do a feature film for the Walt Disney Studios, a big new picture involving animation and live action. It was planned as a follow up to *Mary Poppins*, the large film musical with delightful characters that celebrated free flight into childhood fantasy. Julie Andrews and Dick Van Dyke were the stars of *Mary Poppins*. The stars listed for the new film were Angela Lansbury and David Tomlinson.

"Hello, I'm Bill Walsh. I'm producing *Bedknobs and Broomsticks* and I'm a big fan of yours." "Thank you Mr. Walsh." "Please call me Bill. Can I call you Don?" "Yes, that would be fine." I was excited as I took the open hand extended to me and shook it vigorously. A giant smile lit up the face of the large man standing across the desk. He came around and we took seats in adjacent arm chairs free from the separation of power furniture.

Getting to the enormous studio lot in Burbank had been a nightmare for me. Lea and I were now both owners of automobiles. Mine had been purchased just the night before from a friend who was a salesman at a Ford dealership in downtown Los Angeles. Ronald Colón had given me a great deal on a brand new Thunderbird with a beige and brown exterior and interior, detailed with leather piping on the elegant seats. It was a much larger car than the one in which I had taken lessons and my driver's test. It was also larger than the Toyota Corolla that we had purchased for

Lea. It was a major vehicle. I left myself plenty of time to get to the studio and, in navigating my route from Beverly Hills to Burbank, I assiduously avoided the freeways which filled me with anxiety. Getting the luxurious tank out of the garage was enough of a trauma to me. From the driver's seat, I could not judge the outline of the vehicle and held my breath with every tight maneuver. I turned into the studio entrance on Buena Vista Boulevard and stopped at the gate. "Mr. Walsh is expecting you. Park anywhere along the curb." I looked at the rows of cars in the VIP parking area that guard indicated to me and drove forward until I found a vacant space. As I turned the wheel, I heard a terrible scraping noise and realized it was the sound of metal against metal. I panicked and withdrew, then forged ahead further and further away from my destination, until I found a space on a side street that was an easy straightforward shoe-in entry for my monster vehicle. I got out and went around to view the opposite front fender. The beautiful classy new finish was scarred with an ugly streak. I walked back and stopped at the collision point. The missing paint that formerly belonged to my dented fender was hanging from the corner of the back bumper of a stylish European sports car. Except for the additional dangle of color to its silver exterior, it seemed in perfect condition.

At Walt Disney Studio the highly skilled animators were always given a head start on the arduous, meticulous, and detailed process. My first assignment was to develop sequences for the animated characters in the underwater ballet, "The Beautiful Briny Sea." The action took place in a sea bottom grotto ballroom all a-swish with dancing sea life. Carolyn and I hired Bill Landrum and Maria Ghava as a start up skeleton crew to work on the creation of these study vignettes. To aid us in our discovery process, the Department of Special Effects produced an ingenious rigging that would allow the dancers to approximate floating and had the device installed in our rehearsal space. A series of pulleys guided a rotating arbor that was hung on ceiling-mounted horizontal tracks. The rotating arbor was fitted with parallel cables that hooked on to specially mounted metal plates with grommets that were installed into cut-off jeans. The attached dancer could spin head over heels while floating through space as well as rotate in horizontal circles from a push-off start that would send the arbor into its revolve. The other end of the pulley was mounted with a canvas bag, weighted to the exact poundage of the dancer, forming an exaggerated balance scale in action. We discovered that with a little assistance on the off-camera weighted bag end, the dancer could execute a fanciful series of floating maneuvers. To accomplish this we hired on two more dancers to our small skeleton crew and named them the bell ringers. Al Mello was engaged as dance arranger to develop the song melodies into music for the dances. These character dance studies were then filmed and the clips were delivered to the animators. They would start their work based on our materials and then come back to us with technical requests. "We need at least six more frames to make this action really smooth." We calculated the number of seconds in a bar of music in relation to the duration of each frame and then I would re-choreograph the sequence to meet the requirement. We also designed the swim/dance actions for the leading characters or for their dance doubles if the activity required an athleticism outside the actor's movement skills. The choreography for these sequences and for the small character dances and the large dance production number, "Portobello Road," was drawn on storyboards that were mounted on the walls of the hallways of the directors' building where we went to confer with the film's director, Robert Louis Stevenson.

The dance auditions were mob scenes. Dancers of every age, size, discipline, and nationality crowded in for a chance at employment in the big new Disney film set in World War II London. The Portobello Road sequence allowed for a marvelous amalgam of market people and military personnel from every corner of the British empire. I employed the knowledge from my studies of Indian dance and from my West Indian heritage, and let my imagination fly in designing the dances for the troops on leave amongst the market hawkers and characters of the colorful Notting Hill Gate street emporium in wartime London. I had personally discovered this Saturday street market while working in London on a musical play. I had been engaged by a British producer to choreograph a production based on the famous Dickens' novel *A Tale of Two Cities*. The assignment ranged from choreographing dances on the revolutionary barricades to elegant vignettes in Queen Marie Antoinette's salon. During my work on this unfortunately never-to-materialize musical, Lea, Guy, and I had stayed in a rented maisonette on Kensington Park Road in Notting Hill Gate. Looking out the kitchen window on our first Saturday morning there, we saw a steady track of people climbing stairs and wandering around the rooms inside the buildings facing us across the back alley. We got dressed and went around the block to discover Portobello Road, the most enchanting and bustling market of antiques, books, flowers, instruments, and every imaginable what-not jamming the buildings and spilling out into pushcarts and stalls lining the street. On weekdays the antique market disappeared and street vendors selling foods and produce took over. My intimate knowledge of this neighborhood was a great aid to me in preparing for the kaleidoscopic production number in *Bedknobs and Broomsticks*. The film sequences which emerged jumped from scene to unexpected scene following the story line of the protagonist's search for a missing portion of an ancient book of magic incantations.

Among the many bright moments of this successful and happy experience, there was the one inevitable tragedy, the one prize number that was to end up relegated to the cutting room floor. Angela Lansbury's character had a secret profession. She was a mail order witch. The moment when she received a package from her sponsors, via Her Majesty's postal service, and opened it to discover her first genuine witch's broom, was a moment of jubilation captured in song and dance in a fun filled number called "A Step In The Right Direction." As the fledgling witch went about trying out her new magical acquisition with varying degrees of lack of success, her mangy black cat yawned in boredom and winked large yellow eyes at his mistress's awkward mishaps and lack of finesse. Angela sang and danced marvelously, and the number added a dimension to her character, a private moment. When the final cut was readied with the number completely excised, I was dumbfounded and went to query Robert Louis Stevenson. "Oh yes, my wife also likes the pussy cat number. She says she misses it terribly."

For the huge Portobello Road production I had assembled a large cast: dancers of all ages, character people, and specialty acts. I had also been given a well organized rehearsal and shooting schedule. I brought Michele Simmons and Geri Seignious into the cast to dance the British West Indian segment, set to a steel drum version of the sprightly um-pah-pah tune. Geri Seignious had been in my New York dance company and had gone on the European tour of *Black New World*. I had discovered Michele Simmons in the senior dance class at the High School of the Performing Arts in New York. I had used Michele on the *Leslie Uggams Show* and had groomed her to perform the solo figure in *Rainbow Round My Shoulder* in The Inner City Repertory Dance Company. Michele had a gift for comedy and was equally expressive in dramatic and pure dance roles. Working with her was exciting and brought back to me that special fulfillment I only received from guiding gifted dancers.

Lea, Guy, and I had lived in the new Beverly Hills residence on Wetherly Drive just one month when Michele and Carolyn persuaded me to start teaching. They had arranged for the classes to be held in a large studio run by Karabel, an eccentric woman who sold dance attire from a small room adjacent to the large rental space. The classes quickly attracted a following as the word spread throughout the sprawling Hollywood dance community. One day as I arrived at the studio with Carolyn, I looked up at the metal staircase that led to the entrance door and saw a stream of water seeping over the door sill, splashing from the stairs in a cascade, and forming a large pool in the parking lot. We ran upstairs and found Karabel washing her swollen ankles in an overflowing tub. We called her sister who came by immediately to deal with her and we went on with class. Among the people treading their way through the soggy entrance was Clarence Jackson. Clarence, or Jack as he was now known to his intimates, or C. Bernard Jackson as he was known officially as the director of the Inner City Cultural Center, had heard that I was relocated in Los

Angeles, and was here to invite me to make my classes part of the Inner City Cultural Center's program. It was wonderful to see my old buddy from Club L'Ouverture days in Harlem. Jack's offer also included a home base for a dance company within the Inner City Cultural Center, an organization that could take care of all the administrative freight that had killed my desire to ever have a company again. It was immediately appealing. We laughed and hugged and sealed our agreement to pick up where we had left off so many years ago.

The Walt Disney Studio costume and make-up people were wonderful. Not only did they magically change a perfectly affectionate, fluffy, and fastidious feline into a battle-scarred alley cat, they also transformed the sun-worshipping Hollywood dancers into proper military personnel including British sailors, soldiers, members of the women's naval unit known as WRENS, Royal Highlanders, and Sikhs. Among the turbaned quartet of Her Majesty's sikh guard was Michael Peters who had also been a Donald McKayle Dancer on the *Leslie Uggam's Show* and would go on to choreograph the high-powered music-video *Thriller* for Michael Jackson. I developed dance passages for this international military amalgam based on national dances from each group's country of origin. It was a fascinating quest that led to many discoveries.

Financial management of the huge cast of actors, extras, and staff for the film dictated a shooting schedule that was completely out of sequence. This was a challenge for the principal actors who had to deal with holding onto the integrity of plot and character development while jumping forward and backward in the telling of the story. The last two months that I spent on the film were relegated to shooting the live action that would later be integrated with the animation. After the principal actors were released, the second unit took over with the filming of special effects. This included the battle sequences with antique museum armor that came to life, dancing furniture and clothing, and solo scenes involving the animals.

The precision of planning for the live action with animation was a marvel. I spent about six weeks in what was known as the sodium process. On a special sound stage, in front of a chrome yellow cyclorama, a dual-lens camera captured the action performed on twin rolls of film. One roll caught the actors against a background of black limbo, while the other simultaneously recorded the exact same action in a negative silhouette. The animation was placed on the negative silhouette roll which when overlaid with the live action roll produced the magical results that thrilled and baffled the imagination. All filming was done on the sound stages or on the back lot of the Burbank studio. The rolling English countryside and the white cliffs of Dover seen in the film were all produced by the Matte Department, which painstakingly rendered the backgrounds and wedded them seamlessly to the foreground action.

"Donald, it's Nick Vanoff. I've got a real zinger for you. We're doing a sequence with Diana Ross and the Supremes. We've got Ethel Waters as special guest artist. I want to do a dance sequence for Diana... something that she's never done before, a first on our show. I want to use "The Soulful Strut." It's a hot idea and you're the man to do the job." "Sounds wonderful Nick. I enjoyed working with her on the Ed Sullivan Show." "Yes, Diana asked for you... and... she wants you as her dancing partner!" "What?... Nick, I'm not performing anymore." "Diana said to say... please! You're not gonna turn her down, are you?" "Well, okay... but give me a day to get my nerves together and think about it. When is this for? I'm finishing up a special over at CBS with Dick Van Dyke and Mary Tyler Moore. It's called *Dick Van Dyke and The Other Woman*. They also persuaded me to perform a comedy bit. It must be my year of return to tripping the light fantastic." The next day the phone rang again and I picked it up; Diana Ross herself was on the other end. "Donald, are you going to dance with me?" "Of course. How could I refuse? Only you could bring me out of retirement." The number took full advantage of Diana's slender, expressive, model's body and her wonderful face. I had to work in a way I never had to before, designing and executing simple and stylish pop moves that would look wonderful on Diana. Midway through the final rehearsal Diana ran at me and jumped into my arms for a lift in which I would spin her as she wrapped herself around my torso. Then I would kneel and roll her forward towards the camera, wait for her to assume a seductive pose, execute a leap with both legs tucked up, and land at her side for the finish. As she ran to me, jumped, and wrapped her legs around me, she dug her fingernails into my arms, and I could feel the flesh give way to her lethal talons. Finishing the final pose, I looked to see a trickle of blood on my biceps. A month later after the show had aired, I sent Diana a clip from Ann Barzel's "Looking at Television" column in the April, 1969 issue of *Dance Magazine*, along with my note: "You see Diana, I told you not to dance with me." Ann Barzel was effusive in her commentary... "Donald McKayle, entirely unannounced, turned up on the Hollywood Palace show of March 8 in an exciting dance in the jazz genre. His attractive partner wore a slinky black sequin dress and moved excitingly and in the excitement I missed her name."

I turned the key in the lock of our Beverly Hills' home, and as the door swung open I called out, "I'm home," to no response. I expected to find Lea practicing in the dining room which, with the addition of a floor to ceiling mirror, we had turned into a dance studio. It was perfect for flamenco. I passed through into the kitchen and found a note attached with a magnet to the refrigerator. "Donaldo, William Morris called. Roy Silver wants to talk to you about a second Bill Cosby special. His number is on the pad." I found the pad on the kitchen table where Lea had placed it and dialed Roy Silver. The first Bill Cosby special had been a great success for me and one of the main reasons for the move to Los Angeles. It had been produced in truly opulent Hollywood style. The giant Titan camera was driven into the studio to shoot one sequence, hovering over the jungle gym set like a helicopter. The tab for this maneuver was reported to be ten thousand dollars. The scripts were bound in butter soft leather, embossed with a portrait of Bill and with an attached fringed leather place marker. Souvenir scarves with the same likeness were placed on the back of each seat for the invited studio audience. The show's opening sequence that began with Bill's childhood memories was shot on location, starting in South Philadelphia, and after a cross-country chase, ended on the set at the NBC Burbank Studios. I was still living in New York and was flown out to Los Angeles for the rehearsals and the shoot. I called Margolit Oved and her husband Mel Marshall and asked if I could stay with them in their Brentwood home. I had come out prior to the production schedule for dance auditions and had been put up at the Tolucca Motel next to NBC. I was not thrilled with the arrangement in spite of its obvious convenience. Margolit had stayed with us in our New York apartment on 110th Street when she first arrived from Israel. Every day Bill Cosby's huge chocolate brown Rolls Royce would pick me up from Margolit and Mel's home in the Brentwood Hills and chauffeur me to the NBC Studios. As we coasted along the freeway to Burbank, passing motorists would ogle the impressive vehicle. When they saw the license plate that read "COS," they would speed up and ride abreast of us, peering inside and rubber-necking dangerously, trying to get a glimpse of the celebrity passenger in the back. I would peep mischievously from behind the tinted glass and confound them. I had choreographed a number which included Bill Cosby dancing with the ensemble and had built another dance around Bill's celebrated childhood companion, Fat Albert. The rocking waddle that I devised as the dance signature and the chant, "Heh, heh, heh, Fat Albert," had caught on and been picked up in the discos as a dance craze.

The show was called *The New Bill Cosby Show* and was to feature the Noah story on Bill's new album, a comedy vignette from his night club act. Bill had the remarkable ability to turn the largest casino into his own living room and the hundreds of high paying customers into his personal house guests. The Noah number was unusual for a television dance sequence. It not only contained the entire original monologue with Bill costumed as a white-bearded Noah, but it also had a long and fully produced ballet with a large cast of dancers. I brought Mary Barnett out from New York to dance on the special, and in spite of my resolve following the Brooklyn Academy of Music concert, I again hired Bill Louther as a leading dancer. One of the guests that showed up for final dress rehearsal was Eugene Loring. He had completed a radical face lift and was totally unrecognizable. He stood next to me on the set and waited for me to speak with an impish gleam in his eyes before finally revealing himself to me. Loring had attended the concert I had produced for Lea and was eager to use her to dance in the restaging of his ballet *Capitol of the World* on a special show to benefit his proposed Hollywood company. The performance was to take place in the wealthy Hidden Hills gated community. Lea would dance opposite Roy Fitsell in the role originally created by Lupe Serrano. Lea's strong femininity and sinuous Spanish *port du bras* were perfect for the role.

When we first arrived in Los Angeles, Lea and I made a practice of selecting a restaurant from the plethora of fine eateries and visited a new one each week. Following a generous Chinese meal, Lea and I strolled along Hollywood Boulevard and heard the sound of castanets coming from the open windows above us. We followed the sound up to a studio on the second floor and were invited inside to watch a flamenco dance class in progress. Teodoro Morca was teaching and his partner La Conte was circulating amongst the students giving corrections as Teo demonstrated, dancing at full tilt while gazing intently at himself in the studio mirror. At the end of the class, we introduced ourselves and they both welcomed us warmly and invited Lea to attend the classes. Soon she was taking private lessons, and Teo was choreographing solo dances for her. Using the L.A. Spanish dance grapevine, Lea found Lupe Del Rio, a former dancer with José Greco, and the two of them became fast friends and colleagues. Lea felt ready to debut in her new-found art, and I became the eager producer and costumer for the event. I rented the Assistance League Hall, a small theater with a wonderful wooden interior that reminded me of the Ted Shawn Theatre at Jacob's Pillow. It had all the same warmth of atmosphere and acoustics. Lupe Del Rio was artistic director for the evening.

Donald McKayle

presents

Lea Vivante

in

"Dances of Spain"

I didn't want my name to appear again on the program and so for my assignment as costume designer, I used Lea's pet name for me. The program credit read: Costumes by Don Aldo. Lea had purchased two flamenco gowns from Mariquita Flores in New York. I would design and execute all of the other eleven, which entailed researching the authentic regional styles for the Galician dances choreographed by Lupe del Rio and building the costume for the *Amazona de Guzman*, choreographed by Teodoro Morca to the Sarasate *Zapateado* for violin. I hired Mel Dangcil as pianist and musical director, a violinist for the Sarasate, a singer to bridge the intervals, Benito Palacios, flamenco guitarist, and Manolo Lieva, flamenco singer. I managed to cover all details right down to a dresser to help Lea backstage with the rapid costume changes, but somehow I failed to hire a photographer, and we were left with no pictures of this important event. This was all done while I was working on *Bedknobs and Broomsticks*. After sending Lea off to bed to conserve her energy for the demanding solo performance, I would sew the costumes late into the night. Some nights yards of box-pleats and ruffles rose in mounds on the work table, as the rhythmic action of my hands fed triple layers of trimmings through the pressure foot of the sewing machine. The whir of the motor would lull me to sleep and I would suddenly awaken as my drooping forehead hit the machine.

"May I speak to Donald McKayle, please." "This is he." "Hello, this is Bella Lewitzky, and I want to welcome you to Los Angeles." "How wonderful of you to call. I've always wanted to meet you." "Well, let's do that. A conservatory of the arts financed by funds from the Walt Disney Corporation will soon be starting, located just immediately above Los Angeles in the new community of Valencia. I'd like to talk with you about your possible involvement in the School of the Dance. The conservatory will be called the California Institute of the Arts although, in the last year of planning, the name's already been shortened in everyday usage to Cal Arts."

I had taught master classes and accepted temporary positions at many colleges and universities and had been on the permanent faculty at Bennington College, Bard College, Sarah Lawrence College, and the Juilliard School's Dance Division, but I had never assumed the administrative role I entered at the California Institute of the Arts. I was the associate dean; Bella was the dean of the School of Dance. The new campus in Valencia was not ready for the scheduled opening and the students who had come from all over the country started the initial term in temporary quarters at the Villa Cabrini in Burbank. Four days of the school week were devoted to the pursuit of the student's major art discipline with possible work in any of the other four arts as a minor or as ancillary study. Wednesdays were given over to the humanities in an all-institute program known as Critical Studies. Much of what came out of Cal Arts in those first years of the 1970's was anti-establishment, confrontational, or visionary. It was a credit to the Walt Disney Corporation that they weathered the assault to their tradition bound, family value orientation and continued to support the infant institution.

Yofi was pacing the floor beside our bed restlessly. Her head moved from side to side and her eyes seemed to be searching everywhere. Suddenly the room began to move and the entire house began to roll. The hanging brass reading lamps above the bed began to swing violently overhead. Lea jumped out of bed and ran towards Guy's room. "It's an earthquake... get up... stand in the doorway!" Lea pulled a trembling and wide awake Guy into the bedroom doorway with me. "Dad, get Yofi!" It was suddenly over. The sun was shining as brightly as it always did on each perfect California day. We went around the house checking for damage. All of the art work hanging on the walls was askew. The wrought iron room divider had crashed to the floor. The tropical fish were cruising merrily about their tank. Water had splashed from the swimming pool and wet the deck. We turned on the radio. "A major earthquake of still unmeasured magnitude on the Richter Scale has hit the Southland. Aftershocks of considerable strength continue to rock the area. A section of the freeway overpass has collapsed in Sylmar, which appears to be the epicenter of the shocker...." "Lea, that's right next to Valencia where the new campus for Cal Arts is being built." We suffered no major damage although a shift in the slump-stone retaining wall had sprung a leak in the sprinkler system and a small geyser of water sprayed the driveway. The center joist of the open beam ceiling had also shifted a fraction of an inch. The new Cal Arts campus buildings in Valencia, just minutes away from the Sylmar disaster, were intact, but several of the stucco structures at the Villa Cabrini in Burbank were condemned and off-limits to the Cal Arts community. Months later we moved into the new campus. Bella disliked the windowless dance studios and Paul Boepple, the dean of the School of Studio Art found no use for the traditional artist studios with slanted overhead skylights letting in filtered north light. Resilient floors were laid on top of the poured concrete slab in the art studios and the School of Dance moved in. One of the original dance studios was welcomed as a black box theater by the School of Drama and the Scene Shop inherited the only workroom with a sprung floor where a dropped hammer was purported to spring back into your hand. When Bella's professional career with her company on tour suddenly took off and kept her away from her duties as dean, I was appointed Dean of the School of Dance. Meanwhile my reputation as an industry choreographer rocketed me to the top of the list of constantly employed choreographers in town and I began what was to be a schizophrenic artistic existence: Dean of the Cal Arts School of Dance, Artistic Director of the Inner City Repertory Dance Company, and freelance Hollywood and Broadway choreographer. We had sublet our

New York apartment on 110th Street so that we would not lose our rent-controlled homestead in the Big Apple. Our sublessee also wanted to establish legal grounds as tenant of the apartment. One month in a devious and foolish move, she forwarded the rent directly to the landlord, rather then submitting it to us as dictated in our agreement. The landlord welcomed the opportunity to get rid of the lot of us and legally raise the rent for a new tenant.

James Earl Jones was powerful in the Twentieth Century Fox film version of *The Great White Hope*. He had shaped the role in the original stage version on Broadway and brought all of that recent work to the film. Martin Ritt directed the powerful dramatization and requested me as choreographer. My main assignment on this project was to choreograph the big celebration following the winning of the heavy-weight boxing title by Jack Johnson, the James Earl Jones character. The scene was set in front of the Club Champion, a posh nitery that Jack Johnson had financed to establish his ascendance into society. The high kicking, rollicking dance ended in a dramatic confrontation as a strange neighborhood elder, banging on an ashcan cover, suddenly challenges the motives and allegiances of the new champion. The dancers were hired under the ballet contract of the Screen Extras Guild which guaranteed them specific days of employment. Regular extras were hired by the day and only called back if they were needed for the following day's shoot. Professional extras knew how to work through the assistant directors to get close to the principal actors so that they would be recognizable in the shot and needed for continuity on the following day. The extras were the crowd of well-wishers greeting Jack Johnson and shouting in adulation. As they shared in his personal victory, they surrounded his open traveling car or peered out from windows or down from roof tops to catch a glimpse of their hero. On all the reaction shots in which the cinematographer panned or held the crowd, Jimmy would stand next to the camera and give a charged performance for the extras, equal in every way to the takes in which the lens was trained on him or on the other principal actors. His rich resonant voice filled the Twentieth Century Fox back lot that had been made over from the extravagant *Hello Dolly* set especially for this sequence. It was strange and disquieting to realize that the contracting of dance artists was equated with the hiring of untrained film extras. Dance extras were a step above on the totem pole as they required specific direction. Dance extras receiving the ballet rate were at the top of the scale as they required special rehearsals, most often prior to the filming days, and usually under the supervision of the choreographer or, in the parlance of the film industry, the dance director.

"Choreography to me is hot girls making horny moves." I listened incredulously to the diatribe coming at me from an overly exercised television producer. "No! That's just not me, and I'd never dishonor my profession or reputation in that way. People can turn on *Goldiggers* if they want to see that." "Well, I've got a knock-out looker that I want on the show." "Fine bring her down to the rehearsal tomorrow. Let her watch first and she can see what I do and then I can see what she can do." The young lady arrived unaccompanied the following day, introduced herself, and asked if she could watch the rehearsal. I welcomed her and placed a chair for her to the side-front. At the end of the morning she was still sitting there, wide-eyed and completely absorbed in the rehearsal process. The producer arrived as we were breaking. "Well how did it go?" Before I could answer the young woman spoke up. "Do you give classes anywhere? This is just fantastic." "I only teach advanced students at Cal Arts right now. That's a conservatory for which you audition to be admitted." I went off with Carolyn to the neighboring Farmers Market for lunch. The producer and I never discussed aesthetics again.

"Hey, Don, I've been practicing that step. I think I've got it. Can you use me?" The devilment in the voice and the low chuckle that followed were unmistakable. "George, what's up buddy?" "Something you're gonna love. Get this...I've got the Temptations, the Supremes, and Diana Ross together for a special. We're calling it *TCB* and we intend to really be 'taking care of business' on this one." George Schlatter went on enthusiastically. He had made his reputation with the irreverent *Laugh In*, and we had collaborated together on another TV special, *Soul*. Mark Warren, with whom I had worked on that project, was to direct *TCB*. He was an imaginative and innovative collaborator, and creative sparks began to fly as we sat down to our initial concept meeting. The novelty of the special, which was to feature the highlights of top hits of these super-star pop artists, was to be a solo dance number for Diana Ross. This was obviously a follow through from the success of her dance debut with me on the *Hollywood Palace*. Mark had discovered a technical device that could rotate visual patterns across the screen in a beautiful kaleidoscope. We conceived a number that would utilize Diana's sense of fashion and her mobile and expressive face in tight close-ups opening to full body shots in motion. The patterns rotating across the screen would be highly colored decorative African cottons which would reveal Diana dancing in couture outfits fashioned from these fabrics. The number was called "Afro Vogue." To further pursue the high fashion analogy, I set up a session for Diana and a top fashion photographer with make-up artists, hair stylists, and a conga drummer. For six hours, Diana changed outfits, hairstyles, and make-up as I called out instructions, created moods and elicited motion and emotional responses while the photographer took roll upon roll of photographs. The tight close-ups of her animated facial expressions, when relayed rapidly filling the screen, seemed to dance all by themselves. The individual sequences of movement were all short takes, but when sequenced with the moving patterns and photo clips produced a kaleidoscope that was pure television magic and marvelous media dance. A calm, uninterrupted, and completely focussed rehearsal with The Supremes and The Temptations was almost non-existent. The steady stream of official and unofficial entourage that were coming and going was getting to me. I finally had more then I could take and as I was to enter into a reheasal with Diana on her solo, I cleared the room. "Everybody out! I need absolute quiet! Everybody out! Now!" As the room cleared, referring to the Motown giant that I had just summarily dismissed, Diana looked at me in amazement. "Donald, that was Berry Gordy that you just threw out!"

"Donald, I can feel my heart pounding right through my costume. I am so excited." I looked at Lea standing in front of me and smiled. She was elegant and eye catching in the magnificent black and white striped *bata de cola* that she wore for the "Thank You Very Much" number on the 43rd Annual Academy Award Presentation in 1973. I was the choreographer for the televised "Oscar" show and was responsible for staging the musical numbers. "Thank You Very Much," the song from the film version of the musical, *Oliver* was nominated in the Best Song category and was to be sung in English by Sally Kelerman, in French by Petula Clark, in Italian by Burt Lancaster, and in Spanish by Ricardo Montalban. The set was in the form of a revolving door which rotated to reveal each of the movie stars with a back-up dancer. Lea was performing the Spanish segment with Ricardo Montalban. He wanted to perform a few *paseos* with her and that section was placed last before all the stars stepped forward for the final coda in English with the revolving door still framing the individual dancers behind. Lea's gown with its sweeping long train had been made for her in Spain by Luisillo. She brought it in and showed it to Bob Mackie who was costume designer for the entire show. He loved it and decided to design the entire number around national costumes in black and white for the dancers, with the stars in tuxedoes and black evening wear. For an Israeli girl who had grown up on American movies and film magazines, performing in a show with these almost mythological idols was almost too much for Lea. When Harry Belafonte came down the backstage corridor where Lea was standing with the other dancers waiting to go on and greeted her with a warm embrace and a kiss, the eyes of the onlooking dancers that went wide with genuine surprise. "Can we kiss you where he kissed you?" "You're not gonna wash that spot, are you?"

Harry and Juliet Prowse were featured in a salute to the Beatles and to the movies they had made. Juliet was particularly engaging in the "Yellow Submarine" dance sequence and Harry brought the tribute to a close with "Lean On Me." Six years later on a return engagement with the Academy of Motion Picture Arts and Science's annual event, it was an entirely different artist that held stage as Lea gave a mysterious and mesmerizing performance. It was the year of *Rocky*, and Sylvester Stallone. I was to choreograph a number to the hit-song "Flying High" from the film. Ben Vereen was engaged to star in the sequence performing with the male ensemble. I had to create the dance in the four days that Ben was available. He had an engagement that would keep him out of town until the final dress rehearsal on the day of the show. I had an opening and closing number to stage with Ann Margaret and the dancers and a dance with the female dancers featuring Lea to "*Ave Satani,*" the nominated song from *The Omen*. William Freidkin had taken over the helm as producer and Martin Pasetta was repeating his directorial role as he had done for years. There was a clashing of ideas and artistic points of view from the outset between Bill and Marty. I had worked with Marty previously and had found him completely unsympathetic to the needs of dance and to the proper presentation of movement on camera. My last excursion with him had been a disaster. Bill Freidkin looked over at me. "What's this...'The Donald McKayle Dancers'?" "Well, we can call them the William Freidkin Dancers, if you'd like to do the choreography." "No, thank you." The whole room filled with laughter. I had gotten my point across in a definitive and non-confrontational manner. I knew it was the only way to move my name up to the top of the show and into the audio announcements, and the only way to give the dancers any on-air recognition. There was a long way yet to go to lift dance out of its role as the step-child of the industry.

The schedule had a way of shifting with the coming and going of the stars and personalities who were hosting and presenting awards and those scheduled to perform. Barbra Streisand arrived and while crossing the stage, took one look at the platform built for her song and refused to use it. "It's too small. I feel constricted just looking at it." It was taken away and hastily expanded while the clock ticked away toward air-time. She had Carolyn stand in for her, put a recording of "Evergreen" on, and asked Marty to go through the shots he planned while she watched, changed, or okayed his choices. Then she got into costume and took her place.

Love endless and evergreen...

"I'm wearing a beautiful dress with genuine Fortuny pleating; it's all cut off by the tight follow spot. Change It!..."

...and ever, evergreen

I sat in the control booth watching Marty fume as he was being ordered about and controlled. With each change the number became better. It was an uncanny transformation. Barbra Streisand came back to the control booth to watch a replay of the rehearsal for a final approval but Jane Fonda had arrived with her police dog in tow and was ready to go on. Ben Vareen had come back with great lapses of memory and Carolyn and I took him up to the lobby of the Dorothy Chandler Pavilion to rehearse. I left instructions to call me when it was time to camera-block "*Ave Satani.*" Candy Brown came into the lobby space as we were putting Ben through his paces. "Are they almost ready for '*Ave Satani*'? "Oh, we've done it already. Lea kept insisting that they call you. She refused to go on but they pushed her into place and started." I burst into the control booth in a rage. "What's going on here. You were supposed to call me for '*Ave Satani*'." "I've got a whole show to do here. You've got a schedule to follow." "We haven't been on schedule all morning. I've been up in the mezzanine trying to get Ben ready. He forgot most of the number. You've got twenty pages just hanging around. Why didn't you send one of them up to the lobby for me?" "Look, just get out of my control booth." "This is not your booth. We're all working on this show together, and yelling at me doesn't change anything. You were wrong and you know it. You don't care or give a damn. You're just a hack!" The door to the control booth burst open and Bill Freidkin came in. He had heard the entire confrontation on the headsets as had all of the technical staff and camera personnel. Marty had seventeen cameras for the show, three outside the theater and fourteen of them inside, eight of which were lined up in the wings like soldiers on the battlefield. "I want a production meeting as soon as we break for lunch." Bill and Marty's eyes locked in silence. I left and went to find Lea. "Was that you in the booth?" The cameramen were smiling. I got several strong pats on the back as I passed through their ranks and continued on to the dressing rooms. I found Lea sitting, smoking a cigarette. "I tried to make them call you but they wouldn't. Warren Beatty stopped me and said the number looked wonderful. He said at the end, with my arms crossed over my chest and the down light casting shadows on my face, I look like the Oscar statuette. All the women surrounding me on the floor and reaching toward me seemed to want to take hold of me. He wondered if you were making a comment on this town and a satiric observation about this strange yearly rite of spring."

11

RAISIN

Through all the years that I knew Robert Nemiroff, he always had a remarkable ability to convey his inner state. Sometimes he could mesmerize and completely capture, at other moments he could become immersed in a self-indulgent catharsis and lose his power and potential audience. He was ignorant of how to harness and control this unusual ability. When it was working, it was an amazing gift; when it derailed, calamity often struck.

I returned to the darkened Broadway theater with Walter Nicks and Kathleen Stanford. The house lights had been turned on and additional work-light had been added on the stage for the last-stand showing of *Kicks and Company*. We had returned from Chicago with our tails between our legs after a disastrous opening at the Arie Crown Theatre. Oscar Brown, a Chicago native son and a bright new talent who wrote and performed his own one-of-a-kind special music material, had conceived and authored the musical, *Kicks and Company* with composer, Alonzo Levister. Musical portions of the show had been presented on the *Dave Garroway Television Show* and in an unprecedented move, financing began to pour in. Bobby and an associate Burt D'Lugoff became interested in the maverick project and asked to produce the show. Falling in line with the established practices of show business, they went after a star name to play the title role of Mr. Kicks even though there was the grass root support that followed Oscar Brown's performance of his own material. What should have guided them was somehow discounted in favor of traditional, and therefore irrefutable, logic. Burgess Meredith was cast in the role. Burgess was a wonderful character actor but was alien to the physical suavity and sexual allure demanded by the character of Mr. Kicks, a master of seduction, the devil revisiting earth. Burgess had neither the physical carriage nor sensuality to bring this off. Edith Lutyens Bel Geddes's sleek tailored suits looked rumpled the moment he put them on. His singing voice and rhythmic sense were less then adequate, and the tasty songs as performed on TV by Oscar Brown, which had had people popping their fingers and rocking their heads, never found a groove in Burgess's performance. The new theater on the lakefront that Bobby was so elated to have found was another albatross. It was, indeed, large and modern; with capacity business, it could bring in record box office sales. It was, however, not a legitimate theater but a convention venue, suitable only for industrial sales presentations. We ended up installing a forest of hanging overhead microphones and still the sound was garbled. The other cast members were all quite wonderful and had been selected with care by the show's director, Vinnette Carroll. Lonne Saton was a wonderful leading man with a mellifluous baritone. Vi Velasco, the ingenue, was a stunning, exotic woman with a strong pop sound. Nichele Nichols, who would later go on to *Star Trek* fame as Captain Ohuru, was a sizzling dancer, singer, and actress in the roll of the waitress, Hazel. One of the show's few successful moments was Nichele's number with the male ensemble, "Hazel's Hips." It was also one of the most popular numbers on the *Dave Garroway Show* along with the sardonic, "Mr. Kicks," and the big ballads, "Opportunity Knock" and "Beautiful Girl."

The cast began to file in and take their places on the empty stage. The dancers warmed-up, practicing isolated phrases from the choreography. Walter Nicks had co-choreographed the show with me, and Kathleen Stanford, a physical trainer skilled in the Joseph Pilates' *Return to Health* program, was our assistant. She had enrolled with Pilates after suffering a freak accident while dancing with Claude Marchant in the variety circuit at the Palace theater on Broadway. They played in a vaudeville format between movie showings and were scheduled after an animal act. A wet spot on the stage floor gave Kathy a nasty spill, which wrenched her knee acutely and tore the cartilage. She spent her post-operative recuperation in Pilates' care and was given years of a dance career that would have been over were it not for this remarkable man. Consequently, she was fanatic in the championing of the Pilates method and had joined forces in a private studio devoted to it with another disciple, Carola Trier. Every morning of our rehearsal and short lived performance run, she would take Burgess Meredith, tone his body, and drench out the alcohol from his muscles. He would grunt and complain from behind the screened off area that Kathy had set up for a work space, as she relentlessly pressed him to his task. He would emerge after a forty-five minute workout dripping with perspiration, his eyes clear, and his mind ready for work. Burgess and Nichele Nichols had left the show with the Chicago closing and did not participate in this valiant attempt at resurrection of a good project gone bad. Thelma Oliver stepped in for Nichele and Hal Scott took over the role of Mr. Kicks. Dorothea Freitag and Joyce Brown were set to play the entire show in a two-piano arrangement that they had devised. They looked a little unsteady as they descended into the pit after the lunch break but the sounds that came forth were electric. The audience of Broadway aficionados, theater owners, possible angels, and friends applauded warmly. Bobbie, sensing an opportunity from the receptive spirit that filled the theater, came up from the audience as the applause was peaking and entered into a wild-eyed harangue at how badly the show had been treated in Chicago. As he continued chastising the Windy City critics and repeating their many bad comments which he found unjustified, he succeeded in draining every ounce of good will that hung in the air. "Our producer is a sentimental fool", said Edith Lutyens Bel Geddes looking at me woefully, with the resignation of final defeat written across her face. "Bobby, I think it's time to thank these people for coming this afternoon and to let them go home." Lorraine Hansbury was at the back of the theater as she spoke, and the audience took her signal to rise and exit. Lorraine had taken over the directorship of the show after the damning reviews of the Chicago opening; Vinnette Carroll had left amid a flurry of rancor and blame. Oscar was morose and angry as he watched his dream go up in smoke. Bobby was still talking to whomever would listen as the audience emptied the theater. Our paths did not cross again for years; then suddenly he was on the phone. A jubilant rush of words greeted me. "Bobby, I don't believe it. How are you? L.A. is exciting and full of new adventure, but it's good to be back in New York. Have you been by yet to see The Inner City Repertory Dance Company? We're part of the Modern Dance Festival at the ANTA Theatre." "Donnie, I was there yesterday. The company is wonderful and your works were as moving, as gripping as ever. I've been very busy on an exciting project; I'd like to talk to you about it. Can we meet for breakfast tomorrow?"

"Donnie, I've been working on a musical version of *Raisin in the Sun* and after years of work, I think I've got something powerful. The composer, Judd Wolden, and the lyricist, Robert Brittan, met in Lehman Engle's BMI Workshop and came to me five years ago. When I got this letter from them saying, 'We'd like to have the opportunity to present to you a group of songs we've written for a possible musical dramatization of Lorraine Hansbury's *Raisin in the Sun*... well, I was more than skeptical. I listened to what they had and sent them away to develop a musical statement for Mama Lena Younger that would be as powerful as Lorraine's dialogue. Weeks later, they came back with a song that was thrilling. They had taken a line from Lena's speech to Benetha. You know where Benetha says to Mama, 'That is no brother of mine', and Mama asks her, 'Has you written his epitaph too?' Well the song that came out of that moment, 'Measure the Valleys,' absolutely bowled me over. I was in tears. Five years later I'm here, sitting and talking to you. I've been writing the book in partnership with Charlotte Zaltsberg. You'll love Charlotte. Donnie, I want you not only to do the dances for this show, I want you to direct *Raisin*." Bobbie sat forward on the edge of his chair and leaned across the table looking at me with a rhapsodic expression. As he spoke to me, transported, he drew me along with him.

The road to realization of *Raisin* was a long and tedious series of backers, auditions and presentations for theater owners. Bobby would read the tight presentation script with narrative and snippets of dialogue that he had created with Charlotte Zaltsberg. Judd Wolden would be at the piano and play the songs that were sung by Joe Morton and Ernestine Jackson. Many auditions later and a couple of years down the line from our meeting in the Carnegie Delicatessen, we had a bite. Zelda Fitchandler, the director of the Arena Stage in Washington, D.C., was genuinely interested. She was ready to present the show in her intimate theater in the round, known for its innovative programming. The production of *Raisin* would take place at the end of the season, for a guaranteed six week run in the summer months when the theater was usually dark. Zelda was a hands-on producer and so another decision maker was added to the mix.

Our first task was casting. Bobby was pushing for Claudia McNeil to play Lena Younger, a towering part in which she had triumphed in the original drama. I was adamant that the project not carry any baggage from before. I was eager to find Virginia Capers with whom I had last worked on the film version of *The Great White Hope*. I had known Virginia since we were children in the Harlem River Housing Projects. She had a marvelous rich singing voice and was a fine actor. She had somehow disappeared from show business and gone over to the more reliable security of real estate. Lea had her real estate agent business card. She called up the agency only to find that Virginia no longer worked there, but through persistence was finally able to track her down in another agency. When Virginia arrived at our house in Sherman Oaks, she was driving the full-sized American sedan that was the trademark vehicle of her new profession. She was filled with excitement and gratitude. Joe Morton and Ernestine Jackson, who had done all of the backers, auditions, were signed to play Walter Lee and Ruth. Veteran character actress Helen Martin would be Mrs. Johnson, and I found a wonderful youngster, Ralph Carter, with a natural gift for the stage and a beautiful strong voice to play little Travis. Shezwae Powell was cast in the role of the young rebel Benetha. Rob Jackson was the African student Asagai and Herb Downer the young preppy, George Murchison, a role that was eventually dropped from the show.

Musicalizing a drama with so much text and so many subplots was a difficult proposition. The songs could develop the dreams and aspirations of the characters in a wonderful soaring way; they also took time as did the dances. Something had to give and in this case the preppy subplot was dropped. Crafting the musical for the rectangular space of the Arena Stage with the audience on all four sides and the actors entering up from the four corner vomitories or down through the audience along the aisle steps was an interesting challenge. Taking a play that had been trapped in the claustrophobia of a Chicago ghetto tenement apartment and making it sing and dance was a monumental task. However, the play's physical confinement, was of great metaphoric importance to the dramatic conflict between Mama Younger and Walter Lee. Much of the dramatic action took place around the breakfast table. Pots, dishes, utensils, a refrigerator, toast, eggs, and other domestic clutter, important parts of the play's action, were a nightmare in the free and flowing staging that I wished to achieve. I spent a week with Joe Morton, Ernestine Jackson, and Ralph Carter on the first scene, knowing that the solution for the entire play lay in the handling of this opening. Little by little I removed the props until the action was pared down to rhythmic pantomime. It worked like a dream. Robert U. Taylor followed suit with settings and properties that were wooden units, and levels painted black and free of all decoration or upholstery. The color came in Bernard Johnson's bold costumes.

In the dropping of the George Murchison character we lost a whole side of the Benetha Younger character. Shezwae Powell was not happy with this and became petulant and difficult to work with. She resisted learning new song material. She even carried a crib sheet onto the stage to grab a peek at lyrics she did not want to sing. She was a talented actress and had a wonderful smoky voice; I was annoyed with her misuse of her abilities. The multi-talented dancers included Elaine Beaner with her powerful contralto voice, Al Perryman, Loretta Abbott, Debbie Allen, Chuck Thorpes, Renee Rose, Lettie Battle, and for a few weeks her younger brother, Hinton. Their mother agreed to let him do the show if he kept up with his schoolwork. Lettie tutored the sixteen-year-old Hinton on the side during breaks. Hinton was amazingly loose limbed and limber and possessed a powerful jump. He was ready to burst out and viewed school-work as an impediment. He failed to keep his contract with mother and, as promised, she withdrew him from the production.

We opened with rave reviews for the show, the dancers, and the actors; my work was singled out for praise. The public reaction was so great that Zelda Fitchandler decided to extend the run through the entire summer. Bobbie was busy making deals to bring the show into New York and open on Broadway. We needed a transfer point to remold the show from the round to a proscenium presentation. Bobbie contracted the Walnut Street Theatre in Philadelphia; we were on our way.

Raisin was in the final week of its successful run at the Arena. I was busy working with Robert U. Taylor in his New York studio on the reconceived design for the proscenium version of the show, when I received a call from Bobbie. Shezwae was out sick and her understudy, Debbie Allen had gone on for her. "Donnie, they say the phone has been ringing constantly with people asking, 'Is that new girl who went on last night going on again tonight?' Maybe we'd all better get down to D.C. tonight and see Debbie." Debbie Allen was an alumnus of Howard University, the prestigious black University in Washington, D.C., and knew how to network her friends. Whatever the source of the unprecedented phone inquiries at the box office, the results were that Debbie had the entire creative staff there that evening. She was wonderful. Her reading of the role was beautifully modulated, and she was totally in command. She received an ovation from the audience and from her fellow performers. As of that evening, the role of Benetha was hers in the move to Broadway, and there remained the unpleasant but necessary task of breaking the news to Shezwae. "I'll send her a telegram in the morning." "No Bobbie, it can't be done that way. We've got to meet with her and tell her in person. The show closes Sunday. Let's see her at the office in New York Monday morning. "Okay Donnie, but let's make it at noon." I was in Bobbie's 57th Street office early for the noontime meeting but Bobbie had not arrived. At twelve o'clock on the dot Shezwae arrived. For half an hour I engaged her in conversation. She was outgoing and completely delightful. I was enjoying her expansive openness, and it seemed cruel to continue in this way any longer. "Shezwae, you're such a lovely person, it's hard to bring you bad news, but I must. I had hoped Bob Nemiroff would be here, but I will have to tell you. You will not be playing the part of Benetha any longer." The room that had just been filled with Shezwae's bubbly conversation was suddenly still. The silence thundered. Shezwae's eyes traveled about the space carefully taking in its contents. Her gaze rested on the cityscape beyond the parted blinds at the window and then returned to me. "I knew this meeting was going to be bad." "You should never have let Debbie go on for you. No minor or even major discomfort on your part should have allowed that. But it happened and we were there. After seeing her in the role, there is no way I could put you back into it. The part is hers." Shezwae rose from where she was seated and walked towards the entrance door. I followed after her. "I'm sorry." She turned back to face me. "There's no hard feelings. I'll be rooting for the show. I know it's going to be a real big success. I'll see you opening night." The door closed behind her and Shezwae was gone. I sat down on the couch and looked out the window at the same buildings that Shezwae had searched to find the words that she had just uttered. As I contemplated her amazing bravery, a big lump rose up in my throat. Fifteen minutes later, Bobbie came through the door looking red-eyed and harried with a long commuter's story about the way down from Croton this morning. Though I was angry, I looked at his dismay and let him off easy. "Shezwae's gone. She took it amazingly well." "I'll write her a letter." "Yes, Bobbie, that would be nice."

The Walnut Street Theatre was an excellent transfer point. It was a landmark building, the oldest theater in the historic section of old Philadelphia. Gaslight lanterns still hung on its beautifully restored facade, and its interior was warm and intimate. A short walk brought you to the old society district with its rows of tiny, red, brick two-story houses. Three white marble steps led up to paneled wooden doors hung with shiny brass door knockers. Beyond was Bookbinders restaurant with its large menu featuring fresh seafood and the Port of History Museum on the river front.

The new stage set retained the stark, pared-down look of the original but included a partial second story balcony in the surround. The danced prologue fully utilized this extra elevation. It set up the tough streets and the drug culture from which Mama so desperately wished to escape with her family intact. With the addition of a table and two chairs, the space was transformed into the Younger family apartment, with Travis asleep on the make-down bed and Ruth starting her morning chores. The proscenium staging worked fluidly and though it was pleasant to be able to concentrate on the action without seeing audience members in the background, I missed the magical moment when Travis slid down the aisle railing of the Arena Stage singing "Sidewalk Tree." Once again, we were an unqualified success, and the box office was barraged. On matinees we added chairs into the balcony aisle. The office of the mayor made a last minute request for matinee seats and Mayor Rizzo had to be seated on one of those added straight back oak chairs with its red seat pad. By the end of August 1974, Bobbie had secured the 46th Street Theatre for our Broadway house, and the marquee already was ablaze with a lighted sign announcing *RAISIN*. I had rented a flat in an apartment hotel on Central Park West and 82nd Street. Lea, Guy, and Liane joined me for the week prior to the Broadway opening. Liane was now a part of our California household and the three of them flew out from L.A. to be with me for this special moment.

Opening night was just hours away. Guy was handsome in his new suit and Liane looked lovely and amazingly mature in her beautiful new dress. They went downstairs to the lobby cafe-bar. Guy wanted to show Liane his skill on the pinball machine. Lea and I got dressed in our formal wear and went to collect them. Lea looked unbelievable in a Georgio San Angelo clinging sheath in bone white alix jersey. The bodice was of a fine elasticized net shimmering with rhinestones. Her head was covered with a tight mesh cap completely studded with graduated rhinestones, and a coat of white feathers hung casually over her shoulders. There was no doubt in my mind that she would be the most beautiful woman at the theater tonight. I entered the cafe-bar and found Guy busy at the pinball machine with a crowd of people around, cheering him on. Liane was at the bar sipping a Shirley Temple and some oily lover-boy was putting the crush on my fifteen-year-old daughter. I got rid of him in short order, gathered up Guy and Lea, and hailed a taxi. We piled in and headed down to the 46th Street Theatre.

The reaction from the sophisticated opening-night crowd was ecstatic, and the opening night party was a blast. Bobbie excitedly relayed the early reviews which were all glowing. Topping off the festivities was Dizzie Gillespie and his orchestra on the bandstand for some of the tastiest sounds imaginable. This warm giant of a virtuoso radiated genius, humor, and love. "Donald, will you dance this one with me." I looked at Shezwae smiling at me with her arms open and swept her into the Latin beat that ricocheted around the room. Dizzie was singing a cockeyed Calypso and everyone was chiming in on the choruses. "I'm so glad to see you here." "I told you, I'd see you opening night, didn't I?" Eventually the all important *New York Times* review arrived, and Bobbie read it word for word. A mighty cheer went up and Lea and I went to look for Liane and Guy to take them back to the hotel and to a well earned sleep. Guy was upstairs at the pinball machine and a crowd was again gathered around him. "It's time to go, Guy." "Not now, Dad. I'm on a roll." He dug into his pocket and pulled out a wad of money. "Where did you get money to bet?" "I found ten dollars in the men's room. Here, count it. How much have I got now?" The careless pile of bills added up to over one hundred and fifty dollars. I convinced him that this was the time to stop and was able to ease him away from the pack of petty gamblers intent on breaking his streak and, "cleaning the kid out."

I returned to Los Angeles and the phone wouldn't stop ringing. Jane Chodoroff called from the New York William Morris office to congratulate me again and to inform me that I should expect a call from Norman Lear, the television producer with the golden touch. The call came as predicted, and I went to meet him in his private office at CBS. Norman Lear had broken convention in Hollywood and produced the highly successful *All In The Family* and *Maude*. He was planning a spin-off from *Maude* for Esther Rolle who played a saucy, warm, and intelligent maid. The spin-off was to be set in Chicago in an apartment in the projects and would present the family of this feisty, black, working-class woman in human terms. Norman Lear had seen *Raisin* and wanted me for the new show. "I think what you did with *Raisin* is marvelous. This, in today's terms, is what we want for our show. It'll be called *Good Times* and I want you to direct. Esther Rolle is set and we've got John Amos to play her husband. They're powerful together, and...somebody you know should be here any moment." As he spoke the door opened and Ralph Carter came in with his mother, sister, and his agent, Selma Rubin. I wasn't sure that I approved of Ralph leaving *Raisin* so soon and didn't think it was contractually possible. Norman Lear had made Bobbie an offer he couldn't refuse, and Ralph's understudy would be taking over the role of Travis. There were still a few months before all of this would begin and time enough to make a smooth transition.

Norman Lear was a producer completely involved in all of his many projects. Every major decision was in his hands. Casting was his baby, and while he ran everything by me, it was only to keep me informed. The stand-up comedian Jimmie Walker was engaged as the older brother and soon began to take over the show as the writers pandered to his scene stealing physical comedy, feeding him a stream of loud laughter one-liners in the process. Bernadette Stanislaus was hired as the sister and Janet DuBois as the next door neighbor. I had worked with Janet years before in *Golden Boy* and it was wonderful to work with her again. The talented child actress, Janet Jackson was hired as Janet DuBois's foster child. The baby sister of the famous Jackson family brought a welcome ingenuousness to the cast. We started rehearsing the opening script, and I soon found the three camera situation comedy formula a creative vise. The technical knowledge I was gaining was invaluable, but the prospect of spending twenty-six weeks in this restrictive format was something I did not relish. It would demand, from me, a serious application of what Lea called "character building exercises."

"Donald, *Aba* just called. My mother is very sick, I must go back home." "Oh Lea, I'll go with you." We called Arieh and told him our flight arrangements. I informed the Norman Lear office that I would be leaving for a family emergency and would call them from Israel when I could assess how long I would be away. Meanwhile my co-director would continue with the production schedule. We had four scripts finished, "in the can." The opening segment was aired prior to our departure and was received well in the trade papers and garnered a very respectable slice of the ratings. I was happy and excited about our success but relieved to be going away and never for a moment envisioned my return to the production.

Lea and I were taken, by Lea's sister, to the nursing home in Herzlia where their mother was staying. She looked frail and distant when we arrived. I took her hand. "Pnina, I'm so glad I'm here with you. How are you?" Lea kissed her mother. "*Yma*, you remember Donald, don't you?" Pnina looked directly at me and searched my face. "Yes." "*Yma, at mudaberet angleet!*" Lea's sister, Tamar, was overwhelmed. "She hasn't been speaking at all. Questions go unanswered and she stares off into space. Now to understand it's you Donald and to answer in English. It's like a miracle." Two weeks went by while Lea, Tami, and Arieh visited Pnina regularly coming at different times of the day so that she would have a constant reminder of home. We were staying with Adam and Dalia Mishori in Kfar Shmaryahu which bordered Herzlia and were quite close to the nursing home. Lea had just started dinner when the phone rang. Lea came back into the kitchen where I was peeling vegetables, her face was still and expressionless. She placed the wooden spoon on the counter and sat down. "Lea, what is it?" "That was *Aba, Yma* is dead."

The funeral was arranged immediately with the *Chevre Kaddisha* (the Holy People who take care of the dead) and filled with friends and family. I traveled with Arieh and Lea to the cemetery in Holon for the burial, which was attended only by the immediate family. One of the officiants took a small razor and cut the edges of our shirts and blouses as a symbol of grief and the ritual weeping and rending of garments. Pnina's body was bound in burial swaddling and placed on a trough under a blue velvet covering. I was one of the male members of the family who lifted the trough and carried the body to the grave site. Pnina's wasted body was feather light and the silhouette under the velvet cover looked small and unfamiliar. Along the way a trio of women let out a terrible wailing and followed us a distance, waiting to be invited to join. These professional mourners moved off when the invitation was not forthcoming. We came to the freshly prepared grave where the rabbi and a contingent from the *Chevre Kaddisha* awaited us. The ceremony was brief. Then the attendants lowered the body onto slabs that lined the grave bottom and slid it off the trough. The tiny mummy that rested on the stone slabs was covered with another layer of slabs resting on side supports that created a shelf over the body. The rabbi spoke a few words more as he lifted earth, threw it on the stone covering , and handed the shovel to Arieh. Arieh took the shovel, filled it with earth, and cast it on the grave. He stopped and began to speak in a rhythmic cadence. The rabbi spoke up in objection. "On this day of the year, you are not allowed to speak over the dead at the grave." Arieh turned briefly to face the rabbi and said simply, "If God chose to take her from me on this day, he will allow me a few last words." Arieh spoke, but not a few last words. He spoke for all the things left unsaid and all the deeds left undone. He spoke of the past and envisioned the future. He finished and cast several more shovelfuls of earth before Pnina's brother took the shovel from him and continued. All the men took turns and then Lea took the shovel from me and dug it into the earth and lifted it. The rabbi objected again, as this was not the role of a female mourner, but a look from her eyes stemmed the words in his mouth. She continued and passed the shovel to Tami. The *Chevre Kaddisha* took over and built the funeral mound into a small knoll. Lea, Tami, and all the women took the flowers that they had carried and laid them one by one on the mound until it was a hill of blossoms. We walked away from the grave and as we came to the road leading out of the cemetery, the women made a file on either side of the roadway. The men removed their shoes and stepped barefoot between the silent line of nurturers and walked symbolically forward, back into life.

12

AT HOME ABROAD

"44 Curzon Street, now that's a posh address. You're right in the middle of Mayfair, overlooking Shepherd Market." Dickie Easton, my London connection at William Morris was quite pleased with himself. He had arranged these delightful accomodations with the management of the large new musical that I was to choreograph. People that supervised the management and financial production of theater in London were called directors instead of producers, and producers were what we called directors in the States. The producer who had asked for me on this occasion was Peter Coe, the original director of *Golden Boy*.

The Four Musketeers was to be presented in 1967 at the Theatre Royal Drury Lane in Covent Garden and would star Harry Secombe. It was a send-up of the Dumas novel, *The Three Musketeers*. Harry Secombe possessed a glorious tenor voice and was a favorite entertainer among London theater-goers. The popular forties song-hit, "Mr. Five by Five" aptly described this affable artist ... "He's five feet tall and he's five feet wide." Harry played the romantic D'Artagnan and cut quite an unusual figure. The cast was filled with members from the popular "Carry On" comedy film series. Sean Kenny had designed the set, and it was a marvel of stage architecture with massive motorized units that were propelled about the stage by hidden drivers. Large full-stage stair units rolled forward. Arched colonnades descended from the flies and were linked by lowered bridge units. The density of the colonnades made the staging of tableaus grouped on the upstage stairs a nightmare. No matter where you placed people they would be blocked from view in some part of the house by the thickness of the architecture. The stage traps opened to reveal the steaming mineral baths of Baden-Baden. The costumes had generous silhouettes to balance the massive structures, and the cast was large with a full complement of dancing ensemble, singing chorus, and show girls. We also had four stunt men who would drop from the towers in the sword fight sequences, cushioning their landing by falling into the crunch of corrugated cardboard boxes. Harry rode a broad-backed mare in one sequence and the king and queen arrived in a pony-drawn trap in another. The cardinal stroked a Persian cat and played chess with the king. The game stretched across a mammoth board, and the chessmen were each a fistful to handle. A specialist in sword fighting was brought in, and I began to study this martial art in preparation for the staging of combat sequences.

The elegance of the Italian school caught my fancy. I enjoyed the sweeping lunge of the *pasata sota*, the backward stepping bows, and the doffing and flourishing of plumed headgear. Cloak and dagger work, even with blunted stage instruments, contained a significant risk of danger, but the enthusiastic stunt men gloried in it. Cleaning up after the animals was a job left to the trainer, who had a costume for his occasional stage appearance. In one sequence a group of narrow stairs, that led down from a center tower, swung into a single line midstage creating an imposing descent for the musketeers from stage heaven to earth. They joined D'Artagnan as he sang his eleven o'clock big-ballad rouser at front and center of the apron. At one performance he ventured backward a step too far and was goosed by the insinuating stair unit. He leaped forward and turned around to wag a naughty-boy finger, chiding the inanimate looming dragon behind him, eliciting great guffaws from the audience. The end of the play was Sean Kenny's scenic *coup de théâtre*. Moving units swung into place, sails were lowered, fireworks went off, and the entire stage was transformed into the royal barge as the full cast boarded singing a glorious final chorus.

The influence of the theater critic on the public was markedly different in London than New York. Between morning and afternoon publications, there was a total of ten dailies carrying theater reviews. This guaranteed a healthy mix of opinion and removed the posture of assumed omnipotence from any single voice. It also guaranteed frank discussion among a sophisticated public concerning the merit of what they read. There was, moreover, a fierce loyalty to favored performers that no damning commentary could shake. Although *The Four Musketeers* received mixed notices, it was a runaway hit. The night before we opened, the cast gathered in the pit stalls to listen to last minute notes from Peter Coe. Suddenly one of the dancers gasped and pointed to the royal box and we all turned to look up. A strange light flickered, and the velvet blackout curtain at the back of the box parted. "It's the ghost! She's here with us tonight. We're going to go off like a bomb tomorrow!" A thankful round of applause and a burst of chatter brought the note session to an abrupt close. Tradition had guaranteed that if the ghost of Drury Lane visited the theater the night before opening, the show would be a success, and so we were. Our popularity occasioned the scheduling of a Royal Command Performance. This time the royal box was occupied by the Duchess of Gloucester. The theater was polished spic and span with all the brass fixtures gleaming. A plush red carpet was rolled out on the path to the royal box and a red curtain was drawn across the door that led to the gentlemen's convenience so that the Duchess would not be affronted on her way to her seat. As she entered the box, two young pages came out downstage of the front drape and played a fanfare on long slender brass horns. The orchestra followed with "God Save the Queen," as all eyes trained upon the Duchess, who smiled benevolently.

During the summer months, the European continent was alive with one *Dance Stage* (Workshop) after another. One of the largest and most popular was held in Cologne, Germany, under the direction of Heinz Laurenzen with the support of the municipality. The large sport *Stadion* on Aachnerstrasse was given over to the Internationale Sommerakademie des Tanzes, two weeks of intensive study in ballet, modern, flamenco, character, and jazz dance, and a choreographic competition held in the beautiful modern theater in the town center. The large student body was international, as was the excellent faculty: Mary Hinkson, Antony Tudor, Patricia Christopher, Hans Van Mannen, and Jiri Kylian. In the summers of 1973, 1975, and 1976 I was invited to attend and teach jazz dance. It was an interesting challenge for me, as I had never taught jazz dance before. My field of expertise was in modern dance technique but it was assumed that following my many successes in commercial theater, I would be a knowledgeable jazz dance instructor. Jazz was the most popular technique taught at the *Stage*. Lynn Simonson, and Alvin McDuffie were the other jazz instructors. The classes were held in the several large gymnasia and were all oversubscribed, with sometimes as many as one hundred students in a class. Visiting teachers from many European cities audited the courses, sitting on benches along the walls and taking copious notes. Although it was not permitted, they would sometimes venture an illegal video recording of the classwork to carry back and teach to their own students, without ever having physically experienced the process.

The second summer that I attended, Guy came along with me. We would join Lea in Madrid at the end of the two week session. Guy became fascinated with the trap drum set and the virtuoso playing of the expert French drummer, Jean Claude, who accompanied the jazz classes. Guy sat next to him during the classes and imitated his posture and the rhythmic movement of his upper torso. Jean Claude befriended him and gave him a rubber practice pad and drumsticks. Guy would sit on the grass with the pad between his legs and pound happily away. A short lesson from Jean Claude was a treasured experience that would sustain this unusual self study for days at a time. Guy befriended a little German girl who was staying with her family at our hotel. They would play together, engaging in lengthy conversations, each in his or her own language. Somehow they communicated with each other. The Krone Circus was in town and I decided to take Guy and his new friend. We arrived before the main attraction in the big tent was scheduled to begin and went off to visit the menagerie. The little girl was ecstatic at the sight of the animals and dived under the chain barrier to hug and pet the ponies. I tried to communicate with her to restrain her impulsive behavior. I entreated with her in English to come out and she chattered happily back at me in German; we soon drew a crowd of amused spectators. Finally, Guy went in and took her by the hand and we went off to the big-top, loaded down with sweets and anxious with anticipation. One of the most exhilarating highlights was the lyric beauty of a herd of free horses filling the arena. In their center was a single barebacked rider. The floor of the rink was blanketed by a carpet of smoke. The horses wove, circled, and turned in place, guided by unseen commands from the blithe horsewoman. From the center, she led her steed in a serpentine path; every horse followed her until the last mare trotted out of the arena; the smoke dissipated and was gone.

I returned to the two week intensive course in Cologne, this time with Lea accompanying me. She took the flamenco classes from José de Udaeta and immediately became his favorite. He asked her to demonstrate for his sessions and began to compose *paseos* that the two of them would perform together in front of the class. We had traveled from Israel where, in 1976, I had been invited by the Batsheva Company to choreograph a work in celebration of the United States Bicentennial. They wanted something very American, and I hastened back to the jazz music that I had heard everywhere in my circling of the globe twenty years prior with the Martha Graham Company. No other element of American culture had made such a mark on the world or been so universally adopted. I had come upon a wonderful recording by Dick Hyman of transcriptions for orchestra of a group of Jelly Roll Morton's original jazz piano compositions. I set out to choreograph a happy and celebratory dance. *Album Leaves*, a work in nine segments, was a choreographic collection of snapshots that evokes past friendships, intrigues, and remembered events. The music set a tone of nostalgic and saucy frivolity. With a nod to Jelly Roll's early career as a sporting house pianist in the New Orleans Tenderloin, and in the spirit of "remembered events," I included another version of "The Crave," the sinuous entanglement in the battle of the sexes that I had staged in my 1962 work *District Storyville*. *Album Leaves* was a great success. The Batsheva Company artistic director was ecstatic. "We've got a *shlager*! We'll perform this one for the entire 1976 season. We've already received an offer for a television production." I considered Kai Lothman's happy news. "Wonderful, but wait out the television offer until you've played it everywhere. You might kill your potential concert audience by exposing it on television too soon."

The night after the gala *premiera* we sat with friends for a good-bye dinner, as next day Lea and I would leave for Cologne. Dalia Mishori was holding a seance at which the spirit of a legendary rabbi had entered the circle of seated women. They were all deeply concerned with the fate of the Jewish hostages being held in Uganda. One of the women present had brought news that the Israeli defense minister Ariel Sharon had spoken the night before with the ruthless African dictator, Idi Amin. Ariel Sharon had been a mentor to Idi Amin in the early days of his military studies. The questions asked of the spirit were spelled out in parables as Dalia's fingers floated about the Quija board. At the conclusion of the session, we drove back to Dalia's home in Kfar Shmaryahu and finished our last minute packing. Dalia came into the room and took off her silver chain and gave it to Lea. The chain dangled a tiny purse of metal mesh containing several agate-like stones. "Wear this on your journey tomorrow."

In the morning as we drove to the airport, every radio station was filled with the news of the daring raid on Entebbe by special Israeli forces resulting in the freeing of all the hostages. When we arrived at the Ben Gurion airport, it was mobbed. The rescue plane had already landed and was being held in an isolated area. We took off for Germany amidst the wild elation that filled the faces and voices of the crowd. We landed in Cologne and moved up in line at passport control until it was our turn. We handed the guard our passports. He smiled warmly at Lea. "Congratulations!" "Donald, Dalia's purse has been burning against my chest all morning long." I held the mesh purse in my hand. The stones inside were emitting an unnatural warmth. What an amazing July 4th!

In 1977, the year after the success of *Album Leaves*, I was invited back by the Batsheva Dance Company to mount a work which would incorporate the Panovs with the Batsheva dancers. After a prolonged and much publicized hunger strike, Valery Panov was allowed to leave Russia with his wife Galina and immigrate to Israel. The new work would be a commemoration of their struggle. I had chosen a theme that would celebrate their arrival into the welcoming arms of their new homeland. The work was called *Mountain of Spices* and utilized the full Batsheva company, the Panovs, and Lea as returning guest artist. I was able to wed modern, classical, Yemenite, and Sephardic dance elements in a collage akin to the mixture of cultures that was Israel. Rina Schenfeld, the reigning diva of the Batsheva Company was the only member who refused to participate, perceiving in the presense of the celebrated guest artists a compromise of her stellar position. The opening at The Mann Auditorium in Tel Aviv was a gala in every sense of the word with the audience cheering and covering the stage with a carpet of tossed floral bouquets. Savoring the success of *Mountain of Spices*, we left for Spain where Lea had scheduled an intensive study course with Roberto Ximenez.

The sun was beating down mercilessly on the streets in Lavapies as I entered the basement studio where Lea practiced with Roberto Ximenez, but this room in Lavapies was cool. Lavapies was an old district of Madrid where the flamenco studios were grouped and guitar music, castanets, the quavering sound of flamenco song, and the *jaleos* or shouts that accompany flamenco performance were everywhere. Roberto smiled at me.

"Welcome, Donald, come in." He clapped in resonant *palmas* as Lea danced the *Alegrias* she was learning. "*Bueno*, Lea, now put on the *bata* and we will practice the *jerezana*. It is a beautiful movement for the woman, and you must learn to handle the train with the utmost finesse." I watched as Roberto brought out the delicate and seductive rhythmic configurations from Lea. Like his partner, Manolo Vargas, he was able to teach the intricacies of the female dance movements expertly. Lea had studied with Manolo in New York and had been sent by him to Roberto in Madrid. The two men were each extraordinary artists. Roberto Ximenez possessed a dynamic technique with brilliant footwork, turns, and body carriage. Manolo Vargas was a magnetic performer who captured your entire being and could transport you from your seat in the theater onto the stage and into the dance. The leading female artist in their company, Maria Alba, had been a student of mine at the New Dance Group. Manolo was so taken with Lea that he convinced Roberto to take her on as a student. This was most unusual as Roberto did not accept students easily. Like Manolo, Roberto was very generous with his time. One afternoon I arrived into the pleasant coolness of Roberto's catacomb studio in Lavapies fifteen minutes after the lesson was to be over. Lea and Roberto were still going strong. Lea was flushed and breathing heavily; she had been working for twenty minutes straight on *vueltas quebradas* and had gone past exhaustion to exhilaration. As she spun around with her head low and her eyes spotting the floor in front of her, she swept her arms in a broken spiral about her head, lifting her knee high and placing her lifted foot precisely before snapping into the turn with a swirl of ruffles following the spirited pirouette. "*Olè, bueno!*" Roberto encouraged her further with a barrage of explosive *palmas*. I joined along with his rhythmic clapping and he countered with a *contratiempo*, nodding and smiling in pleasure at my holding strict *compas* against his variation. Lea picked up the festive mood, smiled and tossed her head as she passed in front of us. "*Basta*, enough, let's go for some tapas. We'll continue tomorrow." That evening was the reopening of the Café de Chinitas under the direction of the famous Gypsy dancer La Chunga and Roberto invited us as his guests. We had a table near the stage and settled down to dinner prior to the show. Just before the tableau was to begin the head waiter brought a party to the empty adjacent table, among the group was Rudolph Nureyev and Antonio who had become an international star dancing with his partner Rosario. I smiled at Rudi. I noticed that neither Roberto nor Antonio acknowledged each other and soon surmised that the first one to speak would be placing himself in subservience to the other in rank. I decided to break the ice. "Rudi, you know Roberto Ximenez, don't you?" Antonio immediately picked up the thread and continued the introduction that I had purposely formulated as a question. "Roberto, how are you? Rudolph Nureyev."

Smiles and introduction were made all around and the cafe lights lowered as the stage lights brightened for the beginning of the show.

The week following the star studded opening, Lea and I returned to the Café de Chinitas once again to see the wonderful tableau. La Chunga was a magnificent artist and was renowned for her authentic *flamenco puro* style, her beautiful sinewy arm movements, and her barefoot Gypsy dancing. She also surrounded herself with an excellent company of dancers and musicians. The leader of the *jaleos* was the excellent *palmera*, Teri Maya. She sat in the downstage chair at the edge of the platform and rang out the *jaleos* (calls) to the performers and to the audience, all the while driving the show with a perfect rhythmic clapping: a crackling sharp edged resonance or soft covered thudding. As the tableau moved toward the end, La Chunga began the obligatory *rumba flamenca* and looked around the audience for some man to pull up on stage for a good time and a good laugh. She gestured to me, and I jumped up on the stage and knelt at her feet. The audience roared with applause and the dancers whooped with laughter and burst into a deafening round of *palmas*. I was having the time of my life and my stellar partner was in shock. She had expected a tourist bumpkin. She twirled a handkerchief around my neck and began to lead me offstage. I fell back again to my knees and in an exaggerated back bend followed her out trembling my shoulders in a vibratory quiver to gleeful laughter, wild applause, and a hearty round of *olés*.

Back home in New York, I received a call from Gil Shiva, an Israeli producer that I had met some years ago. "I'd like to invite you to Israel once more. I'm producing a show there in coordination with Amnon Berenson. It will travel around Israel and play in the major cities of Tel Aviv, Jerusalem, and Haifa. The show is written by Ehud Manor and traces American music from Stephen Foster up to today's disco stars like Donna Summers." "That's quite a tall order for one show." "Ehud is brilliant! The show is pure entertainment. It moves at lightning speed from beginning to end." "Well, it certainly sounds interesting." "Good. Could you meet with us at my office on 58th Street sometime tomorrow?"

Ehud was already there when I arrived, and indeed he was brilliant. Not only had he found a way to collage highlights of the history of American song into a two hour, fifteen minute show, he had done it in a marvelously nonlinear way. The show contained portions of some eighty three song titles, in medleys and occassional full versions, grouped around thematic ideas that were novel and surprising. "Donald, I'm so glad you are interested in doing this show. I love your work. *Album Leaves* is one of the best things Batsheva has ever done and they can't stop playing it. All the *kibbutzim* are requesting it. They've never had such a success with the public." "Thank you, Ehud. Lea spoke last night to her father in Tel

Aviv and he is very impressed with your radio show. He says you know just about everything there is to know about pop music. Tell me about the show. What do you call it?" "I call it 'One More Time,' because we are tracing back through all this wonderful material. Like me, most people in Israel grew up on American pop played on English radio. But Amnon is already selling the show with the Hebrew title *Libi Sheyech L'Broadway!* (My Heart Belongs To Broadway!)." "Ehud, if the show should ever come to this country, I don't think it could be called *My Heart Belongs to Broadway.*" "Well, in Israel the word Broadway has a certain magic for the population. Maybe Amnon is right. I see a cast of eight singers and dancers. The opening number I call 'I Got.' All the songs in this section have titles that include the words 'I Got.' Each title would feature one of the performers individually and then a medley would end with everyone together." I listened with growing delight as Ehud explained the constant flow of music from ante-bellum ballads and cakewalks to a sequence he called "Fruits and Vegetables, South of the Border." "It's a melange, a fruit cocktail, if you'll excuse my bad pun, of songs made famous by Carmen Miranda, Josephine Baker, and Harry Belafonte. Then, there's a western sequence that includes a singing horse, a gospel and spiritual medley, a Chicago mob gangster sequence with throwbacks to torch songs, a present day disco medley with quotations from the New Wave of Broadway shows, such as *Hair,* and songs from all time movie favorites like "Somewhere Over the Rainbow." "Ehud, I'm now more than intrigued. Let's start from the top and go stroke by stroke."

Amnon Berenson came into town to meet with me and with Howard Roberts, whom I asked to be musical arranger, and to attend the cast auditions. Amnon was a complete contrast to the sophisticated urbanity of his partner, Gil Shiva. He was a *kibbutznik* and very basic in his outlook and tastes. They were the classic "odd couple." In spite of some beginning disagreements with Amnon, I chose a wonderful cast that everyone, including Amnon, agreed was dynamite. The eight performers were Gregg Burge, Jamie Patterson, Pi Douglass, Wilbur Archie, Elaine Beaner, Bonita Jackson, Yolanda Graves, and Priscilla Baskerville. Margaret Harris was engaged as our pianist/musical director. The other musicians would be contracted in Tel Aviv. We spent three weeks rehearsing in New York with a super high level of creative intensity coming from all directions: from Ehud who was constantly inventive, from Howard who exceeded himself in musical arrangements brimming with wit and texture, from Tom Walsh and Merrily Murray who designed the simple and stylish unit set, roll-drops, and props, and from Rita Weissman who designed costumes that fulfilled all of the humor and sweep of the palette that Ehud and I had created. Ken Billington, who had been stage manager and technical director for my dance company and who had become a very successful lighting designer, would be coming to Israel to do the lighting design for the show. The cast members were triple threat performers. They all sang, danced, and acted, each excelling in one of these areas. Three weeks later we were on an El Al flight to Israel to finish our rehearsals and technical work at Kibbutz Ha Ogan where we would preview, open, and from which we would tour for the remaining half of 1979. Elaine Beaner brought along her daughter, Melissa, who became a full member of the kibbutz, enrolled in its school and was soon happily playing with the children and speaking Hebrew.

In 1978 in Los Angeles, I had directed and choreographed another theatrical anthology, *Evolution of the Blues*, in which Elaine was a featured player. It was a collection of American secular and sacred music, but with a completely different premise than *My Heart Belongs to Broadway*. It was the brain-child of jazz vocalist, Jon Hendricks, and was based on his hypothesis that jazz and the blues came out of the music of the black church. With a brief nod toward African antecedents, he followed the development and growth of this American art form from the theatrical posture of a preacher delivering a sermon, "Everything started in the house of the Lord." Jon Hendricks was also the star performer and showcased his own songs and vocal arrangements. The entertainment value of his work was high, but the essence of the show was side-tracked by his very large ego. Major forces in the evolution of jazz and the blues were given short shrift or completely overlooked while an extended sequence was given over to the work of Lambert, Hendricks, and Ross, performed with his wife and children whom he insisted on having in the show as Hendricks, Hendricks, Hendricks, and Hendricks. Jon had put on the show in San Francisco, where it played weekends at a little theater with an on-and-off schedule. I had flown up to see it at the request of Hal Grossman and Mark Green who wanted to bring the show to Los Angeles and hoped to interest me in developing this material into a full theatrical production. I had met this Los Angeles producing team in a very strange get-together at the law offices of Mark Green and his partner Burton Lane. I was ushered into a dark office lit by a single lamp on a desk behind which sat Hal Grossman. Standing behind in the shadows were Green and Lane. The ring of light that bounced off of the desk blotter illuminated Hal's mustached mouth as he spoke. It was like having an audience with dis-embodied lips. Of course, this was Hollywood and by then I was ready for anything. Other meetings followed with Jon Hendricks, then audi-tions, and finally rehearsals. Jon retained co-directorial credit on the Los Angeles production although he contributed nothing to the vision or detailing of the new production other than his own performance which he brought in tact from San Francisco. As a performer he took choreograhic direction reasonably well and spent the rest of the time during rehearsals involved in the *Los Angeles Times*'s crossword puzzle. Well into the very successful run of the play that continued for a year, beginning in 1978 at the Westwood Playhouse, I dropped in on the show and was amazed to hear Jon in his role as minister, incorporating a commercial for his record albums as part of his on-stage sermon. In the intermission, his wife Judith sat in the lobby in her costume selling these records and promising that Jon would be glad to autograph all purchases at the close of the performance. The cast marched down the center aisle singing with Jon bringing up the rear until the entire cast was assembled at the exit door for the final coda. Jon, as promised, segued in his ministerial garb to the sales booth and began to autograph records as Judith continued to huckster additional sales. I walked over and looked squarely in Jon's face as he reached out his hand expecting another record and gushing compliment. "Jon, I had such respect for you ... I'm sorry I ever met you." As I mounted the last steps of the spiral staircase that led up to the single dressing room that the cast of *My Heart Belongs to Broadway* shared in the theater at Kibbutz Ha Ogan, I heard Elaine's voice. "When Donald gets upset he's another person. You'd better look out. He's after your ass!" I knew she was recalling my disapproval of Jon Hendricks' unprofessional behavior in *Evolution of the Blues* and our fiery confrontation in the lobby of the Westwood Playhouse in Los Angeles. She had accurately predicted my mood and the target of my displeasure. Pi Douglas was protesting innocence as Elaine spotted me and disappeared behind the curtain that divided the dressing room into male and female sections.

"Pi, that was one of the cheapest, most obnoxious, and loathsome displays I have ever seen in the theater." "Donald, what did I do?" "You stood out there in your cowboy outfit working the front row of young boys like a burlesque queen. Your role in that sequence was based on John Wayne, not Mae West. I don't ever want to see anything like that again." Pi's eyes dropped and he fell into an attitude of silent contrition. As I descended the spiral stairs, I heard Elaine's low chuckle joined by other muffled titters coming from the women gathered on the other side of the dressing room behind the dividing curtain. I was to return to Los Angeles to stage the dances for the 1979 Annual Emmy Award show but decided to spend a week vacationing before my departure and headed for Jerusalem. Valery and Galina Panov had invited me for a house warming party at their new flat.

It was in 1984, five years later, that I found myself again on an El Al flight to Israel shepherding a teen-aged company of break dancers to perform in another show produced by Amnon Berenson and conceived by Ehud Manor. Ehud who was now a popular television personality with a weekly show, "Ad-Pop," featuring the best in popular American music. *Dancing in the Streets* would tour throughout Israel, playing major cities and kibbutz theaters. The auditions in New York were unlike any other auditions that I had held in my career. Break Dance was a vernacular expression of city youth and required an athleticism that defied the participation of more mature dancers. Throughout the inner city, in any of the five boroughs of New York, teenagers could be found practicing multiple pirouettes while spinning on their shoulders, backs, or heads with large cardboards from the boxes used to transport refrigerators broken open and spread on the pavement as protective surfaces for these amazing maneuvers. Playground handball courts were favored practice venues and young graffiti fellow artists supplied spray-paint backdrops for this impromptu street dance theater, transforming the poured concrete handball courts into vibrant walls of color. Large, battery charged sound boxes were status symbols carried on the shoulder, blaring forth pulsating rhythmic rap music, while the proud owner executed a slow strutting walk known as bopping. These "ghetto blasters" were placed alongside the cardboard dancing grounds and supplied the accompaniment for the spins, footwork, and freezes that comprised the mostly horizontal break dance vocabulary. The youngsters in Los Angeles had developed a vertical branch of street dancing with chopping arm movements, body isolation shifts in the hips, neck, and ribcage, and sudden low crouches that was called "locking." Locking had an even more forceful variation called "popping" and a sinuous rhythmic variation that took New York by storm. It was called "electric boogie." The eight youngsters on the flight to Israel with me were chosen for their ability in these forms and for their individuality, unique personal invention, and for their skills in improvisation. Of the eight, only two were female: One was a marvelous fifteen-year-old electric boogie dancer who specialized in the sliding dance movements known as "moon walking." The other young woman was a trained jazz dancer and older than the rest. Her role was critical to the show's plot that would eventually emerge from the talent pool that I now looked at sleeping soundly in the cramped body configurations that trans-Atlantic flight necessitated.

"Mr. McKayle, what's he doing?" I looked in the direction indicated by the wide-eyed youth to find an orthodox Jew wrapping around his arm the *tfillin* that extended from the phylactery, a small leather box of prayers resting on his forehead, while covering his head and torso with a large black and white *tallit* (prayer shawl). "Mr. McKayle, I can't get to the bathroom. A whole lot of these guys are back there rocking and blocking the way." "Come with me. They're praying facing in the direction of the temple in Jerusalem that was destroyed hundreds of years ago. When we get to Jerusalem I'll take you to visit the Wailing Wall. It's all that remains of King Solomon's temple and is a holy place for all Jews." We pushed our way through the absorbed ten member *mignon* of worshippers.

"Mr. McKayle, what're these large white moth balls and this pink stuff?" I looked at the box he shoved at me. It contained bagles, lox, and cream cheese. "Phew, this stuff is nasty. Can't I get some corn flakes?" I could see that I had my work cut out for me. Dealing with culture shock would be of primary concern. Amnon had arranged for the rehearsals and pre- views to be held in Kibbutz Kfar Blum in the northern Galil section of the country. Kfar Blum was a kibbbutz settled originally by immigrants from Great Britian so that English was a universally spoken second language there and the youngsters would have no difficulty with communication. A teacher was employed for school lessons that occupied three hours of the morning. The teacher was an American who had returned to ortho- doxy and resettled in a religious community in Israel. The highly individual lessons were not relished by the youths who had expected a vacation from schoolwork.

Ehud and I built the show around the two major street dance allegiances held by the cast. We had three excellent breakers and four electric boogie dancers. One of the electric boogie crew was a superb natural mime and had developed a puppet persona that was remarkable. He called himself Rage, short for outrageous. Ehud and I latched into the ever present competetive bantering between the two crews and built a scenario that had them battling each other in a stalemate situation until the arrival on the scene of the jazz dancer, Monique Van Mannen. Whichever crew could persuade her to join their ranks would emerge on top. In a rap written by Ehud and delivered by Monique in a charming and anacronistic speech pattern flavored by her Dutch upbringing, she explained that if they all got together and pooled their collective talents into a show they could make a financial killing and become stars. The second act was the fulfillment of her plan. Their show existed in outer space with a science fiction fantasy point of view. The production was a tremendous success with the Israeli public and the performers had groupie followers wherever they went. Amnon had titled the show in Hebrew, *Shigaon HaBreak Dance! (Break Dance Madness!)*. A cast trip to a Tel Aviv disco meant a packed house for the owner and carte blanche for the cast. Overnight stardom and Israeli teen-age adulation were almost too much for the kids to handle. They became pampered in every way, making demands that were gladly met by their hosts at Kfar Blum. When things were going their way, everything was "fresh," but when they were displeased with something, it was "flake." Special items were available on the luncheon menu in the dining hall when the kids complained of "all that white food" served on the platters of Kosher dairy dishes spread with yogurt, leben, sour cream, and the like for the community. They were also not used to farmers coming in to eat with all the natural odors of the fields and barns clinging to them. On Friday nights a disco was set up for the young people and the cast had a chance to interact socially with the young *kibbutznik* of their own age. "Mr. McKayle, how do we get to the disco?" "Take the road right outside the main house. Keep straight on it until you come to the cows. Turn left and continue until you come to the chickens. Turn right and in a little while you'll hear the music and you'll be there." "How will we know when we get to the cow barn and chicken coop? It's dark out there at night, Mr. McKayle ... and there're no street lights." "Just follow your noses. You can't get lost."

With Louanna Gardner and Sylvia Waters in *Amahl and the Night Visitors*.
Photo: Lewis Brown.

Sammy Davis Jr. and Jaime Rogers in a scene from *Golden Boy*.
Collection of Donald McKayle.

Debbie Allen, Joe Morton and dancers in a scene from *Raisin*.
Collection of Donald McKayle.

Gregg Burge, Mercedes Ellington, and Hinton Battle in *Sophisticated Ladies*.
Collection of Donald McKayle.

With Diahann Carroll on the set of *The New Bill Cosby Show*.
Collection of Donald McKayle.

With Charles Dubin and Harry Belafonte on the set of *The Strollin' Twenties*.
Collection of Donald McKayle.

With Bill Cosby and Sydney Poitier on the set of *The New Bill Cosby Show*. Collection of Donald McKayle.

With Carolyn Dyer outside CBS television studios, Los Angeles, California. Photo: Ruth Kramer Ziony.

Donald McKayle.
Photographic study by Irving Paik.

Teaching at the Sommer-
akademie des Tanzes in
Cologne, Germany.
Collection of Donald
McKayle.

Teaching at the Sommerakademie des
Tanzes in Germany. Photo: Pieter Kooistra.

Donald McKayle. Photographic study by
Normand Maxon.

13

THE BROADWAY BANANA PEEL

Cyma Rubin flashed her eyes at Lea as we entered Sardi's following the opening night performance of *Raisin*, and spoke to me in an audacious stage whisper. "She's absolutely stunning!" A year later, we were in our Sherman Oaks hillside home and Cyma Rubin was at the door. She had come to Los Angeles to finalize plans for me to direct and choreograph, *Dr. Jazz*, the new Broadway musical she was to produce. I led her upstairs into the L shaped living/dining area with its expanse of glass windows overlooking the valley below. "What a lovely home you have." "Thank you. Can I get you something cool to drink." Lea went off to get the mineral water requested by Cyma, who continued her inspection of the room and then wandered out onto the patio. Lea came up to me as I was about to follow Cyma and handed me an icy tumbler of bubbling water with a slice of lime. "Here, please give this to her, and don't let her into the bedroom. If she wants to use the bathroom, send her downstairs. Guy's bathroom is a mess." "What's the matter, dear?" "I don't know. Call it a chemical reaction. I just don't like that woman. I don't want her around my personal things."

I sat on the stage of the Winter Garden theater playing cards with a few members of the *Dr. Jazz* cast. A newspaper reporter and photographer arrived to record this unusual scene. The cast and creative staff sat around under the watchful eye of the Actors' Equity representative, awaiting the fate of the show which had come to a virtual standstill. Cyma Rubin had run out of production funds and was in negotiations with a wealthy friend who, in a last minute effort to ward off the preemptive closing of the show a fortnight before the announced opening, was selling a Kandinsky painting to pay off creditors and satisfy union bond posting. This was the latest catastrophe in an endless series of mishaps that plagued the production.

"When the fish goes rotten, the stench always starts at the head." Lea spoke to me in a lengthy phone conversation at the end of a day filled with acrimony and confrontation. Cyma had arrived unannounced at the rehearsal hall in the afternoon and insisted on seeing a number that featured her daughter, Loni Ackerman. Loni was a talented performer with a huge voice encased in a diminutive body. Cyma was adamant on her playing the ingenue, a secondary and entirely expendable role. Raoul Pene Dubois, the scenic and costume designer, had been in that morning to see the number at the scheduled rehearsal time, and had reported back to Cyma. Raoul and Cyma were former colleagues from her production of *No No Nanette*, the remounted vintage musical that had captured the hearts of New York theatergoers and whose much rumored behind the scenes melodrama had been chronicled in the infamous tell-it-all book, *The Making of No No Nanette*. I was personally unaware of the climate of animosity surrounding Cyma that permeated the Broadway community, until the day that Cyma and I bumped into Tommy Tune in a restaurant. I introduced Tommy to Cyma and, looking squarely in her face, Tommy answered Cyma's "How'd you do" with "So this is what a Cyma Rubin looks like." Whatever Raoul had said to Cyma that morning had sent her into orbit and delivered her at the rehearsal in a posture of high agitation, with smoking guns drawn, ready to dictate and control. The number in question was a purposeful piece of fluff, designed to point up the contrast between the vapid prevailing popular theatrical entertainment of the twenties and the visceral new music called jazz that had arrived in New York from New Orleans and was trying to break into Broadway. Cyma stamped her foot and wagged her finger at me, but I was not about to subvert the point of the show by giving the vacuous ingenue character an inappropriate show stopper. I recalled Cyma courting me and Paul Carter Harrison for the project at a dinner party in a Los Angeles restaurant. At that time she finessed revealing her true nature, adroitly side-stepping when, in an intended endearment she called us, "my boys," and an immediate icy chill descended on the conversation. Now she was adamant and there would be no retreating. I was equally determined and was quite ready to get rid of the character and the number altogether. Buster Davis, who had conceived the show, wanted to retain both the character and the number. Paul Carter Harrison, who had written the book based on Buster's scenario, wanted to radically change the show's libretto and present the exciting and gritty true facts of the vibrant historical period it purported to honor and abandon the anemic fiction that had been invented from pure cloth to showcase Cyma's tastes. These clashing points of view led to a standoff that Cyma finally broke by removing her daughter from the cast of the show. Loni, the real victim of these maneuvers, was years later able to convince director, Harold Prince, that she had a complete understanding of the dynamics of the Argentine international political superstar, Eva Peron. "Understand her? I've lived with her all my life!" She was granted the role in the Los Angeles company of the musical hit *Evita*.

The casting of principal performers for *Dr. Jazz* was a bicoastal endeavor. Lola Falana was everyone's choice for the female lead. The controversial title role, Dr. Jazz, was a conceptual point of contention that carried over into casting. I reluctantly agreed to interview Cyma's list of West Coast song and dance men. I contacted Donald O'Connor and he proposed that we meet at the Polo Lounge. To my innocent inquiry, "Where's that?," he answered with a simple repetition saturated with disbelief, "The Polo Lounge!" I called Jack Jackson at Inner City Cultural Center and he laughingly directed me to the in-spot at the Beverly Hills Hotel. Donald O'Connor was a no-show and eventually the role went to another *No No Nanette* alumnus and Hollywood second fiddle, song and dance man, Bobby Van. Pop vocalists, such as Margaret Whiting, came to the principal casting call set up at the Inner City Cultural Center with their noses slightly out of joint because of the lack of glamour in the surroundings and completely unwilling and unprepared to audition. The dance calls were held in New York, and I was able to assemble a wonderful company of dancers including Michele Simmons, Bruce Heath, and Gail Benedict from my Inner City Repertory Dance Company in Los Angeles.

This was my third time working with Lola Falana over a period that spanned more than a decade, from *Golden Boy* in 1964 to the television variety series, *The New Bill Cosby Show* in 1968 to this 1975 Broadway musical on trial, *Dr. Jazz*. Troubles started to emerge in rehearsals as Lola's irrepressible street urchin character began to blossom, and Bobby Van's slippery heel of a character grew rancid and distant. Lola was a formidable talent with a lush voice, a voluptuousness in her dancing, and a charismatic stage persona. Bobby's talent was, in contrast, limited. What he did, he did well, but that was the end of the story. He could not learn new material and totally resisted the unfamiliar. Lola's success riled him and the love interest written into the plot became an impossibility. Bobby had one heavy duty, powerful, and revealing moment in the show where he sang a song from the 20s, "It's Getting Very Dark On Old Broadway." This was done in the minstrel show black-face makeup popularized in period shows by Al Jolson. The negative energy that this number would produce was purposely calculated and salient to the show's integrity. Bobby could not handle the audience reaction and refused to do it or to kiss Lola in the intimate love scene. The racial overtones of his stance were not lost on me or on Paul Carter Harrison, as we both had experienced Bobby's difficulty in having two black men in positions of authority over him. I remembered a Hollywood screen musical which had Bobby bouncing on a pogo stick throughout an entire production number and realized that the secret of using him successfully was to frame his limitations with a gimmick that would allow his boyish charm to score. This was possible in staging the title song, "Hello Central Give Me Dr. Jazz," in which Bobby did a series of soft shoe slides traveling backwards across the apron of the stage, singing and beguiling the audience with a captivating smile. The scripted character, however, was multi-dimensional; the monochromatic appeal of this single number could not remedy the inherent problems in Bobby's approach. He had a desperate need to be loved and was playing

a part that the audience basically loved to hate. Polarization and dishar-
mony took over: Joan Copland, a featured actress who played opposite
Bobby was replaced; a new book writer and a new director were brought
in to assuage the fragile ego of our leading man. I continued as choreographer and after the show limped in, opened briefly, then closed, I emerged
from the fray with a Tony nomination for outstanding choreography. Lola
was singled out for praise and Raoul Pene Dubois' colorful poster joined
the grouping of posters from infamous Broadway flops mounted on the
wall of Joe Allen's restaurant, a theater hangout on the West 46th Street
block known as Theatre Row. Included in that display of rogues were two
other posters from shows with which I had had an association.

I'm Solomon, which lasted just two short weeks at the Mark Hellinger
Theatre in 1968, was the Broadway permutation of *Shlomo Hamelek ve
Shalmai Hasandlar* (King Solomon and the Cobbler), a delightful chamber
musical that I had seen in Tel Aviv at the Camari Theatre. Zvi Kolitz, an
Israeli producer living in the United States, believed it would be a bonanza
on Broadway and that the New York Jewish population, which was larger
than that in Israel, would welcome it with open arms. He explained this
estimate at an initial meeting of the cast, creative staff, and production
personnel that preceded the first day of rehearsals. The meeting was held
in Central Plaza, a large rehearsal hall on Second Avenue, the lower East
Side boulevard that had been home to New York's once thriving Yiddish
Theater. The rehearsal hall was directly over Rattner's Dairy Restaurant
and the three producers, Zvi Kolitz, Abe Margolies, and Soloman Sagall
sat behind a skirted banquet table set with pitchers of ice water. The stars
of the show were the comedian, Dick Shawn, and the singer/actress,
Karen Morrow. Carmen Matthews, who had been cast so wonderfully as
the mother superior in the film *Lilies of the Field*, would play Bathsheva,
mother of King Solomon. The luminous Salome Jens would play the
legendary Queen of Sheba. Ernest Gold, who had written the music for
the film *Exodus*, was the composer of the completely new score and Anne
Croswell supplied the new lyrics. In fact as I listened to Zvi speak, I found
hardly anything in his description that resembled the charming show that
I had seen in Tel Aviv. The three producers had widely divergent ideas
of the project, and each extolled the virtues of the show he envisioned.
Zvi Kolitz stood before us in a beautifully tailored Italian suit, addressing
us as if he were delivering an argument in front of the United Nations
General Assembly. Soloman Sagall, a fatherly man, spoke to us in heavily
accented English sprinkled with Middle European Jewish expressions, as
if we were a class of kindergarten children, eager to begin the first day
of school. Abe Margolies, a New Yorker who had made a fortune in the
47th Street jewelry business, rose next and told us in pure Brooklynese
what a great show we had. I sat listening and observing the wide-eyed,

open-mouthed expressions on the dumbfounded cast. It was like being in a scene from a Three Stooges movie. Michael Benthall, the English director of classical theater, had somehow been engaged to shepherd this project. He thanked the trio of producers with a chuckle and told us we would start a read and sing through of the show after lunch, which had just arrived courtesy of Rattner's Restaurant and the largesse of Abe Margolies. I went around greeting the dancers and found Lea, who was my assistant choreographer on the show. I pulled her away from Zvi Kolitz who had her engaged in a Hebrew conversation. "Well, what do you think, dear?" "It's certainly going to be different." Ruben Ter Arutunian, our talented and moody scenic designer, sat to the side watching the proceedings with a baleful, jaded expression.

"Okay, all the dancers on the stage. Try not to bump into the other actors." Michael Benthall was used to working with exquisitely trained ensemble players in British repertory theater and expected scenes to simply emerge from our pick-up company with casual blocking instructions. He also had little knowledge of how to collaborate with a choreographer. "That's enough dancers. Dance off now." "Michael..." Michael turned to me as he heard his name called out. "...I'll take over now that you've sketched in what you want. The choreography can't be just thrown up on the stage. It needs to be designed and rehearsed. Why don't you take Dick and Karen and work on their first scene."

By the time we got to Philadelphia for out-of-town tryouts, the confusion resulting from lack of communication had multiplied into near disastrous proportions. Abe Margolies arrived at the theater as the throne room was being put into place and took great offense at Ruben Ter Arutunian's rendition of King Solomon's marble throne. It had the twelve lions of Judah guarding the kingly seat, resting proudly back on their haunches with fangs bared and penises at full erection. Margolies had the offending members chopped off and Ruben left Philadelphia in a raging fury.

The 1971 poster for *1600 Pennsylvania Avenue* that graced Joe Allen's wall of flops did not bear my name as choreographer nor did it list Frank Cosaro as director. We had both been replaced in Philadelphia, the incongruously entitled City of Brotherly Love, by George Faison and Gilbert Moses respectively. This last ditch effort to rescue a show which boasted authorship by the enormous talents of Alan J. Lerner for book and lyrics and Leonard Bernstein for music did nothing to keep it from toppling under its own weight and pomposity. Other members of Broadway's royal family connected with this much heralded production were producers Roger Stevens and Robert Whitehead. Tony Walton's sets and costumes which faithfully followed the premise of the show were indicative of the production's inherent conceptual weaknesses. The libretto traced the history of the infant United States, the vesting of the seat of federal power in the District of Colombia, the real and fictitious lives of the early tenants of the White House, and the lengthy construction of the presidential residence at 1600 Pennsylvania Avenue. The concept was that the United States is a nation in rehearsal. It was politically idealistic and full of good intention, but historically indefensible. Tony's theatricalized rehearsal sets and costumes were visually boring within the elegant red velvet interior of Philadelphia's Forrest Theatre. There were some glorious snatches of music, intelligent lyrics, and moments of highly sophisticated humor overlaying a fallacious depiction of the heinous American practice of slavery that I found alternately syrupy and insulting. One sequence involving a slave boy picked up along the muddy unpaved roadside by Dolly Madison on her tortuous journey to the unfinished presidential home was particularly offensive. Little Lud grows up as a house servant under Dolly's maternal protection, enslaved yet happy in his dependency, and blindly faithful to his mistress. First lady, Dolly Madison, sings a glorious warm ballad to this emasculated lad, entrusting him with the care of the very nation which legally denies him power, manhood, or self-determination. Lud, the eternal boy-child in the Lerner/Bernstein libretto, is married in the White House and on his wedding night he and his bride are rocked to sleep by the other servants to the cloying strains of an infant's lullaby. Gilbert Price and Emily Yancey played the hapless couple denied their adulthood on this most intimate night of their lives. I refused to stage this scene as conceived and restrained no words in explaining my revulsion. "Was this the way you were treated on your wedding nights? The entire idea is repugnant to me."

During a preview performance, I sat with the two of them at the back of the orchestra on the steps leading up to the mezzanine, watching the first act. Lenny's face was contorted in an expression of ecstasy as he listened to the concluding notes of the first act finale. Alan sat silently, looking morose and troubled. He wore white cotton gloves to restrain him from a nervous habit that caused him to pick at his cuticles, but the gloves had failed in their mission and were covered with blood. As the audience started up the aisle toward the outer lobby, a man noticed the illustrious pair that had authored such beloved classics as *My Fair Lady* and *West Side Story* and spoke out boldly. "Look at the brain trust up there. Couldn't you give us a real show? Does it get any better in the second act?"

The following day, on my way over to Roger Stevens' hotel room for an impromptu meeting called without a specified agenda, I bumped into Zoe Caldwell and her husband, co-producer Robert Whitehead. "Oh, I'm so sorry. You must feel just awful." I answered her with cloaked vagueness as I had no idea to what she was referring, but something inside of me guarded against asking for clarification. Perhaps it was the pained expression on Robert Whitehead's face or the swiftness with which he swept Zoe away, before she could engage me in further conversation. Roger Stevens, on the other hand, was all business, friendly and dispassionate. "Donald, we are going to have to part company on this one. I've spoken with Biff Liff at William Morris to assure him, as I now assure you, that all our contractual arrangements stand exactly as agreed upon." "Roger, we both know there are many serious problems with this show, but my work is not among them. Unless you deal with the real and inherent dilemmas, no one you get will be able to help."

Roger smiled enigmatically. "I hope at some other time we can work together again." Exiting the hotel, I bumped into Frank Cosaro. There was fire leaping out of his eyes. "So you've just got your kiss off. What a crock! I'm glad to be out of it. It stinks to hell!" The show floundered on. Biff Liff intimated that Roger Stevens was questioning him about the possible reinstatement of my version of "The President Jefferson's Birthday March." The Broadway parasites had already hung the show with so much black crepe that nothing could postpone its inevitable funeral. It was too late for any reverse cosmetics and the show folded in a landslide of carnivorous press, media coverage, recriminations, and gossip.

In the winter of 1979, Biff Liff called from Wiliam Morris with some exciting news. "Donald, I've got a real tasty offer for you, a new Broadway show." "Really... who... what... when? Tell me." Biff Liff outlined that the project was a musical on the life and work of Duke Ellington. There was a group of producers involved in the project. They had acquired the rights to Duke Ellington's vast musical output and literary samples to be fashioned into a Broadway musical with eyes on a future Hollywood film. "The producers are Manheim Fox, Burton Litwyn, Sondra Gilman, Louise Westergaard and Roger Berlind. Roger's been around the block a few times, the others are just getting their feet wet. They'd like to have a meeting with you, if you're interested. They've seen your ballet *District Storyville* on the Ailey company and have already made an offer to the leading lady, Judith Jamison."

Duke Ellington, along with Earl "Fatha" Hines and Count Basie, comprised the royalty of the jazz world, but Ellington's musical palette embraced areas that set him apart from the others. This would be my fourth professional encounter with the art of Edward Kennedy Ellington. The first had been the 1957 *A Drum Is A Woman*, the extended work on the history of jazz that had been recorded with Duke reading his own narration between his large orchestral and vocal pieces. It had been made into a television special, and I was the assistant choreographer working with Paul Godkin. Talley Beatty was the lead dancer along with Carmen DeLavallade who played the role of Madam Zajj, Duke's formulation of his muse, the Lady Jazz. This had been followed by my 1965 staging of

Duke's, "It Don't Mean A Thing If It Ain't Got That Swing" for *The Strollin'
Twenties,* featuring Paula Kelly dancing with William Louther and Dudley
Williams. The third encounter in 1978 was *Queenie Pie,* the unfinished
opera buffa that also was to be mounted as a television special. Duke's
untimely death left that project lost in the maze of grasping hands claiming control of his vast estate. I attended several creative sessions organized
by Jac Venza for public television, but the project languished in legal
embroilment and never got off the ground. All of this was to become part
of the theater work I would design as a "portrait of Duke Ellington —
painted in music, dance, and song." Burton Litwin was the first member
of the producing team to meet with me. He flew out to Los Angeles and
presented the scope of the project from his perspective. He promised to
make available to me all records, books, music, and other materials at his
disposal. Burt was the vice president of the music publishing firm, Belwin
Mills, which owned the rights to the early Ellington compositions through
the 1940's. With his interest in theatrical production and his ability to
deliver the rights to this major portion of the Ellington catalogue, he came
into the growing family of producers. Manheim Fox was president of
American Retrospectives and held the rights to important anthologies of
Ellington recordings and writings and was also an aspiring producer.
Manny brought in his rights package and became a member of the team
along with Sondra Gilman and Louise Westergaard, who were engaged
in feature film ventures, and Roger Berlind who had many full-fledged
Broadway credentials. Together, the group was able to acquire the rights
to the 1950s' portion of the Ellington folio from Ruth Ellington, Duke's
sister and owner of Tempo Music, and the rights to the other primary
branch of Duke's musical outpouring from Robbins Music Company.
These acquisitions included almost all of Ellington's some one thousand
compositions as well as his autobiography *Music Is My Mistress.* With this
awesome body of work in hand, I eagerly set to my enormous and exciting
task. Lea's downstairs studio in our home was turned over to me and an
expandable work table was set up and soon covered with research materials as I crafted what I called a choreo-musical with the working title,
Duke. On March 6, 1978, I finally arrived at a music and dance scenario
with intermittent dialogue lifted and paraphrased from Duke's own words.
I happily bound and mailed it to the eagerly awaiting producers.

   A year and a half later I was in New York setting up housekeeping in
a small studio apartment on Claremont Avenue. It neighbored the Riverside Church where Gabrielle and Liane had first attended school and
was just up the street from the old Juilliard building where I had taught
classes prior to the school's relocation in Lincoln Center. I arrived two
weeks before the apartment would be available, and Roger Berlind and
his wife Brooke graciously took me into their East End Avenue apartment

as a house guest. Burton Litwyn gave me a twenty-four-hour pass to Belwin Mills Publishing Corporation's New York headquarters on 57th Street and Broadway. For a year, starting in January 1980, the library music room there was my home away from home. For months, I tirelessly pursued the elusive Mercer Ellington, Duke's son and the inheritor of his glorious orchestra, for copies of songs and orchestral scores that were stored in the "off-limits Ellington warehouse." I spent endless and wonderful days working at the piano with Lloyd Mayer on vocal medleys and dance arrangements of the selection that I had gleaned from the seemingly bottomless well of Ellington music. Finally, I arrived at a first document:

SYNOPSIS

The presentation is a *choreo-musical*, divided into two acts.

ACT I — DUKE'S WORLD

The first act deals with the public man in a roughly chronological sequence, beginning with the original small Ellingtonian group, The Washingtonians, playing Harlem Rent Parties and in Cutting Contests at the Kentucky Club. It then moves into the famous Cotton Club era and the exotic Jungle Reviews. The main body of the first act is Travel. We leave the Cotton Club and take to The Road, passing through the Dance Halls in Anywhere U.S.A. through Hotel Rooms scattered around the world, to the hip centers everywhere, where new audiences were found and finally back in triumph to New York and great success at home base.

ACT II — DUKE'S PLACE

The second act deals with the private man. The first section is called Woman, a constant source of inspiration to a man who loved to love. The second part is Night Life and deals with the fun world of the night person, encompassing many of Duke's best known works. The resolve of the act is in the Sacred Works. The denouement is in the command at the concluding moment of the Second Sacred Concert, Praise God and Dance, which brings us full circle to Duke's beginnings and perhaps his most important commandment — It Don't Mean A Thing If It Ain't got That Swing.

In the preface to the document and throughout the script specific instructions were given detailing design concepts and directions for my other creative colleagues:

> The costuming will cover half a century and will reflect the taste and
> fashion of the man, the world around him, including the entire scope
> of his travels and the changing styles of theatrical dress from the 20's
> to the 70's.
>
> The stage extends over the orchestra pit, thrusting out to meet the
> audience. The evening will be constantly musical, always Duke
> Ellington — even to his use of language, which is as unique as his
> music, as individual and singular. All spoken words will be built upon
> his writings, books, articles, and record liner notes, as well as excerpts
> from his many interviews.

Several meetings and reworkings later, the details and events of my
scenario had slightly altered with refinements and new musical discov-
eries. The title of the show had been the biggest item of discussion and
the quintet of producers all bared their business heads and argued until
a final decision was made. A more "sexy" name was desired and after
plumbing the titles of Duke's best known songs and my refusing to accept
Satin Dolls, the decision to call the show *Sophisticated Ladies* was adopted
by all. At the beginning of July I returned home to spend the holiday. Lea
was throwing a big party for my fiftieth birthday, and the day before the
big event a case of Dom Perignon champagne arrived: "You're the best!
Manny, Roger, Louise, Sondra, and Burt." The honeymoon had now officially begun.

The most important item to any theatrical production is the perfect cast.
I had learned from my years in the arts and entertainment that it mattered
little what you had in your head or on the printed page; it was what was
up on the stage that counted. If it didn't happen there, for all purposes
it didn't exist. The most crucial element in assuring that my creative vision
would come to life was the selection of a cast that was able to breathe and
soar with me. The selection of the creative team and production staff were
of almost equal importance and in any event needed to be accomplished
first. "Peter, I'm doing a most exciting and wonderful new show on the
life and music of Duke Ellington. I've been developing it for the past year
and now we're ready to go. I'd love to have you on board as my production stage manager." "Donald, it's fabulous and everyone's talking about
it. What a coup and no one deserves it more than you! I'd love to do it
but I'm not free ... what a bummer. There is someone I can recommend.
He's fantastic ... the best ... better than me ... Alan Hall." I jotted down
the telephone number that Peter Lawrence gave me. I had worked with
Peter in 1978 on a show which that had run out of money and had to be
abandoned in Philadelphia. It was an American historical drama set in the
waning years of American minstrelsy in a border state where a traveling
troupe of black minstrels known as Black Sally and her Minstrel Trouba-
dours were under siege by a group of black militants who wished to end

what they considered the blatant degradation of the race by white and black minstrels. As the angry mob gathered outside the theater, the frightened troupe of performers went about preparing and presenting their show replete with every stereotyped and hoary cliché of the minstrel tradition: the raising of the roll-drop to reveal a semi-circle of chairs awaiting the rowdy high stepping entrance of the blackface performers, musicians, interlocutor, and endmen to sing the ballads and coon songs, to perform the buck dancing, the exchange of palaver between Mr. Tambo, Mr. Bones, and Mr. Interlocutor and the enactment of comedy sketches, and finally the star-turn second act entry of Black Sally played by Della Reese. The ill-fated production was called *The Last Minstrel Show* and had as its featured player Gregory Hines. I had worked with Gregory before on a television special produced by George Schlatter called *Soul* in which he performed with his brother Maurice and his father as part of the night club act, Hines, Hines, and Dad. He was a performer of wonderful instincts with a whole barrel of talent at his command. He could negotiate a comedy routine with impeccable timing, play an impressive stint on trap drums, sing a ballad with a charming, lump in the throat delivery, and roll off intricate rhythm tap dance improvisations with complete ease. Maurice was the older brother and had a more balletic style, embroidering his tap dancing with pirouettes. Their father backed up the act on the traps, relinquishing his place when the impulsive and engaging Gregory finished dancing and segued to the drums. At those moments, Dad and Maurice would lead the audience clapping on the off beat as Gregory sounded forth on the tom-toms.

The cast of characters for *The Last Minstrel Show* called for performers who could act, sing, and play the musical instruments. I thought a leading candidate for this seemingly impossible casting assignment was Gregory Hines. He was chosen and was wonderful in a role which required him to dance, sing, play drums, perform a comedy sketch in travesty, as well as act the part of a timid and fearful young man cowering in the face of the threat of mob violence and the disdain and wrath of Della Reese's towering reading of the role of Black Sally.

For *Sophisticated Ladies* I planned the cast of eight principals and eight members of a chorus which I called the Soloists Ensemble. Gregory was my first choice to play opposite Judith Jamison. I presented the idea to my agent, Biff Liff at William Morris, who also had Gregory as a client. Gregory jumped at the offer and drove from the Venice Beach hotel, where he was vacationing with his girlfriend Pamela Koslow and their respective daughters, to our home in Sherman Oaks to discuss the project. He was well aware of my unusual approach and extremely enthusiastic. He opened himself up to me gregariously in a stream of conscience conversation filled with anecdotes and personal items.

With the two leading players in place, my next assignment was to secure the right person for the pivotal position of production stage manager. I dialed the number Peter Lawrence had given me. "Sorry I can't come to the phone. I'm taking Miss Havershorn to have her bottom scraped." I chuckled through the message that I left on Alan Hall's answer machine. To what exactly was he referring? I was eager to meet him and immediately hoped he would undertake the production stage manager position. With Alan Hall signed on as production stage manager and his wife Ruth Rinklin as first assistant stage manager, we set up the cast auditions. It was comforting to learn from them that it was their houseboat that Alan had taken to be scraped clean of barnacles and that Ruth had not been in harm's way from some diabolical kinky practice. Simultaneously I entered into the scenic design process with Tony Walton with whom I had collaborated before on two auspicious projects, in addition to the ill fated *1600 Pennsylvania Ave*. They were *Golden Boy* and the 1974 Emmy Award winning children's special, *Free To Be You and Me*. In that television vehicle I had crafted a number for Roberta Flack and Michael Jackson as two children playing on a huge window seat and singing a song that was somehow quite prophetic.

> When I grow up will I be pretty
> Will I be a great big movie star ...

Tony Walton was extremely enthusiastic about having Willa Kim as costume designer for the show. I had seen her work with the Eliot Feld Ballet and her simple but attractive designs for Bob Fosse's *Dancin'*. Her work was largely associated with dance, so I was eager to meet with her and explore the possibility of her coming aboard the design team. Tony, himself, was a marvelous costume designer, and his impassioned recommendation carried great weight with me. We met at her house and I went through her design portfolio as we sat sipping wine in rattan cobra chairs. The San Francisco Ballet was coming to the Brooklyn Academy of Music, and Willa was eager for me to see her designs for Michael Smuin's *Song For A Dead Warrior*. As I said good-bye and rose to leave, a protruding nail in the seat of the chair grabbed hold of my pant leg and tore a sizable gash, leaving a dangling V shaped patch. Willa appeared completely nonplused by the unfortunate incident and had no designer secret to offer to salvage the smart new trousers that I had worn to greet a possible colleague. We agreed to meet at the performance in Brooklyn where, when we went back stage to meet Michael Smuin and to inspect Willa's visually arresting and costly buffalo bodies and feathered tribal array, I was to see the very lively and animated side of this talented and enigmatic woman.

One of the delicious discoveries of the audition process was the amazing Phyllis Hyman. She walked into the room slightly over-animated from nerves and blew us away with the power and stylishness of her voice. She had a sound that was unique and was equally at home with pulsing jazz tunes, skat singing, or a searing ballad. She was a large and attractive woman and would look wonderful in highly theatrical costumes. There was no point in waiting to tell her of a decision that was unanimous and instantaneous. "We'd love to have you in our show." "You mean, I've got the job? For real?" As we nodded and babbled effusively, Phyllis burst into a delightful series of whoops and squeals. Priscilla Baskerville, the magnificent soprano who had been part of the company I had taken to Israel with *My Heart Belongs To Broadway*, was a harder sell to the primarily pop and commercial taste of the group of producers. She was who I wanted and I finally cut through all the commentary and said emphatically, "I will see no one else for the role." It was becoming glaringly obvious that everything was taking ten times as long as necessary with everyone having their say and re-say. This was going to be a long and arduous process. Little personal meetings with the separate producers, with private agendas, were requested. One of them, at Sondra Gilman's east side town house, began quite pleasantly but after a bit too much red wine got downright abusive since I continued to disagree with her point of view. Luckily, I had a dinner date with Liane, who arrived, and I was able to leave the disagreeable and argumentative session. The next day Manny Fox called to have a talk and indicated that he had heard from Louise of the unfortunate incident. He begged me not to take it to heart. "Sondra can get a bit overbearing when she's had too much wine." Louise Westergaard called next to request an audience. The meeting at her upper Fifth Avenue residence/office was one of those events whose visual images, down to the most minute detail, I shall never erase from my memory. She opened the door, welcomed me, and led me into the parlor. I sat in a comfortable armchair facing the window and Louise sat opposite me, sending her Chinese housekeeper to bring drinks. "Mei Lin's one of the family. I just love her." The drinks arrived and Louise began a meandering conversation about the show, my scenario, and what a fan she was of my work. As she plied me with compliments, she commenced to shuck off her shoes and draw her legs up on the couch, with her knees spread widely apart stretching her skirt into a taut frame that exposed Rubenesque thighs. Her voice and manner segued from coy to sultry as she picked at her toenails and then brought her fingers up to her mouth, resting them lingeringly on her bottom lip. This scene was etched on my mind, perhaps to be recreated in the future when a dramatic plot called for some bizarre activity out of the shadowy side of feminine guile and duplicity.

Part of my arrangement with the producers was for a preproduction work period. A pair of dancers and two assistants of my choosing would be hired so that I could prepare material for the show prior to the start of full rehearsals. I was able to convince Mercedes Ellington to accept the position of assistant choreographer over her lingering proclivity to steer shy of projects that immersed her in the embroiled dynamics of the Ellington clan. Mercedes had been a student at Juilliard during my tenure there and had gained fame as a June Taylor Dancer on the Jackie Gleason Television Variety Hour. She was an excellent dancer and could be described in the parlance of Duke Ellington, her famous grandfather, as a *café au lait* beauty. She was the only offspring of her father, Mercer Ellington's first marriage. Mercer, as musical director of the show and the leader of the Duke Ellington Orchestra, would be on-stage conducting. He was on tour with the orchestra and would return in time to commence rehearsals and settle into his suite at the Edison Hotel with his Scandinavian wife and with Mercedes' new five year old brother. Her other siblings, Edward Kennedy Jr. and Gae, progeny of Mercer's second marriage, would show up at rehearsals from time to time to pick up envelopes from their father. Her aunt, Ruth, baby sister of Duke and a contemporary of his son Mercer, was a major player in this Ellington Project, now officially entitled *Sophisticated Ladies*. That Mercedes agreed to my offer, considering the odds stacked against it, was a testament to her belief in my work.

My other assistant was Bruce Heath, a dancer whom I had nurtured beginning with an apprenticeship in the Inner City Repertory Dance Company. He had been introduced to me, as had many alumni of Bernice Johnson's Jamaica, New York dance school, by Michele Simmons, a principal dancer with my Los Angeles concert company. I had taken Bruce and his classmate, Gary Chapman, into the company together and trained them in the repertory. I created several new works while they were with the company, including *Songs of the Disinherited* in 1972, which featured Michele Simmons in the climactic solo "Angelitos Negros." As my work began to encompass an increasing number of television musical variety series, specials, and award shows, Bruce rose to the position of second assistant under the tutelage of my associate and primary assistant, Carolyn Dyer. In 1978, Bruce became my primary assistant and was entrusted with the audition and restaging of the Chicago company of *Evolution of the Blues* which overlapped with my premiere of *My Heart Belongs To Broadway* in Israel. I had arrived in Chicago after a seventeen-hour flight from Tel Aviv and come directly from the airport to a rehearsal in the ballroom of the Ritz Carlton hotel. Bruce had taught all the dances and staged the movement elements of the songs but was waiting for me to translate the material into the new setting. The Drury Lane Watergate theater had seating in the round. The revolving stage was designed by Thomas Walsh as an enormous phonograph record, the center of which could be raised on an hydraulic to become a dais, pulpit, or any platform of importance. I had only two days to completely restage the show which had run previously for a year in the intimate thrust setting of the Westwood Playhouse in Los Angeles.

"Donald, we've got trouble." I studied the consternation on Bruce's face and the worry that filled his large Bambi-like eyes. "Foster's been acting strange and he's been manhandling Eartha in the slave auction sequence." I found Foster Johnson next door in the bar. He greeted me with a smile, his eyes shining in a handsome face surrounded by a ring of silvery hair. "Don, I'm sure glad to see you. Did you just arrive?" "Yes, I've got to go and take a short nap. I didn't get any rest on that endless flight. I'll see you in an hour. Bruce is waiting for you inside." The dynamics were already completely out of control with Foster's alienation from the company. Bruce had not been able to handle the volatile situation and it was but one of the many problems that awaited my solution: the scenery would not be finished in time for the scheduled opening that weekend fortunately giving me an extra few days; costumes had been redesigned by Judy Dearing and would also benefit from the delay; there were some theater management problems ... but first I would have to sleep.

I had grown very close to Bruce, my relationship with him having developed into a paternal bond. At Bruce's wedding, I had walked down the grassy lawn as surrogate father-of-the bride. Just prior to the commencement of the preproduction rehearsal period for *Sophisticated Ladies* Bruce went into the hospital for knee surgery. There was no thought on my part of replacing him; rather, I went to the hospital with the carved African walking stick that had been given to me as a stylish post surgery crutch. It had been nicknamed, Idi Amin's Stick because of the events in Uganda that coincided with my operation. I handed it to him as a talisman for his speedy and complete recovery.

"Let's introduce ourselves to each other. It's a good way of becoming acquainted with what will be your creative family for the next few months of rehearsals and for the years of successful playing that will follow. I'm Donald McKayle, conceiver, director, and choreographer and though I've met you all in the selection process, I know I will get to know you a whole lot better."

"Mercer Ellington ..."

There was a pause as Gregory who was next to Mercer looked a little nonplussed as whether or not to comply with my directive. Perhaps he had envisioned a ceremonious personal introduction to the rest of the cast, followed by a round of applause. This was not the atmosphere of ensemble that I wished to foster for the rehearsal period. I turned to him and waited.

"... Gregory Hines." I was keenly aware of of the imperceptible edge of disquiet that filtered through the cast as they pondered their star. "I'm Judith Jamison." Judy's bright voice cleared the air and dismissed any need for fawning or tribute. Adrian Bailey completely eased the moment as gales of laughter followed his announcement. "And I'm Annette Funicella." As rehearsals progressed, Gregory increasingly distanced himself from me. This was no longer the young man I had worked with from Hines, Hines, and Dad, nor the eager, versatile, and willing actor who had played in *The Last Minstrel Show*. This was a new and ambitious performer who had a definite agenda in mind: becoming a major superstar with this vehicle, whatever it might take. Judith Jamison, whom he had pursued in a macho way as an item of personal conquest, was now an irritant to him. She had been hired first and her contract set limitations on the contracts of any other star performer. It would never allow him his desired singular top billing, above the title. The degree to which this displeasure would emerge in insidious small acts of sedition was soon to become apparent.

My concept of *Sophisticated Ladies* was not easily pigeon-holed, and that seemed to fascinate the writers that flocked to interview me. It also made them nervous and aggressively edgy. It spoiled the neatness of their task and pushed them to persist in questions designed to make me agree that my work belonged to one of the clearly identifiable and practiced forms of musical theater. "Wouldn't you agree that the show is basically a review." "The show is a celebration of the many facets of an extraordinary creative life which defies stereotypes and flip characterization." "But in its formal aspects, the show is closer to a review, isn't it? It's surely not a book show." "There are many things you can say it is not. A book show would be one of those." "Then you do agree it is a review." "The show is a theatrical painting of an unconventional musical talent. It is a canvas that is texturally rich with stylistic variety and utilizes selections from the full portfolio of the music and writing of Duke Ellington. This choreomusical is composed of his earliest composition, 'The Soda Fountain Rag,' some of his most famous works for his orchestra including the perennial favorites, 'Sophisticated Lady,' 'Satin Doll,' 'I Got It Bad and That Ain't Good', and 'Mood Indigo,' works of symphonic texture such as, 'Black, Brown, and Beige,' and 'Three Kings,' portions of his sacred concerts, 'Heaven,' 'Come Sunday,' and 'Praise God and Dance'." All of it is held together by his own words spoken by different raconteurs who step out of the cast of principal performers." "Is Gregory Hines the principal raconteur and the main character telling the story." "Gregory is the initial raconteur, but the story is picked up almost immediately by the Judith Jamison character and transfers fluidly to the characters played by Phyllis Hyman, P. J. Benjamin, Terri Klausner, Gregg Burge, Hinton Battle, and Priscilla Baskerville. I'm afraid you'll just have to deal with the show as I've created it." I could sense that my pronouncement was going down like castor oil and would come back to haunt me. Rumblings of discontent that would persist like a numbing toothache, had already started in rehearsal with Gregory, who wanted an easygoing night club format. Gregory had just finished two stints in Hollywood and the scent of stardom was all around him. He was determined to retain it. We did have some wonderful moments in rehearsal when I was producing numbers that catered to his talent and surrounded him with a chorus of supporting players such as in the tap dance card game to *Koko* in the second act. He was ecstatic and delightful as I designed the New York cabby number around him to "I'm Just A Lucky So and So." That particular number, though, seemed to bring out the territorial instinct in other creative players. I had conceived it with all of its physical details designed and clearly spelled out in the production script. The evening preceding its first rehearsal, I got together with Alan Hall and we devised an ingenious rehearsal prop, which Alan built, that would allow me completely to stage the number with the cast. The taxicab would be formed by four male dancers seated in rolling office chairs back to back, facing in opposite directions and held together with a wooden frame on which a stool was mounted for Gregory as the cabby. The seated male dancers would be bent over at the waist most of the time and with their arms linked would form the doors and chassis of the cab. They would step rhythmically maneuvering the vehicle, rocking on their seats when the motor idled, pressing their feet forward when the vehicle braked, all the while singing a doo-wap accompaniment to Gregory's rolling vocal. It was a great number with an unusual and original staging and Gregory was in seventh heaven. Tony Walton and Willa Kim arrived at different times to formalize the design. Tony worked quickly; we soon had a fully built sleek body frame for rehearsal. Willa was slow and noncommittal in all her design entries, so we would have to wait to see the flashy exteriors that would clothe Tony's structure. When the playbill came out a brief and bold entry was included: "Taxicab designed by Willa Kim."

The speak easy number which featured Priscilla Baskerville as the club proprietor, à la Brick Top, was a production tour-de-force and a marvelous comic turnabout for Tony Walton. Gregory played the doorman sliding the peephole back and forth as he examined and let in only the desired big-spenders. The band musicians were patrons scattered about and mixed with the hoi polloi slumming at this Harlem nightspot where prohibition whiskey was served in coffee cups just in case of a police raid. Tony did that historical idea one better. When the police came knocking at the door and Gregory signaled, the tabletops flipped over. Crosses and hymnals replaced the drinks and in a matter of seconds the nightclub was transformed into a storefront church. Willa took Tony's lead and had Priscilla's costume become a clerical, if besequined, vestment sporting a huge jeweled cross as a necklace. Priscilla's glorious voice rang forth as the music of the "Kentucky Toodle-oo" segued into the beautiful spiritual "Just A

Closer Walk With Thee." As the song turned around into a New Orleans strut, even the police got the spirit and began to join the joyous group shout which ended the number. It was one of the bright spots of the first act but was one of the first numbers to be dropped after the Philadelphia opening. This was done to assuage Gregory, who would play second fiddle to no one and demanded more of a singular presence in the entire proceedings. He wanted to sing a romantic ballad holding stage by himself, backed up by the orchestra. This was not in my plans; I resisted, and an irrevocable friction was set in place. Louise Westergaard was busy promising each of us what she thought we wanted to hear and in the process concocted complete revisions of the same story. Gregory was equally busy on his own behalf, enlisting the support of members of the cast and even my personal assistants. I noticed Bruce Heath distancing himself from me and Claudia Asbury, whom I had chosen as dance captain, greeting my work with an arched and critical eye. Mercedes Ellington was withdrawing into herself as if revisiting a personal nightmare. I suddenly felt all alone in my task. My agent, Biff Liff, was nowhere to be found, and I realized that I was in a hornet's nest. Judith Jamison's big first act number, "In My Solitude," was danced with Hinton Battle. The other principals sang the lyrics to the hypnotic melody, standing under neon lit hotel marquees. Gregory wanted none of this, and the song would finally go to Priscilla Baskerville and become the only remaining solo item in her performance after the beautiful "Come Sunday" and "Praise God and Dance" were dropped. Gregory withdrew from all numbers that dealt with the serious or spiritual essence of Duke Ellington or called for a performance of vulnerability or depth. At the same time, Louise Westergaard let slip to me in a practiced aside that Gregory wanted to perform "Satin Doll" with Terri Klausner in place of P. J. Benjamin. He also began to undermine Judith Jamison's performance of "Black Beauty" in the Cotton Club sequence, adding ad libbed dialogue into his scripted performance. One matinée he went so far with his lounge-act free wheeling lack of theater discipline as to announce to the audience the score of the Eagles play-off football game.

Production meetings abounded to deal with the show's problems, and the producers decided to bring in Gregory's tap dance teacher and mentor, Henry Le Tang, to design some specialty tap numbers for Gregory. They also would bring in Sam Art Williams to replace Duke's words with a book that would feature Gregory as a fictitious character of equal importance to the overwhelming presence of Duke Ellington. This stuck like a jagged stone in my craw, and I refused to participate in this outrageous travesty. This stand was the climax of a spiraling tornado of negative energy that found me at the eye of the storm. Daily meetings with the quintet of producers speaking over one another would dissolve into separate and private agendas. Perhaps the most insidious and devious of these machinations happened in Washington D.C. when I received an early morning emergency call from Louise Westergaard asking me to meet her at her suite at the Watergate Hotel. She stated that she had already contacted Bruce for me and that he would be in charge of the rehearsal reviewing the proposed new show opener, to yet another version of "Take the A Train."

I got to the hotel early, eager to get through with the mystery meeting and back to rehearsal. The show was going at cross purposes with all the added creative personnel and conflicting approaches and the cast was stressed and on a nervous edge that was ready to explode. The receptionist at the desk called up to announce me. "Mrs. Westergaard says to take a seat in the lounge. She'll be ready for you in a few minutes. We'll call you, sir."

After waiting impatiently for fifteen minutes, I went to the house phone and rang up Louise's room. "I'm off to rehearsal. I can't wait any longer." "Didn't they call you. I told them to send you up. Have you had coffee? I have croissants and fruit." The events that followed completely erased any memory of the contents of this meeting. I got to rehearsal and asked Bruce to show me the number. There was a confusing conversation with Bruce and a grumbling from the cast that accompanied a lackluster and seemingly unrehearsed showing of the number that had begun the day before. Alan Hall looked angry and the company was completely out of sorts. "Donald," he said venomously, "they've been working on a totally different version of the same number with Henry for the last hour." I was completely flabbergasted by this information and confronted Henry. "Donny, I thought you knew all about it. That's what Louise told me." When I met Lea for lunch, she recounted running into Priscilla Baskerville on the way over, who described to her with disgust the morning activities and the mood of the cast. With one butcher's stroke, Louise had been able to wrest authority from me and place me in a defensive posture from which I would never recover. When I later approached her in an angry confrontation, she looked at me with a blank face and impassivity replied, "I just had to hedge my bets."

It soon became clear to the producers that Sam Art Williams' new book was not working. Sam went back to New York and the show was to be restored to my original libretto. Gregory flatly refused. He was elated with his new literary importance. "I'm going out there and talk about, 'Duke and me,' just like I've been doing for the last week." The end result of this final insubordination was that the producers let Gregory go and the show was to go on with Gregg Burge in his role and Michael Scott Gregory moved up from the ensemble to cover Gregg Burge's part. At the same time Judith was ill and Winona Smith was to go on for her. Winona was a dynamic talent but petite in stature and could not wear any of Judith's costumes. Willa Kim was off on some other project and not available to deal with the emergency. Lea agreed to lend the show some of her personal wardrobe and frantic calls back and forth to a friend in Los Angeles finally located the sumptuous Georgio San Angelo rhinestone studded alix jersey white gown and cloche that would carry Winona through the white section of the show and could be dressed up further when appropriate with Judith's white fox boa. The outfit was put on a plane flying from Los Angeles to Washington D.C. and it arrived in time for a fitting. The white section had given Willa her mark of identity in the show and a design concept that would eventually earn her a Tony award. The concept, however, was not Wilia's; rather, it was Tony Walton's. It was not until after Tony's elegant show poster came out that Willa arrived at her design concept. The poster showed the young, dapper Duke Ellington in black high hat and tails surrounded by a bevy of female pulchritude wrapped in exquisite white fur collared clutch coats perched on a drum bridge of piano keys. "Tony, why didn't you tell me you were going to do the poster with those wonderful looking women?" Tony smiled at Willa's coquetry. He was an excellent costume designer in his own right, had a complete design vision of the show, and possessed a magnanimous heart and a benevolent nature that was totally lacking in territorial avarice.

The cast had received the announcement of Gregory's dismissal with panic. They were aware of his charismatic hold on the audience and felt abandoned. Mercer offered to speak to Gregory's father to ease over Gregory's defiance and get him to return. Without a word of discussion the producers reversed the stand they had taken with firm resolve only an hour earlier and fell in line. Alan Hall gave in his notice with disgust. "I will not work with that evil man." Alan had been witness to Gregory at work as he crafted his personal ascension and had seen the confusion caused by the producers' actions. I realized, as director of the show, I would eventually have to accept blame for the calamity and anguished over what to do. I had seen the show that I had envisioned and meticulously crafted slowly and irrevocably eroded and knew that under the present circumstances, it could never be recaptured. The producers were looking around for a replacement director, contacting Alvin Alley, Arthur Mitchell, Jerome Robbins, Geoffrey Holder. All of this came back to me via the Broadway underground. Later, Geoffrey was to take Lea and me out to dine at Back Stage where we were seated at a table with a lampshade printed with my name, as he revealed to us his conversation with the producers. "Yes, dear heart, they called me too. I just told them, 'You've already got the best, and you'd better hang on to him and learn how to work with him.' I'll never forget what you did for me in the *Carribean Calypso Carnival* when Mike Mansfield asked you to replace me ... No,

Donny, not me!" My own agent, Biff Liff, had not contacted me through all of this malaise, but was quick to offer the services of another client, Michael Smuin, artistic director of the San Francisco Ballet and longtime colleague of Willa Kim and Tony Walton.

"Donald, what happened in that meeting with the cast and the producers. Bruce is acting like a snake in the grass." I questioned Lea concerning what she meant. "He's smiling from ear to ear, rubbing his hands together, walking up and down the hall, and giving all kinds of neck action." "Why? What did he say?" He said, "I guess the shit just hit the fan." Then he went off laughing.

Betrayal is a hard thing to accept or countenance. Wasn't he the same talented young man, fresh from New York to Hollywood, to whom I had offered a position on a television series, placed in the California Institute for the Arts with a scholarship, featured in the Mark Taper Forum production of Leonard Berstein's *Mass*, worked with intimately as a member of my concert company, and loved like a son, stepped in as substitute father-of-the-bride at his wedding, visited at his hospital bedside with the promise to hold secure his job as my assistant until he was healed, giving him my African walking stick as a talisman of my belief and honor? What could he have been promised by Gregory to explain this behavior? What gnawing ambition could produce such actions and what could defend them? I had yet to learn that loyalty was short-lived in the unstable and insecure world of show business. I could not lose my belief in the inherent beauty of the human spirit and forgiveness with me would always be possible.

Demoralization set in, and I agonized over what to do to preserve the remains of everything that I had worked for and my own sense of worth. I had always enjoyed wonderful relations with casts and considered dancers part of my extended family. I could not understand or accept the finality of the series of events that had produced this moment of truth and after a night of soul searching and discussion with Lea, I drafted a letter to the cast and addressed it to Terri Klausner, the Equity deputy.

Washington, D.C.
January 16, 1981

To the cast of Sophisticated Ladies
c/o Terri Klausner — deputy

Tomorrow, I will leave Washington and return home. I have remained here to try and affect a smooth path and order for the future of the show. This is a project I have worked on for some sixteen months and am directly responsible for its existence — wholly on an artistic level and in a large measure on a business level, as I was the one used to sell it to prospective backers. I am also responsible for each and everyone's position with the show and for some of you only through perseverance.

I have always dealt with the show and the cast with a great deal of caring and love for the project and the people in it. I will continue to do so and can only hope the anxiety and hatred that I saw Wednesday will not consume the project and can be exorcised as quickly as possible. I did not quit the show, nor was I fired. I looked honestly and objectively at what I saw in front of me and asked the producers to find a new captain for a ship that was floundering hopelessly with everyone in panic. There was no other choice. It was not easy but had to be done and if the sacrifice had to be mine personally — then so it would be.

Please galvanize yourselves around the new leadership and put behind all the kinds of activities that led to this situation. You each have a job as a performer and as performing artists you will succeed or fail. Please put all your energies into that tremendous task. For that you are all ably and superbly equipped. When you venture into the other arenas you do disservice to your real work and to your talent and contribute to the terrible environment that you are all wallowing in and from which you must emerge if there is to be a "Sophisticated Ladies."

On the creative staff you have several consummate professionals all of whom I wholeheartedly support and with whom I have had complete and open communication from our initial coming together until now. Please give them the full opportunity to work with you. They are:

1 — Joyce Brown and Lloyd Mayers on the musical staff.
2 — Henry Le Tang who brings a knowledge of so many of the styles and periods encompassed by the show and a strong commercial sense.

There may be a new head brought in. You will probably know this at the same time I do, if not before. There are only a few weeks left to bring together what has always been and still possesses the earmarks of a sensational entertainment.

I wish us all success and an end — pemanently — to the demons that have surrounded us.

With deep feeling,
Donald McKayle

Back home in Sherman Oaks, I received a pained and conciliatory note from Roger Berlind. He was the one real professional in the quintet of producers, a man of integrity and someone whom I immediately befriended.

Dear Donald,

The pain just doesn't go away. I keep wondering what I might have
done to influence the course of events that led to last week's rupture.
If I am guilty of errors of omission or commission, I am truly sorry.

   One of the few joys that have come my way in this project is my
friendship with you, Donald, I sincerely hope it will survive and
flower.

   With admiration and affection.

                                                                Roger

   I had reported my decision to the producers, who agreed with my plans.
True to form the producers had their legal counsel draft a letter to me
claiming damages because of my departure, which they had sanctioned.
The end result of this adversarial posture was for me to engage counsel
in rebuttal. The affair was finally arbitrated through the offices of Burton
Litwin who could not see everything that I had worked so hard for ending
in dissension and rancor. It was also obvious that my enormous contribution to the show that would preview in New York in less than a month
would not be served well by additional public acrimony. The drama
surrounding the show was already the kind of news that sent theatrical
journalists and gossip columnists into a feeding frenzy and "the story"
was all over the papers and persisted past the New York opening. In
reaction I wrote an open letter to the press which somehow never left my
publicist's office. In it I made clear that of the thirty nine musical numbers
in the show, twenty were in the original form that I had created, six others
altered in varying degrees by the new director/choreogapher. Michael
Smuin, had staged only five new songs, some in collaboration with Henry
Le Tang, and most felicitously redone two group choreographies and
made one number completely on his own. I summarized briefly some of
my numbers that I felt illustrated the urbanity and wit inseparable from
what is called Ellingtonia, and added a tribute to the exciting work of
Henry Le Tang. I spoke of the extraneous story, the quest for the "perfect
note" and the artificial character, "Johnny the Entertainer," grafted onto
the production by Sam Art Williams.

   After the successful opening of the show, in an effort to dispel any
thought that they were behind the published fury of gossip, innuendo,
half truths, and falsehoods, the producers called a meeting which brought
Michael, Henry, and me together in the same room for the first time. The
stilted atmosphere was rent almost at the beginning of the meeting by
Michael who declared, "Maybe I should just take my name off the show.
I did no original choreography." Voices around the room echoed as one,
"No." We left the meeting with a sense of some tangible accomplishment,

if only amongst ourselves. Michael and I even went to lunch in the litttle restaurant next to the stage door of the Lunt-Fontanne Theatre to display the spirit of accord. This effort proved to be totally in-house as the media persisted in holding on tenaciously, like a bulldog with an old slipper, to the myth of Michael Smuin's complete make-over of the show. After the awarding of the Tony nomination for Choreography to the three of us, and much to the dismay of the producers, Henry Le Tang and I published an ad in *Variety* and the *Hollywood Reporter* thanking the Tony nominating committee and listing our separate choreographic contributions to the show which by elimination showed clearly the balance of individual choreography that had received the triple Tony nomination. The producers were furious and accused us of actions that were detrimental to the show and could lose it the Tony Award for choreography. Henry withdrew from participation and left me with the complete bill for the ad. After a meeting with the producers at the office of their publicist, where I was kept waiting in the anteroom for half an hour, I was threatened with legal action for utilizing the show logo in the ad. I was advised to withdraw it completely and told that I was receiving bad advice. I gathered by deduction that Henry in a spate of cowardice had put the onus on Rita Salk, a publicist we both retained, and had denied any part in the formulation of what had certainly been a joint effort. No matter the extent of my personal devastation and the cruel residue left on my reputation by the published distortions, I found the resilience of my being and the integrity of my strong creative soul resurging and overriding the misfortune. *Sophisticated Ladies* opened at the Lunt-Fontanne on Broadway on March 1, 1981. On June 6, I received a telegram:

> WIN OR LOSE YOU'RE A WINNER
> BURT LOUISE MANNY ROGER AND SONDRA

Sophisticated Ladies had garnered a plethora of Tony Nominations. On the eve of the award presentation ceremony, the producers had sent telegrams to all the nominees. Lea and I attended, decked out in the requisite formal attire, I in my new Georgio Armani tuxedo and Lea in an asymmetrical black and silver, one shoulder sequined gown and cape of her own creation. She wanted to look sensational and she did. Willa Kim ogled her from head to toe at the awards banquet. The Tony for Outstanding Choreography went to Gower Champion for *42nd Street*. His sons stepped up to receive the award for Gower who had died the day of the show's premiere. On the way out of the theater, Michael Smuin commented to me, "Well, you can't beat a dead man." As the award envelope was opened for Outstanding Actor In A Musical, Gregory Hines jumped up from his seat in a reflex action. He quickly sat back down as Kevin Klein rose to receive the award for *Pirates of Penzance*, turning around to Gregory with a shrug, his palms opened and a diffident little smile across his face.

I was soon back into the swirl of my multi-faceted career staging a night club act for Aretha Franklin, then up to Portland in 1982 for the premiere of *Ricochet* with The Company We Keep, followed by *Solaris* with the Cal Arts Dance Ensemble in 1983, a return engagement with The Company We Keep for the premiere of *Collage* in 1984, followed by *Avatar* for the San Antonio Ballet, and then off to Israel for *Dancing In The Streets*. By June of the very same year I was busily involved in the creation of a revolutionary staging of Eugene O'Neills' *Emperor Jones* for the American Musical Theater Festival in Philadelphia and the Pepsico Summer Fare in Purchase, New York starring Cleavon Little as Brutus Jones and utilizing the Alvin Ailey Repertory Ensemble as the Voodoo Nation in a further distillation of my development of choreo-drama.

"Donald, this is Donovan Marley." I looked up from my lawn chair at the large man coming towards me with a smiling face and an extended open palm. "I've looked forward to this meeting for some time and thanks to Carolyn, it's finally happened." Carolyn had arranged this quiet Sunday afternoon barbecue at her home expressly to bring the two of us together. Donovan shook my hand vigorously as he spoke and Carolyn swept down on him, bearing a wicked concoction of tequila and fruit juice. Donovan was the artistic director of the Denver Center Theatre Company and had previously been in charge of developing the drama school and theater-producing company located at Hancock College in Santa Maria, California, into the Pacific Conservatory for the Performing Arts. Carolyn Dyer, who had performed in my Los Angeles concert dance company and assisted me on all of my television work for over a decade, had choreographed several musicals with Donovan at PCPA. These productions alternated during the summer months between the theaters in Santa Maria and Solveng, that lovely re-creation of a slice of Denmark nestled in the rolling hills just inland from the Pacific coast. Carolyn had wonderful reports of the working atmosphere that Donovan created and of the integrity and artistic richness of the productions under his direction. A delightful easy conversation between Donovan and me led to the mention of my production of *Emperor Jones* and of my work in choreo-drama. Donovan's eyes lit up and his already animated face began to sparkle. "I've been wanting to do a production of *Emperor Jones* for a long time. I think that now I've found it. Would you be interested in coming to Denver and mounting your production. We have an excellent design staff, everything you could need. We are also blessed in Denver with a first rate professional dance company, the Cleo Parker Robinson Dance Ensemble, that would excel as your Voodoo Nation. Cleo is on our board at the Denver Center for the Performing Arts. The theater company is but one branch of a complete performing arts center that includes a symphony at the Boetcher Concert Hall where the orchestra plays in the round so that everyone is in a choice listening environment. We have a film house, a touring house that books traveling Broadway productions, and a research television and voice center. Donald Sewell is our president and we have a board that includes some of the big shakers of national theater such as Roger Stevens from the Kennedy Center." I was caught up in Donovan's enthusiasm and by the end of the afternoon, I had made plans to go to Denver, to direct and choreograph *Emperor Jones*, and also to choreograph a production of *Purlie* in collaboration with one of the resident directors, Randy Mylar, for their 1986 season.

Working at the Denver Center was everything that Carolyn had hinted and that Donovan had promised. It was a highly professional and excellently run operation with every member of the organization personally invested in the artistic product. This was true from the performers to the production staff, the designers, the workers in the scenic and costume shops, the running crews, the administrative staff, and the public relations personnel. I chose Antonio Fargas to play Brutus Jones. I met with Byron Jennings, a member of the resident acting company and a marvelous classical actor, and explained my concept to him. He was eager to assay the role of Smithers as part of his performing season in Denver. I had bumped into Cleo Parker Robinson quite by chance in a restaurant located in the courtyard of my apartment building at Manhattan Plaza in New York City. She was sitting at an outdoor table as I passed by on my way out of the building. Paul Carter Harrison was at the table and called me over. "Donald, come here. There is someone I want you to meet." "Donald McKayle, I don't believe it ... a living legend ... in the flesh." Cleo was a striking person with a commanding presence and a gift for endlessly interesting conversation. "We've got to get you to Denver. We must have one of your works on our company." "It so happens, I'll be there." Cleo was thrilled with the news of my planned work with the Denver Center and ecstatic at the proposal of using her company in partnership for the creation of *Emperor Jones*. This was the beginning of a relationship that would blossom into a permanent home for me. I would no longer have a dance company of my own but I would have several companies around the country that would serve as repositories for my repertoire and true creative residences. They each possessed that one all important ingredient, a visionary artistic director: Cleo with the Cleo Parker Robinson Dance Ensemble; Jeraldyn Blunden with the Dayton Contemporary Dance Company; Alvin Ailey with the Alvin Ailey American Dance Theater; Lula Washington with the Lula Washington Dance Theatre, Dennis Nahat with the Cleveland San Jose Ballet.

My 1986 production of *Emperor Jones* in Denver had grown in richness and nuance since the 1984 Philadelphia version and was an unqualified success. The task of staging the ebullient *Purlie* in the round was just the sort of challenge that set my creative juices flowing. I extended the opening flash-forward funeral scene as an ongoing event throughout the play and, with the addition of other spirituals as musical underscoring, the scenery was changed in front of the audience. The glorious voice of the lead gospel singer, Lita Gaithers, and the choir were a welcome presence as cotton bales, picket fences, and furniture came and went to the beat of anthems, sorrow songs, and gospel shouts.

"Donald, let's talk about next year. We're not letting you get away." I agreed to return to Denver the following season and choreograph *South Pacific* with Donovan directing and to mount a production of *House of Flowers* that I would direct and choreograph. But first, I would have to find the original production script and orchestrations. With the passing of Truman Capote and Harold Arlan, the materials of the show seemed to have vanished. It would take a year of sleuthing and reformatting from sources as varied as the Los Angeles Institute of the Musical Theater and the Library of Congress. My love affair with musical theater which had been so brutalized was in healing recovery and the tenderness of that process rendered me aglow with expectation, dreams, and plans for the future.

Poster for the University of California's Main Library exhibit "Infinite Journey: Donald McKayle's Life in Dance." Poster Design: Sylvia Neinhaus. Photo: Zachary Freeman.

14

ARTIST PROFESSOR

The hour plus drive from Sherman Oaks to the campus of the University of California at Irvine to take my sister-in-law, Tami, to a meeting with a professor in social sciences seemed years ago. At that time she had completed her doctorate and was a professor at the University of Tel Aviv where she was engaged in some special research. Try as she might to explain the contents and ramifications of her studies to me, I was never able to repeat with clarity what she carefully outlined. I had found myself in this scholarly conundrum when I was greeted by a gracious and suprised Janice Plastino. "Donald McKayle, what brings you here to UC Irvine?" "My sister-in-law is visiting from Tel Aviv and has a meeting with one of your professors in the Social Science Tower. I'm actually her conveyance and thought I'd mosey around while I wait, and see what's going on in dance here."

Teaching dance and developing young artists had been a part of my personal interest from my own beginning fascination with the body's possibilities as a vehicle of expression. I had taught creative movement to children when I was a junior counselor at Camp Woodland before I had any formal experience with dance. I just shared my own joy and found great satisfaction in what came back to me. I would formulate creative problems for my eight year olds that would keep them busy and happy for an hour or calm them down after an overly contentious group inter-action in some other activity. "Donald, am I ripe yet?" "No, you're still hard and green. The sun will turn you into a glowing, luscious, ripe tomato, but you have to stay quiet and feel it shining on you and doing its work." "Okay." .... "Donald, are you fooling me?" I had taken this love for creative play into my beginning sessions as a teacher in the Young People's Department at the New Dance Group and watched Bruce Becker, Suzanne Charney, Alan Weeks, and Paula Kelly develop from youngsters into dance artists. Eliot Feld, who at twelve had studied with me at the Deerwood Adirondack Music Camp, performed with my company in *Games* and then took that same work into his company's initial season at the Brooklyn Academy of Music. Daniel Levin danced the Tin Can Solo in Eliot's company, a role which Eliot himself had performed so delight-fully for me. Martha Wittman, Lar Lubovitch, Lester Wilson, and Dennis Nahat had all been at Juilliard when I taught classes under the Graham wing of the Dance Faculty overseen by Martha Hill. Joyce Trisler, Chase

Robinson, and Patricia Christopher, members of the Juilliard Dance Theater, also attended my classes. Carolyn Adams, Meredith Monk, Beverly Emmons, and Lucinda Childs had been at Sarah Lawrence when I commuted between the campus in Bronxville, where the Dance Department was chaired by Bessie Schönberg, and Bard College in Anondale-on-Hudson, where Ana Itelman was chair. Two drama students, Olivia Cole and Chevy Chase were active participants in my dance classes at Bard. My extended tenure at Bennington College had me mentoring the work of Dimitra Sundeen, Al Huang, and Kathy Posin. My work at the California Institute of the Arts had connected me with the future dance artists Lynda Davis, Les Watanabe, Bill De Young, Susan Rose, Gail Benedict, Raymond Johnson, Priscilla Regalado, and Alonzo King. Throughout a full and distinguished career as a choreographer and man of theater, educating dance artists had been a constant. The continual flow of letters and notes penned by former students in response to news items about me was testament to the reciprocity of feeling that we had shared. A card from Margie Jenkins in San Francisco thanked me for remembered words of encouragement. A snide reminder was quipped to me by Tony Christopher, CEO of the Landmark Entertainment Group in Hollywood with his partner, Gary Goddard, another Cal Arts alumnus. "Donald, do you remember what you shouted at me across the classroom when I was cutting up? 'Tony, must you always play the fool?'"

In July of 1989, I joined the faculty of the University of California, Irvine, as Professor of Dance. The year prior to my appointment was filled with inquiries from several universities offering me faculty positions. This sudden rush of recruitment from the academic world caused me to seriously consider accepting a full time position in higher education. Locating in Irvine would keep me close to my parents who were in their twilight years and would need me nearby. I was also very impressed with the quality of the Dance Department at UC Irvine and found the conservatory atmosphere within the research university setting appealing.

In the fall of 1993, the Dance Department moved into spanking new quarters. I had finally emptied all the boxes and felt at home in my fresh surroundings. I chuckled at a letter from Daniel Nagrin with the salutation, "Dear Professor Donald." The wall over my desk was a crazy quilt of award citations. I hung the Samuel H. Scripps/American Dance Festival Award in a remaining space to finish the assemblage.

> To Donald McKayle, performer, teacher, choreographer. His dances embody the deeply felt passions of a true master. Rooted in the American experience, he has choreographed a body of work with radiant optimism and poignancy. His appreciation of human wit and heroism in the face of pain and loss, and his faith in the redemptive

powers of love endow his dances with their originality and dramatic power. Donald McKayle has created a repertory of American dance that instructs the heart.

I had glowed in the radiant warmth of the tumultuous ovation I received as Maya Angelou finished reading the award citation. She smiled and said to me, "You are loved." Gregg Lizenbery and Marilyn Cristofori had crafted a wonderful eleven minute video especially for the June 1992 award celebration. It traced my career in dance and theater with archival clips of me performing: in the 50s in *Games* and *Rainbow Round My Shoulder*; sections of *District Storyville* as presented on Canadian television; snippets of *The Road To Jerusalem* with the Batsheva Dance Company of Israel; snatches from *Sophisticated Ladies*; camera swipes of posters from *Raisin, A Time For Singing, Dr. Jazz,* and *Evolution of the Blues*; photos of Sammy Davis and Jaime Rogers in the fight scene from *Golden Boy*; clips of Juliet Prowse and the Donald McKayle Dancers in the "Yellow Submarine" number from the 43rd Academy Award celebration; Lea dancing at the 49th Academy Award presentation in the Oscar nominated selection from *The Omen*; and shots of me rehearsing dancers around the world. It was a glorious occasion and I was deeply honored to have shared this acclaim with the giants of modern dance who had received it in the preceding years: Martha Graham, Merce Cunningham, Paul Taylor, Alvin Ailey, Katherine Dunham, Hanya Holm, Alwin Nikolais, Twyla Tharp, Erick Hawkins, Anna Sokolow, and the posthumous award to Doris Humphrey, Charles Weidman, and José Limón to establish a scholarship fund for the coming generations of young choreographers.

As Maya spoke, "... this award comes late, but not too late, thank God ....," I heard her warm resonant voice just as it was, over two years prior, from the pulpit at the Cathedral of Saint John the Divine in front of a congregation at the memorial service for Alvin Ailey. Some five thousand people filled the cavernous great hall and spilled out onto the steps and sidewalk. The draped coffin of Alvin Ailey lay in state at the foot of a stage. Present and former dancers of the Alvin Ailey American Dance Theater had performed selections from his repertory in tribute to his life among us. Dudley Williams had sent a departing kiss to the casket as the final gesture in his dancing of *A Song for You*. Alvin's mother, Mrs. Lula Cooper, had set the joyous tone of what could have been a wreath of sorrow rather than a celebration of a life, in her rocking, clapping antiphony to the company's performance of "Rocka My Soul In the Bosom of Abraham". Maya asked God to "... grant him sufficient *pliés* to move him with smooth resilience into the next life." Mary Hinkson, sitting across the aisle from me broke into laughter which spread contagiously through the congregation. I sat with the octet of other pall bearers in the front pew and rocked gently in a rhythmic keening that led me through a personal reverie of my experiences with the man for whose soul we now gathered together to help usher forward. What he left behind will remain here on earth with us and with those who succeed us. A year earlier, almost to the day, the nave of Saint John the Divine had held the body of James Baldwin, another great man snatched away in the prime of life. I remembered my last meeting with Jimmy in Paris in a restaurant on the left bank and years before, my first encounter with a then shy young man working as a waiter in Connie's West Indian Restaurant, a young man whose brilliant literary career would startle the world. I rocked and remembered.

The gathering in the downstairs church hall prior to the ceremony brought together people, many of whom had not seen each other in a long time. It was a solemn occasion for such a grand reunion. The continuity of life's sometime mundane existence in the face of the celebration of its moments of greatness was a welcome, if strange, reminder for me of reality. Brother John Sellers was to be one of the pall bearers, but he arrived in a huff because his name had somehow been left off of the commemorative program. We smiled at each other and allowed him to exhibit his annoyance. As Max Roach sounded the recessional on the drums, the pall bearers gathered on either side of the casket. As it was rolled forward and we walked towards the great doors through which daylight streamed, I reached out and held the hands of those I could touch and nodded at others too distant for contact: Patti Bown with tears filling her enormous eye, Olive John, Shawneequa Baker standing beside Nicki in his wheelchair, Charles Blackwell, Maurice Perres, students, and faithful audience members whose faces I remembered from countless performances. As we arrived at the steps and lifted the casket off of its carriage, the group of us swayed noticeably under its great weight. A weeping and distraught Ulysses Dove who had not been able to sit with the honor guard up front, found his way to our aid as we stepped forward down the broad steps toward the waiting hearse. The throngs outside parted silently and the attendants took the coffin from us and slid it onto its resting bed inside the curtained interior. As the doors closed, Mazasumi Chaya fell into me, burying his face in my chest; my tears dropped uncontrollably onto his shock of black hair as his own sorrow shook his body. I left him and walked back to retrieve my overcoat from the church hall and ran into Arthur Mitchell coming upstairs with my coat in his hands. "I had to leave when I saw you two or I would have been no good." I took my coat from him and together we walked out into the daylight.

I placed the blown glass Samuel H. Scripps/American Dance Festival Award statuette, dubbed the "Sammy," on the mantle piece. It rested between the NAACP Image Award of a kneeling man holding the world overhead, which I had received as conceiver/writer of *Sophisticated Ladies*, and the engraved plexiglass pyramid from the Alvin Ailey American Dance Theater, alongside the laurel wreath decorated Lauds and Laurels Award from the UCI (University of California at Irvine) Alumni Association for professional achievement. I wandered out onto the cantilevered balcony of our Laguna Beach home overlooking the Pacific Ocean, Catalina Island, and the white caps breaking on the sands of Main Beach, and sat sipping a morning coffee.

Coming to UCI in 1989 and accepting a professorship in dance was supposed to be a mellowing step in a long career. Instead, it was but another charging of my active battery which drove overlapping projects that seemed to generate almost spontaneously. My work with the dance faculty and students as Artistic Director of UCI Dance was extremely fulfilling. It was, however, time consuming especially when added to my teaching schedule in advanced modern dance technique and graduate choreography. In fact, my university work served excellently as a laboratory for creative projects that would find professional lives outside the academic setting. Both of the dance works that I had mounted on student casts in my first years on campus had entered the repertoire of the Cleo Parker Robinson Dance Ensemble with great success. They were also strikingly different from one another and represented stylistic departures in my choreographic palette. *Sombra y Sol (Images of Frida Kahlo)*, to a vibrant Aaron Copland score, featured Cleo's senior dancers, Marceline Freeman and Gary Abbott, and *Ring-a-levio*, a study of youth gang subculture to a driving score of Astor Piazzolla, brought the young Karah Abiog to prominence in a passionate encounter with Gary Lewis. I had discovered Karah while fulfilling a commission at Loyola Marymont University and brought her and Cleo together at the American Dance Festival as part of my ongoing personal mission of developing and placing exceptional young talent.

A residency in Buenos Aires with the Argentinean modern dance companies, Nucleodanza and the Ballet Contemporáneo del Teatro Municipal General San Martin and Astor Piazzolla's captivating music had been inspirational for what became a major addition to my creative *oeuvre*.

January 1992 featured overlapping sessions in a downtown Los Angeles hotel of the national conference of Dance/USA and the International Conference of Blacks in Dance. At a joint banquet, I found myself at the same table with Dennis Nahat. We had not seen each other for many years and we engaged in an invigorating meal-full of catching up. The event was hosted by the Lula Washington Dance Theatre and for the occasion Lula's company and Cleo's company from Denver had joined ranks to present an augmented version of "Shaker Life," the last movement of my *Songs of the Disinherited*, one of the works that had been chosen for the American Dance Festival's classic revival program, The Black

Tradition in American Modern Dance. "Donald, that's magnificent!" "Donny, that brings me back to my roots. Thank you, thank you!" The voices of Dennis Nahat and Lester Wilson came at me from either side of the banquet table. "Donald, we must get you out to Cleveland to do a work for the company."

"Dennis, I'd love to. What do you want?" "Anything ... just something from you." At home, I shared the exciting news with Lea. "Do you have something in mind? A new work? Is there a piece of music you've been listening to? I have something that I think would make a wonderful ballet." I listened eagerly to Lea's rush of ideas and suggestions and something lurking in the back of my mind began to insinuate itself forward. "Lea, I've been reading two books that have planted images that keep reappearing, Isabel Allende's *House of the Spirits* and Lawrence Thornton's *Imagining Argentina*." "Oh, they are both magnificent works."

At last, a fully formed mental picture, a remembered incident, was clearly in front of me. It was December of 1989; I was driving from the Buenos Aires airport and had entered the city. The USIA contact that had picked me up had the driver swing through the city center on an introductory tour. We were passing a large pink building. "Who are those women and what are they doing?" "Those are the *abuelas*, the grandmothers. They march in front of the government headquarters here in the Casa Rosada every Thursday. It is part of the fabric that makes up this city and its dramatic story." As the embassy guide kept up a running conversation, the images of the living monument we had just left lingered with me. Women were walking slowly around the obelisk in the Plaza de Mayo, their heads covered with white handkerchiefs and pictures of their loved ones hung from strings around their necks, as if pointing fingers of accusation at invisible leaders inside the Casa Rosada. They marched silently, demanding information on the whereabouts of those who had "disappeared" some twenty years ago during the military repression in Argentina known as "the process." The anguish and courage that had kept that vigil alive for all those years, the demand and need for final closure on this terrible chapter of human history, began to form into the germ of choreography. Lea handed me the disc of Astor Piazzolla's *Concierto para Bandoneon* and reminded me that she had brought it home when I was working on *Ring-a-levio*. "Listen to it now. I think it's perfect for what you want to do." The driving rhythms and haunting melodies took hold of me; movement, design, and patterns began to form. I knew that I had found the musical environment for *House of Tears*. I wrote a scenario and sent it to Dennis.

I traveled to Cleveland to observe the company in rehearsal of Dennis's *Celebrations and Ode* choreographed to Beethoven's Seventh and Ninth Symphonies. That visit gave me a wonderful picture of the variety and strengths of the dancers. I knew that I wanted to work with Karen Gabay and Raymond Rodriguez in the principal roles. I was also excited by the strong male and female corps of dancers and the passion and dedication of the Venezuelan contingent of dancers from the Ballet Nuevo Mundo of Caracas. "Wait until you see Zhandra Rodriguez. She's the director of the Venezuelan company. She joins us as guest artist for *Swan Lake*. I think you may want to use her also." Dennis and Zhandra were old friends and colleagues from Ballet Theatre days. They had kept up their professional bond which had taken the shape of this collaboration between the Cleveland San Jose Ballet and the Ballet Nuevo Mundo. This made possible repertoire and joint performing seasons that could not be done by either company alone. Dennis was also in the process of extending this visionary idea into a triumvirate with Robert Barnett and the Atlanta Ballet.

Working with classically trained dancers was very different than choreographing for a company trained in modern dance. It was something I had enjoyed immensely while staging *Daughters of the Garden* on The Harkness Ballet in 1965 and with the San Antonio Ballet while creating *Avatar* in 1984. The dancers in Cleveland were excellent. Dennis had trained them well and challenged them on many aesthetic levels with a varied repertoire. This made them an ideal choice for my choreographic plans. I had identified roles for individual dancers in which I thought they would be perfect. As I developed the ballet, my predilections succeeded even beyond expectations. Raymond Rodriguez's reading of the despotic general was brilliant and Pamela Raymond's anguished portrayal was harrowing as the distraught woman who returns home to find nothing left of her husband other than his fedora hat, knocked off and crushed underfoot during his abduction. Karen Gabay alternated in the passionate role of the lover, dancing opposite the excellent Olivier Muñoz and the allegoric portrait of the Spirit of Argentina. She shared this part with Zhandra Rodriguez. They each gave a completely different rendition of a tragic picture of trampled heroism. Lea's costume for the Spirit was a white chiffon draping inspired by the kerchiefs of the women that marched solemnly around the obelisk. A gash of blood red outlined the bodice beneath the heart from which the kerchiefs fell, and free flowing washes of blue cascaded from the shoulder. When the Spirit was lifted and carried aloft by the specters of "the disappeared" in the concluding trial sequence, she appeared to be the floating banner of the Argentinean flag flying over the women. The women were garbed in black and the men in shades of gray as they accused the bemedaled general, the villain of the dirty war against humanity. The success of *House of Tears* led to my staging of it in May of 1992 in Caracas. My renewed camaraderie with Dennis was capped by his request for a second ballet the following year.

I had choreographed several works to the music of L. Subramaniam, the brilliant violinist and composer. I had first met Mani at Cal Arts where he was completing his Masters of Fine Arts in music. The choreographies had been done to assemblages of his Indo-Jazz fusion pieces, recorded with excellent artists. *Collage* had been mounted on the Alvin Ailey American Dance Theater, after a preliminary version for the Portland based, The Company We Keep. *Apsaras* was made for the Cleo Parker Robinson Dance Ensemble; *Solaris* for the Dance Ensemble at Cal Arts, a quartet of fine dancers that included, Tina Yuan, Marvin Tunney, James Bishton II, and Loretta Livingston. The new work that I planned seemed perfect for Subramaniam's music, and I decided to call him to see if he had orchestral scores that would be right for my idea. After a lengthy process, I was finally sitting face to face with him in his home in Reseda, listening to his tapes recorded by symphony orchestras in Europe, Asia, and New Zealand. I selected the rhapsodic *Shanti Priya* for the new ballet, which I titled *Mysteries and Raptures*. I set about developing the scenario and working with Lea on the costume designs and with Oliver Jackson on the scenic back cloth. I envisioned the back cloth as a moving choreo-graphic element from which all the players would emerge, which would be manipulated by the dancers to envelope the on-stage action. Lea mailed the costume renderings to me in San Francisco where I was in rehearsal for a work with the San Francisco Ballet.

In the summer of 1993, a telephone message had reached me at the American Dance Festival in Durham from Helgi Tomasson, artistic direc-tor of the San Francisco Ballet. I had originally met Helgi, some twenty years prior, when he was with the Harkness Ballet, and I was glad to renew our acquaintance. The San Francisco Ballet was one of the six top-ranking national ballet companies involved in the John F. Kennedy American Ballet Commissioning Project. Helgi was calling to offer me the choreographic commission. I was excited about the honor and about working with the company. It was large and excellently trained, with a superb classic technique. While I was not sure how the dancers would relate to modern movement, I accepted Helgi's invitation to view the company in their repertory season at the San Francisco Opera. Not only was the company exquisite in Helgi's neo-classic *Handel Concert*, it was dramatically strong in William Forsythe's *In the Middle Somewhat Elevated*, highlighted by a commanding performance by Muriel Maffre. A young corps de ballet dancer, Eric Hoisington, exhibited a striking fluidity in David Bintley's *Job*.

When James Newton joined the music faculty at UC Irvine, he had given me a casette tape of his work. I was fascinated by two electronic pieces, "Senegalesque Dance" and "Wayoyee." My studies and reflec-tions on ancient and traditional human civilizations that lived in close communion with the environment, and on modern technology that excelled in destruction, led me to conceptualize a work I called *Gumbo Ya-Ya*, a Gullah expression meaning "everybody talk at once." I began to delineate movement passages: the ancient dance; choreographic expositions of air, reed, and earth cultures; the contrasting cold and remote movement palette describing the self-aggrandizement of much of modern life; and the callous gentrification that, when overlaid upon simple civilizations, resulted in their demise. I began to unite my findings with James Newton's extended composition which he had fashioned from his two original pieces and my choreographic scenario. The inclusion of his beautifully rendered acoustic flute, playing against the computer driven electronic score gave a richness of texture that exploded in the touching central duet section, "Safe Harbor."

Christina Gianinni, with whom I had worked on several occasions including the East Coast production of *Emperor Jones* and the Israeli show *Dancing In the Streets*, spent an extended half week with me toward the end of my six week summer residency in Durham. She developed her preliminary renderings into costume and scenic elements made from stretch lycra that gave the ballet a unique and completely original environment. Everything was ready for an October 19, 1993 premiere at the Kennedy Center when the wheels of progress groaned to a complete halt. The musicians of the Kennedy Center orchestra went on strike, making it impossible for the company to perform its *Swan Lake*, the other half of its week's program. Cameron Mackintosh, producer of *Phantom of the Opera*, the mega hit scheduled into the Opera House, refused to be held hostage by the striking musicians, and in defiance, continued to play sell-out houses performed to canned music recorded abroad with a German orchestra. This adversarial stand fueled intransigence on both sides. They would neither convene nor arbitrate around the bargaining table. The premiere of *Gumbo Ya-Ya* was put on hold until perhaps 1995, because of a clause, basic to the contract, that insisted that the premiere performance be at the Kennedy Center. With skillful negotiation and clever legal maneuvering, the California premiere, scheduled at the San Francisco Opera in February of 1994, was allowed to take place under the banner of preview performances. It was part of the planned repertory season prior to Helgi's presentation of his full length new *Romeo and Juliet*. The official premiere of *Gumbo Ya-Ya* would thereby remain at the Kennedy Center; it was scheduled for May 17, 1994.

I had just begun rehearsals in San Francisco when Lea called me on August 3, 1993 with a joyous announcement. "Donald, we have a granddaughter. She's beautiful." I could not get away to see the baby or share the happiness with Guy and Donna. I was booked solid and had to fly from San Francisco directly to Hawaii for an exchange professorship with

Gregg Lizenbery at the University of Hawaii at Manoa. I would teach a week and a half for him and he would teach the opening two weeks at UC Irvine for me while I finished my choreographic residency in Cleveland. It segued directly from Hawaii with only a half day stop over at home. Every fiber in my body wanted to abandon my unyielding schedule and rush to see the baby, but I knew it was impossible and that I would have to wait until I returned in six weeks. I had been touched and honored when Guy had asked me to be the best man at his wedding. I had hoped that I had been a good father but to be Guy's entrusted best friend on the eve of his wedding was very special to me. The little boy, who had wanted only to see his new bicycle when I took him home from the airport in New York so many years, was now a man with his own family. Now there was a new little girl, Tyler Kyndra.

"Donald, how did the premiere go? Was *Mysteries and Raptures* a big success?" "Lea, it was wonderful. They danced magnificently and your costumes were exquisite. I have all kinds of compliments for you from total strangers who walked up to me in the theater and remarked on their beauty." "Donald, we have trouble at home." "What trouble ... what's wrong?" "I've been frantic up here in the Washington wilderness. Laguna Beach is on fire! It's all over the television. I've gotten through to Guy but it's impossible to get through to Laguna." Luckily, our home was spared the ravage that took away so much of our community. A neighbor at the end of our *cul de sac* had a pump in his swimming pool. He stood on the roof of his house and watered the surrounding area while the police were evacuating the street. Thanks to his bravery and the calming of the winds, the fire stopped just below us. I had been able to reach Les Watanabe the night of the fire. He was home when I called, having parked his car on Crown Valley Parkway and hiked the seven miles on foot, along streets that were closed to vehicular traffic. He could look up to where we lived and had determined that we were not touched by the conflagration. By the weekend I was able to reach neighbors who had returned to their homes and each added individual details to the terrifying story. Knowing that our home was all right and learning from Lea that our housekeeper, Ferminda, was at the house gave me the calm to take a detour on the way home from Cleveland through New York City. I had scheduled a meeting with Anthony Stimac at Musical Theatre Works to talk about developing one of my large dances into a musical theater work. Driving home from the airport, I was keenly aware of the scent of burnt vegetation. The blanket of night covered the sight of the bald hillsides that stood out in charred relief in the daylight.

Kevin Jeff, the artistic director of Jubilation Dance Theatre, had envisioned *Blood Memories* as a musical when he saw the work at its premiere with the Alvin Ailey American Dance Theater in 1976; he had brought the project to Musical Theatre Works. They expressed interest in pursuing the possibility with me and with Howard Roberts, the composer. The idea was, indeed, viable, but to make the jump from dance theater to musical theater it would need to be completely reconceived. For years, I had been working on a musical drama that had grown out of *District Storyville* and it was now ready to go. I presented the project to Tony Stimac and he jumped at it. My own enthusiasm was contagious and faces began to light up around the room as I unfurled the details of the story and gave a taste of the wit and drama of the lyrics.

In 1981, after the opening of *Sophisticated Ladies*, I had decided to ground my bi-coastal existence properly with a worthy *pied-à-terre* in the Big Apple. Kevin Gebhard, a young producer, contacted me at the New York apartment after seeing *District Storyville* on the Alvin Ailey American Dance Theater, saying that he saw a musical in my ballet. I prepared a scenario which I called "Storyville" and presented it to Alice Childress for consideration. Alice was an active playwright as well as a novelist, whom I had worked with thirty-some years ago in my first theatrical venture *Just a Little Simple* and I had been an ardent fan of hers ever since. While she showed signs of interest, there was no immediate spark of commitment. Kevin suggested that we contact Toni Morrison, the prize winning novelist and master of letters. The meeting with Toni went well and she seemed eager to work on a musical play. She had a close connection to New Orleans and decided to give it her own take, keeping the dance focus but infusing the story line with her mythic characters. She also wanted to try her hand at the song lyrics and I put her together with Dorothea Freitag who had written the score for *District Storyville*. I was also actively engaged in the song development, finding selections from the rich ante-bellum heritage of the Bayous and guiding the balance of energy and musical dynamics. Some of the songs that emerged were wonderful and the language was exquisite, but the play did not hang together. The descriptive passages that appeared on the printed page were an inseparable part of its integrity. Unfortunately these passages would not exist for an audience and even Toni's magnificent presence, reading her own words at the two workshop presentations financed first by Paramount and then Joseph Papp's Public Theater, could not hold the undivided attention of an audience prepared for the action to unfold via the players. This version entitled, *N'Orleans, the Storyville Musical*, languished on my shelf next to the original scenario. A decade later, Mark Green, who had attended all the workshop presentations and who had complete belief in the power and commercial viability of the original premise, kept the project alive and finally united me with a lyricist, Pamela Phillips Oland. We began work on a new version called *Shimmy*, "What you do to get in and out of life's tight places."

Finding the right composer took more than one try. Dorothea had passed away and I had decided to keep her work for the *District Storyville* unique unto itself and not have it or the dance compromised by dilution into another project. Pamela came back from a song writer's association conference in Dallas with enthusiasm for a young composer from Nashville. We began working together, but after a year the desired results had not been accomplished. This was not a work that would fall easily within the limited perspective of song writing. We needed a score and a complete creative partner as the composer, someone with investment and input in the entire project. Pamela, ever resourceful, found another candidate and we started over again. Steven Bramson's sense of melody was rich and varied and his piano reductions promised a vibrant orchestral score and immediately suggested ideas for dance. He also composed beautiful small ballets that were excellent musical paintings of the period. Tony Stimack and his associate, Lois Englund were fascinated with the project and declared all systems go with Musical Theater Works for a fall development process. I left a demo tape of the score with them and departed the next day for an assignment in Moscow.

The snow fell in huge flakes as Lynda Davis and I drove, huddled together in the backseat of the auto that picked us up from the Moscow airport. We were finally freed from the slowly moving queues that had funneled us through passport control and customs. My newly acquired goose down mackinaw, duck-billed ear-flapped cap, down-padded gloves, and wool muffler gave the impression of a large child sent out to play in the snow by an overly protective mother. But Muscovites walking through the snow in their boots and fur hats made me feel quite at home in my attire. The winter wonderland that glistened around us was quite a contrast to the sun drenched scene that I had left just an airplane ride ago. A week later, the streets that had been so pristine on our entry were covered with wet black slush and the automobiles that plowed through the ugly mixture in a continuous helter-skelter, devil-may-care traffic onslaught were all a uniform shade of muddy charcoal. This residency with the Free Ballet was the fourth project in which I had participated under the American Dance Festival's Institutional Linkages Program, an international cultural exchange project sponsored by the Rockefeller Foundation and the United States Information Agency. The other three had taken me twice to Buenos Aires and once to Montevideo. I had already begun the staging of *Rainbow Round My Shoulder* on an ensemble of dancers that Nikolai Ogryzkov had gathered from his own Free Ballet, from the Bolshoi Ballet and the Moiseyev Dance Company, and from the smaller Russian Seasons Dance Company. My contact with the Russians was extremely pleasant, and the students in my burgeoning technique class greeted the beginning of each lesson with a sustained round of applause and beaming faces. National elections in 1993 were just a few days away in this land in transition, but now there were choices for the voters among many political parties.

Nikolai and his wife Svetlana brought Lynda Davis and me back to the apartment we shared. I leaned against the wall in the foyer and removed the massive wool-lined rubber and leather Canadian boots that Lea had given me. I felt like Nanook of the North as I mastered the flat-foot stride that the great boots required. My slippers awaited me on a shelf. The rented apartment in the center of Moscow that had been pleasantly warm when we left in the morning was distressingly chilly. The heat was off and the tap water ran cold. The stove was not functioning, a loose connection in the electric plug seemed to be the problem. After a meal of fruit, blini, caviar, and vodka, I climbed under the heavy comforter in my long-johns underwear and socks and fell into a deep sleep filled with dream fragments that battled for my attention until the trilling sound of the alarm clock awakened me to a room now miraculously warm. I thanked the providential elves who had labored throughout the wee hours of the night in behalf of our comfort and trundled off to begin my morning ablutions.

The large building which housed the Moiseyev ensemble was also home to the Philharmonia and artists carrying instrument cases and dance bags were entering and exiting as we arrived. Lynda, Raisa, our translator, and I followed Nikolai to the garderobe, where we deposited our coats. Choosing not to take the small and claustrophobic elevator, we climbed the stairs. The sound of piano music playing a *milambo* attracted our attention and Nikolai directed us to a first floor studio and gestured for us to enter. "Donald, this is the famous gaucho dance. It was my solo with the company." Igor, one of the dancers learning *Rainbow Round My Shoulder*, was dancing the solo under the tutelage of a small wiry dancer in gaucho boots and spurs, with a short blade held in his belt. Igor looked marvelous in the solo. Nikolai rushed over to him after he finished and demonstrated a correction in the recovery from a pirouette that landed in a deep squat balanced on the inside edges of the boots. As a former soloist with the Moiseyev company, Nikolai was greeted with great respect by everyone we passed. His long tenure with the company had been marked by controversy stemming from his keen interest in western dance forms. The company had been one of the best ambassadors of goodwill from the Soviet Union. It was billed:

THE MOISEYEV DANCE COMPANY
Academic Ensemble of Folk Dance of the USSR

During a tour to Paris, Nikolai had grabbed the opportunity to take classes in jazz dance with American expatriate dance star and pre-eminent exponent of the Jack Cole dance technique, Matt Mattox. One day his lessons absorbed him so completely that he reported late to the theater. This marked the end of his jazz studies abroad. He had been constantly under the observation of two agents of the KGB. The company enjoyed many foreign trips after that time, but one of their leading soloists, Nikolai Ogryzkov, was to remain in Moscow. With the coming of Perestroika, he was one of the first Russian choreographers chosen by Charles and Stephanie Reinhart to participate in the International Choreographers program at the six week summer session of the American Dance Festival. Nikolai had seen my work when the Alvin Ailey American Dance Theater had performed in Moscow and our meeting at the opening picnic on the Duke University East Campus lawn was a genuine dream come true for him. I was deeply moved by his overflowing admiration. He took modern dance technique with me and participated in my repertory class while Mary Corey was Labanotating *Rainbow Round My Shoulder*. He learned the role that I had originally performed and now had gone full cycle, bringing me to his country to stage the work on Russian dancers and taking me to his own dance family at the Moiseyev.

I took Igor Moiseyev's extended palm in both of my hands and, clasping it tightly, paid him my respect and admiration. He smiled warmly and invited me to follow him. He guided us from his office to the next-door rehearsal room where chairs had been arranged for us in front of the dancers. We were greeted with applause from the twenty male and four female dancers assembled. They showed us sections of a sailor's dance, a marvelous depiction of the great metal machinery in the ship's hold, visions of endless fields of bending wheat, and an extravagant Gypsy dance which had the female dancers in luxurious back bends with limpid arms draped in gestures of grief. I looked at Igor Moiseyev sitting next to me watching his dancers, shaking his head when the slapping body percussion sections began to race ahead of the piano accompaniment. He was a marvelous creative artist and one of the most important choreographers in Russia.

Visiting the Bolshoi Ballet School was a very special occasion and an invitation not easily forthcoming. Fifteen little girls stood facing forward in an angled horseshoe arrangement. They were clothed in white leotards, white canvas soft ballet slippers with white socks on their bare legs, and wore a short gossamer skirt fashioned from a single layer of white tulle netting. Their hair was pulled back from their smiling faces in a small knot at the back of their heads and they held their little skirts away from their bodies with extended open arms. The pianist sounded an arpeggio and as one they executed an exquisite *reverence* stepping first to one side, dipping into a small bow, and then with a unison turn of the head, repeating the delicate movement to the other side before coming to a perfect finish with their heels joined in a completely opened first position. They stepped back to the barre and continued the lesson we had interrupted with our entrance. Nikolai had trained at the Bolshoi school and now his younger daughter, Pauline, was a Bolshoi pupil. His older daughter, Kristina, was a student at the Moiseyev school. The new Bolshoi school was a little town in itself. The building was a four story edifice built in an unbroken flow, surrounding a planted courtyard. It occupied an entire city block. Large picture windows looked down from hallways on the snow covered quadrangle and the sound of piano music crept through rows of closed studio doors. We were to observe classes in classic technique from the smallest girls to adolescent girls and a class for teenage boys. The training was carefully codified and disciplined to produce the expertly prepared finished dancer in the Bolshoi style. The carriage emphasized a long straight back, lifted chest, and elegant line of the neck. In the early lessons with the little ones, every position of the feet and limbs was reached with a point of arrest and delineation before proceeding to the next. The prescribed *épaulement* of the shoulders and upper body was carved into the execution of every movement until it was second nature and concentration could be placed on other facets of the technique. I wondered what happened to pupils who, at the beginning, passed the entrance exams and were accepted on their potential and then, as they grew from babyhood, developed physiques that no longer embodied the classical ideal. My musing was soon to be answered when we entered a session held in the school theater. Girls were training on the raked stage. They were clothed in an array of attire that was reminiscent of the trappings found in private studios in New York City, where plastic pants, leg warmers, and wildly assorted colors were de rigueur to disguise both real and imaginary body imperfections. The boys' class was a rehearsal for a special demonstration for the Clintons, the American president and first lady. They had just completed the rehearsal and were in assorted positions of collapse around the room. They rallied bravely and went through the demonstration again for us, executing a full battery of bravura jumps and turns and finishing with an elegant *reverence*. Their class was held in a studio with a floor raked to the same degree as the Bolshoi stage so that they would be completely comfortable with the placement of body alignment in multiple turns executed on an angled base and with mastering the control of the trajectory in leaps going both up and down the tilted stage surface. We continued our tour, entering rooms where costumes were being prepared, passing by the shoemaker, and visiting the library and video viewing rooms. We sat in on a piano lesson in which the instructor dealt one on one with her young pupil. There was a gymnasium, an infirmary, a large cafeteria, a kitchen, and classrooms for academic subjects. The dance instruction included the study of folk dance, character and classical variations, partnering, and repertory rehearsals, as well as the daily basic instruction in classical ballet technique. We waited in the large entry foyer seated on divans by the garderobe until the headmistress was able to see us.

Sofia Golovkina was indeed a personage. She sat behind a desk at the end of a long room. Many chairs were placed against the walls, carpets dotted the wooden floor, paintings hung in display, and a vase filled with fragrant rubrum lilies graced a table in front of curtained sliding doors that in balmy weather were opened onto the garden courtyard. "Good morning, I am pleased that you were able to come." She rose from her chair and came towards us speaking fluently in accented English and extended her hand. Her face was alive with expression as she listened to Nikolai's introduction and shook hands with Lynda and me. "It is a very busy time for us. We are preparing for a visit from Mrs. Gore." She accepted our words of gratitude for the morning visit and began to return to her desk, clearly indicating that the audience was over. "How many pupils do you have in the school?" Her blue eyes lit up even brighter as she turned to answer my inquiry. "We have six hundred students and three hundred on the staff. It is a little city which must care for all its important citizens very well." We made a final farewell and went out to the garderobe where we bundled up before cautiously navigating the icy steps to the street. There we were fortunate to find Peter, the instructor of the boys' class, who gladly agreed to drive us to the military club where I would teach my technique class.

The class had been scheduled to be held on the stage of the literary club, but the students overflowed the tiny platform, and I was forced to demonstrate movements at the very lip of the stage, balanced precariously on the metal covers to electric outlets. Nikolai had found the larger space and apologized profusely for its condition. "Ala, wash the floor, make it clean. If it no good, I look more." In spite of Ala's efforts, years of dust seeped back up from the old parquet and deposited itself on the backs of the students as they learned a fall and recovery. The rear of the large room was stacked with metal wardrobe trunks and was adapted as a changing area by the students. On the second floor, an open small stage area guarded by the watchful gaze of the former communist leaders, Stalin and Lenin, painted on the walls, was presented as a possible alternative studio space. I rejected the drafty, somber environment and chose to stay in the downstairs studio and navigate around the two pillars and through the dust. The decaying building was quite a contrast to the impressively appointed conservatory we had just left.

The rythmic pounding of unison applause and the radiant faces of the audience marked the bows at the conclusion of the performance of *Rainbow Round My Shoulder*. The Russian dancers accepted the warm acknowledgment from the full house of some seven hundred people in the Children's Theatre. This was the finale of the informal showing, the final demonstration of our two-and-a-half-week residency. Lynda and I were greeted with bouquets of long stemmed pink roses as we joined the dancers on the stage for the question and answer portion of the program. This was a first for Russian audiences, and we did not know what to expect. The response was immediate and full; questions and commentary flowed from the audience. The performers from *Rainbow Round My Shoulder* had been joined by the dancers who had performed in Lynda's improvisation and composition class demonstrations and by the children from Nikolai's school who had opened the program. From among them came statements of deeply personal insights and heartfelt wishes for our return. Loaded down with armfuls of be-ribboned and cellophane wrapped flowers, we were whisked away to a magnificent meal at the Moscow Commercial Club. The table was set with great beauty in a lovely private room. A picture painted into the plaster on the wall showed the last czar of the Russias standing with an assemblage of family and foreign dignitaries and the regal dowager, Catherine the Great. We were serenaded by a guitarist/singer, entertained by a magician, and enjoyed excellent conversation with our hostess and her guests. It was a wonderful way to conclude a visit that had revealed many of the different aspects of Moscow life in the new Russia. Andre, one of the dancers, was waiting for us when we arrived at our flat. "I'm sorry I had to miss." I sensed a reticence and hesitation in his voice beyond the search for words in a foreign tongue. I placed my hand on him to ease his composure and felt a pistol in an arm holster. He pulled away instinctively. "Andre, are you a policeman?" "No, I've had a problem. Six attacked me. I am lucky I am alive. They beat me here, and here, and here." He indicated his head, knees, and ribs. "It was dark. They were after robbery. I go to the police for allow to have this." He opened his jacket and showed me the gun. "I am lucky." This was a side of Russian life that had not revealed itself to me in the comings and goings of the people on the street that I passed every day.

My suitcase was packed and closed with a great deal of leaning and squeezing. As I placed my toiletry travel case into my carry-on bag, I heard a jingle from a plastic bagged package that I jostled. I smiled as I opened the wrapping and took out the gaily painted, round-bottomed doll that I had purchased at a gift stand in the Kremlin. The cherubic face was surrounded by floral art work deftly applied in exquisite strokes. When pushed or spun, the bell shaped lady would whirl and tumble with a delightful tinkling sound coming from its internal bell. It was for Mother and I knew it would give her hours of merriment. Mother would be ninety-six in a month and though her eyebrows and shoulders still danced when music played, she could no longer engage in fancy footwork. This little lady would now do her bidding and spin at her command.

"Lynda, is there any ice in the trays?" Lynda had been a godsend, giving me twice daily ice massages on my knees and ankles. They had taken on the appearance of small dirigibles after the first two days of work on the hard floors, demonstrating the highly athletic movement vocabulary that I had created for *Rainbow Round My Shoulder* some thirty-four years ago. "I think we have the makings of one final deep freeze before Nikolai comes to pick us up." "Good, let's just call it one more for the road."

The mantle piece over the fireplace and the adjacent shelf unit at my home in Laguna Beach were filled with the many awards that I had received for lifetime achievement in dance and theater. Framed citations covered the walls of my office at the university. Are they trying to bronze me? I smiled at the thought. Testaments of admiration, praise, respect, and love surrounded me. Somehow, without realizing it, I had moved into the role that now repeatedly characterized my introductions at official presentations, "...that great statesman of the dance...." On my 67th birthday, July 6, 1997, the Balasaraswati/Joy Ann Dewey Beinecke Chair for Distinguished Teaching was added to the honors:

> Concerned with the artist's role in addressing the human condition, he continues his longtime influence on modern dance both as distinguished choreographer and master teacher. His teaching, displaying its hallmarks of dignity, informed sensibility, and sympathetic mentoring, encourages as well as instructs. For dance students, he is an ongoing source of inspiration. A legendary exemplar of the art of dance, Donald McKayle devotedly transmits the spirit of that art in all its variety and vibrancy.

The prior three years had been eventful, crowded with the benchmarks of a mature career and marked with life's inexorable measures. Mother and Dad were well into their nineties. Dad, four years Mother's junior, was dedicated to caring for her. Mother grew increasingly demanding in her need for constant attention. On the second Wednesday of January 1996, I arrived early in the morning to take Dad to have a pace maker inserted to boost his beautiful but ailing heart. The housekeeper had not arrived as scheduled and I was about to ask the next door neighbor to look in on Mother while I drove Dad to the hospital. Suddenly Mother awoke with a violent scream and it was clear that I must stay with her. Dad suggested that he go by taxi and assured me that he would be fine by himself. The cab arrived and he hurried down the hall to the elevator. "Dad, take your cane; slow down; the taxi will wait for you." He smiled and kissed me as he took the cane from me. "Go back with the old girl; she needs you." I watched from the window as he stepped spryly, waving up at me as he went. I would never see Dad that animated or in control again. For the next two weeks, I jockeyed back and forth between home in Laguna, teaching at the university in Irvine, sleeping over to take care of Mother in Inglewood, and visiting Dad in the hospital. Dad came home weak and unable to function the way he had before. The following week, Mother took a turn for the worse. Just three days shy of her ninety-eighth birthday, she passed away. When I returned from the hospital to Dad, somehow he already knew. With his agreement, I moved him to a board and care facility near us in Mission Viejo where Lea and I could visit with him daily. He seemed to like it there; but his condition never improved. Without Mother to care for, he seemed to have no reason to stay around any longer. Fourteen weeks later, he left us. Suddenly, both my parents were gone. In my sixty-sixth year, I was an orphan.

A year earlier, I had begun a new stage of my constantly burgeoning career. I had received a call from Carla Maxwell. Her unmistakable voice on the phone was filled with excitement and purpose. "Donny, the Limón Dance Company is applying for a National Dance Residency Program Grant and we would like to have you as our choreographer." I was equally excited and queried Carla for details. A million dollars from the Pew Charitable Trusts was to be divided equally among ten dance company/choreographer combinations following what would surely be an exhaustive national search. An important part of the application we submitted was my proposed role as choreographer, master teacher, and coach. We were chosen as one of the ten recipients and in 1995 I began a new phase of my career, as artistic mentor and resident choreographer of the Limón Dance Company. The major thrust of the grant was the creation of a new work for the company which I called *Heartbeats*. It was an idea that had been with me for a long time, waiting for the right circumstance to take shape. Here it was, the opportunity to work with an excellent group of artists over a two-year period, rather than the six weeks' maximum time allotment that usually accompanied the commissions offered me as a freelance choreographer. Carla was an excellent artistic director with a clear vision and mission, an all-important ingredient for a successful repertory company. Moreover, I was attracted by the diversity of the dancers. They included artists who had been with the company for some thirty years to those who had just entered. This breadth of experience was essential to my concept: the crossing of the boundaries that divide us as humans, and the revelation of what we share in common. The dance would be set to songs of the heart from around the world. I love to sing and have a formidable repertory of songs. Nevertheless, I plunged into my usual research mode and uncovered many others of great beauty. Lea opened her extensive collection of foreign-language CDs for my listening, pointing out her particular favorites. Once again, I called upon Howard Roberts to join me on this project with musical direction and orchestrations. He also contributed composition, setting Langston Hughes's poem, *Minstrel Man* to music. I worked with the company in their New York studio, on tour when possible, and at their summer residency in the State University of New York at Purchase. I brought them to UC Irvine for a residency in which I could fully realize my dual role as choreographer and professor. These rehearsal periods gave me time to gestate my work properly and to get to know the company in depth as individual artists. *Heartbeats* premiered February 17, 1997 at the San Jose Center for the Performing Arts in a marathon one hour plus of choreographic outpouring. I then set about trimming and refocusing, making the painful but necessary deletion of five sections, arriving finally at a forty-five minute work. It played in July 1997 at Jacob's Pillow and at the American Dance Festival to consistent standing ovations.

I arrived at this rich moment in my life, having passed through some deep trials and being forced to face my own mortality. The second Tuesday of May, 1997, I awoke from a troubled sleep with a pressure gripping my chest. I could not find a comfortable position in the bed nor could I rid myself of this terrible discomfort, the likes of which I had never before experienced. I must have found a way back to sleep because morning light greeted me in a less fearful but still troubled way. I called my doctor and got his answering service. I went off to the university, counseled a student, and was finally on the phone with Dr. Levin who told me to come in at once. "The good news, Donald, is that you're still standing; the bad news is that you've had a mild heart attack. We're taking you into the intensive care unit at Saddleback Memorial Hospital immediately."

The damage to my heart was minimal and no invasive procedures were indicated. The news spread swiftly. I was deluged with messages and phone calls. Flowers poured in from across the country. I never knew how deeply I was loved by so many. On the fourth day, I was sent home. After a week's complete rest, I began the active phase of my recuperation, walking in the surf at the beach, watching small flocks of pelicans soaring overhead, delighting in the playful antics of youngsters on their boogie-boards.

The next week, the doorbell rang and I opened it to Eva Desca. She gave me a warm embrace. I had reconnected with her after some fifty years. Eva was an amazing woman. She and her longtime friend, Sue Nadel, were the directors of a company of senior dancers, five women in their eighties, known as the Emeritus Dance Company. They performed a full program of dance works, highlighted by their signature presentation *Still Kicking, But Not As High*. In 1995, I had invited them and six members of the wonderful children's dance company, the Saint Joseph Ballet, along with six university dancers, to participate in my new work, *When I Grow Up ... When I Was A Child*, uniting the three generations.

Eva sat down next to me. "Take my hand," she said, holding it out to me. "I'm starting something new and I need your advice." The woman who in 1947 had told an eager amateur, "Do the movement and say I am the greatest dancer in the world!", was now requesting counsel from her ardent pupil. I looked into her beautiful and earnest face, framed by a luxurious mane of snow white hair, and a mist came over my eyes.

CHRONOLOGY: CHOREOGRAPHY, DIRECTION, PERFORMANCE

1948
- SATURDAY'S CHILD
  Poem: Countee Cullen
  Costume Design: Donald McKayle
  Original Performer: Donald McKayle
  Club Baron, New York, NY
- DUDLEY, MASLOW, BALES AND THE NEW DANCE GROUP (Performer, 1948–55)
- JEAN ERDMAN DANCE COMPANY (Performer, 1948–53)
- MARY ANTHONY DANCE COMPANY (Performer, 1948–52)

1950
- CREOLE AFTERNOON
  Music: Traditional
  Costume Design: Donald McKayle
  Original Performers: Donald McKayle and Jacqueline Hairston
  Henry Street Playhouse, New York, NY
- SONGS OF THE FOREST
  Music: Lou Harrison
  Costume Design: Donald McKayle
  Original Perfomer: Donald McKayle
  Hunter Playhouse, New York, NY
- EXODUS
  Music: Traditional
  Costume Design: Donald McKayle
  Original Performer: Donald McKayle
  Henry Street Playhouse, New York, NY
- CONTEMPORARY DANCE COMPANY (Choreographer, Performer, 1950)

1951
- GAMES
  Music: Traditional
  Costume Design: Remy Charlip

Scenic Design: Paul Bertelsen
Lighting Design: Pamela Judson-Stiles
Original Perfomers: Dancers: Esta Beck, Eve Beck, Louanna Gardner, Remy Charlip, John Fealy, George Liker, John Nola
Singers: June Lewis, Donald McKayle
Hunter Playhouse, New York, NY

- FRED WARING SHOW: 1951 ("Salute to American Indian Week"–Choreographer–CBS-TV)
Perfomers: Marc Breaux, Donald McKayle, Daniel Nagrin

1952
- FRED WARING SHOW: 1952 ("Jungle Drums"–Choreographer–CBS-TV)
Performers: Marc Breaux, Donald McKayle
- BLESS YOU ALL: 1951 (Performer, Broadway)
Mark Hellinger Threatre, New York, NY
- DANIEL NAGRIN DANCE COMPANY (Performer, Guest Artist, 1951)
- HER NAME WAS HARRIET
Music: Traditional
Costume Design: Donald McKayle
Lighting Design: Pamela Judson-Stiles
Original Performers: Donald McKayle & Company
Elizabeth Williamson, Matt Turney, John Sakamari, Donald McKayle, Eve Beck, Maurite Mair, Osborne Smith, Patricia Brooks, George Liker, Pat Underwood, Irving Burton, John Cobb, Albert Popwell, Shawneequa Baker, John Fealy, Donald McKayle, Matt Turney
Hunter Playhouse, New York, NY
- NOCTURNE
Music: Moondog (Louis Hardin)
Costume Design: Donald McKayle
Lighting Design: Doris Einstein
Original Performers: Donald McKayle & Company
Shawneequa Baker, Esta Beck, Eve Beck, Louanna Gardner, John Fealy, Ed Lum, Donald McKayle, Arthur Mitchell, Joseph Nash
Kaufman Concert Hall, YM&YWHA, New York, NY
- JUST A LITTLE SIMPLE: (Choreographer & Performer, Off-Broadway, 1952)
Club Baron, New York, NY
- NEW YORK CITY OPERA BALLET (Performer, 1952–54)
City Center, New York, NY
- MERCE CUNNINGHAM DANCE COMPANY (Performer, 1952)
- ANNA SOKOLOW DANCE COMPANY (Performer, 1952–55)

1953
- CAIN'S KEEP (Performer, Off-Broadway)
  New York, NY
- FOUR VIGNETTES
  Music: Samuel Barber
  Costume Design: Donald McKayle
  Original Performers: Donald McKayle & Company
  Lee Becker, Kathleen Stanford, Cristyne Lawson, Jacqueline Walcott,
  Alvin Ailey, Donald McKayle, Ernest Parham, George Mills
  Hunter Playhouse, New York, NY

1954
- THE STREET
  Music: Alonzo Levister
  Costume Design: Donald McKayle
  Original Performers: Donald McKayle & Company
  Esta Beck, Eve Beck, Leonore Landau, John Fealy, Wayne Lamb, Donald
  McKayle, Joseph Nash
  Brooklyn Academy of Music, NY
- PRELUDE TO ACTION
  Music: Alonzo Levister
  Costume Design: Donald McKayle
  Original Performers: Donald McKayle & Company
  Wayne Lamb, Donald McKayle, Joseph Nash
  Brooklyn Academy of Music, NY
- HOUSE OF FLOWERS (Performer, Broadway)
  Alvin Theatre, New York, NY

1955
- GAMES (Choreographer, Performer, CBC-TV–Toronto, Canada)
  Performers: (Partial List) Esta Beck, Eve Beck, Leu Comacho, Kevin
  Carlisle, Joseph Nash, Donald McKayle, George Liker
- MARTHA GRAHAM DANCE COMPANY (Performer, 1955–56)

1956
- HER NAME WAS HARRIET (recreation)
  Music: Traditional, arranged by Howard Roberts
  Costume Design: Donald McKayle
  Lighting Design: Marvin March
  Original Performers: Donald McKayle & Company
  Alvin Ailey, Cristyne Lawson, Dorene Richardson, Lee Becker, George
  Mills, Kathleen Stanford, Jacqueline Walcott, Donald McKayle, Ernest
  Parham, Stradella Lawrence, Elaine Baker, Katherine Barnes, Walter P.

Brown, Thomas Caret, Irving Hunter, June Lewis, Lee Becker
Hunter Playhouse, New York, NY

1957
- MUSE IN THE MEWS
  Music: Jimmy Giuffre
  Original Performers: Donald McKayle & Company
  Costume Design: Domingo A. Rodriguez
  (Partial List) Cristyne Lawson, Donald McKayle, Kevin Carlisle,
  Kaufman Concert Hall, YM&YWHA, New York, NY
- ROBERT DE CORMIER SINGERS (Club Act/Concert Review)
- HARRY BELAFONTE (Club Act/Concert Review)
- COPPER AND BRASS (Performer, Broadway)
  Martin Beck Theatre, New York, NY
- WEST SIDE STORY (Performer, Broadway)
  Winter Garden Theatre, New York, NY

1958
- RITA MORENO (Club Act)
- GAMES (Choreographer, Performer, Folio CBC-TV)
- OUT OF THE CHRYSALIS
  Music: Samuel Bloch
  Costume Design: Donald McKayle
  Original Performers: Juilliard Dance Theater
  Juilliard School of Music, New York, NY

1959
- RAINBOW ROUND MY SHOULDER
  Music: Traditional from the Collection of John And Alan Lomax
  Arranged by Robert Dercomier and Milton Okun
  Costume Design: Domingo A. Rodriguez
  Lighting Design: Doris Einstein
  Original Performers: Donald McKayle & Company
  Dancers: Mary Hinkson, Alfred DeSio, Donald McKayle, Jaime Rogers,
  Gus Trikonis, Charles Moore, Harold Pierson, Jay Fletcher
  Singers: Leon Bibb (soloist), Joe Crawford, Joli Gonsalvez, Elijah Hodges,
  Sherman Sneed, Billy Stewart, Roy Thompson, Ned Wright
  Guitarist: John Stauber
  Kaufman Concert Hall, YM&YWHA, New York, NY
- ON THE SOUND (Golden Eagle Award Film)
  Performers: Mary Hinkson, Matt Turney, Donald McKayle
- COME AND SEE THE PEPPERMINT TREE (Vocalist, Narrator, Additional Lyrics, Washington Records)

- RAINBOW ROUND MY SHOULDER (Choreographer, Camera Three–CBS-TV)
  Original Performers: Donald McKayle & Company (same as 1959 premiere)

1960
- ONE-TWO-THREE, FOLLOW ME
  Music: Traditional, Arranged by Donald McKayle
  Costume Design: Donald McKayle
  Original Performers: The Merry Go Rounders
  Kaufman Concert Hall, YM&YWHA, New York, NY
- FESTIVAL OF TWO WORLDS (Spoleto, Italy)
  Choreographer & Performer: Games, Rainbow Round My Shoulder, Syrinx
  Teatro Nuovo, Spoleto, Italy & Teatro Caio Melisso, Spoleto, Italy
- HELEN GALLAGHER (Club Act)
- SOMETIME, ANYTIME (Vocalist, Riverside Records)
- THEY CALLED HER MOSES (Choreographer, Camera Three-CBS-TV)
  Performers: Jacqueline Walcott, Sylvia Waters, Robert Powell, Carmen DeLavallade, Arthur Mitchell, Kathleen Stanford (vocal soloist), Miriam Burton
- SOUL (Choreographer–NBC-TV)

1961
- FREE AND EASY (Director / Choreographer) Amsterdam, Utrecht, Brussels, Paris
  Carre Theatre, Amsterdam, The Netherlands

1962
- DISTRICT STORYVILLE
  Music: Original Composition, Dorothea Freitag
  Authentic Material, Sydney Bechet, Jelly Roll Morton, Tony Jackson
  Traditional Funeral Dirges and Marching Band Music
  Costume Design & Decor: Normand Maxon
  Lighting Design: Nicola Cernovich
  Original Performers: Donald McKayle & Company
  William Louther, Pearl Reynolds, Thelma Oliver, Jacqueline Walcott, Herman Howell, Gus Solomons Jr, Shelley Frankel, Eliot Feld, Louanna Gardner, Mabel Robinson, Alfred DeSio, Kenneth Scott, Esta McKayle, Harriet Clifford, Sylvia Waters, Dudley Williams
  Kaufman Concert Hall, YM&YWHA, New York, NY

1963

- LEGENDARY LANDSCAPE
  Music: Lou Harrison
  Costume Design: Normand Maxon
  Scenic Design: Robert S. Blackburn
  Lighting Design: Thomas Skelton
  Original Performers: Donald McKayle & Company
  Mariko Sanjo, Pearl Reynolds, Gus Solomons Jr, Harriet Clifford, Claire
  Mallardi, Esta McKayle, Sylvia Waters
  Hunter Playhouse, New York, NY
- ARENA
  Music: C. Bernard Jackson
  Costume Design: Normand Maxon
  Scenic Design: Normand Maxon
  Original Performers: Donald McKayle & Company
  Louis Falco, Donald McKayle, Sylvia Waters, Claire Mallardi, Esta
  McKayle, Raymond Sawyer, Dudley Williams
  Palmer Auditorium, New London, CT
- BLOOD OF THE LAMB
  Music: C. Bernard Jackson
  Costume Design: Normand Maxon
  Original Performers: Donald McKayle & Company
  Donald McKayle, Carmen DeLavallade, Dorene Richardson, Gus
  Solomons Jr., Dudley Williams, Raymond Sawyer
  Palmer Auditorium, New London, CT
- TRUMPETS OF THE LORD (Off-Broadway—Director/Choreographer)
  Performers: Cicely Tyson, Al Freeman Jr., Lex Munson, Teresa Merritt,
  and Ensemble
  Astor Playhouse, New York, NY
- THE TEMPEST; ANTONY AND CLEOPATRA; AS YOU LIKE IT (Choreographer, NY Shakespeare Festival)
  Harkness Theater in the Park, New York, NY
- DISTRICT STORYVILLE (Choreographer–Canadian Broadcasting Corporation–Toronto, Canada)
  Performers: William Louther, Pearl Reynolds, Thelma Oliver, Jacqueline
  Walcott, Herman Howell, Gus Solomons Jr, Shelley Frankel, Tommy
  Johnson, Louanna Gardner, Robert Powell, Esta McKayle, Harriet
  Clifford, Sylvia Waters, Dudley Williams

1964

- REFLECTIONS IN THE PARK
  Music: Gary McFarland
  Costume Design: Normand Maxon
  Lighting Design: Nicola Cernovich

Original Performers: Donald McKayle Dance Company
Dancers: Carmen DeLavallade, Gus Solomons Jr, Jaime Rogers, Robert Powell, Raymond Sawyer, Takako Asakawa, Mabel Robinson, Sylvia Waters, Pearl Reynolds
Musicians: Bill Bary, Gary McFarland, Jerome Richardson, Richard Davis, Mel Lewis, Willie Rodriguez, Willie Dennis, Jim Rainey, Sol Schlinger, Bill Lewin, Phil Woods
Hunter College Assembly Hall, New York, NY
- DAUGHTERS OF THE GARDEN
  Music: Ernest Bloch
  Costume Design: Donald McKayle
  Original Performers: Batsheva Dance Company
  Galia Gat, Rena Gluck, Lea Levin, Ehud Ben David
  Habimah Theatre, Tel Aviv, Israel
- GOLDEN BOY (Choreographer, Broadway–Tony Nomination for Best Choreographer)
  Shubert Theatre, Philadelphia, PA
- AS YOU LIKE IT and ANTONY AND CLEOPATRA (Off Broadway–Choreographer)
  New York Shakespeare Festival, New York, NY — Harkness Theater in the Park, New York, NY
- EXPLORING (Baseball Segment–Choreographer–NBC-TV)
- AMAHL AND THE NIGHT VISITORS (NBC Opera– Choreographer–NBC-TV)
- CROSSTOWN
  Music: Jerome Richardson
  Original Performers: Donald McKayle Dance Company
  New York, NY

1965
- INCANTATION
  Music: Joaquin Rodrigo, Arranged by Miles Davis
  Costume Design: Donald McKayle
  Original Performers: Donald McKayle Dance Company
  (Partial List) Lea Levin, Jerry Grimes, Renee Rose, Mary Barnett, Rahamim Ron, Raymond Sawyer
  Brooklyn Academy of Music, Bklyn., NY
- WILDERNESS
  Music: Aaron Copland
  Costume Design: Donald McKayle
  Original Performers: Donald McKayle Dance Company
  (Partial List) Lea Levin, William Louther, Jerry Grimes, Rahamim Ron, Ruth Lerman, Raymond Sawyer, Yuriko Kimura, Connie Burnett, Rodney Griffin

Brooklyn Academy of Music, Bklyn., NY
- THE STROLLIN' TWENTIES (Produced by Harry Belafonte–Choreographer–CBS-TV)
- FANFARE — The Al Hirt Show (Choreographer–CBS-TV)
- JAZZ DANCE — USA (Choreographer–NET-TV)

1966
- A TIME FOR SINGING (Choreographer, Broadway)
  Mark Hellinger Theatre, New York, NY
- TEN BLOCKS ON THE CAMINO REAL (Choreographer–NET-TV)
- BURST OF FISTS
  Music: Howard Roberts
  Costume Design: Donald McKayle
  Original Performers: Donald McKayle Dance Company
  (Partial List) Jaime Rogers, Sally Neal, Raymond Sawyer,
  City Center, New York, NY

1967
- BLACK NEW WORLD (Director/Choreographer)
  Music: Dorothea Freitag and Howard Roberts
  Conductor Pianist: Margaret Harris
  Costume Design: Normand Maxon
  Lighting Design: Nicola Cernovich
  Original Performers: William Louther, Sally Neal, Geri Seignious, Miriam Burton, George Tipton, Mary Barnett, Charles Berry, Tony Callender, Larry Dismond, Rodney Griffin, Jerry Grimes, John Parks, Trina Parks, Richild Springer, Charles Sullivan, Clay Taliaferro, Clyde Turner, Sylvia Waters, Sharon Miller, Thommie Bush, Mabel Robinson
  Kaufman Concert Hall YM&YMHA, New York, NY
  (European Tour: London, Wiesbaden, Holland, Edinburgh, Zurich, Nervi, Hamburg)
- THE FOUR MUSKETEERS (Choreographer, Theatre Royal Drury Lane–London)
- SOUNDS OF SUMMER (Choreographer–NET-TV)
- BLACK NEW WORLD (Choreographer–NET-TV)

1968
- I'M SOLOMON (Choreographer, Broadway) Mark Hellinger Theatre, New York, NY
- THE ED SULLIVAN SHOW (Choreographer–CBS-TV) (with The Supremes and Bobby Vinton)
- T.C.B. (Choreographer–NBC-TV) (Motown Special with Diana Ross and The Supremes and The Temptations)
- THE BILL COSBY SPECIAL (Choreographer–NBC-TV)

1969

- THE GREAT WHITE HOPE (Choreographer, Film–20th Century)
- THE HOLLYWOOD PALACE (Choreographer, Performer, ABC)
- DICK VAN DYKE AND THE OTHER WOMAN (Choreographer–CBS-TV)
  Performers: Dick Van Dyke, Mary Tyler Moore and Cast
- THE LESLIE UGGAMS SHOW (Choreographer–CBS-TV)
- THE SECOND BILL COSBY SPECIAL (Choreographer–NBC-TV)
- AND BEAUTIFUL (Choreographer–Metro Media-TV)

1970

- INNER CITY REPERTORY DANCE COMPANY (Artistic Director 1970–74) Los Angeles, CA
- BEDKNOBS AND BROOMSTICKS (Choreographer, Film–Walt Disney)
- THE 43RD ANNUAL ACADEMY AWARDS (Choreographer–NBC-TV)

1971

- SOJOURN
  Music: Andre Jolivet
  Costume Design: Charles Berliner
  Original Performers: Inner City Repertory Dance Company
  Leslie Watanabe, Barry D'Angelo, Dan Strayhorn, Carolyn Dyer, Ruby Millsap
  Inner City Theatre, Los Angeles, CA
- THE SUPER COMEDY BOWL (Choreographer–CBS-TV)

1972

- MIGRATIONS
  Music: Carole Weber (instrumental ensemble) Gregory Kramer (electronic music)
  Costume Design: Terri Tam Soon
  Original Performers: Inner City Repertory Dance Company
  Michele Simmons, Carolyn Dyer, Regina Bell, Ruby Millsap, Delila Moseley, Jackie Landrum, Sachiye Nakano
  Inner City Theatre, Los Angeles, CA
- SONGS OF THE DISINHERITED
  Original Performers: Inner City Repertory Dance Company
  Costume Design: Donald McKayle
  I'M ON MY WAY
  Music: Traditional, Arranged by Phil Moore Jr.
  Original Performers: Bruce Heath, Lorraine Fields, Gary Chapman
  UPON THE MOUNTAIN
  Music: Traditional, Arranged by Phil Moore Jr.

Original Performers: Georgelton McClain, Cleveland Pennington
ANGELITOS NEGROS
Music: Manuel Alvarez Maciste
Piano and Vocals: Roberta Flack
Original Performer: Michele Simmons
SHAKER LIFE
Music: Richie Havens Stormy
Vocals: The Voices of East Harlem
Original Performers: Bruce Heath, Lorraine Fields, Gary Chapman,
Georgelton McClain, Cleveland Pennington, Michele Simmons
Inner City Theatre, Los Angeles, CA
- THE SUPREMES (Club Act)
- CHARLIE AND THE ANGEL (Choreographer, Film–Walt Disney)
- Leonard Bernstein's MASS (Choreographer, Mark Taper Forum, LA)
- A FUNNY THING HAPPENED ON THE WAY TO THE SPECIAL
  (Choreographer, ABC-TV)
- THE NEW BILL COSBY SHOW (Choreography–CBS–TV)

1973
- RAISIN (Director/Choreographer, Arena Stage, Washington, D.C.)
- THE GRAMMY AWARDS (Choreographer, ABC-TV)
- BLACK OMNIBUS (Choreographer, Metro Media-TV)

1974
- BARRIO
  Music: Miles Davis
  Costume Design: Terri Tam Soon
  Original Performers: Inner City Repertory Dance Company
  Lea Vivante, Maria Ghava, Bill Landrum, Leslie Watanabe, Juleste Salve,
  Georgelton McClain
  Inner City Theatre, Los Angeles, CA
- THE TEMPTATIONS (Act or Concert Review)
- RAISIN (Director/Choreographer, Broadway–Tony Award–Best Musi-
  cal; Tony Nominations–Best Choreographer, Best Director)
  46th Street Theatre, N.Y., NY
- FREE TO BE YOU AND ME (Choreographer, ABC-TV–Emmy Award–
  Best Children's Special)
- GOOD TIMES (Director, CBS-TV)

1975
- DR. JAZZ (Director/Choreographer, Broadway–Tony Nomination–Best
  Choreographer)
  Winter Garden Theatre, New York, NY

1976

- ALBUM LEAVES
  Music: Jelly Roll Morton
  Costume Design: Donald McKayle
  Original Performers: (Batsheva Dance Company)
  Rina Schenfeld, Deborah Smulian, Pamela Sharmi, Rahamim Ron, Yair
  Lee, Roger Bryant, Leah Avraham, Per-Olof Fernlund, Laurie Freedman
  Habimah Theatre, Tel Aviv, Israel
- RECUERDOS
  Music: Heitor Villa Lobos
  Costume Design: Donald McKayle
  Original Performer: Lea Vivante
  Los Angeles, CA
- THE MINSTREL MAN (Choreographer, Film for Television–Tomorrow
  Entertainment Emmy Nomination–Outstanding Achievement in
  Choreography)
- BLOOD MEMORIES
  Music: Howard Roberts
  Lyrics: Maureen Malloy
  Costume Design: Hugh Sherrer
  Original Performers: Alvin Ailey American Dance Theater
  Judith Jamison, Dudley Wiliams, Clive Thompson, Enid Britten, Beth
  Shorter, Masazumi Chaya, Donna Wood, Carl Paris, Warren Spear,
  Ulysses Dove, Tina Yuan, Mari Kajiwara, Estelle Spurlock, Sarita Allen,
  Marla Bingham, Charles Adams, Warren Spears, Marvin Tunney,
  City Center, New York, NY

1977

- MOUNTAIN OF SPICES
  Music: Moondog (Louis Hardin)
  Costume Design: Donald McKayle
  Original Performers: Batsheva Dance Company
  (Guest Artists) Lea Vivante, Valerie Panov, Galina Panov.
  Yair Vardi, Shimon Cohen, David Oz, Pamela Sharmi, Yair Lee, Leah
  Avraham, Nurit Stern, Ruth Kleinfeld, Deborah Smulian, Rahamim Ron
  Mann Auditorium, Tel Aviv, Israel
- ARGOT
  Music: Various Artists (Collage)
  Original Performers: Joyce Trisler Dance Company
  Nancy Collahan, Leslie Watanabe, Miguel Lopez, Diane Grumet,
  Jacqueline Buglisi, Lonnie Morreton,
  Riverside Church Theatre, New York, NY
- CINDY (Choreographer, Film–Paramount)

- THE 49TH ANNUAL ACADEMY AWARDS (Choreographer, ABC-TV)
- THE MAD, MAD, MAD WORLD OF THE SUPER BOWL (Choreographer–NBC-TV)
- THE RICHARD PRYOR SPECIAL (Choreographer–NBC-TV)
- COMEDY TONIGHT (Choreographer–NBC-TV)

1978
- RITA MORENO (Club Act)
- THE LAST MINSTREL SHOW (Director/Choreographer, Broadway)
- EVOLUTION OF THE BLUES (Westwood Playhouse, Los Angeles, CA Drama Logue Critics Award, Best Choreography)
  (Drury Lane Water Tower, Chicago; John F. Kennedy Center, Washington, DC)
- CINDY (Choreographer, ABC-TV)

1979
- ARETHA FRANKLIN (Act or Concert Review 1979–1981)
- ONE MORE TIME (Director/Choreographer, Israel)
- THE ANNUAL EMMY AWARDS (Choreographer, ABC-TV)

1980
- THE JAZZ SINGER (Choreographer, Film–Samuel Goldwyn Studios)

1981
- SOPHISTICATED LADIES (Concept/Musical Staging, Broadway–Tony Nomination–Outstanding Choreography; Outer Critics Circle Award–Best Choreography; NAACP Image Award–Concept/Writer, Best Stage Play)
  Forrest Theatre, Philadelphia, PA

1982
- RICOCHET
  Music: Claude Bolling
  Costume Design: Lea Vivante
  Original Performers: The Company We Keep
  Nancy Matschek, Tami Gray, Sara Grindle, Sandy Matthern, Benny Bell, Patti Benson, Janet Mai, Terri Matthern, Bonnie Nedrow
  Lincoln Hall, Portland, OR

1983
- SOLARIS
  Music: L. Subramaniam
  Costume Design: Lea Vivante

Original Performers: Cal Arts Dance Ensemble
Loretta Livingston, Tina Yuan, Jamie Bishton II, Marvin Tunney
Japan America Theatre, Los Angeles, CA
- COLLAGE
  Music: L. Subramaniam
  Costume Design: Lea Vivante
  Original Performers: The Company We Keep
  Bonnie Merrill, Judy Patton, Catherine Evleshin, Tish Stoppel, Sara
  Grindle, Terri Matthern-McCanna, Sandy Matthern-Smith, Janet Mai,
  Patti Benson, Jackie Bennington-Weiss, Joe Morales, Dane Coles, Dan
  John, Bonnie Nedrow
  Lincoln Hall, Portland, OR

1984
- AVATAR
  Music: L. Subramaniam
  Costume Design: Lea Vivante
  Original Performers: San Antonio Ballet
  Marina Chapa, Guy Bilyeu, Bernie DeLance, David Guzman, Mark
  Hawksley, Paul Vasterling, Robyn Lawhorne, Laura Kedzi, Bronwen
  King, Barbara Kinney, Michele Piquet
  Theatre for the Performing Arts, San Antonio, TX
- THE EMPEROR JONES (Director/Choreographer–American Musical
  Theatre Festival, Philadelphia, PA)
- DANCING IN THE STREETS (Director/Choreographer, Israel)

1985
- VEVER
  Music: Colleridge-Taylor Perkinson
  Costume Design: A. Christina Gianinni
  Scenic Design: Edward Burbridge
  Original Performers: Alvin Ailey Repertory Ensemble
  (Partial List) Michael Joy, Desirée Sewer, Loris Anthony Beckles, Andre
  Tyson, Jonathan Reisling, Ray Tadio, Patricia Jacobs, Ruthlyn Solomon
  Riverside Church Theatre, New York, NY
- LOOKING FOR JERUSALEM
  Music: Sholmo Gronig and Ehud Manor
  Original Performers: The Batsheva Dance Company
- 3 BY 3 – Great Performances – Dance in America (Choreographer–
  NET/PBS)
  Performers: Alvin Ailey American Dance Theater
  Donna Wood, Rodney Nugent, Masazumi Chaya, Michito Oka, Carl
  Bailey, Kevin Brown, Gary Deloatch, Ralph Gillmore

1986
- BENEATH THE BAOBAB
  Music: Sholmo Gronig
  Costume Design: Lea Vivante
  Original Performers: Dimensions Dance Theatre
  Laney College, Oakland, CA
- APSARAS
  Music: L. Subramaniam
  Costume Design: Lea Vivante
  Original Performers: Cleo Parker Robinson Dance Ensemble
  Winifred Harris, Curtis Fraser, Marceline Freeman, Daryl Sneed, Rosalyn Briscoe, Becky Hill, Deedee Hill, Ronnie Wittacker, Elizabeth Scott
- PURLIE (Choreographer, Denver Center Theatre Company, Denver, CO)
- EMPEROR JONES (Director/Choreographer, Denver Center Theatre Company, Denver, CO)

1987
- TWILIGHT
  Music: Villa Lobos
  Original Performer: Gregg Lizenbery
  Laxson Theatre, Chico, CA
- HOUSE OF FLOWERS (Director/Choreographer, Denver Center Theatre Company, Denver, CO)
- SOUTH PACIFIC (Choreographer, Denver Center Theatre Company, Denver, CO)

1988
- STARDUST (Musical staging and choreography, Burt Reynolds Jupiter Theatre, Jupiter, FL)

1989
- PRIVATE DEBTS (Choreographer, Film–Chanticleer Films)

1990
- RING-A-LEVIO
  Music: Astor Piazzolla
  Costume Design: Chuck Goheen
  Original Performers: UCI Dance Ensemble
  Achmed Valk, Tom Smith, Kathy Auten, Isabel Garcia, Margaret Pomeroy, Tracy Douglas, Leslie Hardesty Sisson, Shauna Leehner, Anne Marie Etchepare, Gerise Stripling, April Brannan,
  Village Theatre, Irvine, CA

- DISTANT DRUM
  Music: Astor Piazzolla
  Costume Design: Lea Vivante
  Lighting Design: Beth Thurmond, Bill Brown
  Original Performers: African American Dance Ensemble
  L.D. Burris, Sharone Price, James K. Green III, L. Maurice White, Garmen
  Mejia, René Blackwell, Ava McFarlane, Karen L. Zemek, Toni K. Hall,
  Chuck Davis, Beverly Botsford
  Reynolds Industry Theatre, Durham, NC
- STARDUST (Creative Realization / Musical Staging / Choreography, Pre-
  Broadway)
  Burt Reynolds Theatre, Jupiter, FL

1991
- SOMBRA Y SOL (IMAGES OF FRIDA KAHLO)
  Music: Aaron Copland
  Costume Design: Elizabeth Novak
  Lighting Design: Cameron Harvey
  Original Performers: UCI Student Dance Ensemble
  April Brannan, Jude Clark-Warnisher, Diane Berry, Mary Troy, Ynhi
  Lehoang, Larry Sousa, Rick Crawford, Edouardo Nieto, David Mullins,
  Sheetal Ghandi, Isabel Garcia
  Village Theatre, Irvine, CA
- INFINITE JOURNEY
  Music: Max Bruch
  Costume Design: Lea Vivante
  Lighting Design: Heidi Nicholas
  Original Performers: Loyola Marymount Student Dance Ensemble
  Karah Abiog, Daniele Hooper, Patricia Hudson, LaCey Wheat
  Strub Theatre, Los Angeles, CA
- ROCKIN' WITH RACHMANINOV (Director / Choreographer)
  Music: Horace Silver
  Costume Design: Lea Vivante
  Lighting Design: Kathy Herbert
  Original Performers: (Dancers) Atalya Bates, Maisha Brown, Victor
  Butler, Larry Sousa, Tamica Washington,
  (Singers) Andy Bey, Dawn Burnett
  (Narrator) Chuck Niles
  (Musicians) Ralph Bowen, Carl Burnett, Bob Maize, Andy Martin,
  Michael Mossman, Bob McChesney, Rickey Woodward, Horace Silver
  Barnsdale Theatre, Los Angeles, CA

1992

- HOUSE OF TEARS
  Music: Astor Piazzolla
  Costume Design: Lea Vivante
  Lighting Design: Nicholas J. Cavallaro
  Original Performers: The Cleveland San Jose Ballet Company
  Karen Gabay, Raymond Rodriguez, Alejandra Cobo, Olivier Muñoz, Pamela Raymond, Lisa Alfieri, Luana Hildago, Cynthia Graham, Sean France, Glen Tarachow, Pamela Reyman, Kevin Thomas, Joseph Konicki, Steven Voznik, Dalia Rawson, Gina Domenichelli, Linda Adolphi, Elizabeth Sullivan, Linda Jackson, Ramon Thielen, Hector Montero
  State Theatre, Cleveland, OH

1993

- MYSTERIES AND RAPTURES
  Music: L. Subramaniam
  Costume Design: Lea Vivante
  Scenic Design: Oliver Jackson
  Lighting Design: Christina Giannelli
  Original Performers: The Cleveland San Jose Ballet Company
  Ramon Thielen, Karen Gabay, Alejandra Cobo, Linda Jackson, Holly Morrow, Lisa Alfiere, Corey Colfer, Gonzalo Espinoza, Servy Gallardo, Mark Oltoski, Alexander Hasbany, Glen Tarachow, Deidre Byrne, Meghan Haas, Joanne Jaglowski, Gabrielle Lamb, Nancy Latoszewski, Elizabeth Sullivan
  State Theatre, Cleveland, OH
- RING-A-LEVIO
  Music: Astor Piazzolla
  Costume Design: Michelle Wise
  Lighting Design: Keith W. Rice
  Original Performers: Cleo Parker Robinson Dance Ensemble
  Karah Abiog, Gary Lewis, Gary Abbott, Angelica Edwards, Susan Richardson, Randy Brooks, Cedric Flynt, Michael Medcalf, Morgan Wahab, Marceline Freeman, Pamela Semmler
  New Dance Theatre, Denver, CO

1994

- VIGILS
  Music: Frederic Rzewski
  Costume Design: Bernard Johnson
  Lightning Design: Christopher Hall
  Original Performers: UCI Dance Ensemble
  Kit Ashleigh, Barbra Bean, Sae La Chin, Cynthia Boyett, Jennifer Dawson, Kristin Fox, Sandra Guiterrez, Trisha Hanada Rogers, Mariah Hyde,

Gina Lo Presti, Dana Mandell, Kim Mikesell, Melody McKenney, Sally McAdams, Brook Notary, Si-Hwa Noh, Coleen Clark Patterson, Marisa Pittenger, Francine Schlenker, Diana Stanton, April Strong, Susan Marie Torres
Irvine Barclay Theatre, Irvine, CA
- GUMBO YA-YA (a John F. Kennedy American Ballet Commission)
Music: James Newton
Costume and Scenic Design: A. Christina Gianinni
Lighting Design: Lisa J. Pinkham
Original Performers: San Francisco Ballet Company
Muriel Maffre, Eric Hoisington, Yuri Zhukov, Katita Waldo, Sara Sessions, Jennifer Blake, Yolanda Jordan, Kristin Long, Sedley Chew, Jason Davis, Bernard Courtot de Bouteiller, Jeff Stanton, Jais Zinoun, Jason Crethar, Ikolo Griffin, Askia Swift, Grace Maduell, Michelle Wilson
San Francisco Opera House, San Francisco, CA

1995
- WHEN I GROW UP ... WHEN I WAS A CHILD
Music: Alan Terricciano
Costume Design: Annaliese Baker
Lighting Design: Leslie Bjork
Original Performers: UCI Dance Ensemble, Saint Joseph Ballet, Emeritus Dance Company
UCI Dance Ensemble: Christopher Morgan, Terrica Banks, Sally McAdams, Si-Wha Noh, Melody McKenna, Francine Schlenker
Saint Joseph Ballet: Abel Gaspar, Aide Hernandez, Sonia Melendez, Liz Lira, Sara Lopez, Claudia Romero
Emeritus Dance Company: Eva Desca Garnet, Sue Nadel, Lee Cooley, Janet Steinberg, Mollie Portner
Irvine Barclay Theatre, Irvine, CA

1996
- RAINBOW ETUDE (for the American Dance Legacy Institute)
Music: Traditional, Arranged by Donald McKayle and Alan Terricciano
Costume Design: Bernard Johnson
Original Performer: Ruth Andrien
Skidmore College, Saratoga Springs, NY

1997
- HEARTBEATS
Music: Howard Roberts
Costume Design: Theoni V. Aldredge
Lighting Design: Steve Woods
Original Performers: José Limón Dance Company

Nina Watt, Carla Maxwell, Carlos Orta, Pamela Jones Malave, Francisco
Revulcaba, Carl Flink, Emilie Plauché, Mary Ford, Daniel Charron,
Bradon McDonald, Natalie Desch, Robert Rugala, Jonathan Ridel
Center for the Performing Arts, San Jose, CA
* THE SEVEN DEADLY SINS (Director/Choreographer)
  Music: Alan Terriacciano
  Costume Design: Dwight Richard Odle
  Lighting Design: Tom Ruzika
  Scenic Design: Michael Phillip Yingling
  Choreographers: LUST: Donald McKayle, ENVY: Clifford Breland,
  ANGER: James Penrod, SLOTH: Molly Lynck PRIDE: Nancy Lee Ruyter,
  GLUTTONY: Sean Greene, GREED: Janice Gudde Plastino
  Original Performers in LUST: Richard Elszy, Albert Jones, Mike Muniz,
  Alicia Okouchi, Sheila Russell, Keena Smith
  Irvine Barclay Theatre, Irvine, CA

1998
* IN THE DEEP DREAMING OF MY HANDS
  Music: Ofra Haza and Bezalel Aloni with Vocals by Ofra Haza
  Tadros and René DuPéré with vocals by Francesca Gagnon
  Costume Design: Lea Vivante
  Lighting Design: Tom Ruzika
  Original Performers: Lea Vivante and Achmed Valk
  Irvine Barclay Theatre, Irvine, CA
* DELICIOUS OBSESSION/SWEET BONDAGE
  Music: Nusrat Fateh Ali Kahn
  Costume Design: Dwight Richard Odle
  Lighting Design: Tom Ruzika
  Original Performers: UCI Etude Ensemble
  Amber Bosin, Cherise Bryant, Michelle Camaya, Richard Elszy, Maya
  Culbertson, Gabrielle Ereno, Kimberly Haddock, Albert Jones, Ashley
  Holladay, Leah Langelier, Meadow Leys, Eddie Mikrut, Audrey Prentice,
  Sheila Russell
  Carolina Theatre, Durham, NC
* SUPPLICATION
  Music: Nusrat Fateh Ali Kahn
  Costume Design: Donald McKayle
  Original Performer: American Repertory Dance Company
  Michele Simmons
  Schoenberg Hall, Los Angeles, CA

1999
* CHILDREN OF THE PASSAGE

Choreographers: Donald McKayle and Ronald K. Brown
Music: Dirty Dozen Brass Band
Costume Design: Omatayo Wumni Olaiya
Lighting Design: William H. Grant III
Original Performers: Dayton Contemporary Dance Company
Monette M. Bariel, Ricardo Garcia, Terrence Greene, Veronoca Green, G. D. Harris, Deshona Pepper, Alvin Rangel, Greer Reed, David Reuille, Sheri Williams
Victoria Theatre, Dayton, OH

- DANGER RUN
Music: Frederic Rzweski. Performed by Alan Terricciano
Costume Design: Omatayo Wumni Olaiya
Scenic Design: Kenneth John Verdugo
Lighting Design: William H. Grant III
Original Performers: Alvin Ailey America Theater
Rene Robinson, Uri Sands, Bahiyah Sayyed, Mucuy Bolles, Linda Cáceres, Briana Reed, Dwana Adaiaha Smallwood, Venus Hall, Matthew Rushing, Benoit-Swan Pouffer, Vernard J. Gillmore, Jeffrey Gerodias, Richard Whitter, Clifton Brown, Guillermo Asca, City Center, New York, NY

- MARDI GRASS
Music: Nusrat Fateh Ali Kahn
Costume Design: Dwight Richard Odle
Lightning Design: Tom Ruzika
Original Performers: UCI Etude Ensemble
Alicia Albright, Sandee Barnes, Amber Bosin, Cherise Bryant, Richard Elszy, Danashanti Harter, Ashley Holladay, Albert Jones, Leah Langelier, Meadow Leys, Eddie Mikrut, Jennifer Norton, Samatha Palmer, Jennifer Parsinnen, Sarah Reese, Sheila Russell, Seth Williams
Irvine Barclay Theatre, Irvine, CA

2000
- DEATH AND EROS
Music: Jon Magnussen
Costume Design: Madeline Kozwalski
Lighting Design: Tom Ruzika and Shelly Callahan
Original Performers: Lula Washington Dance Theatre
Keisha Clarke, Tamica Washington, Albert Jones, Jeremiah Tatum, Shameika Hines, Laura-Lisa Rodriguez, Shari Washington Rhones, Nabachwa Ssensalo, Bernard Jackson, Alexander Pelham, Eloise Laws, Kimgsley Leggs, Jon Magnussen, Norman Beede, Lenon Honor, Chris Lancaster, Jay Metz
Royce Hall, Los Angeles, CA

- TANTALUS
  Author: John Barton
  Additional Text: Colin Teevan
  Directors: Edward Hall, Sir Peter Hall
  Choreographer: Donald McKayle
  Lighting Design: Sumio Yoshii
  Denver Center Theatre Company, Denver CO

- JAMNATION
  Musical Direction: Kei Akagi
  Additional arrangements: Kei Akagi and Charles Owens
  Scenic Design: Kenneth John Verdugo
  Costume Design: Linda Davisson
  Lighting Design: Alexis L. Hoeft
  Music:
  1. Direct Current— Christopher Dobrian and K ei Akagi
  2. West end Blues— Louis Armstrong
  3. Bloomdido — Charlie Parker
  4. Agra — Duk e Ellington
  5. Felicidade — Antonio Carlos Jobim
  6. MinorSwing — Django Reinardt and Stephan Grapelli
  7. Blue Bird of Delhi —Duke Ellington
  8. Carolina Shout — James P . Johnson
  9. Be Bop — Charlie Parker
  Original Performance: (Dancers) Cherie Adame, Derrick Agnoletti, Alicia
  Albright, Teresa Avina, Leigh Atwell, Elizabeth Bogdanski, Catherine
  Bonomini, Voetor Borjas, Cherise Bryant, Melody Chen, Christine Crest,
  Candance Coffee, Dorothy Chang, Danielle Daguman, Maya Elbaum,
  Elizabeth Feltman, Nathan Hodges, Lara James, Anna Kaiser, Kurt Kikuchi,
  Piper Lewis, Brooke Melton, Mary Kate Monohan, Maria Mufloz, Wendy
  Nilsson, Seth Williams, Julia Wilson, Timothy Wilson, Adam Young (Musi-
  cians): Carl Vickers, Karl Esquerra, Charles Owens, Justin Cortell, George
  McMullen, Jeff Long, Kei Akagi, Alan Terricciano, Art Davis, Sherman
  Ferguson, Frank Potenza

HONORS AND AWARDS

1963   • CAPEZIO AWARD, New York, NY
1965–81 • ANTOINETTE PERRY (TONY) NOMINATIONS
            1981 "SOPHISTICATED LADIES", Choreography
            1975 "DOCTOR JAZZ", Choreography
            1974 "RAISIN", Direction
            1974 "RAISIN", Choreography
            1965 "GOLDEN BOY", Choreography
1969   • BLACK ACADEMY OF ARTS AND LETTERS, Boston, MA
            — Elected Fellow
1977   • EMMY NOMINATION, Los Angeles, CA
            Outstanding Achievement in Choreography – "THE
            MINSTREL MAN"
1981   • NAACP IMAGE AWARD
            Writer/Concept, "SOPHISTICATED LADIES" Best Stage Play,
            Los Angeles, CA
        • OUTER CRITICS CIRCLE AWARD, New York, NY
            Choreography – "SOPHISTICATED LADIES"
        • DRAMA LOGUE CRITICS AWARD, Los Angeles, CA
            Choreography – "EVOLUTION OF THE BLUES"
1989   • BLACK VISIONS: MOVEMENTS OF THE BLACK MASTERS
            Schomburg Collection, New York City Public Library, New
            York, NY
            Photographic and Print Exhibit Honoring Eleven Artists
1989–93 • AMERICAN DANCE FESTIVAL INSTITUTIONAL
            LINKAGES PROGRAM
            Sponsors: Rockefeller Foundation, United States Information
            Agency:
            Buenos Aires, Argentina, 1989, 1991
            Montevideo, Uruguay, 1992
            Moscow, Russia, 1993
1991   • LEGACY OF THE MASTERS "A Historical Tribute to Alvin
            Ailey and Donald McKayle", Black Choreographers Moving
            Toward the 21st Century, California Afro-American Museum,
            Los Angeles, CA
1992   • AMERICAN BLACK ARTS AWARD In Fine Arts (... for his

choreography for Broadway, Film, Television and Modern Dance) presented by "Ebony" magazine
- SAMUEL H. SCRIPPS/AMERICAN DANCE FESTIVAL AWARD, Durham, NC
- GRIOT AWARD Fifth Annual Conference of Black Dance, Los Angeles, CA
- LAUDS AND LAURELS AWARD (Professional Achievement) UCI Alumni Association, Irvine, CA

1993
- JOHN F. KENNEDY AMERICAN BALLET COMMISSION, Washington, DC, "Gumbo Ya-Ya", for the San Francisco Ballet
- DONALD MCKAYLE DAY, Sixth Annual Conference of Black Dance, Dallas, TX

1994
- MOST OUTSTANDING PROFESSOR: ASUCI/UCI Alumni Asssociation
- LIVING LEGEND AWARD for Distinguished Lifetime Achievement, National Black Arts Festival
- Lehman Award (... for the advancement of dance in our society)
- AMERICAN DANCE GUILD AWARD (Outstanding Lifetime Achievement)

1995
- CHOREOGRAPHY FELLOWSHIP, Naboral Endowment for the Arts
- AMERICAN DANCE LEGACY INSTITUTE, Brown University
  Donald McKayle, subject of the first interactive volume, (CD Rom, hardcopy, video casette),
  Housed in: Smithsonian Institute, Washington, DC; National Museum of Dance, Saratoga Springs, NY
- HERITAGE AWARD, California Dance Educators Association
- RESOLUTION from the COUNTRY OF LOS ANGELES (... a treasured asset to the community he has so deeply moved through his work)
- NATIONAL DANCE RESIDENCY PROGRAM AWARD, with the Limón Dance Company: administered by the New York Foundation for the Arts, funded by the Pew Charitable Trusts.
- Appointed ARTISTIC MENTOR and RESIDENT CHOREOGRAPHER of the Limón Dance Company

1996
- DANCE/USA HONORS (... outstanding lifetime contributions and creative leadership)

1997
- DISTINGUISHED FACULTY LECTURESHIP AWARD for RESEARCH,
  University of California, Irvine
- PROCLAMATION from the CITY and COUNTY OF DENVER

(... October 2, 3, 4, 1997 to be "Masterworks: A Tribute to Donald McKayle Days")

- BALASARASWATI/JOY ANN DEWEY BEINECKE ENDOWED CHAIR for DISTINGUISHED TEACHING, American Dance Festival, Durham, NC
- LESTER HORTON AWARD, Los Angeles, CA

1998
- IRVINE FELLOWSHIP IN DANCE (sponsor, the James Irvine Foundation, administrator, Dance,USA)
- DONALD MCKAYLE'S LIFE IN DANCE
  University of California Main Library
  Muriel Ansley Exhibit Gallery, Irvine, CA
- MARTIN LUTHER KING, CESAR CHAVEZ, ROSA PARKS SCHOLAR
  Western Michigan University, Kalamazoo, MI
- DANCING the DREAM, Lincoln Center Out of Doors "Tribute to Donald McKayle" with Limón Dance Company, Lula Washington Dance Theatre, Cleo Parker Robinson Dance Ensemble, Dayton Contemporary Dance Company
- CITATION from the CITY of NEW YORK
  (in recognition of his many contributions to the world of dance ...)

1999
- IMAGES AND REFLECTIONS: CELEBRATION OF A MASTERPIECE
  Documentary on Donald McKayle's "Rainbow Round My Shoulder"
- BEST CHOREOGRAPHY, Regional Dance America, Pacific "The Rainbow Suite"
- 100 AWARD from the 100 Black Men of Orange County

2000
- UCI Medal (The University of California, Irvine's highest honor)
- AMERICA'S IRREPLACEABLE DANCE TREASURES: THE FIRST 100
  Dance Heritage Coalition/Library of Congress

INDEX

Walt Disney Corporation 207, 208
Walt Disney Studios 199, 200, 203
Walton, Tony 168, 247, 248, 259, 262, 263
Warfield, William 131
Warren, Mark 210
Washington, Lamont 168
Washington, Lula 268
Watanabe, Les 272, 280
Waters, Ethel 204
Waters, Sylvia 120, 149
Wayne, Dennis 193
Wayne, John, 234
Wayne, Paula 160
Weeks, Alan 271
Weidman, Charles 64, 65, 197, 273
Weissberger and Frosch 179
Weissman, Rita 232
West, Mae 234
West Side Story 131, 132, 248
Westergaard, Louise 249, 250, 255, 260, 261
Westwood Playhouse 234, 257
When I Grow Up...When I Was A Child 291
White, Miles 43
Whitehead, Robert 247–249
Whiting, Margaret 245
Widdoes, Kathleen 198
Widman, Anneliese 62, 63, 66
Wilderness 192, 194

Wilderness Stair 35
William Morris Agency 145, 146, 150, 199, 204, 222, 225, 249
Williams, Dudley 121, 126, 149, 150, 180, 250
Williams, Irene 134
Williams, Joe 180, 181
Williams, Lavinia 19
Williams, Sam Art 260, 261, 265
Williams, Tennessee 69, 129
Wilson, Lester 164, 167, 271
Wilson, Mary 188
Wind in the Willows 27
Winter, Ethel 64, 74, 75, 77, 78, 94
Wittman, Martha 271
Woldin, Judd 217, 218
Wood, David 74, 96
Woods, Phil 131

X
Ximenez, Roberto 229, 230

Y
Yancey, Emily 248
Yarborough, Sara 19
Youdelman, Robert 145, 199
Yuan, Tina 278

Z
Zaltsberg, Charlotte 217, 218
Zeigfield Theatre 67

Other titles in the Routledge Harwood Choreography and Dance Studies series: